QUALITATIVE EDUCATIONAL RESEARCH IN DEVELOPING COUNTRIES

REFERENCE BOOKS IN INTERNATIONAL EDUCATION
VOLUME 35
GARLAND REFERENCE LIBRARY OF SOCIAL SCIENCE
VOLUME 927

Qualitative Educational Research in Developing Countries

Current Perspectives

Edited by
Michael Crossley
Graham Vulliamy

Garland Publishing, Inc.
New York and London
1997

Library of Congress Cataloging-in-Publication Data

Qualitative educational research in developing countries : current perspectives /
    edited by Michael Crossley, Graham Vulliamy.
            p.   cm. — (Reference books in international education ; v. 35.
Garland reference library of social science ; v. 927)
        Includes bibliographical references and index.
        ISBN 0-8153-1494-9 (acid-free paper)
        1. Education—Research—Developing countries.   2. Education—
Research—Developing countries—Methodology.   I. Crossley, Michael.
II. Vulliamy, Graham.   III. Series: Garland reference library of social
science ; v. 927.   IV. Series: Garland reference library of social science.
Reference books in international education ; vol. 35.
LB1028.25.D44Q35   1997
370'.78'091724—dc20   96-16786
                                                                              CIP

Printed on acid-free, 250-year-life paper
Manufactured in the United States of America

To Anne and Rosemary

CONTENTS

SERIES EDITOR'S FOREWORD

This series of scholarly works in comparative and international education has grown well beyond the initial conception of a collection of reference books. Although retaining its original purpose of providing a resource to scholars, students, and a variety of other professionals who need to understand the role played by education in various societies or world regions, it also strives to provide accurate, relevant, and up-to-date information on a wide variety of selected educational issues, problems, and experiments within an international context.

Contributors to this series are well-known scholars who have devoted their professional lives to the study of their specializations. Without exception these men and women possess an intimate understanding of the subject of their research and writing. Without exception they have studied their subject not only in dusty archives, but have lived and traveled widely in their quest for knowledge. In short, they are "experts" in the best sense of that often overused word.

In our increasingly interdependent world, it is now widely understood that it is a matter of military, economic, and environmental survival that we not only understand better what makes other societies tick, but that we make a serious effort to understand how others, be they Japanese, Hungarian, South African, or Chilean, attempt to solve the same kinds of educational problems that we face in North America. As the late George Z.F. Bereday wrote more than three decades ago: "[E]ducation is a mirror held against the face of a people. Nations may put on blustering shows of strength to conceal public weakness, erect grand façades to conceal shabby backyards, and profess peace while secretly arming for conquest, but how they take care of their children tells unerringly who they are" (*Comparative Methods in Education*, New York: Holt, Rinehart and Winston, 1964, p. 5).

Perhaps equally important, however, is the valuable perspective that studying another education system (or its problems) provides us in understanding our own system (or its problems). When we step beyond our own limited experience and our commonly held assumptions about schools and learning in order to look back at our system in contrast to another, we see it in a very different light. To learn, for example, how China or Belgium handles the education of a multilingual society; how the French provide for the funding of public education; or how the Japanese control access to their universities enables us to better understand that there are reasonable alternatives to our own familiar way of doing things. Not that we can *borrow* directly from other societies. Indeed, educational arrangements are inevitably a reflection of deeply embedded political, economic, and cultural factors that are unique to a particular society. But a conscious recognition that there are other ways of doing things can serve to open our minds and provoke our imaginations in ways that can result in new experiments or approaches that we may not have otherwise considered.

Since this series is intended to be a useful research tool, the editor and contributors welcome suggestions for future volumes, as well as ways in which this series can be improved.

Edward R. Beauchamp
University of Hawaii

FOREWORD

Meaning is very much a preoccupation of our postmodern era. Increasingly, the infinite differences that exist in how individuals interpret the world and choose to engage with its challenges are being recognized and accepted as legitimate, as well as inevitable. The role played by culture in mediating such interpretations, in defining the membership of particular social groupings and thereby giving some structure to this otherwise chaotic world, is also now recognized.

One of the more significant intellectual manifestations of such recognition has been the steady growth in popularity of an approach to social scientific research that accepts the need to take into account the perspectives of those being studied. The so-called "qualitative" paradigm has as its defining principle a commitment to seeking to understand the phenomenon being studied in the light of the explanations and perceptions of those involved. It places the influence of culture and context center stage and throws down the gauntlet to those who would impose their own interpretations to account for the motives and meanings of others. The introduction of qualitative research methods such as unstructured interviews and observation reflects this desire to capture the participant's perspective, and is rooted in turn in a theoretical orientation that takes as its starting point the existence of a plurality of belief systems. As the editors of this collection make clear in their opening chapter, the adoption of qualitative methods does not, in itself, constitute qualitative research. Rather it is the commitment to the interpretative paradigm that is crucial, to a theoretical position that starts from a recognition of multiple realities and hence the need to understand the salient features of the social context being studied.

This is an important and timely reminder for those interested in research in developing countries. An extensive research literature now testifies to the effects that the thoughtless imposition of the assumptions and practices of other cultures has had on these societies. Such impositions include religion and work practices, farming methods and political institutions that colonial powers have often sought to introduce in the light of their successful development in their own countries. Perhaps the most pervasive and the most powerful of these cultural exports is that of education. Virtually every country in the world now has an education system designed to provide formal schooling along the lines of that developed in Western Europe in recent centuries. Equally pervasive is the examination culture that developed in Europe at the same time and that now reinforces an approach to education that emphasizes the academic at the expense of the practical, competition between individuals rather than cooperation, and universal, rather than culturally specific, forms of knowledge. For many years, research in developing countries has also tended to conform to such universalistic assumptions about the nature of truth. If fools rush in where angels fear to tread, there has certainly been in the past no shortage of individual researchers, government agencies, and international aid organizations ready to define problems and prescribe solutions according to their own priorities and their own cultural assumptions concerning how these may best be implemented. The result has been a checkerboard of success and failure, progress achieved often at the cost of the loss of some other good following the failure to take into account the overall picture and the many different social factors in play.

Hence the recent upsurge of interest in possible alternative approaches for such research. As the field of comparative and international education has become increasingly sensitive to the need to take context into account in exploring the lessons to be learned from the experience of other countries, so those involved in research in developing countries have recognized the particular importance of partnership in the research endeavor; of not imposing values and goals generated elsewhere on their colleagues working under very different circumstances. That this is true at every level of research activity is well illustrated by the various contributions to this volume. From the activities of international aid agencies at one extreme to small-scale projects conducted by individuals at the other, it is clear that there is a new readiness to recognize the value of qualitative perspectives and methods in developing countries. But if these approaches share a common theoretical rationale, they are characterized by a very considerable variety of methods, with the more familiar armory of case studies and evaluation techniques being complemented by the exciting potential of approaches such as action research and ethnography.

This volume is very timely. It will both support and powerfully reinforce the growing interest in qualitative research in developing countries. It provides some excellent guidelines for good practice in a range of different approaches and it offers a detailed and well-argued rationale for why such methods are important. Yet the book is also to be welcomed for its important substantive contribution as well. In it we find many important insights into topics as diverse as school management and educational policy-making, teachers' professional development and curriculum innovation. The contributions are drawn from a very diverse and geographically spread range of countries, so providing a powerful endorsement of the international relevance of the issues being addressed.

I welcome this book. It is important both in the progress it represents and the progress to which it will lead. The editors are to be congratulated for initiating this important project and for carrying it forward to such a successful conclusion.

Patricia Broadfoot
University of Bristol

Acknowledgments

The origins of this book go back to the early years of the 1980s when the two editors first collaborated on qualitative research in the South Pacific nation of Papua New Guinea. Since then we have both pursued an active interest in related methodological issues and in comparative and international studies of education and development. We would therefore like to acknowledge the influence of all current and former colleagues, in both developed and developing countries, who have supported our various research activities. In particular, we thank the contributors to this volume who have worked hard to incorporate our structure and suggestions into their methodological reflections and accounts. The experience of producing this volume has, in itself, been a most creative process—and one that has helped to further our own understanding of the potential of qualitative research in an international context. We hope it will be a source of direct help and of some inspiration to others. Thanks are also due to Maureen Harvey at the School of Education, University of Bristol, for impeccable secretarial assistance during all stages of the book's evolution, to Mary O'Connell and Jan Green for help during the final preparation of the manuscript, to Professor Edward Beauchamp for supporting the project throughout, and to all production staff at the Garland offices in Hamden and New York.

Michael Crossley
Bristol
Graham Vulliamy
York

I QUALITATIVE RESEARCH IN DEVELOPING COUNTRIES

ISSUES AND EXPERIENCE

Michael Crossley

Graham Vulliamy

INTRODUCTION

The origins of this book can be traced back to field research conducted by both of the present writers in the early 1980s. The context for this work was the developing country of Papua New Guinea in the South West Pacific. We had both been invited to contribute to the evaluation of a major secondary sector curriculum innovation by the Papua New Guinean Ministry of Education and the Educational Research Unit at the University of Papua New Guinea. Each of us had a separate brief and focus for his own work, though as coordination with local researchers evolved so too did the extent of our own collaboration. The substantive findings of our research into this particular curriculum project are reported extensively elsewhere (see, for example, Crossley, 1981, 1984a, b; Crossley and Vulliamy, 1986; Vulliamy, 1981, 1985a, b). From the methodological perspective, our joint interest in the application of qualitative research and evaluation strategies in developing countries has continued to inform much of our subsequent work.

Since reflexive accounts and biographical histories are themselves characteristic of the qualitative research literature, it is perhaps pertinent to note that our first joint methodological writing explored the potential of school case studies for the field of comparative education, in the light of Stenhouse's call for detailed fieldwork (1979) and our own Papua New Guinean experience (Crossley and Vulliamy, 1984). Fortuitously, we had both traveled to Papua New Guinea, one directly from the UK and the other via Australia, interested in ways of studying the processes of educational innovation and of documenting the nature and quality of teaching and learning. At that time few substantial qualitative studies of education in developing countries were available in the international literature; but the works of Stake (1967), Stenhouse (1975), Parlett and Hamilton (1977) and other writers then challenging conventional models had already had a broadening influence upon educational research and evaluation strategies in the West. Moreover, the Papua New Guinean authorities were themselves keen to establish a strong and multidisciplinary tradition of educational research (Guthrie and Martin, 1983), and to encourage useful in-depth studies of schools. Our methodological work thus evolved quite naturally to consider the potential and limitations of qualitative research and evaluation for developing countries; and, as we reflected upon our broader field, the importance of related epistemological, theoretical and practical issues for comparative and international studies in education began to emerge increasingly clearly.

In this present volume, published in the Garland Reference Books in International Education series, we aim to build on our previous work, reflect upon relevant methodological developments in the past decade, and draw together useful examples of contemporary qualitative research and evaluation conducted in a selection of developing countries. The book expands on a number of core themes articulated in earlier work (Crossley and Vulliamy, 1984; Vulliamy et al., 1990; Crossley and Broadfoot, 1992), but pursues a wider range of specific methodological issues and debates through the analysis of research experience in a broader sample of developing countries. To enhance the utility of the book most chapters have been carefully planned to focus upon one major research method or issue, in the context of one specific study. Key issues include the importance of fieldwork, document analysis, qualitative interviews, classroom action research, insider fieldwork, ethical problems, case-study evaluation, the planning of qualitative research, dilemmas of teamwork, research capacity building, and north-south collaboration. The studies themselves examine formal and non-formal initiatives, community perceptions, school innovations, teacher training, tertiary education and provision for nomadic communities. Detailed examples of research in practice are drawn from countries in Asia and the Far East, Africa, Central and Latin America, the South Pacific and the Caribbean. Two introductory chapters also deal more broadly with epistemological issues and debates (chapter 2) and the implications and potential of qualitative research and evaluation for educational policy formulation and analysis (chapter 3).

An overview of each chapter is presented below, but here it is appropriate to explain how the structure of the volume is intended to maximize the accessibility of the material for other researchers in a practical but intellectually challenging way. As such we hope the book will be used as both a reference source and methodological text by a wide range of readers interested or involved in research activities relating to education and development. All contributors have been asked to write for an international audience working in both developed and developing countries; and to keep in mind the differing needs, experience and interests of potential readers as diverse as university students, tutors, researchers, policy-makers, educational planners, and specialists with research or evaluation responsibilities in national, international and non-governmental development assistance agencies.

The authors have themselves been chosen carefully to reflect differing intellectual, professional, and cultural backgrounds. All have substantial research experience in developing countries; some are educationalists, but others have different disciplinary expertise; some hold senior administrative positions; some are currently involved in long-term fieldwork; and others are perhaps more accurately described as practitioners. In this way we are, collectively, able to offer a multidisciplinary contribution to the available literature—and one that represents the work of both men and women. Moreover, of particular significance is the fact that a number of our contributors are writing about research carried out within their own home country—so adding important local perspectives to those articulated by foreign researchers. Indeed, collaboration between local and external research personnel is a distinctive characteristic of the present volume and a strategy that, we argue, holds much potential for further research throughout the developing world. The combination of insider and outsider perspectives in qualitative research can, for example, help facilitate studies that are more sensitive to local contextual factors, while retaining systematic rigor and an important degree of detachment from the culture and world view being studied (Crossley, 1992).

At the most fundamental level we hope this book will be of interest and of direct practical help to others planning, or engaged in, educational research of this nature—and that it will contribute in some way to the future quality and relevance of the work conducted, and to the broader process of research capacity building in developing countries.

THE METHODOLOGY AND METHODS OF QUALITATIVE RESEARCH

The first of the key themes we wish to develop from previous work concerns the nature and definition of qualitative research. Discussion of this is in our view frequently bedeviled by a failure to differentiate between a consideration of techniques of data collection, on the one hand, and a consideration of the underlying approach or epistemology guiding the research, on the other. While qualitative researchers tend to use data collection techniques, such as observation and unstructured interviewing, which produce words as data, and quantitative researchers tend to use techniques, such as questionnaire surveys or experiments, which produce numbers as data, such distinctions are not viewed by most qualitative researchers as the crucial differentiating feature. Rather, qualitative researchers usually view themselves as influenced by underlying philosophies and theoretical frameworks that are in conflict with the positivist and postpositivist philosophies which they identify as characterizing much traditional educational research (Guba, 1990b). Such epistemological differences shape a researcher's overall strategy and approach, irrespective of what data collection techniques are adopted. Thus, qualitative researchers do sometimes use data collection techniques that result in quantification and statistical analysis and positivist researchers sometimes use data collection techniques, such as semi-structured interviewing, which are more usually associated with qualitative researchers. Therefore characterizing research debates in terms of a quantitative/qualitative techniques division—as so often continues to be the case, particularly in developing countries—is unhelpful. As Fetterman points out:

> One need only scratch the surface of the qualitative/quantitative debate to understand that the terms "quantitative" and "qualitative" are in themselves misleading. They are commonly accepted handles for both the contrasting paradigms and the methods associated with them. (Fetterman, 1988:5)

While philosophical positions underpinning both positivist and antipositivist approaches in the social sciences have coexisted since at least the late nineteenth century, it is nevertheless the case that the widespread development over the last twenty five years of qualitative research *in education* has been a product of epistemological critiques of the positivist tradition that had hitherto dominated educational research in Western countries in the postwar period. Accepting the limitations of any shortened statement on the methodology of positivism (Halfpenny's 1982 book, for example, delineates twelve different usages of the term), Finch's definition is nevertheless an adequate guide:

> "Positivism" is taken to mean an approach to the creation of knowledge through research which emphasises the model of the natural sciences: the scientist adopts the position of the objective researcher, who collects "facts" about the social world and then builds up an explanation of social life by arranging such facts in a chain of causality, in the hope that this will uncover general laws about how the society works. (1986:7)

By contrast, the critiques of positivism, associated with traditions such as symbolic interactionism (Blumer, 1969), phenomenology (Berger and Luckmann, 1967) and constructivism (Guba, 1990a; Lincoln, 1990) argue that there is a fundamental difference between the study of natural objects and human beings, in that the latter themselves interpret situations and give meaning to them. Schutz (1962) considers the implications of this and argues that any worthwhile sociological explanation must be related to the actual ways in which groups themselves interpret their social situations. This requires a particular standpoint to the research process which Blumer (1971:21) characterizes as taking the role of research subjects and seeing their world from their perspective because "the actor acts towards his world on the basis of how he sees it and not on the basis of how that world appears to the outside observer." Given this, techniques of data collection are predisposed towards those "such as participant observation, in-depth interviewing, total participation in the activity being investigated, field work etc., which allow the researcher to obtain first-hand knowledge about the empirical social world in question" (Filstead, 1970:6).

We therefore find it helpful to distinguish between research techniques or methods on the one hand and what is variously termed a "paradigm" (derived from Kuhn, 1962), "methodology" or "strategy" (where these refer to the underlying epistemology of a research project) on the other. The relative importance of research methods vis-à-vis research strategies is still a subject of considerable controversy (see, for example, Guba, 1990b and Smith, 1989, together with Hammersley's 1992a critique of these books). At one extreme, writers such as Guba and Lincoln (1988) argue that the basic assumptions underpinning the conventional positivist and, what is variously called "interpretive," "naturalistic" or "constructivist" paradigms are totally opposed to each other, and they regard the positivist paradigm as unsuited to the study of human behavior in any context. Consequently, they maintain that while it is possible to mix different research methods within a research project, it is not possible to mix different research strategies. Thus any particular research method means something different, and is used in fundamentally different ways, depending upon whether the research design is a positivist or constructivist one. This distinction between methods and paradigm is made explicit in their attitude to the use of quantitative data where Lincoln reveals that they "have always said that the constructivist ought to be using, where appropriate, quantitative methods," pointing out that "nonpositivist quantitative methods are quantitative methods that don't make assumptions about strict linear cause-effect relationships" (quoted in Beld, 1994:108–109). At the other extreme, writers such as Reichardt and

Cook (1979) suggest that we should move beyond the paradigm debate and use whatever research techniques suit the research questions in hand, arguing that there are no essential differences between the use of qualitative and quantitative methods. An intermediary position is taken by Patton (1988) who, while accepting the force of Guba and Lincoln's (1988) analysis at the epistemological level, nevertheless argues for a pragmatic "paradigm of choices" whereby researchers can mix both research methods and research strategies, even within a single project. There are some rare examples of researchers who have shifted their own philosophical positions substantially on these issues; Hammersley's early work on ethnography in education, for example, leans toward the Guba and Lincoln (1988) end of the above continuum (see, for example, Hammersley, 1979a, b; Hammersley and Atkinson, 1983) while his more recent work leans toward the Reichardt and Cook (1979) end (see, for example, Hammersley, 1992b). However, for most researchers their allegiances to a particular stance on these issues is established early, mainly as a result of their training. Typically, different disciplines or sub-disciplines and different graduate research centers have different emphases. Thus, for example, as a generalization those trained in the psychology of education are more likely to be exposed to a positivist research strategy than an interpretive one, while those trained in the anthropology of education are likely to have the reverse. Sometimes such differences exhibit themselves in markedly varying approaches to different research areas within education. Vulliamy and Webb (1993) argue, for example, that the dominance of psychologists within the special education field has meant that it has been relatively insulated from developments within qualitative research and that this has resulted in a failure to address vital research questions.

The literature on qualitative research methodology suggests that there are several defining features of such research (see, for example, Burgess, 1985:7–10 and Bryman, 1988:61–69). It provides descriptions and accounts of the processes of social interaction in "natural" settings, usually based upon a combination of observation and interviewing of participants in order to understand their perspectives. Culture, meanings and processes are emphasized, rather than variables, outcomes and products. Instead of testing preconceived hypotheses, much qualitative research aims to generate theories and hypotheses from the data that emerge, in an attempt to avoid the imposition of a previous, and possibly inappropriate, frame of reference on the subjects of the research. This implies a far greater degree of flexibility concerning research design, data collection and analysis, with aspects of each of these sometimes occurring simultaneously throughout the duration of a research project, than tends to be the case with quantitative research. In an unconventional but illuminating metaphor, Oldfather and West (1994:22–23) liken qualitative research to jazz:

> The jazz metaphor creates a pathway for making explicit the tacit understandings that enable us to make our way as researchers without fully orchestrated scores. As jazz is guided by a deep structure of chord progressions and themes, qualitative inquiry is guided by epistemological principles, socially constructed values, inquiry focuses, and findings emerging through analytic methodologies such as constant comparison. . . . The metaphor invites exploration of the improvisatory qualities that allow ethnographers to fly free in response to serendipitous events and emerging understandings.

The earlier discussion of research strategies and methods should alert us, however, to the fact that not all researchers recognize such clearcut differences between positivist and interpretive research strategies. Thus those leaning toward the Reichardt and Cook (1979) end of the continuum, which include Preston (chapter 2 in this volume), believe that many of the assumptions made in the qualitative research methodology literature overplay the differences between quantitative and qualitative research approaches, misrepresenting in the process some of the procedures that quantitative researchers follow (see also Vulliamy et al., 1990:7–25, 159–165).

QUALITATIVE RESEARCH AND COMPARATIVE AND INTERNATIONAL EDUCATION

The second key theme we wish to develop from previous work concerns linkages with the field of comparative and international education, and its distinctive traditions and debates. These can be traced back to the French scholar Marc-Antoine Jullien's efforts to produce detailed research guidelines and checklists for foreign studies in education. This was subsequently labeled "Jullien's plan for comparative education" (Fraser, 1964), and marked early efforts (1816–1817) to provide discipline and structure for the "scientific" study of education in an international context. While Jullien's vision is now seen as an inspiration for the twentieth century development of international databases for education by bodies such as the International Bureau of Education (IBE) and UNESCO, his research strategy has also been challenged for being too strongly influenced by the positivistic assumptions characteristic of his day—and for his concern to identify the one best policy and practice for all contexts. Subsequent generations of comparativists, following the lead of Sir Michael Sadler (1900), have repeatedly drawn attention to the dangers and dilemmas of international transfer, and to the importance of contextual factors in the analysis and development of education (Crossley and Broadfoot, 1992). Isaac Kandel's work, for example, dominated this field in the first half of the present century, and central to his research was this argument:

> In order to understand, appreciate and evaluate the real meaning of the education system of a nation, it is essential to know something of its history and traditions, of the forces and attitudes governing its social organisations, of the political and economic conditions that determine its development. (Kandel, 1933:XIX)

This concern with context focuses upon the macro- or national level and it remains of central importance to the field today. It also underpins many of the methodological and theoretical debates and controversies that have emerged in this field in the post–World War II era (Epstein, 1983). At the heart of this are continuing tensions between positivistic and interpretivist research paradigms (Kuhn, 1962), and between those who seek to pursue a "science of comparative education" and those who eschew the search for cross-national law-like generalizations. While such polarization oversimplifies what is a complex issue, and it is inevitable that epistemological debates will continue in any healthy field of study, it is clear that, through its concern with context, the field of comparative and international education has much in common with the core perspectives and assumptions of qualitative research. It is to the implications of these similarities that we now turn, before applying our analysis to the more specific question of qualitative research and its potential for developing countries.

In the contemporary literature Edmund King (1989) is notable for challenging the influence of positivistic assumptions in comparative education, by rejecting the confinement of research to one "correct method" or to the procedures of quantitative social science. For King, a deep understanding of national context is a vital component of effective comparative and international education, and his approach to research suggests that

> we must get inside the skin of other people as nearly as we can. We must learn the "language of life" as far as possible. We must "make sense" of their conditioning and concerns in their idiom . . . a holistic contemplation of a national education system could be compared with the aesthetic appreciation of a work of art: the complete experience is of more value than the discussion of the parts which compose it. (Kay and Watson, 1982:133)

The similarities between this perspective and the methodological rationale for qualitative research are clearly represented in the search for meaning within the culture under study, in efforts to understand education from the local perspective and in attention to a "holistic" appreciation of a national education system. However, it is to other writers that we must turn as we consider the significance of context at the microlevel—and it is at this level that more direct linkages between qualitative research and comparative and international research in education have become increasingly apparent in recent years.

Reflecting broad trends in the field, Kelly and Altbach (1988) set the contemporary intellectual scene well by pointing out that comparativists have actively challenged post–World War II reliance upon quantification, the dominance of input-output models, the use of the nation-state as the exclusive research framework and structural functionalist epistemology. Criticism has also been made of research that has too often been limited to policy studies—for generating limited knowledge of the similarities and differences in educational *practice* across nations (Saunders and Vulliamy, 1983). To take the topic of curriculum innovation, for example, educational researchers have increasingly called for interpretive studies that document the processes of change at the school level, in the hope that findings will be more helpful for the improvement and further refinement of implementation strategies.

Stenhouse's (1979:9) article was one of the first to make this case explicitly for comparativists when he argued persuasively that

> comparative education will miss making an important contribution to the understanding of schooling if it does not participate in the current development of case-study approaches to educational processes and educational institutions.

Since this work was first published others, including the present writers, have added to the debate. These include Heyman's (1979) ethnomethodological perspective, and Masemann's (1982, 1990) plea for critical ethnography in the study of comparative education. Critical ethnography, Masemann (1982:1) argues,

> refers to studies which use a basically anthropological, qualitative, participant observer methodology but which rely for their theoretical formulation on a body of theory deriving from critical sociology and philosophy.

As May (1994:50) demonstrates with reference to multicultural education, critical ethnography attempts to bring together macro- and microlevel analyses by recognizing the interrelationships between theory and data, and acknowledging the "broader social and cultural processes that affect the school setting under study." Very much in tune with traditional approaches to comparative education such "macro-ethnography" (Lutz, 1984) facilitates more diachronic approaches to school case studies that focus

> on the socio-cultural processes within and outside of the school that create the situations within the school. . . . A school culture can no longer be understood by contemplating its navel . . . The ethnographer must develop more of a holistic perspective that focuses upon the interdependence of variables affecting the school—upon structural causes of change within the organisation. (Chilcott 1987:209)

Such combinations of macro- and micro-level studies, both being contextually grounded, accord well with both the traditions *and* the emerging trends of comparative and international education; and offer ways of more effectively linking policy and practice (Crossley and Burns, 1983). Bonnett and Carrington (1995), for example, usefully demonstrate how differing local and national contexts influence social constructions of anti-racism policy and practice in the UK and Canada, and how they have implications for policy development and implementation. Their study also well demonstrates how national-level analysis can be effectively combined with microlevel qualitative research. Such work, nevertheless, remains consistent with the Sadlerian tradition by challenging the uncritical international transfer of ideas and assumptions, and by drawing attention to the limitations of grand theories in the social sciences. Contemporary disenchantment with Marxist theory and centralized state planning as a world system illustrates this latter point well; but so too do the many critiques of modernization theory itself—not least those articulated by postmodernists who argue that all meta-narratives lock societies into totalitarian and restrictive frames of thought (Lyotard, 1984). In theoretical terms, however, the contemporary critiques of meta-narratives add further support to our case for qualitative research. Rust (1991), a former president of the American Comparative and International Education Society (CIES), for example, links the development of postmodernism to the growth of interest in ethnographic research capable of documenting "local criticisms" and "non-centralized" theoretical products. Supporting Masemann's (1990) argument for diversity in research and varied "ways of knowing," he argues:

Postmodernists would support that claim and reject any claim that one way of knowing is the only legitimate way. Rather, they would say our task is to determine which approach to knowing is appropriate to specific interests and needs rather than argue some universal application and validity, which ends up totalizing and confining in its ultimate effect. (Rust, 1991:616)

In adding that "we are witnessing a shift away from universal belief systems toward a plurality of belief systems" (1991:618). Rust gives further legitimacy to the interpretivist paradigm and, in so doing, helps to strengthen the case for the future development of qualitative research in the field of comparative and international education.

RESEARCH CAPACITY BUILDING IN DEVELOPING COUNTRIES

Our third key theme relates more directly to the potential of qualitative research for developing countries, and to the applied nature of much of the educational research conducted in such contexts. Elsewhere Crossley and Broadfoot (1992) have argued that international travel and consultancy work has increased exponentially in recent years, and that, given the limited cross-cultural experience of many personnel involved in this process, the dangers of inappropriate international transfer of educational policy and practice have visibly increased.

These dangers are often most graphically illustrated in developing countries, where cultural imperialism continues to take many forms (Mazrui, 1990), and the success rate of aid assisted educational reform has not been encouraging (King, 1991). Little (1988:19), for example, warns the prospective international consultant:

> Only when prepared to spend the time doing our homework to learn and understand more about the situation on which advice is sought, and only when prepared to share responsibility when things go badly wrong, should we erect our "for sale" signs. International consultancy work is difficult, and time and energy consuming, if it is to be done well.

She goes on to say that truly international theory "cries out for refinement and elaboration by researchers in and from developing countries" (Little, 1988:8). This, we argue, provides strong justification for the strengthening of the institutional profile—and research training—for comparative and international education worldwide. The experience and the literature of this field, as outlined above, has much to offer researchers and consultants from both developed and developing countries—and training in qualitative approaches to research and evaluation, emphasizing respect for cultural factors, we suggest, should play a central role. Moreover, this is especially timely since research capacity building has been adopted as a priority in its own right for international development assistance in the 1990s. This is reflected in the debate surrounding the 1990 World Conference on Education for All, held at Jomtien in Thailand, and in related reports and policy statements (see for example, King and Singh, 1991; Windham, 1992).

Fry and Thurber (1989) add significantly to the consultancy debate by challenging the "cultural arrogance" of many Western "experts" and arguing for increased research training to be conducted within developing countries (see also Van der Eyken, Goulden and Crossley, 1995). They also explicitly recognize the potential of the comparative and international literature and of qualitative research, by calling for more in-depth fieldwork and increased sensitivity to local cultural contexts. The exemplary consultant, they maintain, requires "protean adaptability":

> Many have several operating cultures, and they have a genuine awareness of the critical need to *adapt* both their professional behaviour and their expertise to new situations in other cultures. Failures in the field of international consulting most frequently result from a mindless adoption of Western approaches in non-Western settings. The [ideal] consultants' appreciation and valuing of cultural diversity makes them open and willing to listen and learn from others, whatever their culture or status. (Fry and Thurber, 1989:130)

The contributions to this present volume have been written in the spirit of the above review, and, collectively, they further elaborate the case for the increased application of qualitative research in the context of developing countries. Recent years have also seen increased research of this nature by others working in this field—with greater numbers of studies originating from developing country nationals. The work of Avalos and her associates (1986) is a valuable example of team collaboration that explores reasons for the school failure of poor children in Chile, Bolivia, Colombia and Venezuela; Rockwell (1991) provides a stimulating and critical review of ethnographic research in Latin America; Adamu (1991) applies "illuminative evaluation" to science education in Kano State, Nigeria; and Fuller (1991) combines ethnographic and quantitative methods in southern Africa. International agencies such as the World Bank have also begun to support some qualitative research initiatives. In this respect recent work coordinated by Dalin (1994) is important since it reports a major World Bank sponsored inquiry based on the study of educational reform processes in thirty-one primary schools in Colombia, Ethiopia and Bangladesh—all considered in their regional and national contexts. Reflecting increased support by other agencies, Blackwell (1992), representing the British Council, also calls for qualitative and formative evaluation to enhance aid effectiveness and inform future policy development in the 1990s.

Given the rationale for the present book these are encouraging developments, though, as reviews by writers such as Watson and Oxenham (1985), Wright (1988b), and Prophet (1994) indicate, there remains much to be done if the potential of qualitative research is to be fully realized in many developing countries. In concluding this section it is therefore appropriate to reflect on our own collaborative work and to summarize our rationale for the application of qualitative research in such contexts. In doing this we are well aware of the dangers of promoting yet further international transfer—though, in this case, we believe that qualitative research may be *more* appropriate in developing countries, where literacy and numeracy are less prevalent, than it is in the West. Indeed, to some extent, modern ethnographic fieldwork can be said to have had its origins in non-Western contexts, through the pioneering work of researchers such as Malinowski (1922) in the Trobriand Islands (now a part of Papua New Guinea).

To return to the focus of this section—and of the book itself—we argue that the main strengths of qualitative research in education are its high ecological validity derived from research in natural settings; its appropriateness for the study of the processes of educational innovations, especially focusing on the unanticipated consequences of change; its emphasis upon the chalk face realities of schooling with studies of classroom processes and teachers' and students' perspectives; its ability to probe the policy/practice interface and thus inform policy makers; and its usefulness in supplementing quantitative research by adding depth to breadth, by acting as a preliminary to the design of large-scale surveys and by interpreting the patterns found in correlational research. Qualitative research in education has a special potential in developing countries because, for various historical and cultural reasons, educational research in such countries has, to date, been dominated by positivist strategies. Consequently, there have been many educational research questions in developing countries to which a quantitative research strategy has been applied when either a qualitative one or a combination of the two would have been more appropriate. In addition, some research questions have rarely been addressed at all despite their potential relevance to both the process of policy-making and to the more theoretical study of schooling in the developing world. The narrative style of qualitative research reports can also be more accessible to a wider range of potential readers; and in predominantly oral cultures the advantages of personal fieldwork, in-depth interviews and observation are most significant. Moreover, despite the developments reported above, there remains a tendency in many developing countries for research and policy planning to be based on a systems perspective that still neglects the realities of schooling in an everyday context.

DEVELOPMENTS IN PRACTITIONER RESEARCH AND EVALUATION

A fourth theme that we believe it is important to explore here relates to the broadening of research styles encompassed by the label qualitative research. The work reported by Vulliamy et al. (1990), for example, was all characterized by the fact that an outside researcher was studying other peoples' cultures and practices, not only in the obvious sense of expatriates working overseas, but in the sense that in Bassey's (1981, 1983) terminology it represented "disciplinary" rather than "pedagogic" research. Bassey argues that in much traditional educational research, whether positivist or qualitative, research questions are derived from traditional educational disciplines or areas, such as sociology, psychology, feminist theory, curriculum studies or science education. He suggests that such "disciplinary" research, carried out by specialists and couched in their language, has been rejected by practicing teachers as of little use in assisting them to analyze classroom situations and in devising solutions to practical problems. By contrast, "pedagogic" research, in which research questions are derived directly from the practical experience and concerns of teachers or other educational professionals, has as its main aim the improvement of practice (rather than the contribution to theoretical knowledge within a discipline). The "teacher research" tradition on which Bassey is drawing has become increasingly influential, not only in the West where notions of the "reflective practitioner" (Schon, 1983) have pervaded a number of educational and social professions, but also in developing countries for reasons which we elucidate below.

While the origins of various brands of teacher research go back to the turn of the century (see Webb, 1990a), contemporary approaches are best viewed as being derived from the pioneering work of Lawrence Stenhouse in the 1960s and 1970s. He argued that both curriculum development and teachers' professional development would be enhanced by teachers systematically studying the processes of teaching and learning (Stenhouse, 1975). He questioned the traditional model of the relationship between educational research and educational change, whereby teachers were expected to adopt those curricula and pedagogic styles that had been "proved" by academic researchers to be successful. Instead, he argued that teachers should take the fruits of researchers and curriculum developers as working hypotheses to be systematically tested in order that they might be evaluated, rejected or refined. An early example of this was the use of teacher researchers in the development of the Schools Council Humanities Curriculum Project in England between 1967 and 1972 (see Elliott, 1991, chapter 2). Since that period, and especially in the last decade, the influence of teacher research has grown considerably. While the philosophical and theoretical influences on different approaches to teacher research vary (compare, for example, Carr and Kemmis, 1986; Winter, 1989; Elliott, 1991; Whitehead, 1993), they all share a strong commitment to a qualitative research paradigm.

It is helpful to distinguish three broad approaches to teacher research, the first of which is case study. As a research strategy, case study has a long history in both anthropology and sociology, where it is associated with ethnography and the intensive study, using participant observation, of a particular group or institution. Where schools have been the objects of study, this has led to the development of theories of schooling located either within an anthropological framework (for example, Spindler, 1982) or a sociological one (for example, Hammersley and Woods, 1976). However, Stenhouse specifically distinguished the use of case study in teacher research from its anthropological and sociological counterparts. He argued that, since ethnographers are strangers to the situations they study, this was an inappropriate strategy for teachers and educational researchers who tend to be very familiar with classrooms. Instead of using participant observation, he envisaged that the analysis of schools and classrooms would be based upon an accumulation of documents ("the case record"), which would include those created through interviews and direct observation (Stenhouse, 1978). Compared to the more traditional ethnographic participant observation studies, this involves much shorter periods of fieldwork with greater reliance on data derived from the transcripts of tape-recorded interviews. While interviews usually play a central part in teacher-research case studies, a variety of other research techniques may also be adopted, including observation, teacher and student diaries, questionnaires and the analysis of teachers' and students' written materials.

A second broad approach to teacher research is represented by evaluation studies. Stenhouse (1975) argued that it should be teachers themselves who should play the major role in evaluating the potential of innovations in their own classrooms or schools. However, he was very critical of the traditional "evaluation by objectives" model, arguing that undue attention to learner outcomes and objectives restricted the scope of evaluation. Thus traditional approaches tend to neglect key aspects, such as the actual processes of innovation, the unintended outcomes of innovation and a sensitivity to the context in which innovation is attempted. In this, he shared with a growing body of evaluators, both in the United States and in Britain, a desire to promote alternative qualitative approaches to educational evaluation based upon the disciplined use of case study (for a review of such approaches, see Norris, 1990).

The third broad approach to teacher research is action research. While this term can be used in a variety of ways, within the context of teacher research it has come to be identified specifically with teachers' inquiries which consist of a cycle or spiral involving identifying a problem, devising and implementing a proposed solution and researching the effects of this (see, for example, McTaggart and Kemmis, 1981; McNiff, 1988). Elliott connects this process specifically with the heightened teacher awareness required for improvement to practice: "this total process—review, diagnosis, planning, implementation, monitoring effects—is called *action research,* and it provides the necessary link between *self-evaluation* and professional development" (1981:ii). Action research is always a form of self-reflective inquiry. It is an approach which requires practitioners to use evidence to identify issues and gain understanding of problems with which they are directly concerned. While it can be undertaken by individuals, it is frequently a collaborative enterprise (Oja and Smulyan, 1989; Westgate et al., 1990). This emphasis on collaborative inquiry can make it particularly appealing to groups of teachers, who share common pedagogic, curricular or policy concerns. This is because it facilitates the investigation of a problem from a variety of perspectives and across different subject areas and hierarchical levels. Also, if a number of teachers are involved it strengthens the likely impact and implementation of change, as is evidenced in Stuart's discussion of collaborative action research in Lesotho in chapter 7.

There are several reasons why the past few years have witnessed a growth in the use of teacher research in developing countries. The first has been its increasing popularity in the West and in particular its use on professional development award-bearing courses at master's and doctoral levels in graduate centers, especially in Britain and Australia, to which students from overseas go to train. Models for such approaches have been provided both by recent textbooks describing the wide range of data collection techniques used in teacher research (see, for example, Altrichter et al., 1993; McKernan, 1991) and by recent edited collections reporting the substantive accounts of such teacher research projects (see, for example, Lomax, 1990, 1991; Webb, 1990b; Vulliamy and Webb, 1992). Allied with this has been a growing tendency for encouraging overseas educators, who are doing further training in Western universities, to return for part of their program to conduct fieldwork in their own countries. This has been a response to a growing recognition that the more traditional model of their conducting research in Western educational institutions poses major problems of transferability to the context of their countries of origin (for general discussions of the problems of international transfer in the educational sphere, see Crossley, 1984a; Crossley and Broadfoot, 1992; O'Donoghue, 1994).

Teacher research has been viewed as having a special relevance in developing countries for a variety of reasons. Wright (1988b:41) views it as a positive antidote to "the growing tendency of international funding agencies to conduct studies by 'remote control' from Washington or Paris," continuing to argue that "West African academics are becoming reluctant to pay unqualified obeisance to the 'correlations,' 'rates of return,' and 'levels of significance' reported in such studies, which are not sufficiently sensitive to local peculiarities and often produce results at odds with experiential knowledge of the situation." Such arguments are reminiscent of Bassey's (1981, 1990) distinction between "generalisability" and "relatability," where he suggests that the products of much traditional educational research, while supposedly generalizable because they have been derived from large samples, are perceived by most teachers as unrelatable to the realities of their specific classrooms. By contrast, given the in-depth portrayal of a particular case to be found in teacher research, whether this is the use of a specific curriculum package or a certain classroom management style, then teachers can readily relate aspects of such a portrayal to their own experiences.

Wright (1988a, b) discusses the development of a "Collaborative Action Research in Education" tradition in Sierra Leone, based originally around a team of twelve teacher educators and forty school teachers. Their aim was to research in such a manner that it could have a direct input into the practice of teaching. Thus, for example, they began with specific questions of the "'what is the problem with X' variety where X might be 'popular participation in geography;' 'the implementation of a Core Course Integrated Science Curriculum;' 'the teaching of music;' etc." (1988a:285). Research was then concentrated on a few schools, using a combination of case-study and action research styles, in order to get an in-depth understanding of the issues rather than adopting the more conventional, but more superficial, broad survey approach. Examples are given as to how the input of teachers' own "practitioner knowledge" provided valuable insights into the research process, which would have gone unnoticed in more conventional styles of educational research, whether positivist or qualitative, and of ways in which such research led to specific changes in educational practice.

Such motives for the practical improvement of classroom teaching often form the rationale for the adoption of teacher research approaches in developing countries, as can be seen in the work of Stuart and her collaborators in Lesotho. For others, however, the adoption of practitioner research has had a more explicit political motivation as, for example, in Walker's (1993, 1994) accounts of facilitating teacher research in black township schools in South Africa:

> In South Africa we have a cadre of progressive teachers many of whose democratic politics fail to translate into democratic classroom practice. Action research would be one way for them to address this gap between their values and their practice. . . . My own experience of working with teachers demonstrates that action research promises much that is valuable: teacher empowerment, the generation of endogeneous theories of teaching and learning; educational research which contributes to policy development *and* its implementation; and worthwhile working relationships between universities and teacher communities. As such it bears serious consideration as a strategy for reconstructing *education* in South Africa. (1993:106–107)

At the same time, Walker's work also points to the very real constraints on promoting teacher research in a developing country context and cautions that methodologies need adapting from the Western context from which they were originally derived—a point made also in O'Donoghue's (1994) critique of the manner in which the concept of "reflective practitioner" has been transferred to Papua New Guinea to become a central notion in the country's new three-year program for the pre-service education of community (primary) school teachers.

If teacher research is one departure from the more traditional styles of qualitative research to be reflected in this volume, another is the growing use of "condensed fieldwork" (Walker, 1974) in a developing country context, prompted by shortages of time and resources for more extended projects. Condensed fieldwork is heavily reliant on interviews and the collection of documents, often incorporating only day-long visits to a variety of research sites (see, for example, the chapters by Davies and Harber in this volume). Citing *Bread and Dreams* (Kushner, 1982) as an example of the genre, Atkinson and Delamont (1985) are skeptical of the potential of condensed fieldwork to produce valid case studies, and such approaches have also been dismissed as "blitzkrieg ethnography" (Rist, 1980). However, the value and validity of the data generated by such fieldwork are dependent upon the scope and purpose of the research. Condensed fieldwork is an inappropriate basis for a portrayal of the values, beliefs and rituals of a particular culture—the traditional focus of ethnography. However, it can provide in-depth information and understanding of more limited themes such as a school event, the use of a curriculum package or a teacher's day. It also has the benefit of broadening a sample to enhance population validity as a supplement to the high ecological validity which ethnographers argue typically characterizes the in-depth study of a single institution (Crossley and Vulliamy, 1984). This can be especially important in policy-oriented research where single in-depth case studies may be dismissed as being atypical. Thus, a condensed fieldwork qualitative research strategy involving day-long school visits with classroom observation, in-depth interviews and the collection of documents in fifty schools over a two-year period was used in a national study of the impact of the 1988 Education Reform Act on primary schools in England and Wales (Webb and Vulliamy, 1996).

QUALITATIVE DATA ANALYSIS AND VALIDATION

Our fifth introductory theme relates to the growing emphasis upon the importance of qualitative researchers revealing the processes by which they have analyzed and validated their data—an emphasis which is deliberately reflected in some of the contributions to this volume (see, especially, chapters by Fife and by Davies). Qualitative data have always presented particular problems for analysis since not only do they consist of words rather than numbers, but also fieldworkers have in the past been notoriously reticent about revealing their own procedures. Recent publications have attempted to remedy this. Thus, for example, Silverman (1993) provides a text on the various methods of interpreting qualitative data in the social sciences; Bryman and Burgess (1994) present an edited collection of a variety of qualitative researchers discussing the procedures for analysis that they have used; Wolcott's (1994) book provides an autobiographical account of his approach to the description, analysis and interpretation of ethnographic data; and Vulliamy and Webb (1992) address the issue of qualitative data analysis and validation specifically in relation to teacher research. Throughout these accounts the influence of Glaser and Strauss's (1967) earlier discussion of techniques for generating and saturating categories using a "constant comparison" method remains a dominant one.

The validation of data concerns the processes whereby researchers can both have confidence in their own analyses and can present their analyses in ways which can be independently checked by others. In quantitative research, both of these can be achieved through the cross-checking of numerical data and the use of established statistical tests. However, in qualitative research, raw data cannot be summarized in convenient form and only very few extracts from such data tend to be used in written reports. Moreover, the process of qualitative analysis is itself partly dependent upon the creative insights and conceptualization of the researcher. It is for these reasons that, until relatively recently, the processes of qualitative data analysis tended to remain hidden from readers of the research. To remedy this, over the past decade an increasing emphasis has been placed by many writers upon the validation of qualitative data. Some, such as Miles and Huberman (1994), have argued for more rigorous techniques for data collection and analysis, each of which should be systematically recorded, seeing little difference between their uses in quantitative and qualitative research respectively. Others, such as Lincoln and Guba (1985), argue that the traditional concepts associated with positivist research are not applicable to qualitative studies. Consequently, at the theoretical level, they have suggested a detailed alternative language for qualitative research, where, for example, the concept of "trustworthiness" replaces those of "reliability" and "validity" and where researchers should aspire to establish a study's "credibility," "transferability," "dependability" and "confirmability." At a more practical level, they have suggested a variety of techniques, many of which—such as triangulation—can be found in the much earlier writings of sociologists and anthropologists. Schwandt and Halpern (1988) have developed the notion of an audit trail to provide a validation device which can be undertaken after the completion of a qualitative research project. Using the analogy of a financial audit, whereby an accountant requires access to certain documentation to assess the financial state of a company, an audit trail refers to the documentation required for an independent assessment of such a project. Schwandt and Halpern argue that setting an audit trail serves two important purposes. First, forcing researchers to keep careful records of the details of their research, including the actual procedures used in data collection and analysis, results in researchers approaching their task in a more self-critical and systematic way. Second, it can provide readers with the kinds of information they require to assess the trustworthiness of a piece of research.

A final theme that we wish to elaborate, and one that effectively introduces our overview of the various chapters, has influenced the very composition of the volume. This is the belief that methodological procedures are best conveyed in the context of reflexive accounts of actual research projects. More traditional methods textbooks tend to make the assumption that relatively unambiguous procedures can be laid down for novice researchers to follow, whatever the context in which the research takes place. Burgess (1984) argues that, by reducing research strategy to a series of techniques carried out in compartmentalized stages, this misrepresents the nature of social enquiry and of the practice of research by playing down the importance of the social process and context for research. We believe that this is especially the case with qualitative research strategies, where the social nature of such research is usually explicitly recognized in the underlying epistemology and where, to return to Oldfather and West's (1994) metaphor, improvisatory deviations from the score are the norm. It is also especially evident in developing countries where factors such as limitations of resources, climactic conditions and cultural norms often require researchers to deviate from their own pre-existing procedures (see Barley, 1986). Accounts here of the *actual* procedures used by researchers are therefore used to critique and refine the more generalized discussions of educational research methods to be found in traditional textbooks.

Contributions to the Volume

In the ten chapters that follow the various contributors critically reflect upon their own research experience in developing country contexts as diverse as the small Caribbean state of St. Lucia and the giants of India, Pakistan and China. As already indicated, all but the first two authors concentrate upon one main method or related issue, so providing a separate methodological focus for each chapter. All contributions are well informed by recent fieldwork, and it is our intention that this often vivid and engaging experience should, where possible, speak for itself—revealing both the potential and the limitations of qualitative research in an international context. With this in mind, the following brief overviews of the various chapters are presented as an introduction and advance organizer, to facilitate the flexible and creative use of the book by the reader.

The first chapter by *Preston* is a challenging, and broad ranging, critical review of research paradigms and related epistemological debates. The analysis raises many controversial issues and demonstrates—not least by the stance taken by the author herself—how differing interpretations of the nature and role of qualitative research are held by members of the research community. Central to this introductory contribution is recognition of the significance of the politics and economics of research, most notably in the applied, consultancy work that dominates studies carried out in many developing countries. Preston demonstrates how her argument for the combination of qualitative and quantitative methods has developed in the light of her own research biography—and how her own position differs, on the epistemological continuum outlined earlier, from that of the present writers.

Diversity of views on such matters can, however, be both stimulating and creative, and in this respect the issues raised here add further to the methodological debate that underpins the rationale for the whole volume. Preston's chapter also explores the relationship between the rise of feminist theory and qualitative research; and, using her Latin American experience, the relevance and liberating potential of participatory action research. Indeed, for readers interested in issues of power and influence, research capacity building, neo-colonialism and relations between "rich" and "poor" countries, the material presented here provides a stimulating and informative foundation for the consideration of the more specific issues dealt with in subsequent chapters.

Cheng's contribution also serves as a broad introductory review, but in this case the focus is upon the potential of qualitative research and evaluation for educational policy analysis and formulation. His Chinese experience is used to good effect in arguing for a more equal balance of power between indigenous and foreign researchers in studies commissioned by international development assistance agencies. In doing so he clearly demonstrates both the advantages and disadvantages of outsider perspectives. The importance of all researchers grounding their studies in a thorough understanding of local culture, nevertheless, emerges as a central argument that graphically supports the context theme for comparative and qualitative studies that we have elaborated elsewhere. Phenomenological sensitivities also inform Cheng's analysis of how different people, in different milieu, construct their own interpretations of planning concepts; and how these interpretations influence the work they undertake and how effectively (or not) they communicate with others—including visiting consultants. In sum, Cheng argues persuasively for greater attention to be given to qualitative research and evaluation strategies, while demonstrating, with reference to contemporary Chinese examples, how such work could help to improve the processes of policy formulation and analysis in developing countries.

Fife applies his anthropological training and experience to a study of the importance of fieldwork in educational research, and he develops his thesis with reference to a study of education and social change in the West New Britain province of Papua New Guinea. The reader is

> provided with specific examples of how [he] went about collecting
> evidence regarding individual actions, cultural expressions, and social formations in such a way as to make it possible to produce a consistent, empirically valid argument regarding education and social change in West New Britain.

The chapter usefully demonstrates how micro- and macrolevel analyses can be combined and linked to emergent theory relating to the impact of state-run education on social inequality in Papua New Guinea. Fife shows how background documentary sources can be combined with observation and ethnographic interviews, and how, following general immersion in the field, the progressive focusing of research is informed by the data itself. In doing so we are also given useful insights into the processes of data analysis in the field, and how findings can be related to existing theoretical knowledge.

Linking in well with Fife's fieldwork perspective, *Harber's* chapter pursues the potential of documentary sources in greater detail. Approaching this from the position of a political scientist, Harber demarcates five different types of documentary evidence (secondary sources, newspapers, textbooks, literature and autobiography, minutes) and—with reference to his own research in Africa—illustrates how such material can help to add "flesh and blood" to our understanding of education in context. Since little is written on document analysis in many educational research methods texts, this is a useful contribution, and one that reinforces the search for patterns that emerge from data analysis, and the importance of the arts and humanities-based disciplines for research in the social sciences.

Two of our central themes, the importance of context and the dangers of uncritical international transfer, stand out well in *Davies's* chapter on qualitative interviews and the study of school management. Here she reflects on case studies of the "realities" of school management in Botswana, Zimbabwe, Namibia and Pakistan. Different types of interviews are identified with the qualitative approach being portrayed as a "social event" or "structured conversation." The flexibility of the qualitative process is highlighted and linked, again, to the emergence of categories or themes and the notion of grounded theory. Differences between the cultures studied also stand out well in this comparative analysis as do the limitations of many Western management theories and assumptions. For those considering the use of interviews in their own research projects this is a most insightful, helpful and readable discussion that provides practical advice in an accessible manner.

Moving more directly into the classroom context, *Stuart, Morojele, and Lefoka's* reflections on their collaborative approach to action research in Lesotho presents a rare example of sustained research cooperation over time. The contrasting reflections of the various writers make this an especially interesting piece—and one that has the advantage of indigenous and practitioner perspectives. Their account illustrates not only the very marked contribution to professional development made by action researchers' systematic evaluation of aspects of classroom practice, but also the constraints which need to be overcome if such inquiries are to become an ongoing part of the processes of teaching and learning.

The focus of *Louisy's* contribution is upon the dilemmas of insider research, in the light of her experience in conducting a detailed case study of her own higher education institution in St. Lucia in the Caribbean. Ethical issues also feature prominently in this chapter as the author considers the problems of access, confidentiality and anonymity in a small-state context. The very real dilemmas of researching a familiar setting, and one's own professional culture and community, are discussed—though a strong argument for more developing country "nationals" to be involved in researching their own systems emerges from the chapter overall. As such, the piece helps to show how all involved might best deal with the inevitable problems they will encounter in such work.

Crossley and *Bennett* also reflect upon case-study research in a small-state, but in this instance it is the Central American nation of Belize. The chapter, however, is set more squarely in an evaluation framework, and pays particular attention to the process of capacity building in developing countries. The authors demonstrate how planning for case-study evaluation has been carried out in a collaborative manner, linked to the implementation of contemporary primary sector educational reform. Special attention is given to a review of the organizational framework established for the study and to the mechanisms devised for ongoing leadership, training and support. To date, little qualitative research or evaluation has been carried out in Belize, though research capacity building is seen as increasingly important for the future. As a study in its own right, this initiative is a useful example of a largely qualitative approach to evaluation originating from international collaboration. Belizean needs and personnel were nevertheless central to its initiation, and from the outset it has had a combination of both product (evaluation reports) and process (research capacity building) goals. The achievements of the early years of the study are documented and the problems encountered are identified here—with particular regard to the lessons that can be learned by others planning similar studies—especially in the context of small states where key personnel are inevitably involved in multiple activities.

A major issue that begins to emerge in Crossley and Bennett's analysis relates to the problems faced in planning and coordinating qualitative research that is to be carried out by teams. *Smith* pursues this theme further with specific reference to the problems he and colleagues encountered in the design and implementation of qualitative research in the primary teachers colleges of Pakistan. Systematization and coordination are essential when many different researchers require simultaneous training to carry out a multisite study—but detailed planning can also inhibit the flexibility and initiative that is central to "responsive" qualitative fieldwork. In this light, the Pakistan experience is most revealing.

Finally, *Choksi* and *Dyer* conclude the volume with a chapter that emphasizes the benefits to be gained from North-South collaboration, and demonstrates many of the basic principles of qualitative research in the context of ongoing fieldwork in the State of Gujarat in India. This is a rare and inspiring contribution in a number of ways. First, it is independent work funded by a Northern research council (the Economic and Social Research Council) but carried out in a developing country. Second, the two studies reported involve collaboration between an Indian artist and archaeologist, with an English linguist, academic and journalist. Their work most effectively shows how the combination of insider and outsider perspectives can be especially beneficial. As the authors themselves say:

> The pursuit of social understanding, which lies at the core of ethnographic research, is a process of discovery; this process can be greatly enhanced by collaboration with a colleague whose perceptions of the familiar and strange are so different from one's own; for the outsider's eyes readily see the strange, and the insider's perceptions of the familiar are sharpened.

The two studies reported concern the implementation of primary school innovation (Operation Blackboard), and a literacy project involving both researchers in the migration travels of Vagad Rabari nomads. As with Cheng, these authors note how perceptions of concepts and problems differ across cultures, and how an understanding of language and culture is vital for effective qualitative research. The chapter considers familiar issues such as access and the dilemmas of informed consent; it raises class and gender issues most vividly; and, for work of this nature, provides a most appropriate closing piece for the volume itself.

In conclusion, we hope the nature, variety and quality of the studies presented here will prove to be useful and stimulating for both new and experienced researchers involved in education and development worldwide. The structure of the book has been designed to make the material both accessible for reference purposes, and rewarding to read in its own right. If these characteristics help our work to contribute in some way to improved research capacity building in developing countries, the efforts of all involved will have been well acknowledged.

REFERENCES

Adamu, A.U. (1991) "Science Education as a Development Strategy in Nigeria: a Study of Kano State Science Secondary Schools." In K.M. Lewin with J.S. Stuart (eds.) *Educational Innovation in Developing Countries. Case-Studies of Change Makers.* London: Macmillan.

Altrichter, H., Posch, P. and Somekh, B. (1993) *Teachers Investigate their Work: An Introduction to the Methods of Action Research.* London: Routledge.

Atkinson, P. and Delamont, S. (1985) "Bread and Dreams or Bread and Circuses? A Critique of 'Case-Study' Research in Education." In M. Shipman (ed.) *Educational Research: Principles, Policies and Practices.* Lewes: Falmer Press.

Avalos, B. (ed.) (1986) *Teaching Children of the Poor. An Ethnographic Study in Latin America.* Ottawa: I.D.R.C.

Barley, N. (1986) *The Innocent Anthropologist.* Harmondsworth: Penguin.

Bassey, M. (1981) "Pedagogic Research: on the Relative Merits of Search for Generalisation and Study of Single Events," *Oxford Review of Education,* 7:73–94.

———. (1983) "Pedagogic Research into Singularities: Case-studies, Probes and Curriculum Innovations," *Oxford Review of Education,* 9:109–121.

———. (1990) "On the Nature of Research in Education" (part 2), *Research Intelligence,* 37:39–44.

Beld, J.M. (1994) "Constructing a Collaboration: a Conversation with Egon G. Guba and Yvonna S. Lincoln," *Qualitative Studies in Education,* 7(2):99–115.

Berger, P. and Luckmann, T. (1967) *The Social Construction of Reality.* Harmondsworth: Penguin.

Blackwell, J. (1992) "Research and Educational Aid: The International Perspective." In P. Kutnick and D. Stephens (eds.) *Qualitative Research in International Education and Development: Its Implications for Teaching, Training and Policy.* Brighton: Centre for International Education, University of Sussex.

Blumer, H. (1969) *Symbolic Interactionism: Perspective and Method.* Englewood Cliffs, NJ: Prentice Hall.

———. (1971) "Sociological Implications of the Thought of George Herbert Mead." In Cosin, B.R. et al. (eds.) *School and Society.* London: Routledge and Kegan Paul/Open University Press.

Bonnett, A. and Carrington, B. (1996) "Constructions of Anti-Racism in Britain and Canada," *Comparative Education,* 31(3) (in press).

Bryman, A. (1988) *Quantity and Quality in Social Research.* London: Unwin Hyman.

Bryman, A. and Burgess, R.G. (eds.) (1994) *Analysing Qualitative Data.* London: Routledge.

Burgess, R.G. (ed.) (1984) *The Research Process in Educational Settings: Ten Case-Studies*. Lewes: Falmer Press.

———. (1985) *Strategies of Educational Research: Qualitative Methods*. Lewes: Falmer Press.

Carr, W. and Kemmis, S. (1986) *Becoming Critical: Education, Knowledge and Action Research*. Lewes: Falmer Press.

Chilcott, J. (1987) "Where are You Coming From and Where are You Going? The Reporting of Ethnographic Research," *American Educational Research Journal*, 24: 199–218.

Crossley, M. (1981) "Strategies for Curriculum Change and SSCEP in Papua New Guinea." In A.R. Welch (ed.) *The Politics of Educational Change*. Armidale: University of New England.

———. (1984a) "Strategies for Curriculum Change and the Question of International Transfer," *Journal of Curriculum Studies*, 16:75–88.

———. (1984b) "The Role and Limitations of Small-Scale Initiatives in Educational Innovation," *Prospects*, XIV(4):533–540.

———. (1992) "Collaborative Research, Ethnography and Comparative and International Education in the South Pacific." In R.J. Burns and A.R. Welch (eds.) *Contemporary Perspectives in Comparative Education*. New York: Garland.

Crossley, M. and Broadfoot, P. (1992) "Comparative and International Research in Education: Scope, Problems and Potential," *British Educational Research Journal*, 18:99–112.

Crossley, M. and Burns, R.J. (1983) "Case-study in Comparative and International Education: An Approach to Bridging the Theory-Practice Gap." In B.A. Sheehan (ed.) *Comparative and International Studies and the Theory and Practice of Education*. Melbourne: La Trobe University/ANZCIES.

Crossley, M. and Vulliamy, G. (1984) "Case-Study Research Methods and Comparative Education," *Comparative Education*, 20:193–207.

———. (1986) The Policy of SSCEP. *Context and Development*. Waigani: University of Papua New Guinea.

Dalin, P. et al. (1994) *How Schools Improve. An International Report*. London: Cassell.

Elliott, J. (1981) *Action-research: A Framework for Self-evaluation in Schools*. Cambridge: Schools Council "Teacher-Pupil Interaction and the Quality of Learning" Project, Working Paper No.1.

———. (1991) *Action Research for Educational Change*. Milton Keynes, Open University Press.

Epstein, E. (1983) "Currents Left and Right. Ideology in Comparative Education," *Comparative Education Review*, 27: 3–29.

Fetterman, D.M. (1988) "A Qualitative Shift in Allegiance." In D.M. Fetterman (ed.) *Qualitative Approaches to Evaluation in Education: The Silent Scientific Revolution*. New York: Praeger.

Filstead, W.J. (ed.) (1970) *Qualitative Methodology: First Hand Involvement with the Social World*. Chicago: Markham.

Finch, J. (1986) *Research and Policy: The Uses of Qualitative Methods in Social and Educational Research*. Lewes: Falmer Press.

Fraser, S.E. (1964) *Jullien's Plan for Comparative Education. 1816–1817*. New York: Teachers College, Columbia University.

Fry, G.W. and Thurber, C.E. (1989) *The International Education of the Development Consultant. Communicating with Peasants and Princes*. Oxford: Pergamon.

Fuller, B. (1991) *Growing-Up Modern. The Western State Builds Third-World Schools*. London: Routledge.

Glaser, B. and Strauss, A. (1967) *The Discovery of Grounded Theory*. Chicago: Aldine.

Guba, E. (1990a) "The Alternative Paradigm Dialog." In E. Guba (ed.) *The Paradigm Dialog*. Newbury Park: Sage.

Guba, E. (ed.) (1990b) *The Paradigm Dialog*. Newbury Park: Sage.

Guba, E.G. and Lincoln, Y.S. (1988) "Do Inquiry Paradigms Imply Inquiry Methodologies?" In D.M. Fetterman (ed.) *Qualitative Approaches to Evaluation in Education: The Silent Scientific Revolution*. New York: Praeger.

Guthrie, G. and Martin, N.T. (eds.) (1983) *Directions for Educational Research*. Port Moresby: University of Papua New Guinea.

Halfpenny, P. (1982) *Positivism and Sociology: Explaining Social Life*. London: George Allen and Unwin.

Hammersley, M. (1979a) *Analysing Ethnographic Data*, Course DE304, Block 6, Part 1. Milton Keynes, Open University Press.

———. (1979b) *Data Collection in Ethnographic Research*, Course DE304, Block 4, Part 3. Milton Keynes, Open University Press.

———. (1992a) "The Paradigm Wars: Reports from the Front," *British Journal of Sociology of Education*, 13:131–143.

———. (1992b) *What's Wrong with Ethnography?* London: Routledge.

Hammersley, M. and Atkinson, P. (1983) *Ethnography: Principles in Practice*. London: Tavistock Press.

Hammersley, M. and Woods, P. (eds.) (1976) *The Process of Schooling*. London: Routledge and Kegan Paul.

Heyman, R. (1979) "Comparative Education from an Ethnomethodological Perspective," *Comparative Education*, 15: 241–249.

Kandel, I. (1933) *Studies in Comparative Education*. Boston: Houghton and Mifflin.

Kay, W.K. and Watson, J.K.P. (1982) "Comparative Education. The Need for Dangerous Ambition," *Educational Research*, 24(2): 129–140.

Kelly, G.P. and Altbach, P.G. (1988) "Alternative Approaches to Comparative Education." In T.N. Postlethwaite (ed.) *The Encyclopaedia of Comparative Education and National Systems of Education*. Oxford: Pergamon.

King, E. (1989) "Comparative Investigation of Education. An Evolutionary Process," *Prospects*, XIX(3): 369–379.

King, K. (1989) *Aid and Educational Research in Developing Countries*. Centre of African Studies: Edinburgh University.

———. (1991) Aid *and Education in the Developing World*. London: Longman.

King, K. and Singh, J.S. (1991) *Quality and Aid*. London: Commonwealth Secretariat.

Kuhn, T. (1962) *The Structure of Scientific Revolutions*. Chicago: University of Chicago Press.

Kushner, S. (1982) "The Research Process." In B. MacDonald, C. Adelman, S. Kushner and R. Walker (eds.) *Bread and Dreams: A Case-Study of Bilingual Schooling in the USA*. Norwich: CARE, University of East Anglia.

Lincoln, Y.S. (1990) "The Making of a Constructivist: a Remembrance of Transformations Past." In E. Guba (ed.) *The Paradigm Dialog*. Newbury Park: Sage.

Lincoln, Y.S. and Guba, E. (1985) *Naturalistic Inquiry*. Beverly Hills: Sage.

Little, A. (1988) *Learning from Developing Countries*. London: University of London Institute of Education.

Lomax, P. (ed.) (1990) *Managing Staff Development in Schools: An Action Research Approach*. Clevedon: Multilingual Matters.

———. (1991) *Managing Better Schools and Colleges: An Action Research Way*. Clevedon: Multilingual Matters.

Lutz, F. (1984) "Ethnography. The Holistic Approach to Understanding Schooling." In R. Burgess (ed.) *Field Methods in the Study of Education*. Lewis: Falmer Press.

Lyotard, J.F. (1984) *The Postmodern Condition. A Report on Knowledge*. Minneapolis: University of Minnesota Press.

Malinowski, B. (1922) *Argonauts of the Western Pacific*. London: Routledge and Kegan Paul.

Masemann, V.L. (1982) "Critical Ethnography in the Study of Comparative Education," *Comparative Education Review*, 26: 1–15.

———. (1990) "Ways of Knowing," *Comparative Education Review*, 34: 465–473.

May, S. (1994) *Making Multicultural Education Work*. Clevedon: Multilingual Matters Ltd.

Mazrui, A.A. (1990) *Cultural Forces in World Politics*. London: James Currie.

McKernan, J. (1991) *Curriculum Action Research: A Handbook of Methods and Resources for the Reflective Practitioner*. London: Kogan Page.

McNiff, J. (1988) *Action Research: Principles and Practice*. London: MacMillan Education.

McTaggart, R. and Kemmis, S. (1981) *The Action Research Planner*. Geelong: Deakin University.

Miles, M.B. and Huberman, A.M. (1994) *Qualitative Data Analysis: An Expanded Sourcebook*, 2d ed. Thousand Oaks, CA: Sage.

Norris, N. (1990) *Understanding Educational Evaluation*. London: Kogan Page.

O'Donoghue, T.A. (1994) "Transnational Knowledge Transfer and the Need to Take Cognisance of Contextual Realities: a Papua New Guinea Case-Study," *Educational Review*, 46:73–88.

Oja, S.N. and Smulyan, L. (1989) *Collaborative Action Research: A Developmental Approach*. Lewes: Falmer Press.

Oldfather, P. and West, J. (1994) "Qualitative Research as Jazz," *Educational Researcher*, 23:22–26.

Parlett, M. and Hamilton, D. (1977) "Evaluation as Illumination." In D. Hamilton, et al. (eds.) *Beyond the Numbers Game*. London: Macmillan.

Patton, M.Q. (1988) "Paradigms and Pragmatism." In D.M. Fetterman (ed.) *Qualitative Approaches to Evaluation in Education: The Silent Scientific Revolution*. New York: Praeger.

Prophet, R.B. (1994) "Educational Research in Botswana 1986–1991. Recent Trends and Future Directions." In S. Burchfield (ed.) *Research for Educational Policy and Planning in Botswana*. Gaborone: Macmillan.

Reichardt, C.S. and Cook, T.D. (1979) "Beyond Qualitative Versus Quantitative Methods." In T.D. Cook and C.S. Reichardt (eds.) *Qualitative and Quantitative Methods in Evaluation Research*. Beverly Hills: Sage.

Rist, R. (1980) "Blitzkrieg Ethnography: On the Transformation of a Method into a Movement," *Educational Researcher*, 9(2):8–10.

Rockwell, E. (1991) "Ethnography and Critical Knowledge of Education in Latin America," *Prospects*, XXI(2): 156–167.

Rust, V.D. (1991) "Postmodernism and its Comparative Education Implications," *Comparative Education Review*, 35(4): 610–626.

Sadler, M. (1900) "How Far Can We Learn Anything of Practical Value from the Study of Foreign Systems of Education." In J.H. Higginson (ed.) *Selections from Michael Sadler*. Liverpool: Dejall and Meyorre.

Saunders, M. and Vulliamy, G. (1983) "The Implementation of Curriculum Reform. Tanzania and Papua New Guinea," *Comparative Education Review*, 27: 351–373.

Schon, D.A. (1983) *The Reflective Practitioner*. London: Temple Smith.

Schutz, A. (1962) "Concept and Theory Formation in the Social Sciences." In M. Natanson (ed.) *Schutz's Collected Papers Volume 1*. The Hague: Nijhoff.

Schwandt, T.A. and Halpern, E.S. (1988) *Linking Auditing and Metaevaluation: Enhancing Quality in Applied Research*. Beverly Hills: Sage.

Silverman, D. (1993) *Interpreting Qualitative Data: Methods for Analysing Talk, Text and Interaction*. London: Sage.

Smith, J.K. (1989) *The Nature of Social and Educational Inquiry: Empiricism Versus Interpretation*. Norwood, NJ: Ablex.

Spindler, G. (ed.) (1982) *Doing the Ethnography of Schooling*. New York: Holt, Rinehart and Winston.

Stake, R.E. (1967) "The Countenance of Educational Evaluation," *Teachers College Record*, 68: 523–540.

Stenhouse, L. (1975) *An Introduction to Curriculum Research and Development.* London: Heinemann.

———. (1978) "Case-Study and Case Records: Towards a Contemporary History of Education," *British Educational Research Journal,* 4:21–39.

———. (1979) "Case-Study in Comparative Education. Particularity and Generalisation," *Comparative Education,* 15(1): 5–11.

Van der Eyken, W., Goulden, D. and Crossley, M. (1995) "Evaluating Educational Reform in a Small State: A Case Study of Belize, Central America." *Evaluation: The International Journal of Theory, Research and Practice,* 1 (1): 33–47.

Vulliamy, G. (1981) "The Secondary Schools Community Extension Project in Papua New Guinea," *Journal of Curriculum Studies,* 13:93–102.

———. (1985a) *A Comparative Analysis of SSCEP Outstations.* ERU Report 50, Waigani: University of Papua New Guinea.

———. (1985b) "The Diversification of Secondary School Curricula: Problems and Possibilities in Papua New Guinea." In K.M. Lillis (ed.) *School and Community in Less Developed Areas.* London: Croom Helm.

Vulliamy, G., Lewin, K. and Stephens, D. (1990) *Doing Educational Research in Developing Countries: Qualitative Strategies.* Basingstoke: Falmer Press.

Vulliamy, G. and Webb, R. (eds.) (1992) *Teacher Research and Special Educational Needs.* London: David Fulton.

Vulliamy, G. and Webb, R. (1993) "Special Educational Needs: from Disciplinary to Pedagogic Research," *Disability, Handicap and Society,* 8:187–202.

Walker, M. (1993) "Developing the Theory and Practice of Action Research: a South African Case," *Educational Action Research,* 1:95–109.

———. (1994) "Professional Development Through Action Research in Township Primary Schools in South Africa," *International Journal of Educational Development,* 14:65–73.

Walker, R. (1974) "Classroom Research: a View from SAFARI." In B. MacDonald et al. (eds.) *SAFARI: Innovation Evaluation Research and the Problem of Control.* Norwich: CARE, University of East Anglia.

Watson, K. and Oxenham, J. (eds.) (1985) *Research, Co-operation and Evaluation of Educational Programmes in the Third World.* Special Issue of the *International Journal of Educational Development,* 5(3).

Webb, R. (1990a) "The Origins and Aspirations of Practitioner Research." In R. Webb (ed.) *Practitioner Research in the Primary School.* Basingstoke: Falmer Press.

———. (ed.) (1990b) *Practitioner Research in the Primary School.* Basingstoke: Falmer Press.

Webb, R. and Vulliamy, G. (1996) *Roles and Responsibilities in the Primary School: Changing Demands, Changing Practices.* Buckingham: Open University Press.

Westgate, D., Batey, J. and Brownlee, J. (1990) "Collaborative Action Research: Professional Development in a Cold Climate," *British Journal of In-service Education,* 16:167–172.

Whitehead, J. (1993) *The Growth of Educational Knowledge: Creating Your Own Educational Theories.* Bournemouth: Hyde Publications.

Windham, D.M. (1992) *Education for All: The Requirements.* Paris: UNESCO.

Winter, R. (1989) *Learning from Experience: Principles and Practice in Action Research.* London: Falmer Press.

Wolcott, H.F. (1994) *Transforming Qualitative Data: Description, Analysis and Interpretation.* Thousand Oaks, CA: Sage.

Wright, C.A.H. (1988a) "Collaborative Action Research in Education (CARE)—Reflections on an Innovative Paradigm," *International Journal of Educational Development,* 8:279–292.

———. (1988b) "Internationalising Educational Research Paradigms: a West African Perspective," *Compare,* 18:39–51.

2 INTEGRATING PARADIGMS IN EDUCATIONAL RESEARCH

ISSUES OF QUANTITY AND QUALITY
IN POOR COUNTRIES

Rosemary Preston

INTRODUCTION

The introductory chapter to this volume has made a case for encouraging qualitative research in education in less developed parts of the world. This chapter provides a bridge between this introduction and the chapters that follow, exemplifying the methods by which such research might be done. By deconstructing some of the tensions latent in the terms quantitative and qualitative, when linked to research method and the methodology in which it is embedded, the chapter develops a very different line of argument to endorse the editors' position.

It is taken as given that research methods are not peculiar to disciplines and that, within and across disciplines, there is little essential difference in the information that may be obtained using one or another method. Instead, the observations of which different methods are capable and the purposes they serve may be the same. The argument is that methods are suited to the particular circumstances of a study so that, to ensure high quality work, researchers should have some skill in all methods if they are to make informed judgments about the work they appraise and undertake in different contexts.

Differentiating method from methodology, the chapter takes the position that the history of the development and use of method has as much to do with rhythms of change and vested interests as with the intrinsic merit of research outcomes derived from one approach or another. Preferences will differ in time and place in respect, for example, of industrial and post-industrial, colonial or neo-colonial societies. In this process, it is possible for the language used to denote the merits of different kinds of research activity to be at variance with what, with hindsight, is achieved.

A long-term, broad brush-stroke historical view presents research as essential human endeavor. This leads to discussion of the dominance of one or another kind of method since, in eighteenth-century Europe, the popular recognition of scientific rationality. Closer to the present, a case is made to link choice of method in different contexts to the current state of tension in development theory and practice. This tension lies in the uncertainties over the extent to which global and supra-national influence or individual and local participation have a greater part to play in the achievement of social and economic well-being.

To triangulate, in a way that is in keeping with contemporary thinking about qualitative research, an account is given of the personal experience of the author. This highlights the contradictory ways in which she and others perceive her work in terms of the methods on which it has been based.

The articulation of the politics of language and economy to preference of method in different contexts, combined with the possibly contentious use of highly subjective autobiographical experience of educational research, goes some way toward a holistic analysis of method as it relates, in this case, to educational research in poorer parts of the world.

SETTING THE SCENE AND CLARIFYING TERMS

To make sense of their environment, people categorize and label the things around them and the ideas which confront them. Chairs are different from tables; they are inseparable as furniture. Philosophy differs from history, but they are inseparable as modes of inquiry.

Research is based on the analysis of relationships between categories. It can create an impression of the separateness from each other of concepts or objects within different categories. It can also separate one category of concepts or objects from another. Sometimes, such separation is a device to assist researchers in the description of relationships and processes in respect of different aspects of the same phenomena.

While the creation of opposites leads to descriptive comparison, it does not immediately lend itself to analysis, in this case, of the use of particular types of method of research in particular types of country. For this to be possible, there are fundamental questions which have to be answered. They include, among others, *who* asks *whom* to do *what, how* and *why*. These questions relate to the execution of the research and to the purpose it is intended to serve. The question *when* means that some account should be taken of the ways in which political, economic and other environments affect decisions about the styles and substance of research at different points in time.

Raising issues such as these allows for researcher understanding of the chosen methods and their underlying assumptions to be articulated.

Methodologically, this brings into play the effect of researcher world views about how the political and economic organization of society interacts with individual or group action.[1] Taking such an approach provides an additional dimension to the simple comparative framework, making it possible to reason the case for different methods of research in respect of particular subject areas in different parts of the world.

Before beginning, there has to be some understanding of the key terms used in this chapter. They include education, educational and other research and what is implied when countries are said to be developing.

Without clarification of the scope of the word education, the perceived dominance of quantified educational research in poor countries may be mistaken. For reasons that will be discussed below, the structure of funding and size of formal systems of education lend themselves in some cases to highly visible research of this kind. However, there have been, throughout this century and before, what may be seen as qualitative studies of schooling in countries said to be developing, while research into other forms of education has rarely been otherwise.

In developing countries and elsewhere this includes research into the primary socialization of children (Mead, 1942; Nieuwenhuys, 1994); the internal processes and external dynamic of non-formal education for out-of-school youth and adults (Klaasen and Kleijer, 1993); studies of professional development, outside education, in public and private economic sectors (Jinkerson et al., 1992); studies of personal learning through community development (Damodaram, 1991); continuous informal learning throughout life (Antikainon et al., 1994).

It is suggested that investment in informal and non-formal educational activity surpasses many times that in formal systems. Its invisibility is explained in part by its continuous, diverse and often fragmented, forms of delivery. The concentration of interest in schooling and higher education and the visibility of research associated with them relates to the high priority (both public and private) given to the preparation of the young for future economic roles in industrial and post-industrial economies.

Categorizing educational research, it may be seen as a field of social inquiry susceptible to analysis at any level (from the individual to the global) and from single or multiple disciplinary perspectives. The point is that educational research does not have methods that are unique to it. In this vein, Guthrie (1987:5) describes his collection of papers, *Basic Research Techniques*, as "an introductory text for students starting to learn about carrying out research into their profession. It draws upon social science research methods commonly used in Papua New Guinea research in education."

Lewin (1990:46) is clear that "Educational research is inevitably cross-disciplinary and traditions within it vary over a broad spectrum that includes ethnographic work, case studies, psychometric approaches, experimental approaches, and survey methods. All of these have impeccable credentials, most are well-established in one or other of the social sciences."

Within this range the use of terms such as quantitative and qualitative becomes problematic. Clarification is needed over the extent to which qualitative research refers to the study of non-numerical attributes of a phenomenon or whether it refers to the methods of analysis undertaken.

For the purposes of this chapter, studies, whatever their methodology, may be undertaken of both quantitative and qualitative aspects of educational development using a range of recognized quantitative and qualitative techniques. However, as will be seen below, quantitative techniques may be applied to qualitative analysis; qualitative methods may be used in what appear to be quantitative studies; sometimes the two are seen as one. Such confusion is exacerbated when it is taken to infer significantly different epistemological interpretations between the producer and the users of the same piece of research.

The case for the cross-national use of any recognized technique, however categorized, assumes that the principles of socially scientific method are not susceptible to cross-cultural, political or economic influences. Logically, if methods of research within and between groups within countries are not altered by the characteristics of the individuals or groups being studied, the same has to be true cross-nationally, regardless of country or country cluster characteristics. There will be complex contextual differences that will affect the conduct of any study and the characteristics of information to be gathered. Nevertheless, in a comparative analysis of women and men attending the same professional development courses in banking, the range of methods available to collect and process information will be the same in, for example, Namibia, Australia or Cuba. The methods of oral history among marginally literate groups will vary little in the U.S., China or South Africa.

If the logic of method applied across cultures, nations and states is constant, other explanations have to be found for its variable application. This chapter is concerned with explanations for choice of method in countries that have been loosely dichotomized according to their social and economic characteristics. The labeling of these categories, in terms of development, has to be done with care. Each of the terms in common use (developed, developing, more or less developed, underdeveloped, rich and poor) provides information about the users' world view, their political assumptions and their awareness of theories of change.

Describing some countries as developing may imply that other countries are not developing. This may be because they have not embarked on the path to development. It may be because they have achieved it. In the past, industrial countries of Europe and North America were sometimes described as developed. They were seen to have achieved and maintained high levels of income and social well-being. Developing countries were those seeking to emulate this development through the industrialization of their economies. In the 1990s, the liberalization of the global economy has seen the social and economic exclusion of growing numbers of people in industrial and post-industrial societies. It has consolidated the position of cosmopolitan commercial and agribusiness elites in countries where the majority of people struggle to survive on the yields from crop and livestock production in increasingly impoverished sectors of rural economies. In each case, this marginalization is a feature of a political and economic system which prevents integration of those at the periphery.

With exceptions, industrial and post-industrial societies represent the rich world with high levels of Human Development (UNDP, 1994). Countries with little industry and weak trading positions are typically poor with low Human Development scores. End-of-century economic and political uncertainties make it optimistic to assume that such states will improve their position or that previously stable affluent states will not collapse.

Mindful of the rapidity and unpredictability of current trends and of the social variations within states indicated above, this chapter uses the terms less-developed, low income and poor interchangeably and more-developed, high income and rich to examine the conditions under which the characteristics of nations and states might affect approaches to educational research within them.

The paragraphs that follow speculate across time about the evolution of method and preference fashions before proposing a definition of the distinction between qualitative and quantitative information. This leads to a discussion of the implications for different kinds of educational research in rich and poor countries.

THE RESEARCH ENDEAVOR IN HISTORICAL PERSPECTIVE

Research is a systematic process of gathering, interpreting and communicating information. For researchers and for the receivers of their findings, it is always an educational experience. In studies of the ways in which people behave and think, the provision of information is likely to enhance understanding, as participants confront an aspect of their lives from an angle not previously considered. Informants may also gain insights into themselves by tailoring what they say to the image of themselves that they wish to project.

In societies without written systems of communication, such information gathering, synthesizing and sharing has been the basis of technological development. This can be inferred from the human ability to process material through trial and error and develop skills to optimize the use of the goods produced, so as to facilitate survival. The making of pots from clay, the spinning and weaving of fiber into cloth, the extraction of salt from grass, would all be outcomes of such technological inquiry.

Of a different order, oral and pictorial history represent a form of research endeavor in these contexts. Elders will have passed on details to aid storytelling and rock and cave paintings, in places as far apart as Papua New Guinea, Scandinavia, France, Zimbabwe and Australia. In pre-literate societies, research of this kind was grounded in experience and local need. As soon as encoded forms of information conservation and dissemination technologies (writing, reading, printing) are developed, there is the possibility of the production and widespread dissemination of human information as we know it today (Deutsch, 1966; Goody and Watt, 1968).

From the civilizations of Ancient Egypt, Greece and Rome, through the Middle Ages in Europe, and into New World colonization in the fifteenth and sixteenth centuries, precise measurement and statistical data collection were essential for building, land control and taxation (Hayes, 1971; Price, 1986). More qualitative records were kept of military strategy and history (Caesaris, 1954; Walsh, 1974), while the study of philosophy and logic with its emphasis on rhetoric, dialectic and mathematics flourished in modes which are, broadly, still in use today (Bowen, 1972).

From sketchy examples such as these, the capacity to recognize, evaluate and capitalize on innovation, using a range of methods, emerges as a human trait. It is always a social process. The nineteenth-century European designation of the study of human behavior as social science did not herald the beginning of intrinsically new methods of social research. In the wake of the scientific enlightenment of the previous centuries, it did have a major impact on the esteem accorded to different kinds of approach, the effects of which continue to influence research in all parts of the world.

CONTROLS, FASHIONS AND METHODS

While everyone has the capacity to make research-based discovery, access to the coding systems required to process and transmit new knowledge has, throughout history, been regulated by levels of technology and by vested political and economic interests. In addition to the frequent restrictions on access to information circulated in written reports, the availability of paper, print and the skills to use them continue to be controlled.

The revolution in social thinking that occurred in Western Europe in the eighteenth and nineteenth centuries saw the development of what became known as the positivistic approach to the study of society. This simulated the styles then thought appropriate to research in the physical and life sciences and represented the ways in which enlightened social thinkers harnessed fashionable concepts of rationality and objectivity to their work. Counting and statistical analysis became the most visible and publicly esteemed form of processing social information, as influential people subscribed to the rhetoric of mathematical rigor and ability to test hypotheses and reveal truth free from bias. The belief was firmly encouraged that the understanding derived from such systematic research would in due course have a more beneficial effect on social behavior and well-being than knowledge produced by other means (Wallerstein, 1991).

The focus on the counting and calculating aspects of what is, in effect, the study of relationships between items of information is common among researchers who came to lead social science across the emerging disciplines from the mid-nineteenth century. This was as true of social anthropologists as it was of sociologists and economists. Warwick makes the point that Malinowski's anthropologies of village life in the South Pacific in the early twentieth century were heavily statistical, for all their contribution to the understanding of qualitative method (Malinowski, 1922; Warwick, 1993). As late as the 1960s one-third of the articles in the American Anthropologist over a five-year period were based on studies employing survey instruments and statistical analysis (Bennett and Thaiss, 1967, quoted in Warwick, 1993). I quote anthropology because in the mid-1990 mindset, as Vulliamy (1990) reminds us, it is the discipline most frequently associated with qualitative approaches to data collection and interpretation. In practice, although much debated, peculiar to the disciplines is their field of study, and not their modes of analysis.

Wallerstein (1991:265) argues the lack of methodical difference, not only between anthropology and sociology, but between all the social science disciplines. "The holy trinity of politics/economics/society-culture has no intellectual heuristic value today. It probably never did. . . . Economic historians are recognising this increasingly by becoming 'social historians'. . . . Let us study the dynamics of family history, but let us not forget price curves in the process . . . and also let us analyse specifically the politics of price curves, or of family history. . . ." Wallerstein's point is that political, economic and social phenomena are inseparable, a seamless web. He sees the separation of social reality into three arenas: ". . . as a terrible legacy of the nineteenth century; . . . a nonsense in terms of how the world really works. No one subjectively has three segregated motivations, economic, political and socio-cultural and there are no institutions that are exclusively in one arena" (Wallerstein, 1991:264).

From this perspective, social science disciplines serve as a mechanism to help the understanding of the complexity of phenomena. Contemporary interest in research that is inter-disciplinary, cross-disciplinary, multi-disciplinary or multi-method, implicitly or explicitly, addresses its inseparability.

This line of argument makes it inevitable that research referring to non-quantified aspects of social processes continued, using what may have appeared as less systematic means of data collection, during the period of the popularization of rational sciences of society and after. As was previously the case, during the Enlightenment and since, the production of knowledge can be seen to derive from the spectrum of techniques available for the analysis of all aspects of data at any level. Even in nineteenth-century France, the early positivists stressed the importance of accounting for context and process, physical and metaphysical, in the interpretation of the significance of social data otherwise treated to scientific analysis (Comte, 1851–54). To this extent a positive science of society is predicated on theories of history and relativity as is any other.

This seems to suggest that explanations for what may appear to be no more than changes in fashion should be sought in other domains, possibly in the complexity of the historically intimate relationship between esteemed knowledge and power. This brings the argument back to the question of who decides what research will be done, with what resources and for what purposes, and the extent to which changing preferences in method are explained by historical, political or methodological rationality.

RESEARCH LEVELS, SCALE AND THE KNOWLEDGE PRODUCTION PROCESS

Accepting the seamlessness of disciplines and the common purpose and capacity of method, it remains to identify contexts in which one approach rather than another may be preferred. As Wallerstein (1991) reminds us, history has seen the growth of economic and social spheres from systems at the household and community level, to those at the level of the province, state and globe. However, along with research that reflects this at national and supra-national levels there has been an uninterrupted need, worldwide, for microlevel studies of intra- and inter-familial, community and organizational relationships.

These studies may inform local practice, but frequently their data are aggregated to provide information for variation within and between wider areas. For all their mundanity, it is not so much at issue that they provide a combination of both quantitative and qualitative information, in either rich or poor countries, but whether or not the knowledge they produce is seen to be based on research.

Within school systems, anywhere in the world, teachers recording the daily attendance of children are collecting information. As soon as they seek to identify and explain patterns of attendance (at different times of the year, according to the sex, age, social origin, motivation or attainment of their pupils) an element of research is present. Head teachers who synthesize class teacher observations, when compiling periodic reports to government about their school and its activities, are participating in a structured research process. It enables a situational analysis (locally, regionally, nationally and eventually globally) on which resource allocations and policy reformulation will be based. Highly applied, such reports depend on a combination of statistical and qualifying descriptive information. A decision to reduce staff levels in the face of falling rolls will be inappropriate without an explanation. Mass emigration from the area might warrant such a move. A severe epidemic or poor quality teaching would not.

Day-to-day research of this kind is a centuries-old aspect of continuous reflection on performance without which organizations, private as well as public, would lose their sense of purpose and achievement. The grey literature produced in this way may represent the meeting of the ways between the academic researcher and the practitioners who write it. That academic researchers, concerned with generalizations at levels far removed from (but umbilically linked to) the practitioner, fail to regard the production of such material as research has become an indictment of their self-perception as intellectual elites.

For similar reasons, the academic researcher may feel equal or greater ambiguity about the knowledge produced, not only by salaried employees of public or private organizations, but by consultant researchers contracted at daily rates to perform client-specified tasks. Again it is seen to be the lack of overt engagement with social theory that discredits research of this kind, although of necessity, it tends to demonstrate a range of techniques, at several levels of analysis. The nonacademic affiliation of many such researchers is a further, usually unspoken, indictment of their work. Typically from rich countries, they will be contracted for work at home or abroad depending on experience. Although increasing, the number of poor country consultants employed internationally is small. There is no history of their advising on rich country development. Open to question is the extent to which books such as this one and a growing number of other publications, often published by non-governmental organizations (NGOs), represent a challenge to or reinforcement of the elitist stance of rich country academics and their control of research method principles (Feuerstein, 1986; Nichols, 1991). These straightforward texts on different aspects of the research process aim to enable nonacademic research workers to monitor what they do and to modify their own action to make it more effective. In the main, written by rich country natives and published in either rich or poor countries, by rich country natives, the methods proposed do not vary from those recommended in less accessible texts, for all that they may emphasize participative process and quality. In marketing terms, there is seen to be an international demand for the information they contain, particularly in less developed parts of the world.

Returning to the theme, if routine applied research for organizational process and outcome monitoring uses both quantitative and qualitative approaches, the question arises as to whether other kinds of study are more fastidious in the type of method they require. Once again, there is doubt that this is so.

Large-Scale Studies

It is axiomatic that large-scale research is costly and that those who harness the resources to pay for it are found in positions of influence. While there is some stereotyping of the relationship between scale and methods of research, the theoretical necessity for this is far from certain. Equally, researcher world view will determine the extent to which the knowledge produced by different methods of research is seen to be grounded in different epistemologies or serves, in the long-term, different social and political purposes.

There is no doubt that survey methods and statistical analysis of data lend themselves for economic reasons to studies of large numbers of people. National censuses of population provide baseline information about demographic, social and economic trends which assist government planning and studies by international organizations of the comparative advantage of nations. Including education and occupational data, censuses are critical instruments in human resource planning and the development of education and training systems.

Large-scale studies require a high degree of control of both those who provide and those who gather information. Questionnaires are constructed in ways which minimize error on completion, whether by respondents or by interviewers. Typically, choice of response is seen to be forced, requiring the selection of one of a small number of prescribed responses. Information provided by respondents, which qualifies the responses made, will be ignored. This has major implications for the validity of the research if only the forced response is counted.

At the same time, it is fallacious to imply that large-scale surveys use only closed questions to gather data suitable for statistical analysis. Many include open questions for information that cannot be previously categorized. Until recently such data may have been unsuitable for statistical procedures once the survey was complete. Today, computerized systems allow for the analysis of qualitative survey data, to the extent that the quantification of qualitative data is commonplace. Once again the scientific rigor of survey methods comes into question.

In studies of literate populations large-scale surveys may require respondents to complete questionnaires themselves. When few respondents are literate, survey information including census data will be gathered by specially trained interviewers. The ability of interviewers to maximize the reliability of the data they collect will depend on the extent to which the instrument successfully measures error their commitment to the intrinsic value of the study, and the extent to which they remain sensitive to what they are doing.

I have suggested above that all methods of data collection and analysis were common before scientific rationality became the guiding principle of social research. The production of knowledge derived from the statistical analysis of survey data is sometimes taken to require relations of production analogous to those classically used in industrial manufacturing. Tasks are highly specified and routinized as much as possible so as to reduce error and increase output. Workers may have little understanding of the significance of their contribution to the overall production process and so lack interest in its quality. Just as the profit from manufacturing will be invested in owners and managers, so too the use to which such research will be put will share the interests of sponsors and clients and the dominant social economic interests that they represent. Rarely will they benefit those who provided the information on which their research was based.

In rich countries, surveys of social deprivation and the identification of strategies for its alleviation carried out by altruistic intellectuals of the nineteenth and twentieth centuries can be construed as contributions to the understanding of the social dynamics of production by people whose funds come from the purse of industrial and landed elites who interpret the realities they observe in terms of otherness from their own. The work of Charles Booth and Beatrice Webb on poverty in London (Booth, 1891–1903) and Engels's (1952) studies of factory life in nineteenth-century Manchester would be examples of studies of this kind. Regardless of their original intention, such studies have led to policy to increase productivity through strategy to improve the social well-being of the poor. In the past such strategy has included the increased provision of education.

The use of large-scale surveys by metropolitan powers to facilitate administration of their colonial dependencies makes transparent the commercialization of knowledge production that takes place as, for example, literate subsistence producers are contracted to complete pre-constructed questionnaires with data taken in interviews from neighbors for national censuses of population, education, health or economic well-being.

The many studies of the influences on individual modernity which were popular in poor countries in the late 1960s and early 1970s would be recent examples of the genre. Most included complex attitudinal and behavioral surveys and with few exceptions were carried out by North Americans or national researchers who had been trained in the United States. Examples include the six-country study of schooling and factory work conducted by Inkeles and Smith (1974) and the studies in South America on geographic and social mobility in which schooling was a critical variable (Kahl, 1968; Balán, Browning and Jelín, 1973).

Industrialization as a strategy for economic growth in primary commodity producing countries, with expected trickle-down improvements in social well-being, legitimized the import of quantitative studies based on neoclassical economic and later welfarist models of development. From the late 1950s, neo-colonialist, policy-oriented studies included elaborate quantitative appraisals of human resource needs and the capacity building policy for education and training that would enable them to be met. Ecuador was one of many countries in 1970 that used international bank loans to research manpower needs and human resource development strategies that would enable industrialized planned targets to be met (Junta Nacional de Planificación, 1970, 1978). More recently Papua New Guinea, along with other countries, has followed the same route in the new wave of internationally sponsored, market-led human resource analysis (Government of Papua New Guinea, 1986).

The assumptions underlying this strategy were that theories of social organization, production and change derived from experience in the industrial world would be relevant to growth and wealth elsewhere. Training sections of the population so that the workforce had the range of skills found in such rich, modern societies would facilitate industrial development and subsequent wealth in countries as yet less technologically advanced (Harbison and Myers, 1964). Large-scale surveys were deemed the most efficient way of identifying educational and training needs and achievements.

Funded by metropolitan organizations, such studies have over many years received much criticism (Bowman, 1966), but continue to be done. They have typically been carried out by expatriate researchers employing local people to gather and process data. They use analytical techniques and present reports that are often beyond the comprehension of those in government who would be responsible for the implementation of their recommendations.

In sum, there is no prerequisite for large-scale studies to emphasize either quantitative or qualitative approaches to research. There is ample evidence to suggest that, whatever the method, there can be no guarantee of rigor in what are necessarily complex processes of data collection and analysis. Colonial history and development inspiration have seen the importation by poor countries of large-scale research that confirms the social and educational distance to be traveled on the road to development. Led by expatriate statisticians, if meaningless to local people, the quality of the process and outcome of such work becomes irrelevant, no matter how well, in the eyes of the researcher, it has been executed.

SMALL-SCALE RESEARCH

It would be misleading to infer that data from small-scale research does not lend itself to statistical analysis derived from questionnaire surveys. Brief questionnaires, small samples and quantification are commonplace. It is equally misleading to suggest that qualitative research is necessarily small scale, although stereotypically it is seen to be so. Similarly it is not the case that non-quantitative studies ceased to be done with the popular acceptance of scientific rationality and social research that was based on its principles. Applied to education in Europe, it is clear that there has always been routine monitoring of educational and social development using both quantitative and qualitative techniques. Thabault (1971), referring to school, parish and government records, was able to construct the development of village schooling in Mazière en Gâtine in France from 1789 to 1914. His explanations are in terms of the diversification of the French economy, the social and economic situation of the community and the quality of individual teachers and their commitment to the school. It is clear that from the beginning there was a systematic recording and analysis of all these issues.

In Britain, by 1850 the government had commissioned studies of the quality of teaching and parliamentary reports, among others, linking this quality, in part at least, to the wealth of the parish and its commitment to the schooling of the young (Watkins, 1846). Such writing is copious and typically on a small scale. It provides detailed information about what was provided and how and what those involved felt about it. In many countries, it is richly supplemented by literary contributions derived from the authors' childhood and teaching experiences. They include, in Britain, Dickens (1892), Brontë (1847) and others.

Elsewhere the early histories of colonial schooling in Latin America, Africa, Asia and the Pacific have been constructed from the notes, reports and diaries of state and church representatives and sometimes local people as well (Jiménez de la Espada, 1881–1897; Jinks, Biskup and Nelson, 1973; Altbach and Kelly, 1978). On the basis of writing such as this, metropolitan revisions to colonial educational policy were made. More visible small-scale research on educational processes in poor countries includes famous anthropologies such as Mead's (1942) work in the South Pacific and that of Spindler (1963) in Mexico, as well as studies of multi-lingualism, administration and policy.

Recently, policy-oriented research emphasizing qualitative techniques is to be found. In Papua New Guinea, they include research into curriculum development by Crossley (1990) and Vulliamy (1985), as well as a cross-national study of primary school teaching in Latin America by Beatrice Ávalos (1986). There are now many studies of indigenous language and schooling (see for example the work of the Instituto de Estudios Peruanos and the Instituto Bartolomé de las Casas in Cuzco) (Godenzzi, 1992) and of schooling and many forms of social continuity and change, such as Nasson's (1986) work in South Africa. Autobiographical novels from writers in newly independent states provide detailed insights into educational experience in places as far apart as Namibia (Diescho, 1988, 1992), Papua New Guinea (Eri, 1970; Soaba, 1977) and Somalia (Farah, 1985).

All in all, as with large-scale educational research, small-scale studies in colonial and neo-colonial contexts have mirrored those of the metropolis. In this, the early and continuing routine monitoring reports ceded visibility to large-scale research. The present pressure to raise the profile of studies that emphasize the qualitative dimensions of development is again in the wake of a rich world movement, one that started nearly two decades ago, but explanations for this are complex and partially obscure. They only partly relate to the critiques of quantitative research indicated above. They are also linked to events in the global economy and to thinking about the implications of these for development.

Changing Emphasis in Development Theory and Research
The failure of rich countries to sustain their own industrial base and of de-

velopment strategy elsewhere raises questions about the relevance of scientific planning to meet specified human resource needs. Combined with neo-Marxist research initiated as to why this should be (Baran, 1957; Cardoso and Faletto, 1969) there has been what is now labeled a crisis in development theory (Hettne, 1990), as evidenced by its inability to theorize the failure of development strategy, including educational strategy, or to formulate ideas for effective new policy. In negotiating this impasse there has been a shift away from states as the focus of planned development to sub-state multi-level development on the one hand and supra-state initiatives on the other (Hettne, 1990; Booth, 1993).

The contemporary movement to rediscover and give value to qualitative approaches to the study of social process is associated with efforts to redress these failures, as well as with the changing pattern of global political and economic relations over the past twenty years. This has seen the arrival of the basic needs approach to development and small-scale self-help projects as the means by which they are to be met. Research associated with these is typically small-scale and less than generously funded, often by resource-stretched NGOs. Such research would in many cases be described as qualitative. Social and gender planning techniques aim to ensure the participation of all stakeholders at each stage of a project cycle, from identification to summative evaluation (Conyers, 1982; Feuerstein, 1986; Marsden and Oakley 1990; Nichols, 1991; Moser, 1993). These processes, developed in response to demand for local control over internationally resourced local development, aim to enhance local capacity in needs identification and action planning and implementation. Without care, they may also ensure continued external control of activities intended to build local leadership and administrative skills.

Many cite Paolo Freire as a catalyst for this kind of development thinking. Without doubt his writing about ways in which to raise awareness of the political dynamic of poverty and oppression was the stimulus for much non-formal education in the 1970s and 1980s. Few question the origins of his thinking and the way it has been influenced by French philosophy (Taylor, 1993) or by the history of participatory adult education and its ability to challenge political and social inequality that has, for more than a century, been a feature of popular resistance in industrial Europe, North America and even pre-industrial Japan. At the other extreme from local participation are supra-national regional alliances to regulate trade and other cultural commerce. Research is commissioned in their interest as a prerequisite for investment in large-scale development. Stereotypically it is quantitative. An example would be a recent World Bank study of women in higher education (Subbarao et al., 1994).

These differences are significant in that they affect the status of the research and those who have access to its findings, within and beyond, the country to which it relates. In large-scale, cross-national quantitative research informants, excavated for the information they contain, are seen to assume roles which are passive, non-reflective and determined by the researcher. They may learn nothing in the process of the study nor of its findings or the use to which they are put. Frequently, the data on which reports are based are exported by funding organizations and are not available locally either to governments or ultimate users of action taken as a result.

From writing such as that synthesized in the opening section of the book by Vulliamy and colleagues (1990), there is clear awareness of the early dualistic critiques of quantitative research and of the complementary virtues of qualitative techniques. These were to the effect that one was informed by pre-set hypotheses, the other committed to their generation; one provided decontextualized fact and the other facilitated the understanding of process and contextual influence; one served to produce easily accessible insensitive information, the other to penetrate sensitivities otherwise undisclosable. In this, the virtues ascribed to quantitative studies in the nineteenth century are described as vices by those who extol softer, less scientific, more reflective and avowedly subjective approaches. The naturalistic paradigm is cited in contrast to those of rationalism, positivism and scientism.

At the same time, as well as writing which criticizes the claim of a-theoreticism in qualitative research, there is as we have seen a body of literature that challenges the notion that one method of data collection is inherently more suited to gathering particular types of information. Critics claim that surveys do not provide access to the meaning for the respondent of the behavior reported or to details of the factors that caused it. This is not necessarily so. The careful survey researcher will have included either open or closed questions to elicit such qualitative information should it appear relevant to the project.

Similarly, challenging formerly conventional wisdom (Rose, 1982), there are occasions when face-to-face methods fail to achieve the disclosure of sensitive information as effectively as a survey. At a 1993 seminar on research methods, sponsored by the Economic and Social Research Council, it was reported that the anonymity of questionnaires may be more effective than in-depth interviews as a means of obtaining accounts of difficult personal experience (Brannen, 1992).

THE FEMINIST CHALLENGE: ATTACK AND COUNTER ATTACK

The contribution of the feminist movements to restoring the visibility and status of qualitative research is fully acknowledged by Vulliamy (1990). Its argument has been that understanding of women's reality may be improved by giving value to women's subjective experience. Such understanding is held to be one of the prerequisites for women's empowerment.

Inevitably, the political threat that arises when oppressed groups find ways to give themselves voice leads to new silencing strategies on the part of those in positions of power in relation to them. It is a short step from images of soft femininity to charges of lack of rigor in qualitative feminist research. Cotterill and Letherby (1993, 1994) received strong attacks on their work, after a summary of their autobiographical research on women had appeared in Britain's *Times Higher Education Supplement.*

To redress the tendency for this discriminatory backlash to undermine such research, typically against women who write on women, Nelly Stromquist in a recent book *Women and Education in Latin America* includes quantitative as well as qualitative feminist studies, aiming to repudiate the stereotyped linkage of qualitative, soft and womanly (Stromquist, 1992). In similar vein is the call by Sprague and Zimmerman (1989) for a reconstruction of feminist research that integrates quantitative and qualitative approaches.

An alternative undermining strategy is for those in positions of authority to appropriate as their own action by subordinates that comes to threaten their position. The participatory ethos of popular development initiatives with its implications for action research, in educational activity in particular (Hall, et al., 1982), is now incorporated as part of the development rhetoric of national governments and supra-national organizations (Overseas Development Adminstration, 1994; Quarles van Ufford, 1993).

The language is of user awareness and choice and of delegation to local authority of the responsibility for the provision of services. Meanwhile, economic restrictions reduce options and the capacity to meet demand from local resources. In this there is paradox. Decentralization (however rhetorical) does mean some localization of research and a new focus on the building of indigenous capacity to generate knowledge, analyze situations and identify need. However, the mass of information gathered has still to be reduced into the conventional prose forms required to attract funds for development activity. This then becomes the point at which the control of locally generated knowledge passes from the community to those skilled in brokering information in such ways (Preston and Arthur, 1995).

COMBINATION, INTEGRATION OR FUSION?

The value of combining methods has long been accepted as a legitimate research strategy. It is not always articulated. People will often not describe as qualitative the work of preparing instruments which will collect data for statistical analysis. They will not categorize as a qualitative aspect of research the task of identifying who informants should be. Likewise, the time spent reflecting upon why the statistics describe relationships as they do is a process of tracing links from the data back to what is known of the contexts in which they were found. It is exactly analogous to the processes undertaken in respect of data that have not been treated quantitatively. Vulliamy (1990:17–18) refers to a sequential process in which concern with issues of quality and quantity alternate as the work progresses.

For Warwick (1993) such multi-method, but not necessarily ordered, research and the triangulation of techniques amounts to integration of method. To move the debate along, I want to suggest that the starting point is one of fusion. Research may be the process of disaggregation, of providing explanations for different aspects of the same, sometimes very complex, phenomena.

At issue, in the context of educational research in poor countries, is the extent to which research is undervalued if it does not give salience to the numerical qualities of phenomena and the extent to which such quantification reduces the visibility of its non-quantitative parts. I want to suggest that the qualitative and quantitative nomenclatures represent user interests in separating the inseparable, which makes it impossible to define a qualitative as opposed to a quantitative datum. It can be said that the qualitative dimensions of any item of information are many and include its numerical attributes. In this, number and quality are inseparable in information that may carry labels of either type.

This alone suggests a strong case for modifying the way in which we discuss the characteristics of research. One solution may be to assume the above fusion of quantity and quality and refer to the balance of verbal and numerical description and analysis within any study. This would be on the understanding that either can be achieved by several means and depend upon a variety of underlying assumptions.

Support for such a strategy comes from statisticians' perceptions of the quantitative/qualitative divide. Miller and Wilson (1983: 89) clarify the issue with reference to systems of a number in a way that appears to take researchers back to their first lesson in statistics. "Measurement or classification at the nominal level where observations are assigned to categories with no implications of relative value or size is qualitative measurement. If numbers are used to code observation categories then they have no more significance than do words, although they are more convenient for processing."

The implications of this are many. It is common for university research method courses to teach how to quantify qualitative discourse and observational data using a range of both non-parametric and, somewhat surprisingly to the novice, parametric statistical techniques.[2]

Thirty years ago, the factor analysis of Guttman scales and personal construct grids were commonly cited examples (Guttman, 1950; Bannister, 1962). Today similar concerns are apparent as computer packages for the management and processing of non-quantified data become ever more sophisticated (Looker et al., 1989). Nominal and ordinal[3] survey data analyzed statistically are also qualitative as are dichotomous dummy variables in regression analysis. Presumably, interval and ratio data not subjected to parametric statistical analysis may also be described as qualitative. In essence, the overlap may be total.

An illustration may help to clarify the above confusion. The data collected for my doctoral thesis using an interview schedule was subjected to computer analysis using SPSS. I understood that the exercise was quantitative and suppressed many of the descriptive contributions from informants that had not been so analyzed. My examiner, feeling that I had completed a piece of ethnography, commented that I had not done myself justice (Preston, 1981). In the same study, I used grid reference techniques to code personal constructions of the relationships between education and different forms of migration. I described my observations, but chose not to submit them to factor analysis on the grounds that the assumptions of equality between intervals between ratings on grid axes were spurious and so invalidated the requirements for parametric statistical procedures (Preston, 1981). In practical terms, at the level of data, there is uncertainty as to which meet the criteria for either qualitative or quantitative study. Arguments are proposed and widely accepted that allow the application of statistical procedures to data apparently not strong enough to permit this.

So What for Paradigms?

Kuhn (1970) proposed the paradigm as the working assumptions, procedures and findings that define a stable pattern of activity for a group of scholars and that help to identify that community. Such a position makes it possible to argue within a pluralist framework that so-called quantitative and qualitative approaches to research are located within different paradigms. Many political economists would claim, using modes of analysis at a different level of abstraction, that both are products of the same system, within a single paradigm, one that is at present oriented to the creation of a global consumer culture alienated from primary production capacity. Accepting the validity of each position means accepting the idea of paradigmatic hierarchy. If ultimately the same point is made based on information gathered using diverse methods, can it be said that the motive underlying the choice of one technique or another, or the purpose to be served by the research using either one, is essentially different? The logic of the method chosen (whether quantitative or qualitative) lies in debate such as this. It lies in the world views of researchers and in their understanding of the dynamic of social cohesion and change. In the end, it is a question of preference.

I know that my own capacity to polish my responses to market researchers collecting data that will be fed into either quantitative or qualitative statistical analysis is normal practice. What I feel to be a highly personalized structuring of my realities in other, apparently less structured, research encounters is also common to the population as a whole. Without being able to confirm the acceptability of the margins of distortion thus incurred, I have to confess doubt about the greater reliability of data using one approach or another. In like vein, while protesting objectivity in house-count sample selection, I know that in Ecuador, confronted with a barking dog outside one of two equidistant houses in my count path, I used to be hard put not to find a good reason for selecting the unguarded house.

As these behaviors are commonplace in research that will have high levels of both verbal and numerical description (Casley and Lury, 1981; Murthy, 1978; Paneff, 1988), the question that has to be posed is: whose interests are being served by the rhetoric of technical rigor applied to inevitably unreliable research. Cynicism immediately says it is tied to the legitimization of the use of money. Large-scale technologically sophisticated studies are likely to serve one set of interests. Small-scale research with minimal infrastructural requirements will serve another. This is not necessarily so.

Stereotypically, the former might derive from the need of state or supra-national organizations whose funding allocation criteria require specific forms of nationwide information before disbursements can be made. The World Bank working through national governments might be an example. A case in point is the Bank's complex reanalysis of statistical data (collected earlier for other purposes) in six countries. The Bank uses the same econometric techniques to predict the probability of positive economic returns to investment in education for women (Herz and Khandker, 1991).

The second case would be exemplified by community level, participatory, sometimes action research (in which adult education researchers were pioneers), which aimed to raise awareness of the political dimensions of social disadvantage and stimulate action to redress them. Key words in this approach are local and relevant, but thinking is usually externally derived, as is the typically modest funding. The approach is radical in that in theory it empowers the oppressed, whether rural or urban poor, women or members of subordinate ethnic groups (Hall et al., 1982; Fals Borda et al., 1991). However, while the rhetoric and interest of the two schemes are wholly different, it could be said they serve complementary purposes, oriented towards the same ends.

Incorporation of women in the labor market, beyond the involvement that is possible from within the domestic arena, can be justified on the grounds that it will make a significant contribution to economic well-being, beyond what would be achieved if the target of such investment were men. For the women, they would bring home a salary, increase household income and so acquire elevated status in relation to men in the family. In the longer term, extending and improving the quality of education for women will also affect fertility and the quality of education and life chances of daughters. The opportunity cost may be further blows to family cohesion and care (with its implications for long-term change in the management of social reproduction), but this is not built into the model. On the contrary it is assumed that women will want to fall in with social pressure and take advantage of all such opportunities.

In the case of participatory action research, terms such as empowerment and well-being have to be understood and defined operationally. Writing such as that of Archer and Costello (1990) on *educación popular* in Latin America suggests that the purpose is again education for skills that will bring in more income, so as to increase status and well-being at the level of the household and, by aggregation, of the community. What appears different is the discourse in which such action is embedded. It is committed to principles of raising awareness about the complex nature of poverty and other forms of oppression as a prerequisite for effective popular action. Such knowledge is to some an end in itself. For others it leads to participatory research and further action. To ensure the relevance and quality of action, diagnostic and evaluatory activities will involve local people in surveys and the collection of data for statistical analysis by project members, on site or elsewhere.

Such approaches require low levels of investment and are usually funded by international charitable and humanitarian organizations. They are frequently implemented, through or bypassing the state, by local NGOs or churches. It is difficult to see how, conceptually, their structure or purpose is any different from that of the World Bank and bilateral donor countries operating within and between sectors through national governments. In isolation, the ability of small local projects to affect policy at regional and national levels will be less.

Without linkages to resource-bearing networks the activities of community-based development projects are difficult to sustain. Participatory Action Research networks, such as those in different parts of the world described by Fals Borda and Anisur Rahman (1991), are not large. Without detailed information on their funding and the ways in which the knowledge they generate is converted to action it is difficult to appraise their viability. To some extent, their very purpose can appear to be the survival of the idea of the network without making transparent the material means by which this is achieved. To many, the project is invisible. As such, its success in raising awareness about the political determinants of social reality, as a prerequisite to change, is seen as a subversive counter flow, threatening dominant interests. As with feminist research described above, the reaction is often to marginalize the activity, by starving it of funds and institutional support or to appropriate its rhetoric into what is often described as the political economy of mainstream development (Hettne, 1990).

I first came across the process of appropriation in the 1950s and 1960s when a Bolivian popular education movement, initiated by peasant unions, was co-opted by the national trades union movement (Pearse, 1973; Preston, 1985a). In Ecuador, I witnessed the introduction of government sponsored consciousness-raising education for adults based on curricula developed at a North American university. Such co-optation—it has occurred particularly widely with non-formal education, as now with participatory action research—produces a state controlled activity couched in words and ideas of liberation and independence.

The extent to which bilateral and multilateral funders pay more than lip service to the participation of representatives of client states in for example the development of their regional development plans is open to doubt. They are sometimes challenged for assuring no more than a physical presence and for still not heeding the voice of the people. It is a moot point whether the representatives of the people in such meetings have already been co-opted or whether, doing their best to put forward the message of those for whom they speak, their words are unheard (Quarles van Ufford, 1993).

EXPLANATIONS

How is it possible for there to be so little clarity about the essential differences between approaches and methods dependent upon them and yet have highly competent theoreticians and practitioners espousing one cause and undervaluing the other? The typical polarization of approaches to a study as either quantitative or qualitative appears to allow scope for change along this continuum when the capacity for innovative activity using the currently popular label has dulled and change is sought by shifting toward use of the other. This may be associated as much with a bid to effect a shift in control of the field as with changing conventional wisdom. Certainly, some of the country papers in a special issue of *Qualitative Sociology* (1988, 11, 1–2) locate their discussion of research development in terms of global social, political and economic change. With reference to Israel, Italy and India, among others, they suggest that the recent development of qualitative research is a response to trends already set elsewhere (Cohen, 1988; Corradi, 1988; Oomen, 1988; Reinharz-Schulamit, 1988).

Such trends have nothing to do with whether countries are more or less developed. A strong element of Lewin's (1990) contribution to the book by Vulliamy and colleagues is the recognition of the inevitability of both quantitative and qualitative dimensions to all research and of the desirability of multi-method, multi-component studies. This is indicative of a growing reaction to the puritanism of much of the separatist debate. Accepting overarching common goals that the results of research from whatever approach will go some way to attain means that there is complementarity of purpose and not conflict, regardless of method. While some time may be required to interlink the apparently opposed dyads of objectivity and rigor (as properties of quantitative aspects of research) and subjectivity and description (as belonging to qualitative dimensions), these labels are essential as rhetoric that serves to mask the common, economically determined ideology in which they are all embedded. With education and development, research has become critical in the process of legitimating the continuing cultural transition required, if political and economic goals are to be met.

BIOGRAPHY

At this point, by way of triangulation, I personalize events that led me to formulate the previous arguments about the confusion surrounding the division between qualitative and quantitative approaches to research. Later, with reference to factors that influence the production of knowledge in poor countries, I raise issues relevant to the interests of my coauthors and their concerns to increase local awareness and skill in doing qualitative research.

Within a month of embarking upon my first degree, I knew that I would make a career in research. It was not until later that I realized that modern language degrees of the 1960s gave little preparation for such work. The mechanisms that I used to become a researcher included in the first instance the institution of marriage and only secondly institutions of learning. As a young woman student with small children living with a development researcher, matters of method and interpretation were part of the daily domestic, rather than public, fare.

An intended study of linguistic change among migrants from rural areas of Bolivia to towns came to nothing, in part because of family demands, but more because of lack of skills and supervision in planning and executing the work. A sensible detour into high school language teaching helped with the transfer via education from something called arts to something called social science. It also gave me time to attend classes on theory and method. As associate to a study of the impact of migration on agriculture in five communities in Ecuador (Preston et al., 1981), I collected supplementary educational data for my doctoral dissertation (Preston, 1981).

My failure to locate this work as non-quantitative social anthropology is explained by several factors. My reading on qualitative methods had been concerned to demonstrate how to quantify qualitative data. I found this ethically dubious and alienating. My supervisor, with limited experience of community studies and none of research in poor countries, was unable to help. For her, comparative education was a discipline not wholly compatible with sociology, although, when the time came, she did identify a social anthropologist as one of the examiners of my work.

Unlike Lewin (1990), I felt that I was grappling alone with the exciting ideas of political economy and sociology of development as they applied to education in the 1960s and 1970s, trying to locate them within my nascent understanding of social science, applying them to what had become to me a quantitative study of educational process and effects. Reinforcement of this assumption came from the fact that I used the data from two projects, migration and agriculture and migration and education, to learn to explore the scope for computer assisted analysis. Designing coding frames, punching cards, writing and managing SPSS programs, I lost sight of the non-quantified work that had brought us that far and of the faithfully copied notes of meetings and other kinds of observation. Later, using these notes to write about nuclearization, non-formal education or gender ideology and women's groups in Ecuador, I was to feel strong doubt about their validity (Preston, 1985a, 1985b). My observations had, I thought, been casually made and were not part of a planned research project. With hindsight I see them as the outcome of participant observation and not as the jottings of an opportunistic journalist.

I now accept that the substance of my research to date has fallen as much within qualitative and interpretive frameworks as quantitative. This was first brought home to me with the comments made about the missing descriptive material and, shortly afterwards, when invited to write about qualitative methods on the grounds of my experience. Since then I find myself described by others as a social anthropologist so that sometimes I apply the term myself.

In this way my own research training, which was on educational issues in a country then said to be developing, did not force me to side with either party in the separatist debate on quantity and quality. Instead, I had to make sense of the fact that the same piece of work was perceived by some as a qualitative study and by others as statistical research. In doing this, I came to challenge the assumptions of essential differences between the explanatory rhetoric for each approach.

In the process of my research, I came to understand that my priorities and those of the people among whom I was moving were the same. In a hut on a mountain ridge near the Ecuadorian frontier with Peru, a woman in homespun turned drying coffee beans and talked, in Spanish more halting than mine, about her visions for herself and, hopefully through the education system, for her children. Her words, ideals and sense of obstacles to be met on the way were no different from those of material well-being and probity that I held myself. Our starting points on the journey, geographically and socially, were an ocean apart, as were the points we expected, in the end, to reach.

This sense of sameness, of being people from very different positions sharing common human experience in our networked world, has come to underpin my approach to research in rich as well as in poor countries, with rich as well as with poor people, in quick and dirty consultancy and more protracted, carefully crafted social and anthropological research. It is this that makes it difficult for me to accept the altruistic language that masks the politics of development, within as much as between states.

Such thinking raises doubt about the ethics of researcher intervention into poor people's lives. Only occasionally is it assuaged, sometimes on parting at the end of a conversation, such as that with the Ecuadorian woman. Normally, I feel a combination of gratitude for the time, hospitality and information given and guilt at my sense of my intrusiveness, the uncertainty of accurate *reportage* and the unknown uses beyond my control to which the outcome of my research might be put. On occasions this vanishes as my host, with a tone of reflective surprise, supplements the customary "It was my pleasure, a mere nothing," by adding words to the effect that the learning experience had been shared: "I enjoyed it. It was interesting. All these things are part of my daily life. I've never looked at them in this way before" (Preston, 1976).

IMBALANCES AND RESEARCH CAPACITY

I do not doubt that if my first research excursions had not been to poor countries I would have learned these lessons in similar conversations structured around research done at future dates in Britain, elsewhere in Europe or North America (Glossop et al., 1984; Gibney et al., 1993). What differentiates such work by expatriates in less developed countries, regardless of method, is its anticipated contribution, however modest, however inexperienced the researcher, to something called the development of the host state. This is as true for self-initiated research said to be undertaken primarily for its intrinsic value as for studies contracted from the outset for their contribution to policy.

In this there is disequilibrium. It is unlikely for novice transient researchers from one rich country to do applied research that will affect the internal policy of another, but this is expected of transient, even student researchers from rich countries working in those that are poor. It is very rare for even senior academics from poorer parts of the world to take part in such transient activities in rich countries, although this is where most have at some time been trained. Instead, with the exception of the minority who become channeled into the select streams of the global research elite, many social science postgraduates from poor countries in rich country universities write dissertations related to development needs at home and may learn little about practices elsewhere in their specialist fields of interest. Among the exceptions would be Iamo, from Papua New Guinea. His doctoral dissertation in the anthropology of North American culture and law was in some measure stimulated by a desire to turn the tables (Iamo, 1986). From a country on which many expatriate anthropological careers had been made, he was moved to acquire and apply the same skills in a Californian, rather than a Melanesian, garden.

Imbalance in research training is perpetuated in imbalance in employment opportunities available to professional researchers. It is the lack of local researchers deemed skilled to internationally acceptable standards that leads funding organizations to heed the reports of research led by international consultants and leaves poor countries so thirsty for expatriate expertise.

Worldwide, the changing structure of employment sees many of those claiming skill in research working freelance, outside universities, frequently overseas. In poor countries the quality of expatriate research and the extent to which it provides a model of excellence for the local researcher depends on many factors. They include the political intent of the job in hand and the extent to which the research process itself, as much as its product, is seen as developmental. These factors dictate the quality of the researchers hired and their ability to make use of the resources provided, to think not only operationally, but creatively, about the problem in hand and how to train local people to do the same (Arthur and Preston, 1995).

In such cases the quality of the work will depend on the researcher skill in critical contextual analysis (documentary and statistical reviews, comparison of the activity in the country in question with its scope and experience elsewhere) and the gathering of new information with which to interpret and evaluate the implications for well-being of present and modified strategy at the level of analysis required.

Most consultants are hired not to be creative but to recommend ways in which to modify strategies being introduced elsewhere, so that they become locally relevant (Preston, 1994). As individuals, most work under great pressure to the limits of their capacity (Arthur and Preston, 1995; Preston and Arthur, 1995). Caught in a web of stakeholder relationships, Murni and Spencer stress the lack of power of the consultant (1995, forthcoming). Most are forced to take the work that is offered at low rates of pay because they have families to feed and mortgages to pay. I was able to refuse a consultancy in Pakistan that would have given me four days to write a plan for non-formal education in the slums of Islamabad, without inquiring if the four days included return travel from England. Someone else will have been pleased at the chance to accept what seemed an unrealistically short period of time for a complex project.

Without the opportunity to reflect on the treadmill on which they find themselves (by signing away their rights to publish their work in academic journals, for example), such international consultant researchers provide the grounds for decisions, the politics of which escape them. Their methods of data collection and analysis are rarely inspected. Feedback to them on their performance, from either client or broker, is virtually unknown (Arthur and Preston, 1995).

In these conditions, there are many impediments to consultants making a successful contribution to the research capacity of poor countries. Counterparts are appointed more often than not to serve as assistants to the consultant, for initiating interviews and providing access to documents. Many consultants do not know how to pass from this point to provide counterparts with skills to turn to good use for themselves the opportunities that they (the counterparts) have provided. Undeniably the structure of consultancy funding militates against such time-consuming investment in local human capital and opportunities are rare to provide on-the-job research training.

If there is a bias in donor demand for governments to provide quantitative data for national and regional studies, with token allowance for other forms of information, this combines with conventional approaches to research methods training. These progress from theory to number, statistics and finally interpretation. The curriculum of research methods courses is often overcrowded so that non-quantitative approaches are poorly practiced. By implication, this lowers their status. With rare exception, these factors lead local people, who are training to do research across the disciplines, down the path of (usually very simple) quantification, at least initially. Nevertheless, even in the poorest of countries, there is a growing research capacity with awareness and experience of a range of formal and informal methods. Their opportunity for work at home will vary with funder perception of their personal qualities, their organizational capacity and external factors, such as the level of corruption and degree of political stability in the state in question. Most usually, local researchers come to work as, often junior, members of cross-national research teams. Where participatory models are used, they quickly learn whether or not they have a voice that is heard. Often they find that, in spite of participatory management of projects, control and comparability of data and its analysis are thought to be more easily achieved with numerical rather than with verbal description and with expatriate rather than with local labor.

IRONIES

There are many ironies in this. In Andean America, the South Pacific and southern Africa I have seen verbally articulate field workers struggle to read out a prescribed survey question and laboriously record the response before repeating the process. Fully preoccupied, without eye contact, they have no sense of informant loss of interest, declining response validity or of the quantity of supplementary information they might have obtained, if they had been able to keep the conversation flowing. To some extent the collection of national census and similar data has to be done in this way, at least with marginally literate groups unable to complete forms themselves. In poor countries very high proportions of populations are unable to write or read. Their planning systems require collectors of data with at least some training. The quality of both their schooling and this training will explain in part their limited capacity.

Beyond this, however, the oral skills of local researchers should not be underestimated. Nor, for fear of atrophy, should they be underused. A colleague of the then Educational Research Unit of the University of Papua New Guinea had demonstrated remarkable interview skill in a social anthropological study of local management of schools, intended to triangulate a brief national survey (Preston and Khambu, 1985). The study included reviews of policy and other primary documentary material, as well as in-depth interviews in thirteen remote rural schools in a single province. With a list of topics to guide our separate conversations with pupils, teachers, board and other community members, he tapped a considerable depth of knowledge, without writing a word.

Like me, my colleague was an outsider. Although Papua New Guinean, he was from a region and language group different from those of the people studied. He was very well able to report verbally and record the information in writing at different levels of abstraction. He was not able to write English in the style deemed appropriate to official reports. In contrast, my own use of English was criticized for its complexity: no one challenged its accuracy or ultimately its relevance.

In such ways the neo-colonial tyranny of language and report form combine to atrophy consummate descriptive and interpretive skills and reify those unobtainable by local people. They doom the local researcher to endless assistantships and minimal experience as leader or initiator of work (Arthur and Preston, 1995). This in itself leads to further deskilling and demotivation. Researchers may become expert in adapting to the styles of successive project leaders, but are prevented from deepening their understanding of specialist fields of knowledge as they shift from, for example, the study of curricula to finance or housing and health.

CONCLUSION

In poor countries programs of national development are essentially educational. They teach people to aspire to particular forms of material and so spiritual well-being in ways that further global interests as much or more than their own. They teach ways in which those goals might be obtained.

Within the paradigm of capitalist consumerism, research is applied to justify courses of action that will stimulate further imports (experts, materials, machines) and orient people to make even greater efforts to stimulate the cash economy. This is as true of schooling of the young as it is of agricultural extension or continuing professional development in the upper echelons of the public service. In this the approach to research is immaterial as is the extent to which it is overtly policy-oriented or only latently so. Alternative strategies that survive do so because they have been appropriated by or marginalized from the dominant mainstream.

The development of high level research and related capacities to increase the independence of low income countries is not yet in the interests of those who control world finance. International technical assistance and consultancy is a means of overcoming local skill deficits and of ensuring external control of research and its consequent action. Simultaneously, the export of expertise is a mechanism for quieting rich country surpluses of skilled labor and reduces the alienation of aid funds. Rich country poaching of local people who do have high levels of research skill, developed sometimes at enormous local cost, is a device to further maintain this imbalance.

It is within parameters such as these that action has to be envisaged to optimize the quality of local research and ensure its widespread acceptability. For poorer countries, the most critical need is to develop a strong local capacity to appraise and challenge the quality and relevance of proposed research, particularly when externally initiated; the skill and experience of those intended to design and execute it; its scope for developing independent local researchers with skills across the range of methods appropriate to cross-disciplinary studies.

Whatever the method, this infrastructural capacity is crucial if the research is to be efficient and locally effective. It should be able to contribute to the formulation of critical questions and identify appropriate ways in which to answer them. To achieve all this, texts such as those in the present volume on different approaches to qualitative research in education in poor countries are a crucial counterweight to those dedicated to a more numerical method.

Maintaining consistently high standards in the production of knowledge, making clear the interdependence of quantitative and qualitative dimensions, is the surest way to raise the value placed on holistic rather than selectively blinkered modes of analysis. Ensuring that this is done with understanding of the purposes and interests to be served by the research is the best that can be desired. Unwise decisions, resulting from a poor understanding of the politics of research and a lack of ability to resist external pressure, make all the effort futile.

NOTES

1. The chapter differentiates methodology and method. Methodology refers to the epistemological and ontological positions which inform a study. Method refers to the techniques used to gather and analyze information, whatever its methodology.

2. Parametric statistical techniques require the high resolution of interval or ration data. Non-parametric techniques are suitable for all data.

3. Data without any inherently ordered relationship are nominal: gender, house numbers. Rank ordered data without fixed intervals are ordinal: social class classifications. Data spaced by regular intervals are described as interval data: temperature scales. Ratio scales are those with a known zero which permits valid statistical comparisons: heights, weights.

REFERENCES

Altbach, P. and Kelly, G. (eds.) (1978) *Educational Colonialism.* London: Longman.
Antikainon, A. et al. (1994) *In Search of the Meaning of Education: Life Course, Generations and Education in Contemporary Finland.* Papers from an Interdisci-

plinary Residential Conference at the University of Sussex, *Life Histories and Learning-Language, the Self and Education*, Brighton, 19–21 September.

Archer, D. and Costello, P. (1990) *Literacy and Power in Latin America*. London: Earthscan.

Arthur, L. and Preston, R.A. (1995) *The Changing Nature of International Consultancy in Human Development: Report to the British Council*. International Centre for Education in Development: University of Warwick.

Ávalos, B. (ed.) (1986) *Teaching the Children of the Poor: An Ethnographic Study in Latin America*. Ottawa: IDRC.

Balán, J., Browning, H. and Jelín, E. (1973) *Men in a Developing Society: Geographic and Social Mobility in Monterey, Mexico*. Austin: University of Texas Press.

Bannister, D. (1962) "Personal Construct Theory: A Summary and Experimental Paradigm." *Acta Psychologica*, 20: 104–120.

Baran, P. (1957) *The Political Economy of Growth*. New York: Monthly Review Press.

Booth, C. (1891–1903) *Life and Labour of the People in London*. London: Macmillan, vols 1–8.

Booth, D. (1993) "Development Research: From Impasse to New Agenda." In F.J. Schuurman (ed.) *Beyond the Impasse: New Directions in Development Theory*. London: Zed Books.

Bowen, J. (1972) *A History of Western Education, Vol I, The Ancient World, 2000BC-AD1054*. London: Methuen.

Bowman, M.J. (1966) "An Assessment of the Work of Harbison and Myers." In M. Blaug (ed.) *Economics of Education* (2). Harmondsworth: Penguin Books.

Brannen, J. (1993) *Research Issues in Mixing Methods*. University of Warwick, ESRC seminar.

———. (ed.) (1992) *Mixing Methods: Qualitative and Quantitative Research*. Aldershot: Avebury.

Brontë, C. (1847) *Jane Eyre*. London: Smith and Elder.

Bulmer, M. W. and Donald, P. (eds.) (1993) *Social Research in Developing Countries: Surveys and Censuses in the Third World*. London: University College Press.

Caesaris, G. I. (1954) "Commentarium de Bello Gallico." In H.E. Gould and J.E. Whitely (eds.) *Caesar Gallic War III*. London: Macmillan.

Cardoso, F.H. and Faletto, E. (1969) *Dependencia y Desarrollo en America Latina*. Mexico: Siglo XXI.

Casley, D.J. and Lury, D.A (1981) *Data Collection in Developing Countries*. Oxford: Clarendon Press.

Cohen, E. (1988) "Qualitative Sociology in Israel: A Brief Survey," *Qualitative Sociology*, 11 (1–2): 88–98.

Comte, A. (1851–54) *Système de Politique Positive*, Vol. II, p. 181. Quoted in S. Lukes (1983) *Emile Durkheim, His Life and Work: A Historical and Critical Study*. Harmondsworth: Penguin Books.

Conyers, D. (1982) *An Introduction to Social Planning in the Third World*. Chichester: Wiley.

Corradi, C. (1988) "Notes on Qualitative Sociology in Italy," *Qualitative Sociology*, 11 (1–2): 77–87.

Cotterill, P. and Letherby, G. (1993) "Weaving Stories: Personal Autobiographies in Feminist Research," *Sociology*, 27 (1): 67–79.

———. (1994) *The "Person" in the Researcher*. Seminar presented to the Centre for Education Development, Appraisal and Research, University of Warwick.

Crossley, M. (1990) "Curriculum Policy and Practice in Papua New Guinea," *Compare*, 20 (2): 141–154.

Damodaram, K. (1991) "Measuring Social Development Through Qualitative Indicators," *Community Development Journal*, 26 (4): 286–293.

Deutsch, K.W. (1966) "Peoples, Nations and Communication." In K. W. Deutsch, *Nationalism and Social Communication*, 86–106 Cambridge MA.

Dickens, C.J.H. (1892) *The Life and Adventures of Nicholas Nickleby.* London: Macmillan.

Diescho, J. (1988) *Born of the Sun.* Cincinnati: Friendship Press.

———. (1992) *Troubled Waters.* Windhoek, Gamsburg: Macmillan Press.

Engels, F. (1952) *The Condition of the Working Class in England in 1844.* London: Allen and Unwin.

Eri, V. (1970) *The Crocodile.* Milton: Jacaranda Wiley.

Fals, Borda, O and Anisur Rahman, M. (eds.) (1991) *Action and Knowledge: Breaking the Monopoly with Participatory Action-Research.* New York: Apex Press.

Farah, N. (1985) *Maps.* Harmondsworth: Penguin Books.

Feuerstein, M-T. (1986) *Partners in Evaluation: Evaluating Development and Community Programmes with Participants.* London: Macmillan.

Gibney, M., Oliver, M. and Preston, R. (1993) *Centre for Refugee Studies: Mid-term Evaluation for CIDA.* Toronto: York University.

Glossop, G.A., Warwick, D. and Preston R. (1984) *The Measurement of Home Background and School Effects. Final Report to the DES.* School of Education: University of Leeds.

Godenzzi, J.C. (ed.) (1992) *El Quechua en Debate: Ideología, Normalización y Enseñanza,* Bartolomé de las Casas, Cuzco: Centro de Estudios Andinos.

Goody, J. and Watt, I. (1968) "The Consequences of Literacy." In J. Goody (ed.) *Literacy in Traditional Societies.* Oxford: Oxford University Press.

Government of Papua New Guinea (1986) *National Manpower Assessment, 1982–1992.* Waigani: Department of Finance and Planning .

Guthrie, G. (1987) "Approaches to Research." In G. Guthrie (ed.) *Basic Research Techniques.* ERU Report 55, Port Moresby: University of Papua New Guinea.

Guttman, L. (1950) "The Basis of Scalogram Analysis." In S. Stouffer (ed.) *Measurement and Prediction.* Princeton: Princeton University Press.

Hall, B. et al. (1982) *Creating Knowledge: A Monopoly? Participatory Research in Development.* Toronto: ICAE.

Hammersley, M. (1993) *Opening up the Quantitative-Qualitative Divide.* University of Warwick, ESRC seminar.

Harbison, F.H. and Myers, C.A. (1964) *Education, Manpower and Economic Growth.* London: Hutchinson.

Hayes, W.C. (1971) "The Middle Kingdom in Egypt: Internal History from the Rise of Heracleopolitans to the Death of Ammenemes III." In I.E.S. Edwards et al. (eds.) *The Cambridge Ancient History: Early History of the Middle East,* Volume 1 part 2. Cambridge: Cambridge University Press.

Herz, B. K. and Khandker, S.R. (eds.) (1991) *Women's Work, Education and Family Welfare in Peru.* Washington, DC: World Bank Discussion Paper 116.

Hettne, B. (1990) *The Three Worlds of Development: The Crisis in Development Theory.* London: Longman.

Iamo, W. (1986) *In Search of Justice and Shelter in Mix-town, USA.* Unpublished Ph.D. dissertation, University of California, Berkeley.

Inkeles, A. and Smith, D. (1974) *Becoming Modern.* London: Heinemann.

Jiménez de la Espada, M. (1881–1897) *Relaciones Geográficos de Indias.* Vols I–IV. Madrid: Hernandez Hijos.

Jinkerson, D.L. et al. (1992) "A Case Study of Methodological Issues in Cross-Cultural Evaluation," *Evaluation and Program Planning,* 15 (3): 273–285.

Jinks, B., Biskup, P. and Nelson, H. (1973) *Readings in New Guinea History.* Sydney: Angus and Robertson.

Johnston, R. et al. (1988) *The Dictionary of Human Geography.* Oxford: Blackwell.

Junta Nacional de Planificación (1970) *Plan Para el Desarrollo de los Recursos Humanos,* Vols. I and II. Quito.

———. (1978) *Plan Ecuatoriano Para el Desarrollo de los Recursos Humanos,* Vols. III and IV. Quito.

Kahl, J.A. (1968) *The Measurement of Modernism: The Study of Values in Brazil and Mexico*. Texas: Austin University.

Klaasen, C.A.C. and Kleijer, K. (1993) "The Marginal: New Developments in the Sociology of Youth and Socialisation," *Sociologie-Gids*, 42 (2): 82–92.

Kuhn, T.S. (1970) *The Structure of the Scientific Revolution*. Chicago: Chicago University Press.

Lewin, K. (1990) "Research Design in Retrospect: Malaysia and Sri Lanka." In G. Vulliamy, D. Stephens and K. Lewin *Doing Educational Research in Developing Countries*. London: Falmer Press.

Looker, D., Denton, M.A. and Davis, C.K. (1989) "Bridging the Gap: Incorporating Qualitative Data into Quantitative Analysis," *Social Science Research*, 18, 4, 313–330.

Malinowski, B. (1922) *Argonauts of the Western Pacific*. London: Routledge and Kegan Paul.

———. (1966) *Coral Gardens and Their Magic*, Vols. I and II. London: Allen and Unwin.

Marsden, D. and Oakley, P. (1990) *Evaluating Social Development Projects*. Development Guidelines 5. Oxford: Oxfam.

Mead, M. (1942) *Growing up in New Guinea*. Harmondsworth: Penguin Books.

Miller, P. McC. and Wilson, M.J. (1983) *A Dictionary of Social Science Methods*. Chichester: John Wiley.

Moser, C.O. (1993) *Gender, Planning and Development: Theory, Practice and Training*. London: Routledge.

Murni, D., and Spencer, S. (1995) "Consultants and Counterparts." In W. Savage and B. Kenny (eds.) *Language and Development: Teachers in a Changing World*. London: Longman (forthcoming).

Murthy, M.N. (1978) "The Use of Sample Surveys in National Planning in Developing Countries." In N.K. Namboodiri *Survey Sampling and Measurement*. New York: Academic Press.

Nasson, B. (1986) "Perspectives on Education in South Africa." In S. Burman and P. Reynolds (eds.) *Growing up in a Divided Society*. Evanston: Northwestern University Press.

Nichols, P. (1991) *Social Survey Methods: A Field Guide for Development Workers*. Development Guidelines 6. Oxford: Oxfam.

Nieuwenhuys, O. (1994) *Children's Lifeworlds: Gender, Welfare and Labour in the Developing World*. London: Routledge.

Oomen, T.K. (1988) "In Search of Qualitative Sociology in India," *Qualitative Sociology*, 11 (1–2): 44–54.

Overseas Development Administration (1994) *Aid to Education in 1993 and Beyond*. London: ODA.

Paneff, J. (1988) "The Observers Observed: French Survey Researchers at Work," *Social Problems* 35 (5).

Pearse, A. (1973) "Structural Problems of Educational Systems in Latin America." In R. Brown (ed.) *Knowledge Education and Cultural Change*. London: Tavistock.

Peet, R. and Watts, M. (1993) "Introduction: Development Theory and Environment in an Age of Market Triumphalism," *Economic Geography* 69 (3): 227–253.

Peil, M. et al. (1981) *Social Science Research Methods: An African Handbook*. London: Hodder and Stoughton.

Preston, D.A., Taveras, G.A. and Preston R.A. (1981) "Emigración y Desarrollo Agrícola en la Sierra Ecuatoriana," *Revista Geográfica* 93, 7–35.

Preston, R.A. (1976) *Fieldnotes*. Ecuador.

———. (1981) *Education and Migration in Highland Ecuador*. Unpublished Ph.D. thesis, University of Leeds.

———. (1985a) "Popular Education in Latin America: The Case of Ecuador." In C.

Brock and H. Lawlor (eds.) *Education in Latin America.* London: Croom Helm.

———. (1985b) "Gender Ideology and Education: Implications at the Ecuadorian Periphery," *Compare,* 15 (1): 29–40

———. (1994) Interview with T. Edmundesen and N. Kemp, British Council. Manchester.

Preston, R. and Arthur, L. (1995) "Knowledge Societies and Planetary Cultures: the Changing Nature of Consultancy in Human Development." Paper presented to the conference Education and Development: Tensions Between Economies and Cultures, Department of International and Comparative Education, University of London Institute of Education, May.

Preston, R. and Khambu, J. (1985) *Between the Community and its School: Boards of Management in Papua New Guinea.* Report for the National Department of Education, Waigani, ERU: University of Papua New Guinea.

Price, S. (1986) "The History of the Hellenistic Period." In J. Boardman et al. (eds.) *The Oxford History of Greece and the Hellenistic World.* Oxford: Oxford University Press.

Quarles van Ufford, P. (1993) "Knowledge and Ignorance in the Practices of Development Policy." In M. Hobart (ed.) *The Growth of Ignorance: An Anthropological Critique of Development.* London and New York: Routledge.

Reichardt, C.S. and Cook, T.D. (1979) "Beyond Qualitative *Versus* Quantitative Methods." In T.D. Cook and C.S. Reichardt (eds.) *Qualitative and Quantitative Methods in Evaluation Research.* Beverly Hills: Sage.

Reinharz-Schulamit, C.P. (1988) "Qualitative Sociology in International Perspective: Editor's Introductory Essay," *Qualitative Sociology,* 11 (1–2): 8–12.

Rose, G. (1982) *Deciphering Sociological Research.* London: Macmillan.

Soaba, R. (1977) *Wanpis.* Port Moresby: Institute of Papua New Guinean Studies.

Spindler, G. (1963) *Education and Culture: Anthropological Approaches.* New York: Holt Reinhart and Winston.

Sprague, J. and Zimmerman, M.K. (1989) "Quality and Quantity: Reconstructing Feminist Methodology," *American Sociologist,* 20, 1, 71–86.

Stromquist, N. (ed.) (1992) *Women and Education in Latin America: Knowledge, Power and Change.* Boulder and London: Lynn Rienner.

Subbarao, K. et al. (1994) *Women in Higher Education: Progress, Constraints and Promising Initiatives.* Discussion paper 244. Washington: World Bank.

Taylor, P. V. (1993) *The Texts of Paolo Freire.* Buckingham: Open University Press.

Thabault, R. (1971) *Education and Change in a Village Community: Mazières en Gâtine, 1848–1914.* London: Routledge and Kegan Paul.

UNDP (1994) *Human Development Report.* Oxford: Oxford University Press.

Vulliamy, G. (1985) *A Comparative Analysis of SSCEP Outstations.* ERU Report 50 Waigani: University of Papua New Guinea.

———. (1990) "The Potential of Qualitative Educational Research Strategies in Developing Countries." In G. Vulliamy, K. Lewin and D. Stephens, *Doing Educational Research in Developing Countries: Qualitative Strategies.* London: Falmer Press.

Vulliamy, G., Lewin, K. and Stephens, D. (1990) *Doing Educational Research in Developing Countries: Qualitative Strategies.* London: Falmer Press.

Wallerstein, I. (1991) *Unthinking Social Science: The Limits of Nineteenth Century Paradigms.* Cambridge: Polity Press.

Walsh, P.G. (1974) *Greece and Rome: New Surveys of the Classics.* Oxford: Clarendon Press.

Warwick, D.P. (1993) "On Methodological Integration in Social Research." In M. Bulmer and D.P. Warwick (eds.) *Social Research in Developing Countries: Surveys and Censuses in the Third World.* London: University College Press.

Watkins, F. (1846) Report on Schools in the Northern Districts; Minutes of Committee of Council on Education for 1845, *Parliamentary Papers, XXXII,* 298.

3 QUALITATIVE RESEARCH AND EDUCATIONAL POLICY-MAKING

APPROACHING THE REALITY IN DEVELOPING COUNTRIES

Cheng Kai-ming

INTRODUCTION

This chapter demonstrates how qualitative research may help to inform effective educational policy-making and how the lack of such research may lead to distorted information and false conclusions in the policy formulation, implementation and evaluation process.

To begin with, the title of the chapter itself could be controversial and some remarks are necessary. The term qualitative research is now widely used in the literature, but many readers will realize that qualitative studies need not be confined to qualitative data alone (see chapter 1). The term in its fashionable sense is frequently defined through being contrasted with statistical research and hypothesis-testing, which is inevitably quantitative. In this paper, the term qualitative research is used to mean research of which the primary purpose is to identify "native" perspectives (or local culture) so as to illuminate a policy issue. The general process in such qualitative research is to allow the researcher's thinking to be shaped by field data and to generate hypotheses, conclusions or theories therefrom.

The term developing country also deserves attention. First, the adjective "developing" is a polite form for "poor," and often assumes a unidimensional measurement of national development: the GNP or GDP. This assumption encounters challenge when other developmental dimensions, such as those favored by UNDP, are taken into consideration. Economic wealth is but one dimension of national development that includes health care, literacy, educational, spiritual and other social dimensions. Second, the developed-developing (or north-south) dichotomy is too broad a generalization that artificially polarizes nations in the world. It has difficulties in accommodating countries such as the newly industrialized economies (NIEs) in East Asia (Cheng, 1991b) and the newly converted nations of Eastern Europe. Third, much of the literature about developing countries, including that on education, is written by people in developed countries. There is, in this sub-field, often a tacit "donor-recipient" paradigm where the "wise" of the north explore the exotic south. This reflects the fact that the majority of known research projects in the south are supported by money and personnel from the north.

Problems with the word reality are even more fundamental. People may have totally different perceptions about their social reality and the nature of knowledge. At the one extreme, one may argue that reality is nothing but human creation. At the other extreme, one may believe in a reality which is external to the researcher and is fully accessible and comprehensible. In between, there are various ways of conceiving what reality is and of understanding the researcher's capacity to fully comprehend it. Lincoln and Guba (1985: 82–87) present a useful discussion of these epistemological issues as do other contributors to this volume. Talking about reality is, nevertheless, always risky but, while it is not intended to pursue philosophical or epistemological issues in this chapter, it is essential to say that most policy-related research assumes that (1) there is an objective reality and (2) such a reality can be better understood by the policy-maker through research. By policy-related research here we mean "research for policy" rather than "research *on* policy." The former is meant to inform policy-making which demands realistic solutions to practical problems. Epistemological assumptions, however, may face challenges when research is about human organizations where policy is built upon interpretations of human perceptions. This is particularly an issue when the researcher works across cultures, and even more so when those from the developed world are looking at developing countries.

In the light of the above, it is the purpose of this chapter to address issues encompassed in the title by evaluating examples and problems in policy-related research; and to illustrate how qualitative methods may help improve our analyses. In so doing, the chapter draws upon experience from China and Hong Kong, the part of the world the writer is most familiar with. Following qualitative conventions, discussions that follow are illustrated by details of specific cases, and where examples are politically sensitive, pseudonyms are used to maintain confidentiality.

PROBLEM DEFINITION AND IDENTIFICATION

Rational policy-making comprises problem identification, solution searching or development and solution selection. Although rational processes are only one dimension of policy-making, problem identification is a useful and practical starting point for any policy process. A first question is then: whose problem are we dealing with? Problems so often have to do with what people expect. It is also argued here that problems, as identified, should reflect or acknowledge local perceptions. This is not always appreciated by researchers coming from outside the community in question. Often, outsiders identify problems, with considerable expertise, from their own frames of reference. In so doing, many ungrounded assumptions are made suggesting that there are universal yardsticks that can be used to measure or evaluate any education system. If visiting researchers are not conscious of their limitations as foreigners, and pay little respect to the local context, they are likely to identify problems which are foreign to the specific context, and their input may not serve the local community well.

By way of illustration, a mission team (of which the writer was a member) was recently sent by an international funding agency to the less-developed province of Shaanxi in China to identify target projects for a substantial loan. It was winter and children were seen shivering in thick clothes, with running noses, in classrooms at freezing temperatures. Heating was not available because the province was not in a region eligible for heating subsidy from the central government. The mission team thought this should become a priority project. Some calculation was done and it was found that for a heater to be installed in a classroom the cost would be around U.S. $71, including a simple stove and chimneys made of iron plates. This would last for three to five years. However, there were 145,579 classes in that province alone at the time of the visit. Heaters for all would cost over U.S. $10 million, and this was disproportionately expensive. This did not include the running costs for coal, and coal was expensive because it was not produced locally. In time the mission team decided to drop the idea of launching such a project.

Subsequent discussions outside the formal visit, however, revealed that the local educational planners and school administrators had been unenthusiastic about the heating proposal from the very beginning. "This is not *our* priority," said the local planners. "We have been learning under the same conditions for generations," said the teachers. "If we had money," both groups said, "we'd rather pay the teachers." Most of the teachers were community employees paid by the local community, and due to recent policies of decentralization, the underdevelopment of the local economy rendered many of them underpaid, or their paychecks were long overdue. However, because funding agencies are never attracted to support recurrent expenditure, the local educators and planners did not raise an initial objection to the heating project.

In this case, there was a marked difference between what was perceived as a problem by the mission team, and by the local educators and planners. There was a difference in expectations. The visiting team, given the brief to fund nonrecurrent items, and with their experience of heated environments back home in winter, naturally focused upon the temperature of the classrooms. The local people had taken the coldness for granted. Cold was expected of life there in any room in the locality. It was not that they did not want warm environments, but for generations they had realized that heating was an expensive item, and it was therefore not a realistic expectation. In other words, heating was not a problem to the local community and was not on their policy agenda, or it was low on the priority list.

Had the mission team tried harder to understand the local perspective by using a more qualitative approach to their study from the very beginning, they might have arrived at proposals more suited to local expectations. Unfortunately, this is not the usual convention with many funding agencies. Too often, international teams tend to regard developing countries as backward; backward not only in their economic conditions, but also backward in their overall development perspectives. In this context, there is a tendency for visiting researchers to "discover" problems for the local community, and this itself is regarded as a valid contribution. In other cases, visiting researchers negate problems that are identified by the local people, and identify policy priorities conforming to an imported framework that they have taken for granted, but which may be totally incompatible with local needs and perspectives.

How Can Planning Indicators Help?

Consultants who visit a developing country often have to rely on planning indicators of acknowledged international significance so that situations in the country in question can be assessed through comparison with those elsewhere. However, education is practiced differently in different countries and the same indicator may reflect very different stories. It is therefore argued that such indicators should be used with greater caution, or else they may prove deceptive and be misleading.

In the early and mid-1980s, for example, researchers who went to China were often amazed by the shortage of qualified teachers on the one hand, and the "over-generous" student/teacher ratios on the other. A World Bank report thus made the following observation:

> The student-teacher ratio has . . . gone down from 27:1 in 1979 to 25:1 in 1983 (the median ratio for other LDCs is about 35:1). The class size has been kept almost constant, at around 34, which implies

that teachers' weekly workload—by international standards, already a low 20 periods—has gone down further. (World Bank, 1985:9)

These policy analysts therefore concluded that there would be a general surplus of primary school teachers in the years to come if the existing policies were to be maintained. The World Bank subsequently recommended that the student/teacher ratio should be increased to 34:1 and there should be a gradual closing of some primary teacher training schools (Ibid.:34–35). Berstecher's (1986) case study of the province of Sichuan arrived at similar observations and comments:

> From a student/teacher ratio of currently 32:1, the plan framework for basic education proposes to go towards a ratio of 18:1 by 1990. By any standards, this policy implies an amazingly generous use of precious and costly human resources. What is more, there is hardly any evidence to suggest that a massive lowering of student/teacher ratios will really pay off in terms of better educational achievements. . . . Thus, it is reasonable to ask whether Sichuan's plan to go all out for an improvement of student/teacher ratios in primary schools is really the best or the only alternative. Does it strike a proper balance between quantity and quality? (Ibid.:46–47)

These observations, criticisms and recommendations are sound as long as one stays at the macrolevel and looks at average figures. The picture becomes different when analysis moves to the microlevel. In a case study of two counties in the province of Liaoning (Cheng, 1991a), for example, the writer acknowledged a shortage of qualified teachers and an increasingly generous student/teacher ratio. Using a qualitative approach to research, however, it was possible to trace the planning process in greater depth and conclude

> for at least two reasons, the demand for teachers was not decided by a simple calculation of overall figures. First, rural classes were normally smaller than the standard class size of 50 and hence calculation by simple teacher-pupil ratio would arrive at very unrealistic results. Second, there were specialised teachers for Language and Mathematics in Primary 5 and 6. Hence, a simple class-teacher ratio, again would not lead to meaningful planning. The actual "planning" was done through careful school-by-school and subject-by-subject calculations. (Ibid.:42)

In this case, because of the policy of universalizing primary education, more but smaller schools were built to comply with the national norm of 2.5 km as the maximum student travel distance (or alternative requirements to guarantee neighborhood attendance). The net effect was that although there was a decline of population, there were more schools because of the sparse distribution. Indeed, there were extremely crowded classrooms in towns and cities (the largest of which held over 100 pupils), but there were extremely small classes (of just a few children) in remote schools. Hence, although many of the rural teachers were unqualified, they were still very much needed in scattered small schools. Average figures at the national or provincial levels could not possibly reflect the huge disparity in sizes among classes, and greater depth of research in context was required.

The expensive reduction in the student/teacher ratio was also seen by local planners as a problem. However, it was inevitably brought about by the broader policy of compulsory education. The decline was not intended. But this is only one part of the story. The workload of twenty periods per week as identified by the World Bank should not lead to the conclusion that teachers share a light workload. Over the years, the writer came to understand that Chinese teachers lead a more demanding life than their counterparts in many other parts of the world. Given an opportunity to systematically study this issue in the province of Zhejiang, an in-depth case study of five sites was conducted (Cheng, 1996, chapter 7), and the following extract is taken from the forthcoming final report:

> The task facing a teacher in China is complex. First, teaching is formal and requires *formal preparation*. In all schools almost without exception, each lesson is taught with a detailed lesson plan. It has become a strong tradition considered by teachers as part of the professional conduct. . . . The lesson plan is considered part of the teacher's performance. It is constantly inspected by the principal, read by peers and is part of the appraisal when it comes to promotion or awards. Even for very experienced teachers, teaching without a lesson plan is thought to be irresponsible if not inconceivable. Repeating last year's lesson plan is also considered as indecent. . . . Preparation of lessons therefore consumes a large part of teachers' time.
>
> Second, teaching is *target-oriented*. That is, students are expected to perform according to targets. This is based on the Chinese tradition which treasures *effort* rather than *ability*. In practice, it means that the teacher is expected to supervise the class of students to work towards some achievement targets. The tacit belief is that if students

work hard, they can always achieve. The implication of this is that apart from classroom teaching, the teacher may spend enormous time to individually help students to pass examinations, for example . . . In the case of China, there is a requirement that over 80% of the students at primary six in rural schools have to pass their graduation examination. The required passing percentage is 95% for cities. Apparently, these targets are actually reached . . . Hence, there is a basic assumption that teachers' performance is the predominating factor that determines students' performance. This significantly adds pressure to the teachers' workload.

Third, the pastoral aspect of a teacher's job is again a heavy load. Most teachers in China are class teachers. . . . A class teacher in the Chinese context is the adviser to the class association which is a student organization. In practice, the class teacher is responsible for the development of all the students in the class. The class teacher is therefore an organizer, a leader, a social worker, a counsellor, a remedial teacher and sometimes a private tutor to the academically weak. In short, the class teacher is responsible for the comprehensive development of each student in his/her class. The general holistic approach to education has also made the class teachers' task more complex than their counterparts elsewhere. For example, home visit is a general routine of the class teacher. The usual practice is that the class teacher is expected to visit the home of each student in the class at least once per term in a two-term year. This really means that for a class of 40, the class teacher has to pay 80 home visits in the year. These are quite apart from the special visits paid to the family due to irregularities in the students' performance.

The rather lengthy quotation above illustrates how Chinese teachers are not underemployed or underutilized. The traditional expectations of each teacher are already very demanding. Moreover, these observations are further confirmed by quantitative data generated from the same study. Teachers, rural and urban alike, showed an average of 40.2% of their time in a day spent on work, 12.1% on housework, 14.0% on self-study/reading and 33.7% for rest/leisure.

From the above it is argued that pupil/teacher ratios and the number of teaching periods alone are not good indicators of the teachers' workload. Real workload can be better understood by qualitative studies of their actual lives. Consequently, policy suggesting a change in the number of active teaching periods may require an overhaul of the concept of classroom teaching and the role of the teacher if change is not to threaten real quality. Indeed, in recent years, some urban schools have achieved an "improvement of internal efficiency" by increasing teachers' contact time, but this has been done at the expense of home visits and the pastoral role of the teachers.

There are also factors in the larger educational context which limit the extent of change possible. Even if there was a will to change the pupil/teacher ratio, the employment system in China would make such a change extremely difficult. To date, with the exception of highly developed regions, what is practiced is still largely a policy of full employment. Schools are staffed with quotas that they are obliged to fill. Although there are national and provincial norms for pupil/teacher ratios, actual staffing is often governed by the requirement to fill the quota regardless of the student numbers. In practical terms, it is difficult to reduce the number of teachers in a school, although it is often equally difficult to increase the number. Such factors are not visible or understandable simply by looking at educational indicators from afar.

The lesson here is that statistical indicators that are convenient for international comparison may not serve effectively for national policy-making. Indicators may reflect factual data well, but education is more of a process. Statistical indicators are rarely meaningful for national policy-making unless the underlying educational processes are also revealed and studied. This is the strength of qualitative research. In pressing this case there is no intention to deny the value of quantitative research and associated indicators. Such data are often good starting points for in-depth inquiry that inevitably entails greater attention to qualitative methods.

The Potential and Limitations of Mathematical Models in Policy Research

Mathematical models can be powerful tools for forecasts and policy simulations. Popular applications are estimations of school dropouts and forecasts for manpower supply and demand. The power of such models lies in their rigor in mathematical deduction that allows extrapolation of past trends into the future, or the collation of local trends to provide a global picture. However, there are two primary limitations with mathematical modeling. First, there are many assumptions underlying each model, and the validity of such assumptions is not always verifiable by the model itself. Second, mathematical models rarely take into account trends that are emerging, but which are not yet significant mathematically. Such emerging trends, however, may well be commonsense for those in the field, and can be identified through qualitative study. Without such contextualized study, mathematical modeling runs a very real risk of producing results that soon become obsolete.

An illustration of this can be taken from China, which, in 1983, launched the world's largest scale manpower forecast for the planning of education up to the year 2000. The manpower forecast was geared to planning higher and technical education. The forecasting exercise adopted a then novel bottom-up approach. Instead of starting from growth in national output and deducing manpower implications for various sectors, industries and work units, this exercise started from work units. For the purpose of manpower stock-taking, full population surveys (covering 99.5% of working personnel) were conducted in seventy-two industries in which work units were visited and their manpower structures studied on the sites. For forecasting, the collected data then underwent mathematical modeling in order to produce forecasts for the year 2000, for example, for the whole of industry in various regions. However, the planners, who had been used to statistical methods, were not content with a purely quantitative approach. The results of the forecast were then scrutinized by a modified Delphi approach such that over 100 experts in each industry went through multiple back-and-forth "voting" to arrive at some consensus (see descriptions in Zhou, 1990: 77–85; Cheng, 1991a:11–13). In hindsight, this multi-method forecast from 1983 provided a reliable broad outline of manpower trends in China and efficiently informed policy-making in higher and technical education in the following decade.

This type of combination of qualitative and quantitative methods clearly has much greater potential. Hong Kong, for example, has undertaken manpower surveys in selected industries since 1973. The surveys are employer-oriented and the detection of manpower shortages is the prime objective. Conducted biennially, the surveys start with full-population site visits for manpower stock-taking in a particular industry, plus an element of employers' opinion survey for future needs. The latter is qualitative in nature. The data, together with earlier records, then undergo mathematical modeling in such a way that more recent data carry greater weight. This modeling provides only a family of curves showing the range of possibilities from the most optimistic to the most pessimistic scenarios. It is then up to the industry's Training Board to meet and decide qualitatively which of the possibilities is the most realistic (see details in Cheng, 1985). Occasionally, qualitative "insider" knowledge of the industry persuades the Training Board to decide to select outside the range provided by mathematical modeling, for example, at times immediately after or before recession.

The two cases mentioned above suggest that while mathematical models may provide an essential basis for policy-making, in practice, many policies are made on the basis of more qualitative data and analyses. It is important not to equate rational decision-making solely with quantitative methods. This is particularly important in the developing world where context-free decision-making is far from unusual among research consultants visiting a new country for a short period.

The following example illustrates the case further. The writer joined an international consultancy team that was sent by a funding agency to look at basic education in a poor province in China. The official net enrollment ratio for the entire country was 97.4% in the year when the visit was done. This is an extremely high figure by international standards and naturally invites all sorts of skepticism among observers. The team visited a large number of villages. Among various things that the team looked at enrollment records were examined in most villages, and these sites were selected by the team not by the local officials. Questions were also asked about dropouts and repetitions in various villages. It was found, for example, that primary school dropouts were more common in some pockets, such as among girls in minority areas and in remote mountains. Otherwise, primary attendance was impressive and was an accepted part of the order of life. The province set down a ceiling of 5% for repetition at each grade, but with a few exceptions, teachers in most villages said this was often not met and not necessary. The team also noticed that at many sites the primary school principal, who was virtually the educational planner for the village, kept a "cultural registration" of all children born because these would be his future students. Fieldwork thus revealed healthy attendance in practice.

However, in the official consultancy report, it was concluded that 30% of the children who enrolled in schools never attended and that only about 50% of those who started school in the first grade ever reached the fifth grade (the final grade in these primary schools). None of these findings reflected field experience but the report admitted that these were estimations based upon models that had yielded effective results in Latin America!

Today, this report may easily gain the attention of readers who have no experience of the Chinese education system, and it may satisfy those who prefer to distrust official figures, particularly from China. However, these data present a picture which is far removed from reality and this has subsequently led to misconceived policy recommendations. The 30% non-attendance and 50% non-completion rates are inconceivable for anybody who has life experience in Chinese villages. In the majority of villages in China, non-attendance at primary school level has become socially unacceptable. There may be some distortion in the official figures, but the extent of the distortion should neither be overstated nor understated. This is not to say that mathematical modeling should not be used. Rather, if conflicts occur between statistical results and field experience, then the conflicts should be a starting point for more in-depth qualitative study to understand the reasons for this. If modeling data are inevitably to be given greater weight than information generated by field visits, then perhaps visits should not take place, and the resources spent in organizing them should be used to help improve schools.[1]

Secondly, much more in-depth but largely unacknowledged research has been done by local researchers on the issue of dropout and repetition. In a survey of this literature on rural education (Cheng and Paine, 1991: 9–10), approximately thirty studies were thus identified and we concluded:

> The studies in this area have seen a general trend of moving from impressionistic speculations based on limited data (e.g. Zhang 1985), to rather sophisticated approaches combining quantitative with qualitative techniques (e.g. Ma, 1984; Yang and Han, 1991). In the earlier studies, there were implicit assumptions of linear causality between dropouts and educational reasons (e.g. Zhao, 1987; Chen, 1988), hence attributing school dropouts to planning or instructional factors. Later studies include economic considerations (e.g. Shen, 1988), . . . The work by Zhou et al. (1987) is perhaps one of the earliest attempts to explore the reality in an intensive case study . . . with the preparedness to adopt multiple perspectives.

The more recent of these studies produced within country display a number of significant trends. First, a movement can be detected away from reliance upon statistical and macrolevel analyses. Second, multiple perspectives on policy issues are increasingly acknowledged and documented. Third, more descriptive and qualitative studies are being carried out and are gaining recognition.

In particular, Yang and Han (1991) conducted a valuable mixed-method study with a high degree of rigor that included questionnaires, in-depth case-study and focus group discussions. This report was submitted to UNESCO as a country paper. A useful study was also conducted by the Education Committee of Hebei Province (1990) which involved (a) a past trend analysis of thirty-nine years, and a statistical projection of future scenarios, (b) a full-population survey among a sample of nineteen counties and (c) a three-year backward tracer study of a random-sampled cohort of 103,887 primary students and 77,171 junior secondary students.

Many of these local studies were under way while the international consultancy visit referred to above was being made. Had the visiting team inquired into the Chinese literature and paid more respect to what was being done in country, their own report would have been more useful and more accurate. Indeed, the studies done by Chinese researchers arrived at conclusions that refute many of the results of the mathematical model developed in Latin America. In some cases the methods adopted are highly sophisticated and can stand any international scrutiny. The UNESCO-sponsored study, for example, followed a general framework defined for international comparison and the Hebei provincial tracer study was a large-scale cohort analysis combined with qualitative probing. Here it is pertinent to note that had the visiting team included a qualitative element (such as several case studies) in its own study, or surveyed the local literature, more realistic conclusions about dropouts and repetitions in Chinese primary schools would have been produced. Mathematical modeling might have been used in a more cautious way that compared initial results with real situations, as was done in Latin America when the model was first utilized. The team might thus have been in a better position to make use of their experience in the field to create a new model more appropriate to the situation in China. Then, and only then, could the conclusions and recommendations made by the team have played a more positive role in tackling the real problems of basic education in China.

Culture and Environment

In educational policy-making, solutions to a problem can be viable only when the causes of the problem are correctly identified and understood. Problems may look alike in different countries and different parts of a country, but their causes and nature may differ considerably. Accordingly, solutions must often vary and problem identification should not stop at the discovery of discrepancies. It is essential to understand the processes by which such discrepancies are formed and the contexts or environments in which such processes take place (see Crossley and Broadfoot, 1992). An understanding of processes and environments requires attention to the local culture; and the study of such processes, environments and cultures is a strength of a qualitative approach to educational research.

Illustrative of this point is a recent study of an ethnic minority area in China. In Miao villages, girls' attendance is exceptionally low. These are the "difficult spots" or, as mentioned above, what the planners call "pockets" where universal primary education was difficult to achieve. In a survey done in one of the prefectures (sub-divisions of a province) that are inhabited by minorities (Wen, 1988) it was shown that although average female enrollment in the prefecture was over 70%, there were counties (sub-divisions of a prefecture) where the enrollment rate was as low as 31%. Meanwhile, the boys' enrollment rate was almost 100%. In addition, only about 27% of the girls ever completed primary school. In some of the schools we visited, there were only one or two girls among a whole school of several hundred children. These are called the "monk" schools. Low attendance among girls has led to low output of female graduates, which in turn leads to a shortage of female teacher trainees and hence female teachers. This has become a rather stubborn vicious circle because parents are reluctant to send their girls to schools with only male teachers.

The same report identified four causes for the low enrollment: economic underdevelopment, parents' discrimination against girls and early marriage, high private cost for parents, and the irrelevance and low quality of schooling. Recommendations to overcome low enrollment are therefore reduction of private costs, expansion of the public schools sector, development of vocational education, and propaganda and education to discourage early marriage.

Home visits were paid to families as part of our research strategy and a general picture began to emerge from such fieldwork. Most importantly this revealed that girls in the Miao ethnic group are expected to take embroidery most seriously. Skills and knowledge of embroidery lore are a demonstration of their talents and hence an indicator of their social prestige. This in turn determines their future in terms of finding a good husband and explains the famous and splendid costumes the Miao girls wear. Each girl wears only costumes that are products of their own manual skills. Embroidery is therefore so important in their social life that girls learn embroidery as soon as they can hold the needle. At ages of twelve or thirteen, girls are expected to do embroidery for their future husbands, and a little later, they do pieces for their future children. Some of these girls become engaged as young as eight or nine years old.

Such qualitative research, within the local culture, revealed previously overlooked but important causes for the non-attendance of girls in school. In this context embroidery skills bear a much higher "economic" value than schooling. Indeed, girls who attend schools incur an opportunity cost which they cannot afford. There is a basic contradiction in the relations between education and the local economy. On the one hand, education is basic to the long-term development and well-being of the Miao communities. At the time of the research, the literacy rate for girls in the prefecture was just over 28%, in strong contrast to that of 71% for boys, and development in the local economy is inevitably hindered by low educational attainment. On the other hand, the social structures and lifestyles of Miao communities present formidable hurdles for the schooling of girls.

In this case, the local planners are aware of the situation and the embroidery issue is fully described in Wen's analysis. However, the difficulties generated by this were classified by external policy analysts as "discrimination against girls" and "backward traditions," hence the proposed solutions lay in "educating parents" and "promoting the Marital Law." The planners were thus thinking in the framework of universalizing basic education and hence anything that presented obstacles to such a course needed to be rectified and changed.

Qualitative fieldwork through the home visits, however, helped the writer not only to understand how the emphasis on embroidery skills had become a problem, but also to assess the importance of culture among the Miao communities. To the Miao parents and the Miao girls, schooling is something imposed on them because of an importance that is not felt within their community. Meanwhile, in order to attend schools, they have to put aside their embroidery exercises, and because of that they worry about their future. Schooling causes problems for girls with immediate effect. From a local perspective, it is therefore not embroidery that is causing problems, but compulsory education that is disturbing their normal lifestyle and culture.

This qualitative study has shed new light on the issue of girls' attendance in Miao communities. If social conditions and cultural expectations are not changed in these Miao villages, there does not seem to be an easy way to improve girls' attendance. The cultural issue that has to be given attention in order to make compulsory education possible is much greater than the problem of compulsory education itself. If the Marital Law (which permits legal marriage only after age eighteen) is difficult to implement in the villages, then the Law of Compulsory Education is a secondary issue. The question before policy-makers is then: is it realistic, and culturally acceptable, to ask such villages to achieve compulsory primary education in the near future? In recent years, some educators in China have advocated a reconsideration of the uniform target of nine-year compulsory education applied throughout the country. The Miao girls have further demonstrated the necessity for such a reconsideration. As a pragmatic measure, national policy has moved away from 100% coverage of compulsory education throughout the nation. The social situation in the Miao villages further challenges policy-makers with questions such as: if all girls in Miao villages can be helped to receive four (or even two) years of school education, is that not a significant target in its own right? What is the most realistic and culturally appropriate policy option?

Clearly, it is often legitimate for central government to make policies for parts of a country to comply with. In the case of compulsory education in China, for example, national policies have made essential contributions to the improvement of basic education in the past decade. In this sense, uniformity in national policies has been a positive factor in educational development. However, uniformity in policies inevitably encounters problems among diverse localities, and where national policy is not so relevant to local needs, imposition may bear little fruit—and in some cases may arouse resentment. Policies are thus viable only when they are realistic, but they are realistic only when they are seen as realistic by the local community. In other words, local perspectives are important in the policy formulation and implementation process. In this respect, qualitative research, which accesses and identifies local views in context can, and should, play a crucial role for policy makers.

MULTIPLE INTERPRETATIONS OF POLICY-RELATED CONCEPTS

Policy-related research often works with concepts that are attractive to policy makers. Concepts such as efficiency, equity and quality are particularly common in the literature and efficiency looms high on the policy agenda. Efficiency is also a priority of donor agencies and international organizations who are concerned about whether or not funding channeled to developing countries is used in the most economical way. The measurement of efficiency may seem unambiguous to planners. To many, efficiency is either measured by input-output analysis or cost-benefit analysis. Such concepts and procedures are, however, more appropriate to industrial enterprises and, when applied to other systems (including education), require more careful modification and application than is often the case in practice. Much research and evaluation is thus conducted at the expense of real understanding of the language with which the system operates.

Such problems were encountered in a project carried out in 1993 in three provinces of China to study the internal efficiency of basic education in rural villages.[2] The research team was drawn from a local research institute, the Shanghai Institute of Human Resource Development. During a preliminary discussion before the research the team arrived at the conclusion that, given the disparity among different parts of China, it was impossible to set a uniform measure for output of the school system. According to members' experience in various parts of the country, the expected output of primary schools may range from "attendance rate for the required years," "high passing rate at graduation" to "high enrollment rate in secondary schools."

In each case, the expected rates again vary. Using any unified yardstick to measure educational output with such a variety of expectations did not seem to be sensible. The team therefore decided to adopt a notion of "minimum acceptable quality" as a benchmark of educational output in the various counties to be studied. This is a floating benchmark that is locality-specific. What this actually means had to be identified during each of the case studies. As such, the case studies were designed to include strong qualitative components. Apart from the collection of financial data and interviews with local officers and planners, each case study included in-depth interviews with school principals, focus group discussions with parents and observations of classroom teaching. The question to be addressed about output was: what is seen as the minimum acceptable quality in this locality?

Discussion about notions of output thus encouraged the research team to be more sensitive about local perspectives. With this preparation and orientation the team discovered a number of other issues that were beyond their expectation, but that were essential to understanding efficiency issues in the villages. First, local planners and educators were more concerned about inadequacy rather than efficiency. Some went as far as saying that efficiency is an issue only when funding is adequate. In a team meeting after the first interviews, members came to the consensus that for the local planners and educators, efficiency *(xiaoyi)* was taken to mean benefits. When they say a school is efficient, they mean the school can do a good job. A further analysis of the situation revealed that a reason for this local perception of efficiency was that the parties who received funds were different from the parties who spent the money. In other words, those who were responsible for the output and those who were responsible for the input never interacted. Not that they did not meet each other physically, but the two groups were not related in a dialectical way. When the input parties did not find enough to spend, they asked for more; when the output parties were asked for more, they tried to find more. This helps to explain why the notion of inadequacy prevails over efficiency. The research team concluded that this is a reflection of traditional thinking in operation in a planned economy.

Second, in addition to the separation of input from output, there was also a "compartmentalization" of funding. That is, all funds were earmarked for specific expenditures, and a convention in China is that different expenditures are taken care of by different sources of funding. In the case of primary schools in villages, the state is largely responsible for salaries of public teachers, educational levies are used for community teachers, and donations are sought for physical constructions (Zhou, 1992). In addition, schools may also generate income through school-owned factories or other economic activities. What was discovered in the research, even by those who had long been familiar with the basic conventions, was that because of the earmarking convention, school principals and local education officers were not given discretion for mixing available funds across budget categories. They also never considered ways to mobilize funds from one "compartment" to another in order to maximize their utilization, largely because this was not expected under the planning system.

Accordingly, the research team made recommendations which pointed to reforms that would be fundamental to the system. Their recommendations included an increase in the discretion for principals in reallocating funds, freedom for schools to raise salaries in exchange for heavier teaching loads to create an incentive mechanism, creation of differential learning targets to motivate the largest majority of students, and the replacement of formal science experiments by low-cost life-related activities.

This is an example of how qualitative research may touch upon the crux of policy issues that are not always assessible through the collection of quantitative data and macrolevel information. The institute in charge of this research was well known for producing national annual reports of educational finance. They were not short of system-level information and they did make very insightful analyses based on the quantitative data. However, efficiency is something that is improved mainly through changes in practice in schools and by the people who work in them. As such, the team rightly emphasized qualitative aspects of the study and therefore began to better understand local perspectives (and misconceptions) of efficiency. This provided sound grounds for making more realistic policy recommendations.

If such recommendations were put into practice, it is argued there would not only be an improvement of efficiency in schools, but also a clarification of the notion of efficiency among local educators and planners. The benefits of the latter would be far-reaching in themselves.

CONCLUDING REMARKS

As argued at the beginning of this chapter, much educational research in developing countries is funded by development agencies operating from developed countries. Too many studies are either carried out by consultants from the north, or they are conducted by local researchers who have to shape their research agendas according to the expectations of the donor agencies. Very often, projects adopt a functionalist point of view, assuming a linear relationship between education and development and, often despite very good intentions, a deficit model of developing countries. Endeavors to identify strengths in education provision in developing countries are rare and only recent (see, for example, Filp, 1993). Such tendencies often trap researchers in unhelpful intellectual and planning frameworks that result in findings which are unrealistic for the specific context.

To illustrate how preconceived ideas can predetermine analysis we conclude with a brief comparison of China and Japan. These two countries share a similar education tradition and are fairly close in their educational practices. If we examine research funded and published by the major aid agencies, research about Japanese education tends to highlight its strengths whereas, until recently, research about Chinese education tends to identify difficulties. One can argue that this is natural because research on China is used mainly to justify loans, which is not the case for Japan. There is a tacit functionalist assumption that Japan's economic strength is attributable to its sound education; while China's poor quality education reflects its low level of economic development. It is, nevertheless, significant to note that publications that are based on qualitative research are often more realistic and fairer to educators in both countries (for example, Lynn, 1988; White, 1987; Rohlen, 1983 for Japan; and Cleverly, 1991; Gardner, 1989; Ross, 1993 for China). Qualitative research and evaluation, emphasizing an ethnographic approach, is thus a valuable mode of investigation for policy makers willing to challenge ethnocentric assumptions, and other preconceptions, that may limit the effectiveness and relevance of educational plans and proposals.

Moreover, our review of the literature produced by researchers visiting developing countries reveals little reference to findings of local research. Even when members of visiting teams have developing country origins, the fact that they are sent by a "northern" funding agency often locates the visit in a north-south relationship, and the study is likely to adopt a strong "donor-recipient" paradigm. Too often there is also tacit disrespect for whatever is generated by local research efforts. Indeed, acknowledging the existence of expertise in the host developing country may limit the future role of visiting consultants.

Under these circumstances, quantitative methods can provide a safe shelter for visiting researchers, and for international funding agencies. The mathematical model cited earlier, for example, had been successful in Latin America and became a convenient vehicle for visiting teams to fulfill their duties elsewhere. In this case there is multiple beauty. First, the model generates a considerable level of sophistication, requires high-tech skills and is seen as "scientific," and "impartial." Second, it has already proved successful in the developing world. Third, results point to a negation of official information about dropouts and so provide the visiting team with considerable legitimacy to maintain its expert position and deliver an authoritative report. How many students actually drop out from schools in China is perhaps less of a real concern for the team, or for the funding agency as a whole, than many would wish to acknowledge.

While this may be an overly cynical and provocative perspective, more criticism in this arena of policy research is required if we are to improve our chances of realistic policy formulation and successful implementation—and qualitative research and evaluation clearly has much to offer, especially in developing countries.

NOTES

1. In that particular visit, per evening per team member in a five-star Beijing hotel cost about U.S. $100. The visit report estimated that the per-student unit expenditure per year in that particular province was about U.S. $16.

2. The project, known as TSS-1, was sponsored by UNDP with the assistance of UNESCO. The writer was the external consultant.

ACKNOWLEDGMENT

The writer would like to thank Mark Constas, his colleague, for reading through the text and making useful comments.

REFERENCES

Berstecher, D. (1986) *Provincial-level Educational Planning and Management in China: A Case Study of Sichuan Province.* Paris: UNESCO/UNICEF Co-operative Program (Mimeograph).

Chen, H.D. (1988) "Bufada Dqu Shisi Jiunian Yiwu Jiaoyu de Xuezhi Wenti (The School System for Implementation of nine-year Compulsory Education in Under-Developed Areas)," *Jiaoyu Yanjiu,* 6:10–12.

Cheng, K.M. (1985) *Forecasting in a Free Market: Manpower Survey in the Planning of Technical Education.* Paper presented in the Second Annual Conference of the Hong Kong Educational Research Association, November 16.

———. (1987) "Where are the Trainees?—Trainers' Plans Versus Students' Aspirations in Hong Kong." In E.D. Fortuijn, W. Hoppers and M. Morgan (eds.) *Paving Pathways to Work.* The Hague: CESO.

———. (1991a) *Planning of Basic Education in China: A Case Study of Two Counties in the Province of Liaoning.* Paris: International Institute for Educational Planning.

———. (1991b) "Challenging the North-South Paradigm: Educational Research in East Asia." In International Institute for Educational Planning and Institute of International Education, Stockholm University (eds.) *Strengthening Educational Research in Developing Countries.* Paris: International Institute for Educational Planning

———. (1996) *Quality of Basic Education in China: A Case Study of the Zhejiang Province.* Paris: International Institute for Educational Planning.

Cheng, K.M. and Paine, L. (1991) *Research on Education in Rural China: A Survey of the Literature.* Plenary paper delivered at the International Conference on Chinese Education of the 21st Century, November 19–22, Honolulu.

Cleverley, J. (1991) *The Schooling of China: Tradition and Modernity in Chinese Education* (2d ed.) Sydney: Allen & Unwin.

Crossley, M. and Broadfoot, P. (1992) "Comparative and International Research in Education: Scope, Problems and Potential," *British Educational Research Journal* 18(2): 99–112.

Filp, J. (1993) *The 900 Schools Programme: Improving the Quality of Primary Schools in Impoverished Areas of Chile*. Paris: International Institute for Educational Planning.

Gardner, H. (1989) *To Open Minds: Chinese Clues to the Dilemma of Contemporary Education*. New York: Basic Books.

Han, Q.L. (1990) "Woguo Zhongxiaoxue Xuesheng Lushi Zhuangkuang de Fenxi he Duice (The Analysis and Solutions for the Problem of School Dropouts in China)," *Jiaoyu Yanjiu*, 2:20–23

Hebei Education Commission, Office of Policy Studies (1990) *Hebeisheng Xiaoxue Chuzhong Liushi Liuji Zhuangkuang de Diaocha Yanjiu Zonghe Baogao (A Comprehensive Report of the Study of Dropout and Repetition in Primary and Junior Secondary Schools in Hebei Province)*. (Mimeograph). Also reported in *Zhongguo Jiaoyu Bao (China Education Daily)*, February 7, 1991.

Lincoln, Y.S. and Guba, E.G. (1985) *Naturalistic Enquiry*. Beverly Hills: Sage.

Lynn, R. (1988) *Educational Achievement in Japan: Lessons for the West*. London: Macmillan.

Ma, Y.Q. (1984) "Dangqian Nongcun Xiaoxue Liujilu Wenti Diaocha Yanjiu (A Study of the Current Rate of Grade Repetition in Rural Primary Schools)," *Jiaoyu Yanjiu*, 9:47–51.

Rohlen, T.P. (1983) *Japan's High Schools*. Berkeley: University of California Press.

Ross, H. (1993) *China Learns English*. New Haven: Yale University Press.

Shanghai Institute of Human Resources Development (1994) *Internal Efficiency of Educational Finance in Rural Primary Schools in China: Report of a Research Based on Case Studies*. Prepared for UNDP and UNESCO. (Mimeograph).

Shen, G.M. (1988) "Sunan Nongcun Xuexiao de Liusheng Wenti ji Duice (The Problems of Dropouts and the Solutions in the Rural Schools in South Jiangsu Province)," *Jiaoyu Yanjiu*, 7:43–46.

United Nations Development Program (various years) *Human Development Report*. New York: Oxford University Press.

Wen, B. (1988) *Qiandongnan Miaozhu Dongzhu Zizhizhou nü Ertong Ruxue Zhuangkuang, Wenti ji Jianyi (Girl Attendance in the Miao and Dong Autonomous Prefecture of Southeast Guizhou: Situations, Problems and Recommendations)*. (Mimeograph).

White, M. (1987) *The Japanese Educational Challenge: A Commitment to Children*. New York: The Free Press.

World Bank (1985) *China: Issues and Prospects in Education*. Washington D.C.

Yang, N.L. and Han, M. (1991) "Xiaoxue Chuzhong Xuesheng Cuoxue Liuji de Yanjiu (A Study on the Drop-out and Repetitions in Chinese Primary and Junior Secondary)," *Jiaoyu Yanjiu*, 3:45–57.

Zhang, J.Y. (1985) "Dangqian Nongcun Zhongxue Liusheng Wenti de Diaocha (A Survey of Rural Secondary Student Dropout)," *Jiaoyu Yanjiu*, 8:33–36.

Zhao, J. (1987) "Chuzhong Yanxue Xuesheng de Xingqu (An Investigation into the Interests of Junior Secondary School Students Who are Sick of Schooling)," *Jiaoyu Yanjiu*, 7:59–62.

Zhou, B.L. (1990) *Mianxiang Ershiyi Shiji de Zhongguo Jiaoyu: Guoqing, Xuqiu, Guihua, Duice (China's Education for the 21st Century: Situations, Demands, Planning and Decisions)*. Beijing: Higher Education Press.

Zhou, N.Z. (1992) *Reinforce the Connections between Education and the Economy:*

Major Issues and Solutions in China's Education Reform. Paper delivered at the International Conference on "Education, Social Change and Regional Development," June 23–25, Hong Kong.

4   THE IMPORTANCE OF FIELDWORK

ANTHROPOLOGY AND EDUCATION IN PAPUA NEW GUINEA

Wayne Fife

INTRODUCTION

Open up any introductory textbook in socio-cultural anthropology and you will find a lecture on the importance of holism. The author will typically explain that anthropologists are usually more interested in gaining an understanding of the total context of human lives than they are in delineating "variables" or "factors" from those lives in order to arrive at a generalization or "law" regarding human behavior. This is particularly true of ethnographic researchers, who traditionally make use of the participant-observation method in their work. Two key terms for an ethnographer are context and pattern. The goal is to formulate a *pattern* of analysis that makes reasonable sense of human actions within the *context* of a given place and time.[1] This task of holism may seem simple enough when a student is reading an introductory textbook, but when the same person turns into a researcher he or she is inevitably confronted with the following two questions: (1) How much context do I have to cover?, and (2) How will I recognize a pattern when I see it? These are other ways of asking how a researcher who follows a qualitative, ethnographic strategy can ever know when a "holistic" understanding has been satisfactorily achieved.

Unfortunately, there is no straightforward answer to this question. The answer can never be fully determined for the simple reason that socio-cultural anthropology is both an art and a science. As a science, empirical evidence must be gathered so that readers of the anthropological product can weigh the evidence for themselves and thereby judge the ethnographer's analysis; as an art, the author of this information must make an aesthetic judgment as to when the context that has been presented is "whole enough." Because of the latter requirement, it is not possible to provide a single answer for the research questions noted above that could be considered valid in all contexts. What can be done, however, is to provide examples of the decisions that particular researchers have made under specific circumstances.

In this chapter, I will outline some of the decisions that I made in 1986–87 when I undertook a year-long research project concerning education and social change in the province of West New Britain in the Pacific island nation of Papua New Guinea. Along the way, I will explain how I arrived at what proved to be workable answers to the two questions listed above. The reader will also be provided with specific examples of how I went about collecting evidence regarding individual actions, cultural expressions, and social formations in such a way as to make it possible to produce a consistent, empirically valid argument regarding education and social change in West New Britain (for an overview of this argument see Fife, 1992a). Due to the constraints of length, only a very small portion of this argument can be reproduced in this chapter. Because of this I have chosen to focus on one particular aspect of my research. This concerns the question of the impact that the implementation of a state-run educational system has had on social inequality within Papua New Guinea. Throughout the chapter we will return often to the question of social inequality, as an illustration of the kind of analysis that can be formulated within each methodological level of the total research project.

It is important to begin by noting that individual, cultural, and social effects are of course equally present and important at both micro- and macrolevels of analysis. However, each will be overemphasized in importance during specific phases of the project, depending on the exact method of research being utilized. Broad social patterns, for example, will normally become most clearly visible when concentrating on macrolevel research; while individual differences usually show up most readily at the microlevel of the project. There is nothing wrong with these tendencies, as long as the researcher continues to remind him or herself that these are methodological artifacts and *not* natural occurrences. What this means at the practical level is that the researcher must be sure to bring *all* of the necessary elements for a good analysis back into the work as part of the final overall interpretation.

THE MACROLEVEL OF RESEARCH

It is easiest for most researchers to begin their work at the macrolevel. In this way, useful work can be done preparatory to on-site fieldwork. Gathering information at the macrolevel has become an important part of any ethnographic fieldwork project. In terms of education, this means that it is no longer enough to treat individual classrooms or schools as if they formed independent "cultures." Education must be seen within its total context and considered in relation to other important social institutions such as economics or religion. We cannot really understand what a particular school is about unless we are also able to interpret something about the kind of role it plays in education as a whole and the way a specific educational system has been constructed (for good examples of this more contextual approach see Singleton, 1967; Haig-Brown, 1988; Weis, 1990; Lofty, 1992; Pomponio, 1992). Macroresearch can be divided into sources of information that come from either the historical or contemporary domains. In anthropology today, both are considered necessary to do a proper job of framing the more intimate research of the more traditional style of ethnography (e.g. Herzfeld, 1991; Taussig, 1991; Thomas, 1991).

In order to construct a model of how a contemporary educational system came to take its present form it is necessary to begin with a history of that system. In an ideal world, the researcher would be able to follow an initial study of secondary historical resources with a study of primary historical sources during the actual fieldwork stage of the project. This is a feasible project within Papua New Guinea, for example, as the University of Papua New Guinea contains valuable historical archives on early education in that country. However, for most of us, funding limits and the concomitant time constraints that this imposes renders an extensive use of primary sources impossible. In my own work, I was forced to rely extensively on secondary sources alongside of the few primary works that had been published. Luckily, Papua New Guinea has a rich secondary literature on the history of education (e.g. Griffin, 1976; Meek, 1982; Dept. of Education, 1985; Pomponio and Lancy, 1986; Smith, 1985, 1987). Through this literature I was able to see that there had been three main phases of educational policy: (1) 1873–1945: an era of almost total missionary control over rudimentary education for the purpose of Christian "salvation," (2) 1945–1960: a period of rapid expansion in the primary school system for the purpose of "basic education," during which the government and missionaries began to work more in partnership with each other, and (3) 1960–present: a final period in which first the colonial government of Australia and then secondly the independent government of Papua New Guinea took over primary responsibility for the organization of the total educational system (see Fife, 1992a: 111–187). It was during this latter period that large amounts of money were invested in the rapid expansion of secondary and tertiary level education in order to prepare an educated "elite" for independence in 1975. An important impact of this trend has been the creation of a school system that fueled regional, urban vs. rural, and the beginnings of class inequalities within the country (e.g. see the papers in Bray and Smith, 1985). By reading some of this material before beginning the on-site phase of the project, I was able to realize that the basis for these emerging inequalities would have to appear within the primary school system and that they should show up during actual microlevel research. Later in the chapter, it will become evident that this was indeed the case. The researcher will normally have only a short period available to read historical material before beginning fieldwork and he or she should concentrate on the broadest outlines of the development of the educational system at this stage of the work. After the fieldwork has been completed, the researcher can then return to either secondary or primary sources and look more closely for material that speaks directly to the development of the most important educational themes discovered during the research. During my later research, for example, I was able to find cultural themes that had emerged within the missionary-dominated phases of education that led me to argue that much of the hidden morality embedded in teachers' attitudes toward students' behavior had their origin in missionary influences (e.g. Fife, 1989, 1994a). This was true even though this research was purposefully limited to three secular, urban-oriented primary schools. Without some knowledge of missionary endeavours within education I would never have been able to recognize these cultural themes when they appeared within the interactions between teachers and pupils in the classrooms of West New Britain.

It is also important to consider some of the contemporary material available at the macrolevel both prior to and during the course of fieldwork. Before beginning direct research, the educational investigator will benefit immensely by taking a little time to read one or two overviews that explain the basic economic structures present in the country in which they are going to conduct their study. Alongside the publications of private scholars, overviews of the general economic conditions of developing countries are often published by the various offices of the United Nations or the World Bank. These sources[2] provide invaluable raw data about employment in the cash economy that, when taken alongside of more analytical works such as Kenneth Good's *Papua New Guinea: A False Economy* (1986), allow the researcher to gain an initial impression of where education fits into a particular country in relation to other important social institutions. In my own work, I was eventually able to show that because of severe structural limitations affecting the potential growth of employment in the various sectors of the cash economy, even students who graduated from high school were going to find it harder and harder to secure any employment in this increasingly competitive arena (e.g. Fife, 1988). This could then be coupled with information from the historical sources that showed an increasing desire on the part of Papua New Guineans to participate in the cash economy to suggest that many of the contemporary educational structures in place were inadvertently aimed at producing employees, even though only a very small minority would ever have a chance of finding direct employment in the cash economy. In short, the culture of education that had been developing over the last several decades in Papua New Guinea did not fit the economic reality of life in that country. Without some understanding of the contemporary structure of economics and employment I would not have been able to recognize the possibility of constructing this argument, nor understood its significance for pedagogical practices within the classrooms of West New Britain.

Before we get to these practices, it is worthwhile to spend some time discussing the kind of macrolevel information that can be gathered regarding the contemporary situation while conducting the actual field research in a developing country. The exact research situation will of course differ from country to country (e.g. compare the cases for Papua New Guinea, Malaysia, Sri Lanka, and Nigeria in Vulliamy, Lewin, and Stephens, 1990), but some things can be said about the general situation of macro research that will remain useful within many different settings.

Vulliamy has pointed out that qualitative studies can not only serve as good starting points for quantitative investigators who are interested in identifying more locally appropriate topics for their research designs (1990b: 18), but can also address themes raised by the prior analysis of quantitative and statistical data (1990a: 42). Thus, when I first entered the capital city of Port Moresby in Papua New Guinea one of the first things that I did was make the rounds of the various offices of the federal bureaucracies (e.g. the bureaucrats responsible for the national level for education, primary industries, development, and so forth). A number of these offices had useful publications, including overall statistical information that is often either not available outside of the country or is only available in an outdated format (a common situation for statistical information about developing countries).

Visits served two purposes. The first one was to gather statistical information that would both quickly inform me of larger social trends in the country and would also serve as background data for my writings when I had time to make a more detailed analysis after the on-site research period was concluded. The second purpose was to arrange informal discussions with bureaucrats or other government people (including academics) who were responsible for the provision of education in that country. These discussions are excellent ways to familiarize oneself with what the local experts consider to be the main educational issues within a given country. This helps correct the research agenda, which all too often has been outlined without regard to local concerns as to the usefulness of any results that might accrue. In my own case, for example, an initial desire to study both primary and secondary schools in West New Britain was altered in favor of research into primary schools after a local academic convinced me that secondary schools in this area had already received sufficient attention, but community schools (the local term for schools that cover grades one to six) had been neglected by researchers. One of the tools that he used to convince me was a computer readout that illustrated widely divergent results on the national grade-six examinations. These examinations are the single most important event determining who will attend secondary schools within the country (only a small minority) and who will be limited to a maximum of grade six (the vast majority). This information made me aware that some schools performed far better than others in preparing their pupils for the grade-six examinations and that an obvious question to try to answer in terms of social inequalities was why this was so. Second, it also made me wonder about the majority of pupils in the country. What kind of an education were they getting if "success" or "failure" was being measured by their inability to pass into a secondary education and of what use was it to their future lives as adult citizens? The raw statistics clearly indicated that community schools that were located in or around urban areas consistently posted much higher success rates in the national examinations than those located in the rural areas. I therefore decided that instead of attempting to compare urban and rural schools (an almost impossible task to undertake using a qualitative methodology given the limitations of time, money, and a single researcher) I would focus my attention on three urban-oriented community schools that were considered a success in local terms. This would give me a chance to see how teaching proceeded within the "best" rather than the "worst" situations and allow me to consider what the majority of students were receiving under optimal conditions even though roughly half of these were still not passing the grade-six examinations.

Newspapers are another source of information that is often available within developing countries, although these are too often ignored by researchers. In the case of Papua New Guinea, because my study was carried out in or around two of the most important towns in West New Britain it became possible consistently to collect newspaper articles, letters to the editor, and editorials. Over a six-month period I systematically clipped pieces that involved any of the following themes: education, domestic or other forms of individual violence, social disputes (e.g. fighting between groups), gender issues, government policies, government or bureaucratic corruption, and development issues. All of these topics are relevant to education. Violence and/or corruption, for example, are often behind school closings in both rural and urban areas (see Fife, 1992b). My intent in this case was not to gather material for a formal media analysis, but rather to (a) gain a broader understanding of issues that were considered newsworthy and therefore of public concern in the country as a whole, and (b) gain a background that would allow me to place the more parochial concerns of West New Britain against these wider issues. A warning must be issued here. Anyone who has ever been interviewed for a newspaper article can tell you that these sources do not always report information accurately. Newspaper articles should be thought of by researchers as excellent places to discover public attitudes toward specific issues, but they should not be trusted as sources for specific information (e.g. statistics) about these issues. Reporters simply do not have the time to check their facts with anything like the accuracy that is expected from professional social scientists. Specific information, therefore, must be checked (e.g. with the appropriate social agency) before it is assumed to be accurate and usable for purposes of educational research. To give an example of the possible uses of newspaper articles, I will briefly discuss a little of the information that I was able to gather regarding the theme of development and suggest how this affected my study.

In the early stages of the study, while conducting informal interviews with parents[3] it quickly became obvious that most viewed education as desirable only if it led to a direct job in the cash economy. If the child was going to grow up and make a living, as the vast majority of adult Papua New Guineans do, as part of the subsistence-based horticultural economy of the villages then most parents expressed a preference for pulling their sons or daughters out of school after a few years before it "ruined" them for the life of the village. The problem was to know which child to invest in for the future. During discussions with parents, I found very few who understood the historical changes that had made it possible for a small number of Papua New Guineans to gain well-paying jobs just prior to and after independence in 1975, but that rendered it highly unlikely that any but a tiny minority would have such opportunities for this kind of employment in the future. Newspaper reports verified my conjecture that a split was developing between the official government position of education for both urban and rural life and the overwhelming cultural projection among parents that education was development and therefore should by definition guarantee a son or daughter graduating from secondary school a place within the cash economy. Newspapers were full of letters to the editor from disappointed parents and students who lamented the lack of opportunity to participate in "development" through a job in the cash economy, even when they had become educated. A good example is the high school student from Chimbu province whose letter appeared in the *Post-Courier* on August 15, 1986, complaining about members of the national parliament. "It is four years since the last national election, but Gumine is still underdeveloped. . . . I am confused whether our MPs understand the word development. If they do, please implement it. They have promised that certain things will be done, but where are they?" A similar letter to the editor in the *Tok Pisin*[4] newspaper *Wantok* on May 17, 1986 by a frustrated young man complains that high school and even university educated people are having difficulty obtaining employment in the government or business companies. His solution is to suggest that (my translation): "The government must give a man or a woman ten years work inside of a company or the government. If a man or a woman is lucky enough to have this time, they must then resign so that a new man or woman can take their place."

In reply to these letters and the more general dissatisfaction expressed by many parents and students, elected government officials began writing newspaper articles or editorials in which they extolled the virtues of independence, hard work, and self-sufficiency. Deputy Prime Minister and Finance Minister Sir Julius Chan, for example, wrote in the *Post-Courier* on July 22, 1986 that Papua New Guineans were getting reputations as people who took the "easy way out" instead of "meeting problems head on with hard work and sacrifice." "Only hard work solve(s) problems—there is no one to blame for failures but ourselves." While a little over a month later, on August 29, the Prime Minister wrote in the same newspaper that ". . . it is now time to bury dependent thinking for good. We will restore confidence, respect the ethic of hard work, and renew the caring and sharing habits of our ancestors. . . . Why should the tax money that comes in from those who are growing cocoa, and coffee, and oil palm go to help people who are not doing any work? Why should the tax money of a few hard working people build schools and hospitals and roads for people who do not lift a finger to make any contribution at all?"

Armed with these preliminary interviews with parents and bureaucrats, supplemented by newspaper accounts that suggested a fundamental split between citizens and the government about who was responsible for development in their country, I could then look to the community school classrooms of West New Britain to try to see where these attitudes were coming from. Were students, for example, somehow being taught that a life in the cash-based, urban-dominated economy was a necessity that must be provided by the government? If so, how was this related to the emerging social inequalities in the country?

THE MICROLEVEL OF RESEARCH

These questions can only be answered at the microlevel of research. This level, which normally involves intensive participant-observation and focused interviewing, will comprise the vast majority of an ethnographer's on-site field research. In my own case, this occurred over a one-year period and included three different community schools in the town areas of West New Britain.

The immediate problem in a study of this kind is to try to find a methodological tool that will help the researcher bridge the gap between the macro- and microlevels of information gathering and analysis. I found such a tool in the writings of anthropologists and others who are concerned with the "hidden curriculum" of education (e.g. Postman and Weingartner, 1969; Gearing, 1979; Gearing and Epstein, 1982; Feinberg and Soltis, 1985; Omokhodion, 1989). Hidden curriculum, which might be thought of as the culture of a specific school or classroom, normally becomes visible to the researcher through an investigation of the way education is organized and enacted within the daily context of schooling. This involves the forms of interactions observable, for example, between teachers and pupils. It also includes the interactions of other members of the educational community, such as parents and members of the school's administration. However, it is not limited to direct interactions and can also be found in the decorations that appear on classroom walls, the spatial formations of a class or assembly, the discourse surrounding what makes a "good" versus a "bad" student and what to do about them, and so forth. In short, hidden curriculum refers to all of the ways that the verbal and nonverbal organization of education affects the production of an ethos or form of consciousness among students.

Identifying an ethos or consciousness (and there may be more than one) occurs through a careful process of gathering data at the microlevel. In my opinion, this process is best begun by simply attending classes as an observer. The researcher should obtain permission from the educators involved to simply sit down at the back of a different class each day for a minimum of two weeks in each school and record as fully as possible the context of education in that class. This includes detailed descriptions of the physical environment of the classroom and the school as a whole; the spatial arrangements of objects, educators and students; and the verbal and nonverbal interactions of teachers and students as well as students and students. Of course no one can actually compile anything approaching a full record of the context of education within a classroom or school, but observers are often surprised at how detailed and accurate their note taking becomes with a little practice. The goal here is to provide oneself with a general record of what is occurring in real classrooms before the observer begins to narrow the ethnographic focus to accommodate his or her more specific research interests.

After the first few weeks of notetaking has been completed, it is generally useful to pause and re-read these notes with an eye toward recognizing the more thematic interests that govern a specific project. The notes can then be coded so that they may be drawn upon in the post-research phase when writing up results. Coding can be done in any number of ways. For the short term, color coded pieces of Post-It Notes can be used to write short labels on (such as "aggressive behaviour," "enforcing gender differences," "valorizing urban life," etc.), which can then be placed next to the actual fieldnote. For the long term, you may want to develop a card system in which separate index cards are created for each topic or theme that has been identified as important in your project. These will include page, paragraph and date references for individual examples that can be found in your research notes. Alternatively, simple databases can be created using computer software.

Re-reading earlier notes can also be useful for determining how the next stage of the project should proceed. Let me give the reader a few specific examples from my own research to show how this can actually occur.

In each of the three community schools in which I conducted my study it quickly became obvious through re-reading my notes that a great deal of attention was paid at all levels of schooling to the importance of form (see Fife, 1994b). Straight lines were used both inside and outside of the classroom to "keep order" (e.g. marching lines during early morning assembly that divided students by gender; sitting lines that divided the classes up into ability groups—each with its own leader—within the class). It was my repeated descriptions of spatial organization in different contexts that enabled me to see how important this repeated form was to the organization of these schools. Once envisioned, it led me to read notes concerning classroom interactions to see if a similar reliance on form over content existed. It should be noted here that in order to protect myself against a false reliance upon idiosyncratic events or interactions I made it a rule during analysis of the materials to only make use of themes for which I had actual examples for all three schools, as well as a minimum of two examples within each school. In practice, almost all of the materials that were utilized could have been represented by dozens of specific naturalistic examples from the classrooms in which I conducted research. Selecting a minimum standard for thematic behaviors is useful to guard against selecting spectacular or exotic examples and over-representing them in the final product.

It did not take me long to find specific examples of "linear" behavior in the material. Notes involving one math lesson, for example, contained a detailed description of a teacher who became angry when one of her students began to do subtraction and addition problems in his head rather than using the much more laborious method of counting out the answers on the floor through the use of sticks and stones. She told him in no uncertain terms that he was a "bighead" and wiped out his answer (even though it was correct), telling him to do it again the "correct" way. Similar examples permeated my notes for a number of different contexts in every classroom, suggesting that many of the teachers took the formal instructions of their curriculum handbooks far too literally. Individuals of course differed in this respect, and I was able to use these differences in a later analysis to develop the notion that what I call a "secondary form of hidden curriculum" exists alongside of the primary forms in these particular classrooms (see Fife, 1992b). More will be said about secondary forms later, but for now I would like to continue discussing the primary form of consciousness in these particular community schools in West New Britain.

When I asked myself how an over-determined concern with form might affect the formation of students' consciousness and the developing social inequalities that were discernible though the macrolevel of data, several possibilities occurred to me. I will only discuss one of these now. Many teachers and other educators seem to convince themselves that they are creating a meritocracy in which only the "best" students pass the grade-six examinations through a mastery of the content of education (such as written or mathematical skills) without taking into account the effects that an emphasis on form has on who will and who will not be able to develop these skills. In the example mentioned above, one of the brightest boys in the math class was disciplined for showing off rather than following the correct form for solving a problem. My notes indicated that certain types of individuals were repeatedly corrected in this way. It is not hard to see how at least some of these students, who often seemed to me to be among the brightest boys in a class, might lose interest in mastering skills if this meant that they were not allowed to explore problems and answers in their own ways. In contrast, this form of individual exploration is widespread and expected for male children within the majority of cultural traditions of West New Britain and other areas of the country (e.g. see Chowning, 1973). It also means that the less than 20% of students who originate from urban areas rather than rural parts of the country are likely to have experienced significantly more exposure to the kinds of "linear" forms that developed out of Australian and other Western cultural traditions of education (for examples of ways that both verbal and nonverbal codes of conduct can affect a child's chances in schools, see Bernstein, 1974; Bourdieu and Passeron, 1977; Apple, 1980; Willis, 1981; Bruner, 1982; Gearing and Epstein, 1982; Apple and King, 1983; Freire, 1983). It is easy to see that if a large number of teachers have somehow reached the understanding that "education" can best be defined through a fidelity to linear form, any difference between urban and rural students' cultural predispositions to assimilate such forms would have massive implications for the development of social inequalities through education in that country.

After the initial weeks of ethnographic observation and a reassessment of the research notes, the investigator is in a position to refine and focus his or her qualitative methodology according to these preliminary findings. One example from my own research involves the development of simple counting schedules in order to serve as a test of the validity of my more informally recorded classroom observations (see Fife, 1992a for a fuller explanation of this methodology). These cannot serve as a test in the statistical sense, because simple counting schedules are not meant to be statistically valid but rather to serve as a more focused method of micro-observation. For those who wish to combine quantitative with qualitative methods, however, they can also serve as a trial run from which statistically valid methods can be developed. In my own case, interest lay in refining what an already more focused form of notetaking was telling me about certain themes of interaction in the classrooms. Schedules were constructed for disciplinary actions in the classroom, teachers' interactions with male versus female students, and the use of *Tok Pisin* versus English (the latter being the official language of education). As the first schedule touches most directly upon the material presented in the chapter up to this point, it will be used as an illustration of this method of ethnographic focusing.

Originally, I decided to develop a counting schedule regarding disciplinary actions for two reasons. The first was that my notes seemed to indicate a significant difference in the amount of time that teachers in the first few grades versus the later grades spent worrying about the form of students' behaviors (i.e. disciplining them). The second involved my reasoning that if a substantial amount of hidden curriculum actually served the purpose of instilling a "Western" style of formal bodily control and if this was internalized by students at the collective level, then it must be behaviorally evident in the amount of time teachers spent disciplining children's actions in lower versus higher grades. Because I lacked video equipment, I decided to focus on only the more easily observable verbal interactions. For my purpose, I defined "disciplinary action" as a verbal command, instruction, or response by the teacher that indicated a negative valuation of a student or students' behavior in the classroom that also led to an immediate response by the student or students. Given the way classes are organized in community schools, it was not possible to hold observation times across schools or even classes as exactly equal. My solution was to divide disciplinary actions by the actual observation time to achieve a disciplinary action/per hour ratio that is more comparable across classes. In all cases, actual observation times totaled between seven and eight hours of classroom time. Selecting a grade two, four, and six class from each school, I further divided the disciplinary actions between the number of times the class as a whole was disciplined (e.g. "There's too much noise in here") versus the number of times individual students were disciplined (e.g. "John, stop that right now!"). I then sat in the classes for the requisite period of time and kept a running tally of these forms of interaction. The interested reader can find the total results reported in my doctoral dissertation (1992a: 268). I give a few simple examples of the findings below in order to illustrate the usefulness of this form of ethnographic focusing in a qualitative study.

Overall, the results show quite clearly that the use of verbal discipline drops dramatically in all three schools from grades two to four to six. It also suggests that individual styles of discipline differ between teachers. A grade-two teacher at one school, for example, favors disciplining individuals rather than the class as a whole, while a grade-two teacher at a different school shows a very even balance between the times she disciplines individuals or the class as a whole. However, regardless of individual preferences, the general pattern shows a uniform movement toward student internalization for an understanding of the kinds of behaviors teachers will or will not tolerate in the classroom. By the grade-three level, the vast majority of students learn how to fulfill teachers' expectations regarding the forms of acceptable behavior.

I have already noted that there are individual differences in the ways that teachers enforce discipline within their classrooms. Notice that this does not affect the collective formation of a pattern nor the effectiveness of this type of hidden curriculum upon the students. This small example is in fact part of a much larger pattern of cultural formation that is occurring in the urban-oriented community schools of West New Britain. These primary forms of hidden curriculum parallel broader social changes that have been formulating over the last one hundred years in Papua New Guinea; changes that began with the missionaries and continued with the increasing penetration of the world market system and the rudimentary development of wage employment in that country. In the specific example of hidden curriculum that I use above, a parallel can be seen between the development of a form of social organization in the urban areas of the country that emphasizes the boss-worker style of social relationships over the more "traditional" forms of non-capitalistic social relationships that remain prevalent in the villages.[5] There are many other forms of hidden curriculum in the classrooms that coincide with this parallel (many of them can be found as far back as early missionary education), such as the use of group leaders to act as "junior executives" or "sergeants" in the class (see Fife, 1992a: 260–264). In my opinion, this overall educational formation reinforces the message of social inequality that suggests that it is "natural" to live within social arrangements in which a minority of individuals are given overall authority (teachers/ bosses), others gain a place for themselves as those who assist the people with overall authority (group leaders/middle management), and the vast majority are expected to live out their adult lives as those who take orders (most students/most adult workers). This parallel has often been pointed out for the way education helps to reproduce the class-based system in developed countries (e.g. see Bourdieu and Passeron, 1977; Apple, 1980; Willis, 1981), but it is particularly ironic to see it happening in the schools of developing countries such as Papua New Guinea where the vast majority of students seem to be receiving preparation for a social future that simply will not ever exist for them as adults. It should be noted here that I do not mean to imply that there is anything inevitable about this educational process. In Papua New Guinea, for example, there have been a number of educators and researchers who have repeatedly urged various governments to recognize and respond to this contradiction. One of the results was the development of SSCEP (Secondary Schools Community Extension Project), an ongoing attempt to transform at least some secondary schools into educational experiences that are more relevant for an agriculturally-based economy (see Cummings, 1982; Crossley and Vulliamy, 1986; for other relevant projects see Weeks, 1985). However, it is one thing to run special projects and another to transform a whole school system, particularly at the primary school level, in a period of diminishing financial resources. As long as the academic model of education that has been imported from Australia continues to provide the basic prototype for the form of primary schooling, most students will continue to experience this contradiction at its most fundamental level.

Roughly halfway through the on-site research period I decided to see if what I had been observing inside of the classrooms translated into a systematic cultural language among those who were most immediately involved with education: teachers, students, and parents. In other words, is there a pattern that can be discerned between the contemporary forms of classroom interactions, social changes over the last one hundred years, and the ways that real people talk about education today (i.e. the collective consciousness of the educational process)?

Interviews had already been conducted with some education officials and discussions held with some parents near the beginning of the research period. Therefore, concentration in this middle stage turned to conducting formal interviews with all twenty-nine of the teachers in the three community schools, as well as a more focused attempt to obtain students' ideas concerning their own educational experience and how it related to their future lives (gathering a "native exegesis" in this manner is always necessary as part of the participant-observation method in order to gain some understanding of the inside point of view regarding the subject of inquiry; see Geertz, 1973). Due to space limitations, I will concentrate on only a few of the findings with regard to teachers and students in order to illustrate the usefulness of two specific methods of research: (1) the formal, open-ended interview, and (2) the use of written self-reportage.

One of the questions included within the formal interview schedule asked teachers to comment upon a typology of students that I had gleaned from earlier observations. Each teacher was asked: (1) "Could you briefly describe what a good pupil is like?" and (2) "What about a pupil who is not very good?" (Results are reported in Fife, 1994b.) The similarity of answers to this question both surprised and convinced me that most teachers did have a habit of slotting students into either one or the other of these well-defined, though covert, categories. The three major requirements that students must display in order to be considered a "good student" by the majority of teachers included: (1) that the student is obedient and listens to the teacher, (2) that he or she behaves well in the classroom, and (3) that he or she is a quiet person who concentrates well. Notice that these are all variations of a single cultural theme that fits the pattern of hidden curriculum in the classrooms as described above. In both cases, teachers seem to be developing a primary cultural orientation within which an educational form that emphasizes discipline and authority takes precedence. This form then becomes projected as an essentialized understanding of the character of individual students. Students who are comfortable with or at least who outwardly conform to the standards of this new social form are said to be "good" students; those who resist it are "bad" students. Again, this suggests that students from urban areas will have a large advantage since they are the most familiar with institutional arrangements in which a linear style of hierarchical discipline is prevalent. It will similarly disadvantage many of the brightest students who come from rural settings, where it is often expected that children should exercise their own aggressive judgments regarding how they can best fit into the cooperative social forms of village communities. Not one teacher, for example, suggested to me that a good student might sometimes question a teacher's or anyone else's authority. And while only one teacher felt that a good student should also be bright, seven mentioned that a bad student can often be very bright. The fact that specific children were often used as examples by teachers to illustrate to me what a good or bad student is like suggests that this categorization is not an abstract or neutral exercise, but rather something that is likely to have very real consequences for specific students in relation to their learning experiences. Teachers enforce these categories through the use of both corporal punishment and verbal shaming. In community schools, then, I would suggest that many pupils are experiencing their first taste of what life might be like should they actually land one of the desired jobs in the cash economy as adults. Rewards will be handed out according to how well the hired worker fits an employer's image of the good worker versus the bad worker, much as they are in the classroom for the parallel images of good versus bad students.

On a more subtle level, the hidden curriculum of classroom organization is teaching large numbers of students not only how to adjust to a particular form of hierarchical social relationships but also to internalize a desire for life inside of these forms. This is a life that can most often only be found inside of the urban areas of the country and that implies direct employment in the cash economy. One way that I decided to test the observational and interview data that had led me to this conclusion was to ask teachers to administer a self-reportage exercise[6] for students in the form of writing an essay as a normal part of grade-five and six English classes on the theme "My Future Work." With this exercise, I was looking for the development of a conscious set of expectations that either resonated with the overall pattern that has been described above or contradicted it. It was as if I were asking the question: Has the hidden curriculum of hierarchical form been internalized to such an extent that it affects future expectations? If so, what does the cultural future look like and how do students expect to participate within it? A full set of results for this question can be found in another work (Fife, 1994b; it is also useful to compare this with a large survey of grade-ten students that is reported in Cummings, 1982). As previously, only a few results will be reported here to suggest the usefulness of the exercise.

Perhaps the single most important finding was that out of a total of 112 grade-five students and 96 grade-six students, only eleven pupils indicated that they saw their future lives as involving working in village agriculture. The overwhelming majority of these senior primary students desired a future in what they saw as the "modern" sector of the developing economy. They wanted to be teachers, members of the police force, taxi owners and mechanics, pilots, clerks, and so forth. Almost every job specifically described in these essays involved a direct and intense involvement in the cash economy, a form of involvement that it is most possible to obtain through living in one of the urban areas of the country. Even an occupation such as school teacher that is practiced in both rural and urban areas involves long years in secondary and tertiary education in or near one of the main towns. The expectations that are displayed in these essays leave little doubt about whether students see their adult lives as occurring primarily within urban or rural areas of the country. Good examples are a grade-five boy who even though he wants to train in the fisheries, wishes to do this so that he can get a job with "the Shell Oil Company." Or the Ewasse boy who wants to be a geologist, an occupation that requires exploration for minerals "in the bush"; he goes on to explain that his desire for this job stems from hearing that these people make a lot of money, which will allow him to pursue the good life (by which he means the kind of life that can only be found in urban areas). Many others simply state that they see their future as occurring in Bialla, Kimbe, Port Moresby or one of the other urban areas in West New Britain or Papua New Guinea.

Again, notice that although students seem to be making many individual choices regarding their future adult lives, there is a very visible collective pattern that suggests the development of a consciousness in at least the town areas of West New Britain that strongly favors an urban-based, cash-economy form of life over the largely rural and village-based way of life that is organized around the quite different forms of social relations that are more suitable for subsistence horticulture. As in the hidden curriculum discussed above, the cultural formation that is displayed here contradicts the reality that by even the most generous estimate that I can make, a minimum of 70–80% of all students who attend primary school will be required to live and work primarily within the framework of the subsistence economy of their home villages.

Before we leave the microlevel of ethnography and analysis, I would like to briefly consider the implication of the individual variations that qualitative methods almost invariably record. As stated at the outset of this chapter, two key terms of any research organized around the participant-observation method can be summarized with the words "pattern" and "context." In the above examples, the overall patterns that are rendered visible at the microlevel of interactions and discourse are constantly played off against the larger context of both historical and contemporary pressures for an overall change in social organization (especially the pressures of the cash economy). These patterns particularly involve what I identified as two of the three necessary components of holistic research: social formations and cultural expressions. The third component, individual actions, has appeared several times within the microlevel of analysis but has not yet been dealt with in any detail. I will undertake to do so now, as an illustration of the kinds of results that can be obtained most effectively with a qualitative research methodology.

Differences in individual actions have been mentioned three times in the descriptions above. They involve: (1) individual variations in the extent to which teachers emphasize the importance of form over content, (2) differences among individual teachers regarding their styles of enforcing discipline, and (3) the individual images that students have about their future work lives. In each of these cases, I suggested that the overall pattern of the primary form of hidden curriculum is only minimally affected by these individual differences and that valid conclusions can still be drawn regarding these patterns. This remains true, but it is also true that my research indicates the existence of what I eventually came to call a secondary form of hidden curriculum. I hinted at this above when I mentioned individual variations regarding the extent to which each teacher enforces a primary form of "correct" learning behavior. It is also implied in the section in which teachers were shown to use cultural labels to divide children into "good students" versus "bad students." In order to have a situation in which students are categorized as "bad," it is necessary to have overt behavior and verbal expressions that rebel against the disciplinary form of classroom interactions. Most students may internalize a disciplinary form to a considerable degree, as the simple counting schedule suggests, but some students do not. Some students resist these and other primary forms of hidden curriculum. (For detailed discussions of the meaning of student resistance, see Willis, 1981; Haig-Brown, 1988. A more general discussion of the term can be found in Scott, 1985.)

Along with student resistance, a careful check of my observational notes during a more intensive analysis after the on-site fieldwork was completed led me to an understanding that there is a second overall, though much weaker, pattern of interactions and attitudes and that this can be said to form a cultural pattern of resistance to the enactments that made up the primary form of hidden curriculum.

It is important to note that unlike the primary form of hidden curriculum, which becomes firmly embedded within the organizational structures of education, secondary forms of hidden curriculum remain more idiosyncratic and rely on an ever changing accumulation of private decisions by individual teachers, students, or others to render them into coherent patterns (see Fife, 1992b: 215). As such, the latter tends to be weaker and seemingly less permanent than the former. Although secondary forms of hidden curriculum can be said to formulate a kind of resistance to the primary forms, as in most such forms of resistance they must also be understood as working within the overall hegemony of the dominant educational culture rather than as something that overturns that culture (see Willis, 1981; Scott, 1985; McLaren, 1986; Haig-Brown, 1988; Fife, 1992c).

A few of the examples that I found in the urban-oriented primary schools of West New Britain include the following: (1) a number of teachers allow boys to exhibit more overtly aggressive behavior than girls under certain conditions, (2) individual teachers occasionally decide to cross the boundaries that normally divide overt curriculum during individual lessons (e.g. bringing religion into math class), (3) some teachers periodically emphasize cooperative individualism over the much more common lessons of competitive individualism, and (4) every once in a while, individually or collectively, teachers will allow students to fail to return to the classroom to continue lessons after recess (i.e. allowing the class or classes to "dissolve" outside of the normal boundaries of the school timetable) (see Fife, 1992c).

What is often held in common in these secondary forms of hidden curriculum is that they resonate with cultural norms that can be found on a widespread basis among the many different village societies of West New Britain (see, for example, Blythe, 1978; Valentine and Valentine, 1979; Zelenietz, 1980; Scaletta, 1985; Counts, 1985; Maschio, 1989). Let us take the example of what is referred to above as "cooperative individualism" versus "competitive individualism" and consider it in the context of urban versus rural social inequalities.

In the primary forms of hidden curriculum, competitive individualism is encouraged in order to prepare students for taking the national grade-six examinations. Teachers normally berate students for sharing their answers with each other (a form of behavior that has great salience within most of the "traditional" cultures in the region), offer verbal and corporal punishment for failure to abide by the individualized question/answer format of lessons, offer messages about the importance of individual property (including intellectual property), and actively encourage students to compete among themselves to attract the teacher's attention during lessons. Taken together, these suggest to students that life is a zero-sum game in which they must compete for the rewards that go with attaining an individual place for themselves in what appears to be the natural social environment of hierarchical relationships.

This is a message that contradicts the type of "cooperative individualism" that becomes emphasized within most indigenous cultures of West New Britain (as well as Papua New Guinea as a whole). It is not surprising, therefore, that teachers and pupils do not show a total consistency in either putting the message of competitive individualism forward or in accepting it as a legitimate cultural form. The grade-four teacher who patiently waits while two of Matias's close friends look up how to spell a word in their books so they can whisper the answer to him (although all can clearly see and hear what is occurring) and then congratulates Matias on the correct answer is encouraging the secondary form of cooperative over competitive individualism. In a similar manner, a grade-two teacher in a math lesson who chastises two individuals for consistently attempting to pre-empt the group chanting the answers to arithmetic problems in unison is imparting a lesson that is given daily in the village context about the importance of collective relations over individual performance. In this form of individualism, a person cannot win individual rewards that he or she does not have to share with the rest of the group. Rather, individuals must learn to bend their aggressive actions and attempts for gaining individual reputations in such a way that any rewards they might garner are fed back into the group and not kept solely for self-aggrandizement.

The fact that secondary forms of hidden curriculum such as "cooperative individualism" occur on a much more infrequent basis than the primary forms of hidden curriculum and that they will become expressed on an ad hoc basis even by those teachers who seem most committed to enacting the primary forms suggests that they play an important if less dominant role in schooling. I have suggested elsewhere (Fife, 1992b) that secondary forms of hidden curriculum that resonate with traditional forms of village life express a kind of aesthetic critique of the dominant messages contained within the primary forms of hidden curriculum. This critique, while not seriously challenging the most hegemonic forms of education, nevertheless provides both teachers and pupils with a certain amount of emotional space within which they may find some personal relief from the driving messages of social change that are perpetuated by the dominant form.

CONCLUSION: THE CHALLENGE OF HOLISM

When using qualitative methods to conduct educational research in developing countries it is important to use both macro- and microsources of information. At the microlevel of research, which is the level that investigators will spend most of their on-site fieldwork pursuing, complex patterns emerge out of individual behaviors. It is best to begin by recording these behaviors through raw ethnographic descriptions, proceeding slowly as the study progresses to refine this raw material through a continual re-reading of the research notes until thematic patterns can be discerned. In my own case, these themes included both a strong and a weak set of patterns which I eventually resolved through the analysis of primary versus secondary forms of hidden curriculum. As the patterns become more evident during the course of research, they can be used by the researcher to focus the remainder of the study more narrowly along what have already proven to be fruitful lines of inquiry. This focus can be achieved through such qualitative methods as thematic notetaking (both in and outside of the classrooms), counting schedules, and techniques of self-reportage. Interviews, both formal and informal, are valuable during all stages as a way of continually comparing the investigators' own reflections about his or her observational data against the "inside" understanding of educators, parents, teachers, and pupils. When major discrepancies exist between the investigators' more external understanding and the inside views of others, the analysis must then involve an explanation of this difference. This explanation is often achievable through the use of macrolevel information. A good example would be explaining the discrepancy between West New Britain parents' perceptions of the relationship between education and employment in the wage economy through the use of the changing historical conditions that helped give saliency to these perceptions and then made a mockery of them.

This is another way of stating that fieldwork can no longer be limited to the microlevel of concern. Too many analytical situations require an understanding of both the contemporary and historical conditions that embed not only education but also other important social institutions that affect education within a given time and place. Macrolevel information must be gathered about the changing political economy that envelops and is in turn impacted by changing educational institutions. Individual schools and classrooms are not isolated phenomena; what occurs in them is affected by and affects other social institutions in any developing country.

When the macro- and microlevels of research are brought together into a single qualitative research project, the investigator gains a much greater ability to discover the ways that individual behaviors are influenced by social relationships, as well as how these become expressed as cultural understandings. It is only through a holistic ethnographic approach to research that the mediating role of education in the larger society can be both appreciated and rendered visible by the investigator.

NOTES

1. The test of ethnographic research that is carried out in the qualitative tradition is verisimilitude, a pragmatic understanding that must balance three levels if it is to achieve a holistic interpretation: individual actions, cultural expressions, and social formations. By "verisimilitude," I am referring here to "the appearance of truth." This is similar to John Dewey's notion of "warranted assertion" (see Dewey, 1982 reprinted in Thayer: 316–334), in which truth becomes defined through the kind of inquiry or research project that is formulated by the investigator. In a pragmatic sense, truth remains an artifact of the research construction.

2. If possible, researchers should provide a place within their budget for the purchase of books and local publications within the country in which their study is to be carried out. Being Canadian, for example, I often find it difficult to obtain books on Papua New Guinea that are published in Australia. It is even more difficult to obtain the reports and other publications that are produced by the various agencies within Papua New Guinea. A good strategy is to simply purchase and ship home works that *might* prove to be relevant.

3. Although I had originally constructed several formal, though open-ended, interview schedules (one each for teachers, parents, students, and government officials) before I began the on-site phase of the study, it soon became obvious that these schedules were only appropriate for the interviews that I conducted with teachers. Parents and pupils alike were very uncomfortable answering specific questions and I soon learned to collect information through open-ended discussions with individuals or groups. Government officials did not have a similar difficulty with the more formal interview, but I found that a set format was not capable of covering the wide range of duties and experiences that officials had within education. A modified schedule that contained only a very few thematic questions was subsequently used for government officials, in which I proceeded to build each new question upon the answers that had been offered for the opening themes (e.g. What are your main duties?).

4. *Tok Pisin* is the name for the pidgin language that is spoken by roughly half of the people in Papua New Guinea and it is one of the official languages of the state. It began as a trade language and remains important in a country in which the usual estimate is that there are over 700 separate languages. A small literature is developing in *Tok Pisin,* including the national newspaper *Wantok.*

5. This distinction is of course far from absolute. The cash economy, for example, affects the lives of all Papua New Guineans, whether they are involved in it through the form of a full-time job or, as the majority are, through a greater or lesser participation in growing agricultural commodities for external sales. The point that I am making here is simply that, in my opinion, forms of social relations that are intimately related to the development of capitalism are beginning to predominate in the urban areas of the country, while social relations that resonate with subsistence production retain great saliency in the rural parts of the country.

6. There are many other ways that this could be done besides the one that was chosen. The exact choice of method should depend upon its appropriateness for the local situation. In this particular case, students were already used to being asked by their teachers to write short essays on assigned topics within their normal English lessons. In another situation the investigator might ask students to make drawings, or ask students to keep a one-day or one-week diary of certain types of activities. Ethnographic investigation requires imagination, coupled with a sensitivity toward what might be appropriate for a particular group of people in a specific

time and place. For this reason, I would suggest that on-site research should normally take place over at least a six-month period. One year is closer to the norm within anthropology, with two years being not at all uncommon. These long periods of time are necessary to gain the methodological sensitivity spoken of above.

ACKNOWLEDGMENTS

I would like to thank the Social Sciences and Humanities Research Council of Canada which provided me with Doctoral Fellowships from 1986–1988, as well as a Postdoctoral Fellowship for 1993–1995, thereby making possible the research upon which this chapter is based. I owe a great debt of gratitude to the people of West New Britain, who were extremely cooperative during the period of research that is utilized within this paper. I would also like to thank the faculty at the University of Massachusetts at Amherst who have welcomed me into their midst during my postdoctoral years and made it possible for me to engage in writing in a congenial atmosphere. Michael Crossley and Graham Vulliamy must also be mentioned, for without their vision and encouragement this work would never have come to fruition. Lastly, to my wife and colleague Sharon Roseman, I owe the usual debt of fine-grained editorial services combined with the kind of emotional support that makes it possible to take the leap of courage into publishing words of one's own. As always, the responsibility of errors and omissions remains solely with the author.

REFERENCES

Apple, M. (1980) "Curricular Form and the Logic of Technical Control: Building the Possessive Individual." In L. Barton, R. Meighan, and S. Walker (eds.) *Schooling, Ideology and the Curriculum.* Sussex: The Falmer Press.

Apple, M. and King, N. (1983) "What Do Schools Teach?" In H. Giroux and D. Purpel (eds.) *The Hidden Curriculum and Moral Education.* Berkeley: McCutcheon Publishing Corporation.

Bernstein, B. (1974) *Class, Codes and Control.* London: Routledge and Kegan Paul.

Blythe, J. M. (1978) "Following Both Sides: Processes of Group Formation in Vitu." Ph.D. thesis, Dept. of Anthropology, McMaster University, Hamilton, Canada.

Bourdieu, P. and Passeron, J. (1977) *Reproduction in Education, Society and Culture.* Beverly Hills, CA: Sage Publications.

Bray, M. and Smith, P. (1985) *Education and Social Stratification in Papua New Guinea.* Melbourne: Longman Cheshire.

Bruner, J. (1982) "The Language of Education," *Social Research,* 49:835–853.

Chowning, A. (1973) "Child Rearing and Socialization." In I. Hogbin (ed.) *Anthropology in Papua New Guinea.* Australia: Melbourne University Press.

Counts, D. A. (1985) "Tamparonga: 'The Big Women' of Kaliai (Papua New Guinea)." In J. K. Brown, V. Kerns and contributors (eds.) *In Her Prime: A New View of Middle-Aged Women.* South Hadley, MA: Bergin and Garvey Publishers.

Crossley, M. and Vulliamy, G. (1986) *The Policy of SSCEP: Context and Development.* ERU Report No. 54. Port Moresby: University of Papua New Guinea.

Cummings, R. (1982) *A Review of Research on SCCEP: 1978–1981.* ERU Report No. 41. Port Moresby: University of Papua New Guinea.

Department of Education (1985) *Growth of Education Since Independence: 1975–1985*. Papua New Guinea: Department of Education.

Dewey, J. (1982) "The Pattern of Inquiry." In H. S. Thayer (ed.) *Pragmatism: The Classic Writings*. Cambridge: Hackett Publishing Co.

Feinberg, W. and Soltis, J. (1985) "The Hidden Curriculum Revisited." In *School and Society*. New York: Teacher's College, Columbia University.

Fife, W. (1988) "Education and Employment in Papua New Guinea." Paper presented at the Canadian Ethnological Society Conference, May 21, Saskatoon, Canada.

———. (1989) "Moral Education in Papua New Guinea: From Overt to Hidden Curriculum." Paper presented at the Canadian Ethnological Society Conference, May 14, Ottawa, Canada.

———. (1992a) "A Certain Kind of Education: Education, Culture and Society in West New Britain." Ph.D. thesis, Dept. of Anthropology, McMaster University, Hamilton, Canada.

———. (1992b) "Crossing Boundaries: Dissolution as a Secondary Message of Education in Papua New Guinea," *International Journal of Educational Development*, 12 (3):213–221.

———. (1992c) "A Question of Resistance: The Example of Education in Papua New Guinea." Paper presented at the Canadian Anthropology Society Conference, May 10, Montreal, Canada.

———. (1994a) "Creating the Moral Body: Early Missionaries in Papua New Guinea." Paper presented at the Northeastern Anthropological Association Conference, April 8, Geneseo, New York.

———. (1994b) "Education in Papua New Guinea: The Hidden Curriculum of a New Moral Order," *City and Society*, Annual Review:139–162.

Freire, P. (1983) *Pedagogy of the Oppressed*. New York: The Continuum Publishing Corp.

Gearing, F. (1979) "A Reference Model for a Cultural Theory of Education and Schooling." In F. Gearing and L. Sangree (eds.) *Toward a Cultural Theory of Education and Schooling*. The Hague: Mouton Publishers.

Gearing, F. and Epstein, P. (1982) "Learning to Wait: An Ethnographic Probe into the Operations of an Item of Hidden Curriculum." In G. Spindler (ed.) *Doing the Ethnography of Schooling*. New York: Holt, Rinehart and Winston, Inc.

Geertz, C. (1973) *The Interpretation of Cultures*. New York: Basic Books.

Good, K. (1986) *Papua New Guinea: A False Economy*. London: Anti-Slavery Society Report No. 3.

Griffin, J. (1976) "The Instant University." In E. B. Thomas (ed.) *Papua New Guinea Education*. Melbourne: Oxford University Press.

Haig-Brown, C. (1988) *Resistance and Renewal: Surviving the Indian Residential School*. Vancouver: Tillacum Library.

Herzfeld, M. (1991) *A Place in History: Social and Monumental Time in a Cretan Town*. Princeton: Princeton University Press.

Lofty, J. S. (1992) *Time to Write: The Influence of Time and Culture on Learning to Write*. Albany: State University of New York Press.

Maschio, T. (1989) "Metaphor, Ritual, and Expression: The Person in Rauto Discourse and Ritual Practice." Ph.D. thesis, Dept. of Anthropology, McMaster University, Hamilton, Canada.

McLaren, P. (1986) *Schooling as a Ritual Performance: Toward a Political Economy of Educational Symbols and Gestures*. London: Routledge and Kegan Paul.

Meek, V. L. (1982) *The University of Papua New Guinea: A Case Study in the Sociology of Higher Education*. Brisbane: University of Queensland Press.

Omokhodion, J. O. (1989) "Classroom Observed: The Hidden Curriculum in Lagos, Nigeria," *International Journal of Educational Development*, 9 (2):99–110.

Pomponio, A. (1992) *Seagulls Don't Fly Into The Bush: Cultural Identity and Development in Melanesia*. Belmont, CA: Wadsworth, Inc.

Pomponio, A. and Lancy, D. F. (1986) "A Pen or a Bushknife? School, Work, and 'Personal Investment' in Papua New Guinea," *Anthropology and Education Quarterly*, 17 (1):41–61.

Postman, N. and Weingartner, C. (1969) *Teaching as a Subversive Activity*. New York: Dell Publishing.

Scaletta, N. (1985) "Primogeniture and Primogenitor: Firstborn Child and Mortuary Ceremonies Among the Kabana (Bariai) of West New Britain, Papua New Guinea." Ph.D. thesis, Dept. of Anthropology, McMaster University, Hamilton, Canada.

Scott, J. C. (1985) *Weapons of the Weak: Everyday Forms of Peasant Resistance*. New Haven: Yale University Press.

Singleton, J. (1967) *Nichu: A Japanese School*. New York: Holt, Rinehart, and Winston.

Smith, P. (1985) "Colonial Policy, Education and Social Stratification, 1945–1975." In M. Bray and P. Smith (eds.) *Education and Social Stratification in Papua New Guinea*. Melbourne: Longman Cheshire.

———. (1987) *Education and Colonial Control in Papua New Guinea: A Documentary History*. Melbourne: Longman Cheshire.

Taussig, M. (1991) *Shamanism, Colonialism, and the Wild Man*. Chicago: The University of Chicago Press.

Thomas, N. (1991) *Entangled Objects: Exchange, Material Culture, and Colonialism in the Pacific*. Cambridge, MA: Harvard University Press.

Valentine, C. A. and Valentine, B. L. (1979) "Nakanai: Villagers, Settlers, Workers and the Hoskins Oil Palm Project." In *Going Through Changes: Villagers, Settlers and Development in Papua New Guinea*. Port Moresby: Institute of Papua New Guinea Studies.

Vulliamy, G. (1990a) "Planning Case-Study Research in Schools in Papua New Guinea." In G. Vulliamy, K. Lewin and D. Stephens. *Doing Educational Research in Developing Countries: Qualitative Strategies*. London: The Falmer Press.

———. (1990b) "The Potential of Qualitative Educational Research Strategies in Developing Countries." In G. Vulliamy, K. Lewin and D. Stephens. *Doing Educational Research in Developing Countries: Qualitative Strategies*. London: The Falmer Press.

Vulliamy, G., Lewin, K. and Stephens, D. (1990) *Doing Educational Research in Developing Countries: Qualitative Strategies*. London: The Falmer Press.

Weeks, S. G. (1985) *Papua New Guinea National Inventory of Educational Innovations*. ERU Report No. 52. Port Moresby: University of Papua New Guinea.

Weis, L. (1990) *Working Class Without Work: High School Students in a De-Industrializing Economy*. New York: Routledge.

Willis, P. (1981) *Learning to Labor*. New York: Columbia University Press.

Zelenietz, M. (1980) "After the Despot: Changing Patterns of Leadership and Social Control in Kilenge, West New Britain Province, Papua New Guinea." Ph.D. thesis, Dept. of Anthropology, McMaster University, Hamilton, Canada.

Using Documents for Qualitative Educational Research in Africa

Clive Harber

> Documentary sources of information, of all kinds, figure centrally in the research of sociologists. Official statistics on crime, income distribution, health and illness, censuses of population, newspaper reports, diaries, reference books, government publications, and similar sources are the basis of much social research by academics and their students. Yet these materials have rarely been given the attention they deserve in accounts of sociological research methods. Questionnaires and participant observation figure centrally in texts on courses on research methods, but documentary sources are considered in only a fragmentary way. (Scott, 1990: ix)

INTRODUCTION

My academic backgound is in the social sciences and in political science in particular. However, professionally I have been both a teacher and a teacher trainer and so it is perhaps not surprising that my research on African education, which began in 1977, has focused on education and political socialization and on schools as political organizations.

This research has involved the use of a variety of methods including questionnaires, interviews and various types of observation. However, the use of different forms of documentation has had a particularly prominent role in the research because it has a number of advantages, given the constraints of the contexts in which the work was carried out. With the exception of doctoral research carried out over a two-year period in Nigeria, constraints of time and money have meant that the research has taken place during short study visits, typically of three to four week's duration, to Kenya, Tanzania and Namibia twice each and to Zimbabwe and Botswana. Five types of documentary evidence gathered during short research periods are discussed in this chapter—secondary documents, newspapers, textbooks, novels and autobiographies, and committee minutes.

These documents have been used qualitatively rather than quantitatively. They have been used both to try to gain realistic insights into various contexts, issues and organizations and to analyze and interpret the meanings transmitted by certain types of documents. All such documents are subjective to a degree, as has been my interpretation of them. However, as with the qualitative use of other research methods, they can contribute "flesh and blood" to our understanding of the often ambiguous and problematic nature of education in developing countries (and elsewhere) that is difficult with ordered, tidy and generalizable statistical data based on controlled sampling.

Documents have certain important advantages—they are convenient to use; are often free or available at only a small cost; can be collected during a shorter space of time than interviews, questionnaires or data based on observation; and can be analyzed when institutions such as ministries and schools are closed. Documents such as the minutes of meetings or past copies of newspapers can also provide information about such phenomena as meetings or speeches that cannot be observed either because they have taken place before the research commenced or to which the researcher may have difficulty getting access for reasons of sensitivity or geography. Finally, in some African countries the political and/or bureaucratic context can mean that it is extremely difficult or enormously time-consuming to get official permission to carry out research involving access to educational institutions. (In Nigeria it took one whole year.) However, gathering documentation such as school textbooks, newspaper articles and policy documents avoids the research permission required for interviews, questionnaires and observation in public institutions.

Of course documents must be used carefully and with sensitivity to the possible biases and mistakes of both the writer and the researcher. They also have a major limitation in that they describe what is said rather than what is done but, as will be discussed below, they can both be a useful support to other research methods and, with due acknowledgment of the need for triangulation, a valuable research method in their own right.

SECONDARY DOCUMENTATION

A distinction is often made in discussion of social science and historical research methods between primary data obtained directly either from people themselves or eyewitness, first-hand accounts and secondary data that are non-original, second-hand information which already exist. Examples of the latter would be government statistics or an existing research report. Documentation can belong in either category depending on its nature and how it is used. For example, school textbooks usually contain secondary information, but if the content is being analyzed for political values then they become primary sources.

However, the difficulty of obtaining documentary material on Africa often makes getting even secondary sources feel more like gathering primary data. First, publications relevant to African education do not exist in overabundance. While there are more publications on some countries than others, there are still many gaps in the literature and virtually no published material seems to exist on some countries at all. Second, despite the shortage of commercially published material, other very useful and up-to-date published documents on education, such as government reports, will invariably exist on the country concerned but they will be very difficult to get hold of outside of the country and sometimes even in the country itself.

However, there are a number of visits that can be made (the Ministry of Education, the Education department at the University, libraries and bookshops) in order to discover what exists in a short space of time. Some of these visits are likely to be considerably more fruitful if some sort of personal contact already exists in the institution concerned—in my case these have usually been former students or research fellows or friends thereof. This can also help to get around a problem noted by the Education Commission in Ghana in relation to educational research:

> Researchers often find that in many places records are not kept at all, but even where they exist there are sometimes problems in getting them. This may be due to the uncooperative attitude of officials because they do not appreciate the value of information or they may mistakenly believe that the information sought may be classified. (Republic of Ghana, 1986: 52)

Another very important source is the dissertations written by education students at the university. As one book on research methods for development workers put it:

> Countless students throughout the world are obliged to write dissertations as part of their university course. Third World students will often write short studies of their own communities, or of another in which they have some contact through family or other connections. These can provide good sources of information on otherwise poorly documented districts or communities, and may provide real insider knowledge, from the writer's commitment and long familiarity with local people. . . . Some university libraries will keep these dissertations

and index them and can assist a search through them using a key word. Academics themselves will often be able to recommend particularly relevant pieces of work by their research students.(Pratt and Loizos, 1992: 49)

As this suggests, the small-scale research for these dissertations is often done in the student's home community and can provide realistic descriptions and insights in relation to the ways in which schools and classrooms actually operate. For example, while doing research in Nairobi in 1988 on social studies education in Africa, use was also made of dissertations on social studies teaching held at Kenyatta University library. These revealed useful information on the persistance of traditional teaching methods, the shortage of teaching resources and the quiet and passive subversion of new forms of pedagogy (Harber, 1990).

NEWSPAPERS

In Africa national newspapers can be useful sources of information on schools for two main reasons. First, education is taken very seriously and stories, feature articles and letters on it appear regularly. Second, national newspapers in Africa not only deal with educational issues but they also deal with events at particular schools. They can thus help to provide realistic insights into what is actually happening inside schools as opposed to what official documents, government representatives, generalized statistical surveys or bland textbooks on educational administration say is happening. Newspapers have therefore been very valuable in the research on school management in conditions of severe financial stringency that I have been carrying out with my colleague Lynn Davies though, as she describes in chapter 6, in the interests of triangulation they have been used in conjunction with semi-structured interviews and a certain amount of informal observation. Newspapers, for example, can provide graphic illustrations of the difficult conditions in which heads, teachers and pupils operate in many African non-elite schools. The following is from a Kenyan newspaper:

> Students at Nginda Girls High School in Murang'a are consuming water that has been declared unfit for human consumption by a government chemist. The School's headmistress Mrs. C.W.Gitu said that this had led to a marked increase of waterborne diseases among the students. . . . Whenever the water pump broke down, Gitu said, students were forced to fetch water from the stream two kilometres

away. . . . She said lack of teachers' houses forced the school to spend Sh18,000 annually to ferry them to and from Maragua town where they lived. She also said that the school urgently needs laboratory equipment which was vital in the teaching of science. It also requires a school bus and electricity so as to reduce fuel bills. The headmistress said that if the teachers lived in the school they would have enough time to prepare their lessons which would improve the performance of the school in national examinations. (*Daily Nation*, 11/4/92)

This concern with the reality of management and administration in African schools began with doctoral research on schools and political socialization in northern Nigeria. I was interested in the organizational model put forward by Nigerian schools and in particular the contrast between the bureaucratic model bequeathed by colonialism and the way in which schools actually operated. In order to investigate the question participant observers kept diaries in two schools, but this was supplemented not only by regular conversations with fellow teachers but also reading two years' worth of copies of the *New Nigerian* newspaper in order to get a wider, national view. However, as I was then new to African education, neither the instructions to the participant observers nor the analysis of the newspapers could begin until I had both lived in the country for a while and done a throrough literature review of existing texts on school management and organization. Only then was it possible to be fairly confident about the organizational features of school life that would be relevant. Moreover, when later analyzing notes based on the newspaper articles, letters, editorials and news reports it was important to make sure that a potentially relevant phenomenon was not just a one-time incident. To be included in the final written product incidents such as pupil violence, staff absenteeism or cheating in examinations therefore had to appear on a regular basis and to form a pattern with what was happening in the participant observers' schools and those of friends and colleagues teaching in other schools.

The research did in fact reveal many ways in which schools did not operate according to the classic Weberian model of bureaucracy as there were widespread problems of absenteeism and lack of punctuality; corruption, bribery and cheating in examinations; non-payment of staff; promotion anomalies; arbitrary transfer of staff; staff shortages and a high staff turnover and violent protests among pupils (Harber, 1989: chapter 7). For example, the analysis of the *New Nigerian* newspaper revealed the following insights into some of the problems of corruption, bribery and cheating in Nigerian education:

In Rivers State, the Teaching Services Commission announced that eight headmasters would have an embargo placed on their salaries until they turned up and showed their certificates at promotion interviews. The Commission commented that most teachers in the state do not have the certificates they claimed to possess and prefer to remain in their grades without any promotion. It also noted that 159 disciplinary actions ranging from warnings to dismissal had been taken against its staff. It thought that the absence of a code of conduct for teachers in the state had given rise to embezzlement of funds, certificate forgery and immoral relations with female pupils (2/2/79). In Lagos State during the second half of 1978, the Akibo-Savage Commission of Inquiry was set up after 5340 teachers withdrew their services in protest at alleged corrupt practices and nepotism in the teaching service. The Commission found that teachers received salaries unrelated to qualifications and experience and that there were fictitious names on the payrolls (31/7/78; 15/12/78). . . . General Obasanjo (then Head of State) referred to leakages of examination papers as a "national emergency" and set up a tribunal to look into the problem (13/7/77; 3/11/77). The tribunal gave various instances of people stealing and selling examination papers, including the case of a policeman who accused a herbalist of casting a spell on him which made him go and steal the papers (7/11/79; 9/11/79). The overall scale of the problem was indicated, however, when the West African Examinations Council announced that it was witholding 33,000 Nigerian results because of malpractices such as cheating, having foreknowledge of the questions, collusion etc. (3/11/77). (Harber, 1989: 117/8)

Newspapers can, however, also be a quick means of beginning to familiarize oneself with the issues surrounding education when on a first research visit to a country. In 1990, for example, I visited Botswana to do some research on the work of headteachers. The main idea was to get examples of the problems actually faced by headteachers as opposed to the generalized and prescriptive accounts of what they do found in books on educational administration. The principal method used was interviews, but time spent going through recent editions of daily newspapers held at the University of Botswana was a form of triangulation that provided some useful information that was used to ask questions in the interviews and in the publications stemming from the research (Dadey and Harber, 1991). For example, one key group of people with which heads have contact is parents. A report in the Botswana *Daily News* (15/1/89) noted that many children who pass the primary school leaving examination fail to find a secondary school place. The senior education officer in the Department of Secondary Education said that parents should start looking for vacancies for their children two weeks before school opened as by then headteachers should know who had not turned up. Thus, as the interviews then made clear, for the period preceding the first term of the school year, and for two to four weeks after, many secondary heads face a procession of parents who had come to persuade, beg and cajole to get their children into school.

SCHOOL TEXTBOOKS

The school textbook is the classroom teaching aid used above all others. In America, for example, 75% of the time elementary and secondary school students are in the classroom they are using textbooks and this figure rises to 90% for homework (Goldstein, 1978: 1). In developing counties their importance is even greater:

> Textbooks stand at the heart of the educational enterprise. Teachers rely on them to set the parameters of instruction and to impart basic educational content. Students' school work often begins (and in some schools ends) with the textbook. Texts constitute the base of school knowledge, particularly in third world countries where there is a chronic shortage of qualified teachers. In many instances teachers adhere closely to texts, using them as the sole source of school knowledge, assigning students lessons contained in the text and testing students only on the knowledge contained in the texts. [Yet] most third world countries have been so immersed in the problems of providing schooling to children on the primary level and, to a lesser extent, on the secondary level that they have paid little attention to curriculum development and even less to the content of school textbooks. (Altbach and Kelly, 1988: 3,10)

The role of school textbooks in the transmission of sociopolitical values has been a recurrent theme of my research on political socialization in Africa. School textbooks transmit political values not just openly but also by omission, biased presentation of the "facts" and indirectly when the values are hidden in an exercise or task to be done. Moreover, as Zimet (1976) reported, textbooks do actually seem to affect the social and political values of school pupils.

Social and political values can occur in textbooks written for any school subject. The following, for example, is a math question from Tanzania:

> A freedom fighter fires a bullet into an enemy group consisting of 12 soldiers and 3 civilians all equally exposed to the bullet. Assuming one person is hit by the bullet, find the probability that the person hit is (a) a soldier (b) a civilian. (McCormick, 1980)

The research I have carried out, however, has used qualitative content analysis to focus on textbooks for the humanities subjects (English, history, geography and social studies).

One advantage of using textbooks is that research permission is not necessarily required. Textbooks can simply be bought and then analyzed later. However, it is first necessary to establish with some authority which books are recommended and being used in schools. This is not always straightforward. In Kano State in northern Nigeria the education authorities did not produce a single list of prescribed books and so I asked both teachers at the primary and secondary schools where I was administering a questionnaire and local inspectors and thereby gradually built up a picture of books that appeared to be widely used (Harber, 1982: chapter 7). In Kenya it was necessary to visit the Ministry of Education and the Kenya Institute of Education before I could establish which books were recommended. While this proved successful in the end, one official did indeed treat me as though I were a spy after secret military information rather than an educationalist after a list of school textbooks (Harber, 1989: chapter 3). In Zimbabwe, on the other hand, post-independence history textbooks carried an "approved by the Ministry of Education and Culture" label while a visit to a school traditionally for whites in Harare produced a copy of the history textbook most widely used before independence (Harber, 1989: chapter 7).

Content analysis itself has been defined as "a multipurpose research method developed specifically for investigating a broad spectrum of problems in which the content of communication serves as the basis of inference" (Cohen and Manion, 1985: 60). It can be used, for example, to learn more about who has written certain documents and why and to analyze style and patterns of communication. My concern, however, has been with the content of communication—to demonstrate that school textbooks in Africa (as elsewhere) contain political values and to investigate if some political values are more dominant in certain political contexts than others.

Content analysis can be used quantitatively for this purpose. For example, in investigating the extent to which Kenyan textbooks reflected the National Goals of Education I was interested in their presentation of the "traditional" and the "modern." This was because two national goals are that pupils should have the knowledge and skills to contribute to "building up a modern and independent economy" and that "children should be able to blend the best of traditional values with the changed requirements that must follow rapid development." A count of the number of times different occupations were portrayed in a widely used English language series revealed that the emphasis was very much on the modern. People were portrayed in "modern" occupations (teacher, police officer, nurse) sixty times while "traditional" occupations (farmer, tailor, shopkeeper) were featured only twenty-two times (Harber, 1989: 46). However, the research on school textbooks has mainly been carried out in a qualitative manner by a subjective interpretation of the nature and balance of the text with validity and reliability addressed by precise referencing of the texts and by supporting arguments with evidence from the text in the form of frequent quotations.

The first step in this form of content analysis is the need to be throughly familiar with the themes to be analyzed. In the case of my own research this has meant sensitivity to and awareness of what is "political," i.e. that the author is directly or indirectly dealing with a topic that is not "factual" (even though it may be portrayed as such) but is controversial in that there are two or more viewpoints about the issues concerned. Such sensitivity does not necessarily come quickly or easily and requires considerable prior reading both on the general political sociology of school subjects (see, for example, Whitty and Young, 1976 and Tomlinson and Quinton, 1986) and on previous analyses of school textbooks (see, for example, Klein, 1985; Mbuyi, 1988; and Scrase, 1992). It is important to have a firm grasp of the idea of all school subjects as socially constructed rather than in some way "natural" or "inevitable," in order that school textbooks are also seen as social artifacts embodying particular values and interpretations of social reality. So that, while analyzing school textbooks also requires familiarity with the country concerned, wide and thorough background reading is perhaps even more important in order to see past the taken-for-granted values which may be so dominant in a certain society that they are not obviously or immediately controversial to somebody coming from that society. Until relatively recently, for example, issues of gender inequality would not have seemed immediately controversial in many African societies.

In analyzing school textbooks for such political values and messages what is said by the authors is obviously important, but often equally important is what is not said. Also important is the language that the author uses. History textbooks used in pre-independence Zimbabwe (Rhodesia), for example, used negative and derogatory language to describe Africans and positive language to descibe the colonizers (Harber, 1989: 107–110). Pictures should also not be overlooked as they can be significant in terms of what is or is not included, the captions used to describe pictures and the balance of pictures across a book.

The following is an example of a piece of content analysis. In Kenya in 1985 a sample of primary and secondary English, geography and history textbooks was selected from the list of key texts recommended by the Ministry of Education and which were widely available in bookshops. Where a series was recommended to cover a range of school grades, two books were selected from the series. In qualitative research of this nature done by an outsider, there is always the potential problem of the imposition of external perpectives onto a context in which they are not relevant. This problem can probably never be completely overcome but there are ways of mitigating it through familiarity with the context concerned—by thorough background reading of the work of academics and serious journalists, by reading local newspapers and by reading the work of novelists such as (in this case) the Kenyan writer Ngugi wa Thiongo. The textbooks could have been analyzed in one of two ways—either according to a pre-existing coding frame or set of categories or by allowing the data (in the form of quotations) to generate their own categories for analysis. In this case the problem of outsider perspective was also further reduced because the humanities textbooks were deliberately analyzed in terms of how they portrayed a number of themes of the official National Goals of Education. Eleven books were analyzed in all. (For a fuller discussion and references see Harber, 1989: chapter 3.)

One such theme was social equality and so the textbooks were analyzed in terms of their representation of men and women. This was an issue much discussed in the Kenyan press at the time as there was a major international women's conference taking place in Nairobi. The textbooks clearly portrayed a sexual division of labor with women occupying domestic and low-status roles. In one English language textbook *(Safari English Course, Book 1)*, for example, in an exercise entitled "What are they doing?" females are described as sweeping the floor, working in the fields, sewing, cooking and ironing while males are in school, eating, resting, reading, playing a game and running. An English language exercise on completing sentences in another book *(English in Use, Book 1)* says:

Either (for men)
After I establish myself in my career. . . . When my wife has three children . . .
Or (for women)

After. . . . I shall perhaps get married . . . when I shall have a child/ three children.

In geography textbooks occupational roles were given as fact and "normal," thereby reinforcing stereotypes of male and female jobs. One geography book, for example, stated:

> the men are responsible for clearing the fields and building huts. The women plant and harvest the crops. Fishing and hunting is also done by the men while women weave baskets and make pots. . . . What do people in your village do in the evening? Very often men go to beer parties. Women often go out to visit their neighbours. (Kitui, 1978: 20, 58)

In a civics book the reader is informed that "girls can become nurses, teachers, office workers or be better wives because of education" (Hannigan, 1981: 25)—not apparently managers, politicians and doctors or in other positions of control and authority.

In terms of attitudes toward other countries, the textbooks tended to be pro-Western but to avoid controversy. Geography textbooks, for example, described mining in South Africa with no mention of apartheid or racism and ujamaa villages in Tanzania without mentioning their socialist political orientation. Similarly, corruption in public life was ignored and public officials were portrayed in a uniformly benevolent light:

> The Azande now live in villages built close to footpaths. This makes it easy for government officers to help the farmers.
> The District Commissioner has an office in Machakos. He is a very busy person. He looks after the whole district.
> Is there a police station?
> Yes, there is one. The police help the D.C. to keep the peace in the district.
> Are there any other people who help the D.C. to look after the district? Yes. There are Education Officers, Agricultural Officers, Veterinary Officers and Trade Officers in the district. They help the government to improve agriculture and education in the district. (Kitui, 1978: 29, 54)

The tendency for children to idealize authority roles and to see them as benevolent is a widely documented phenomenon with a number of possible explanations (Dawson et al., 1977: chapter 4). This research, together with work done in Nigeria (Harber, 1982) and America (Marshall, 1981) suggested that another explanation is that benevolent images of authority are transmitted in pupils' books.

Kenya is a developing capitalist country. Therefore, it was not surprising that in Kenyan textbooks the message is clear—all that is required for success is enterprise and initiative. If individuals fail they have only themselves to blame. For example, one English book *(Safari English Course, Book 3)* has a story about a boy who passes his certificate of primary education but who can't go to secondary school because there aren't enough places. He cannot find a job and is advised to become self-employed so he sets up in poultry farming where the future looks promising; i.e., despite problems of education and employment, initiative and enterprise will win through. Later in the same book a shopkeeper decides to modernize his shop to make it like those in Nairobi—hard work and efficiency lead him to make more money. Another English language textbook *(English in Use, Book 3)* has a passage about a young man, Gacuiri, who leaves school and gets a job, but he wants to be independent and so he sets up in self-employment and is a success. A few pages later there is a poem called "The Song of the Common Man" about the pressures on an ordinary person and how the fate of such people is decided not by themselves but by others with more power. The book comments with some indignation "Can you imagine Gacuiri complaining in this way?" and asks pupils to write a counter poem expressing the freedom of the individual to achieve. In other words structural constraints of power and wealth do not exist and there is equal opportunity for all to achieve through effort and initiative.

LITERATURE AND AUTOBIOGRAPHY

Plummer in his book *Documents of Life* (1983) makes a strong case for "humanistic" qualitative research based on life documents, such as autobiographies and literature. In particular he quotes Nisbet (1976:16):

> How different things would be . . . if the social sciences at the time of their systematic formation in the nineteenth century had taken the arts in the same degree they took the physical sciences as models.

Plummer himself adds:

> Of course affinities between art and science may be found, and for sure some social scientists see their work as profoundly inspirational:

but the baseline is firm. Its major journals speak to abstractions, hypotheses, explanations, proof, samples, theory, objectivity, distance—and although it is constantly at war with the enemy of positivism, in the very battle it reveals what ultimately matters to it. Nobody wages war with Dostoevski or Dickens, Balzac or Bellow, Austen or Auden. Their mode of experiencing, feeling, interpreting and writing sets no standards, provides no models, makes no sense to a discipline that has always aspired to science. (1983: 6)

Yet novels are a valuable source of sociological insight. One writer on qualitative research methods in education, for example, has argued that:

Some of the most acute observers of the human scene have been the realistic novelists and playwrights. Although their work is fictional, that is, imaginative, one of the criteria for judgement of their work is the degree to which they have captured in their imagination profound elements of the human condition. (Smith, 1988: 45)

Modern African literature provides a rich source of insights into the social and cultural context of the operation of schools. While it would be possible to do a complete study of the representation of education in African literature and while it would also be possible to analyze particular novels as they have teachers and education as a major part of the plot (e.g. Ngugi Wa Thiongo's *Petals of Blood* set in Kenya and Bessie Head's *Maru* set in Botswana), I have used extracts along with evidence stemming from other research methods to support discussion of educational themes. Therefore this has in no sense been systematic or comprehensive research, since reading African novels has stemmed from my own interests and my desire to increase my understanding and awareness of Africa. My choice of extracts has therefore been selective and subject to the biases of the books I have chosen to buy and read. However, of importance in research methods is what is claimed for the method used and in the case of literature it has been used to illustrate an argument rather than as conclusive proof and has been used in conjunction with other forms of research evidence. For example, in a recent discussion of the nature of educational administration in developing countries I was interested in the contradictions and tensions caused by the coexistence of "traditional" and "modern," imported values and practices in social structures and in schools in particular (Harber, 1993b). The general nature of these tensions is vividly captured in extracts from two Senegalese novels. In Miriama Ba's *So Long A Letter* the main character says:

We all agreed that much dismantling was needed to introduce modernity within our traditions. Torn between the past and the present, we deplored the hard sweat that would be inevitable. We counted the possible losses. But we knew that nothing would be as before. We were full of nostalgia but were resolutely progressive. (1987: 18/19)

Sembene Ousmane in his novel *Xala* describes one of his characters in the following way:

El Hadji Abdou Kader Beye was what one might call a synthesis of two cultures: business had drawn him into the European middle class after a feudal African education. Like his peers, he made skilful use of his dual background, for their fusion was not complete. (1976: 3/4)

One aspect of these contradictions and tensions, for example, is corruption, which can affect schools as well as other institutions. The following two extracts are from a novel set in Nkrumah's Ghana:

It is well known that the supervisor was once, before coming to the railway administration, a bursar at one of the Ghana national secondary schools. As is the custom in this country, he had regarded the job as an opportunity he had won for making as much money as he could as quickly as he could, and his handling of the school's finances had soon made his intentions clear. The students complained to the Ministry of Education. The Ministry, as is usual in this country, had searched for the students most responsible for the drafting of the letter of complaint and dismissed them for gross insubordination. The remaining students had rioted. The Ministry, looking for more students to dismiss, had closed the school down. There had been no financial probe, of course, but none would have been possible since a fire had gutted the bursar's entire office during the rioting. Very shortly after that the Railway Administration was advised from above to appoint the bursar to his new job. He had brought the allocations clerk with him, and there was every likelihood that it was he who let it be known that the fire in the bursar's office was not the work of students.

The woman put her hand to her throat in a swift movement of disgust, then smiled. "No," she said, "I don't like made-in-Ghana spirits. But there are good drinks in the country still."

"Only in the homes of big shots and Party socialists."

"They must get them from somewhere . . . You must know

people who could get you these things. After all, people don't go to school for nothing." (Armah, 1969: 128, 135)

Away from the world of fiction, autobiography can also provide some interesting insights. The following extract describing the Cameroon again concerns the theme of corruption:

> It was the same in the schools. They are all weighed down with an incredible bureaucratic apparatus for strictly determining which pupils shall be expelled, which promoted and which obliged to take a year again. The amount of time spent in the abstruse calculation of "averages" with arcane formulae is at least equal to that spent in the classroom. And at the end of this, the headmaster arbitrarily decides that the marks look too low and adds twenty across the board, or he accepts bribes from a parent and simply changes marks, or the government decides that it has no need of so many students and invalidates its own examinations. At times it becomes bad farce. It is impossible not to smile at the sight of question papers being guarded by gendarmes with sub-machine guns when the envelope they are in has been opened by a man who sold the contents to the highest bidder several days before. (Barley, 1986: 135)

The personal accounts provided in autobiographies are particularly useful in adding flesh and blood to historical analysis for, just as Plummer notes in regard to gathering life histories:

> A proper focus on historical change can be attained in a way that is lacking in many other methods. Such a focus is a dual one, moving between the changing biographical history of the person and the social history of his or her life span. Invariably, the gathering of a life history will entail the subject moving to and fro between the developments of their own life cycle and the ways in which external crises and situations (wars, political and religious changes, employment and unemployment situations, economic change, the media and so forth) have impinged on this. A life history cannot be told without a constant reference to historical change, and this central focus on change must be seen as one of life history's great values. (1983: 70)

In a recent study of the political history of education in Namibia (Harber, 1993a) I used a number of extracts from the autobiography of John

Ya-Otto (a leading member of the South West Africa People's Organisation—SWAPO). The first of the following two extracts describes the teaching of history in the late 1950s when Ya-Otto was at secondary school and the second describes the period when he was both a SWAPO activist and a teacher.

> My favourite subject in school was history, but our textbook contradicted the stories every Namibian child is told by the elders. The Germans had never been "invited by warring tribes" to bring peace and prosperity to our country, neither had South Africa brought us prosperity. True, we had fought among ourselves, and the Germans had taken advantage of this to conquer us all. The text, however, said nothing about our grandparents' resistance and about the terrible slaughter of the Hereros and Namas that followed the conquest . . . But it no longer surprised me that our schoolbooks were lying; the whites simply wanted us to think that they were more intelligent than we were, that they were a superior race and that, consequently, they were entitled to rule.
>
> Katjimune's school must have given the school board constant headaches, because they frequently sent us inspectors who would appear in the classroom without any warning. The inspectors were looking for us teachers to slip up, for some pretext to fire us. To them our school was a SWAPO nest, a hotbed of subversive ideas. They were right, of course, but I was always careful that my students were ahead in all their subjects before I talked about politics . . . It was often difficult to separate our dual roles. Our country's history is one of oppression, and no person of conscience could teach that history as the South African texts presented it. Nor could we ignore our students' questions about independence in other African countries and how we could win ours. (Ya-Otto, 1982: 30, 63, 64)

COMMITTEE MINUTES

In researching the realities of school management in Africa, as well as carrying out interviews with staff and pupils, I have also tried to obtain relevant documentation about the school concerned. These have included school prospectuses, school rules and school newsletters and magazines. However, particularly useful in helping to understand the daily life of the schools are the minutes of meetings which headteachers have usually been willing to provide during the course of an interview. The following extracts from a meeting of the Board of Governors of a rural junior secondary school in Botswana, for example, give some idea of the material/educational mixture of the problems facing a headteacher in a small community at least two hours away from a town of any size:

> *Repainting of Classrooms.* The classrooms were internally redecorated at the end of last year. We are now trying to obtain quotations for the external repainting of all buildings. So far no contractor has shown any interest.
>
> *New Deputy Head.* The man appointed did not arrive in the village. Presently, this post is vacant.
>
> *Uniform.* Bothakga seems to have gone out of business. Another supplier has been found and it is thought that the uniform will arrive shortly.
>
> *Water Pump.* A water pump has now been installed to pump water from the tank to the staff houses.
>
> *Rent of Teachers' Houses.* The school board has instructed the headteacher to change the rent on the houses which had so far been incorrect and to recover the arrears due from those concerned.
>
> *Vacant Industrial Post.* The messenger deserted in December. The headteacher does not feel he should be replaced, due to the little work available. It was suggested that we get a kitchen hand instead.
>
> *Bank Account Problems.* At the start of this year there were great difficulties in getting the bank to change the signatory of the account to the new bursar. This problem has not occurred in previous changes. The Board resolved that the bank should be informed that in future the signatories to the accounts could be changed on receipt of a letter from the headteacher and the production of new specimen signatures.

Similarly, while recent research on pupil participation in school decision-making in Tanzania (Harber, 1993c) used interviews as a research method, the minutes from school meetings were also useful in getting a better feel of how the system worked in terms of what was (and what was not) discussed at each level and the roles played by the different participants. However, as noted in the introduction to this chapter, such documentation is about what is said and in practice this can be different from what is actually done and sometimes documentation can be deliberately written in such a way as to alter perceptions of what happened according to a particular perspective; hence, the importance of using other research methods in conjunction with documents. In the above two examples, given the shortage of time, interviews were used, as was a certain amount of casual and informal observation. Ideally, however, observation of staff and other meetings over a longer period of time would provide fuller and more accurate accounts of the institutions concerned.

CONCLUSION

Documents play an important, though sometimes unacknowledged, role in educational research. Indeed, "the use of documentation" is often a topic ignored or skated over in educational research methods courses and textbooks and content analysis, in particular, tends to get played down. This is also reflected in the scant attention it has so far received in books on educational research methods. Yet, as this chapter argues, a great deal of communication about and within education comes in a written form and the resulting documentation offers a potentially rich source of qualitative research insights into education and does not have to be used only in the traditional "literature review" chapter of dissertations and theses. Indeed, analyzing and interpreting meanings, messages and signals in documentation such as school textbooks or government publications can itself be the major focus of a piece of research. For educational researchers in developing countries, both expatriate and indigenous, they merit more serious and conscious attention in research design.

REFERENCES

Altbach, P. and Kelly, G. (1988) *Textbooks in the Third World* . New York: Garland.
Armah, A. (1969) *The Beautiful Ones Are Not Yet Born*. London: Heinemann.
Ba, M. (1987) *So Long a Letter*. London: Virago.
Barley, N. (1986) *The Innocent Anthropologist*. Harmondsworth: Penguin Books.
Cohen, L. and Manion, L. (1985) *Research Methods in Education*. London: Routledge.
Dadey, A. and Harber, C. (1991) *Training and Professional Support for Headship in Africa*. London: Commonwealth Secretariat.
Dawson, R., Prewitt, K. and Dawson, K. (1977) *Political Socialisation*. Boston: Little, Brown.
Goldstein, P. (1978) *Changing the American School Textbook*. Lexington, MA: D.C.Heath.
Grant, N. and Wang'ombe, C. (1979 and 1980) *English in Use*. Nairobi: Longman.
Hanningan, A. (1981) *Civics for Kenya Schools*. Nairobi: Kenya Literature Bureau.
Harber, C. (1982) "School Children and Political Socialisation in Kano State, Northern Nigeria." Ph.D thesis, University of Birmingham.
———. (1989) *Politics in African Education*. London: MacMillan.
———. (1990) "Education for Critical Consciousness?: Curriculum and Reality in African Social Studies Education," *International Journal of Educational Development*, 10 (1): 27–36.
———. (1993a) "Lessons in Black and White: 100 Years of Political Education in Namibia," *History of Education*, 22 (4): 415–424.
———. (1993b) "Prismatic Society Revisited: Theory and Educational Administration in Developing Countries," *Oxford Review of Education*, 19 (4): 485–497.
———. (1993c) "Democratic Management and School Effectiveness in Africa: Learn-

ing from Tanzania," *Compare,* 23 (3): 289–300.

Kitui, P. (1978) *Around and About Africa.* Nairobi: Kenya Literature Bureau.

Klein, G. (1985) *Reading Into Racism.* London: Routledge and Kegan Paul.

Marshall, T. (1981) "The Benevolent Bureaucrat: Political Authority in Children's Literature and Television," *Western Political Quarterly,* 34 (3): 389–398.

Mbuyi, D. (1988) "Texts and National Integration in East Africa," *Prospects,* 14 (4): 545–556.

McCormick, P. (1980) "Political Education as Moral Education in Tanzania," *Journal of Moral Education,* 9 (3): 166–177.

Nisbet, R. (1976) *Sociology as an Art Form.* London: Heinemann.

Ousmane, S. (1976) *Xala.* Oxford: Heinemann.

Plummer, K. (1983) *Documents of Life.* London: Allen and Unwin.

Pratt, B. and Loizos, P. (1992) *Choosing Research Methods.* Oxford: Oxfam.

Republic of Ghana (1986) *Report of the Education Commission on Basic Education.* Accra: Ministry of Education.

Safari English Course, Books 1 and 3 (1973) Nairobi: Department of Curriculum Development, Kenya Institute of Education/Ministry of Education.

Scott, J. (1990) *A Matter of Record.* Oxford: Blackwell.

Scrase, T. (1992) "Education and Cultural Reproduction in India: A Content Analysis of Selected Textbooks." In R. Burns and A. Welch (eds.) *Contemporary Perspectives in Comparative Education.* New York: Garland.

Smith, L. (1988) "Broadening the Base of Qualitative Case Study Methods in Education." In R. Burgess (ed.) *Conducting Qualitative Research.* London: JAI Press.

Tomlinson, P. and Quinton, M. (1986) *Values Across the Curriculum.* Lewes: Falmer Press.

Whitty, G. and Young, M. (1976) (eds.) *Explorations in the Politics of School Knowledge.* Driffield: Nafferton.

Ya-Otto, J. (1982) *Battlefront Namibia.* London: Heinemann.

Zimet, S. (1976) *Print and Prejudice.* London: Hodder and Stoughton.

6 INTERVIEWS AND THE STUDY OF SCHOOL MANAGEMENT

AN INTERNATIONAL PERSPECTIVE

Lynn Davies

INTRODUCTION

The context of this discussion on interviewing is primarily a research project on "School Management in Contexts of Stringency," directed by Clive Harber and myself. The project arose from teaching educational management to teachers and managers from developing countries and from the realization that much Western management literature was of dubious relevance in situations of extreme shortage. We knew from our experience of various schools in Africa and Southeast Asia that when there are minimal resources, when teachers have not been paid, when children are taking turns with desks, chairs and classrooms, and when complex patterns of family obligation and political deference constrain administrative behavior, then "rational" models of Total Quality Management appear inapplicable. Daily financial and cultural survival may demand very different management models.

Our research therefore had the aims, first, of collecting case study material on the "realities" of schools in developing countries and, second, of establishing the strategies headteachers and other managers actually used to run their institutions. The overall intention was to produce training materials for ourselves and others, and to further our writing and thinking around the management of "effective" schools in developing countries.

The methodology for the research was the usual mixture of planning and opportunism. We spent periods of two to three weeks in Botswana, Zimbabwe, Namibia and Pakistan interviewing and observing in schools; we engaged research students on similar topics, thus getting data from Ghana, Tanzania, Sierra Leone and Barbados; whenever we were anywhere in the world we would visit a school and interview the head. This became something of an addiction: while other people went to game parks and museums, we would head for the nearest educational institution and crave a conversation. Students taking classes at Birmingham University also gave us wonderful examples, particularly when in discussion on teacher deviance and corruption. Our task has been to collate and make sense of all the mass of material, evidenced as well as anecdotal, in order to derive useful models and frameworks for analysis. So far we have produced work on the job of the headteacher in Africa (Dadey and Harber, 1991); school power cultures under economic constraint (Davies, 1992); teacher resistance (Davies, 1993); managing effective schools (Harber, 1992); and the management and mismanagement of school effectiveness (Davies, 1994a). Two full books also use much of the material (Davies, 1994b; Davies and Harber, in press). This particular chapter will look at interviewing as a key component of the research methodology, although inevitably touching on some of the eventual findings and the emergent analytical themes.

In some ways structuring this account is like the way schools are compared on effectiveness itself, that is, input-process-output. The "input" here is the initial preparation, the interview schedule and gaining access; the "process" is the interview itself, establishing trust, recording the setting, using techniques for opening up and validation; the "output" is the analysis of the interview data, exploring language use and deriving themes. However, some of the issues cut across all three stages, and the structure is not clear cut. But then qualitative research is a messy business, and artificially tidy research accounts would be arguably suspect. While trying to keep roughly to the chronological process, there will be times when the holistic and interwoven nature of research will become apparent, and I will jump about between the topics.

The Interview Design

Conventionally, distinctions are made between structured, semi-structured and unstructured interviews. The implication is that there is a single-line continuum from a tightly bound situation that is no more than a spoken response to a questionnaire, through to an unpredictable chat whose direction is controlled by the respondent. An example of the first is the survey type interview, where market researchers stop you in the street with a clipboard on which are multiple choice boxes for them to tick. They are not interested in your hesitations, your choice of language for reply, your feelings on being interviewed. The last thing they want is to get beneath the surface. At the other end of the continuum might be the "life history" interview, where the aim would be to enable respondents to reflect as they wish on their career, their life-long values, or the intersection between free will and social constraint. For this it might be crucial for respondents to decide the direction of the discussion, in order to locate the themes they perceive to be central to their lives, and which therefore condition their current behavior.

It is perhaps unfortunate that the term "interview" is used for both of these markedly different types of investigation. The derivation of much social science research in "hard," scientific exploration has left a legacy of the image of an interviewer as simply a neutral conduit through which facts and opinions can be noted—a kind of intelligent tape recorder. Yet what should distinguish an interview from a written questionnaire is the presence of the unscripted input, the steerage, and the personality, background and motivations of the interviewer. Interviews in educational research are rarely the stimulus-response, knee-jerk reactions noted in physiology. From the very beginning they are a social event, and governed by a very complex set of social rules, understandings and obligations. For this reason, I prefer the term "structured conversation" (Hammersley and Atkinson, 1983). This gives the essence of the two-way interaction, and underscores the fact that a relationship has to be established even for the simplest interchange to take place. That this relationship may be unequal, or contain power elements, does not detract from the fact that two or more people are talking, and using and interpreting language in a constant conscious and unconscious process.

We did—initially at least—use quite a lengthy and tight interview schedule to engage in conversation with headteachers. This reflected some of the "factual" aims of the research, for we were interested in basic data such as size of school, teacher-pupil ratios, the formal organizational structure, the material problems of books, transport, covered classroom space, teachers' salaries and so on. However, each of the questions was hedged around with the interpretation of how far this was perceived as a "problem" and what the coping strategies of staff or students were. The areas we wanted comparative data on came under the headings of:

• material conditions—equipment, parental contributions, transport, use of school facilities by outside bodies;
• staffing—allocation of responsibilities, teaching methods, staff appointments and promotions, staff training, turnover, accommodation, balances between expatriate/local and men/women, communications, discipline, morale;
• students—admissions, rules, rewards and punishments, prefect systems, student contribution to school maintenance, participation in decision-making;
• external relations—meetings with parents, relationship with local authorities;

- management skills—particular skills needed in the culture concerned, and dual functions for heads of boarding schools.

We did not frame direct questions about the head's own management style, but preferred to ask what they saw as the major styles in the country, and what were seen as qualities for the successful head. Others of our researchers (Ngegba, 1994) did ask the head what style he or she used in the main. I will talk later about inferences from direct and indirect questions. The main purpose behind having a structured set of areas for discussion was to obtain some comparability from the interviews Clive Harber and I were conducting in different countries, and also because some areas (for example, boarding problems) were so underresearched that it was crucial to elicit views on them. The aim of parallel questions was not, however, to be able to draw quantitative inferences, to be able to say "76.9% of the schools studied had prefect systems." Instead, we were designing the questions as triggers to generate a reaction from a head, so that we could later look at, say, how a prefect system was described or what the underlying ideology was behind the use of students in positions of power.

In practice, we found that we used all the thirty-two question areas increasingly less. Inevitably, once heads start saying the same things—particularly about the problems of resource shortages—we found we could go directly to the more particular questions of strategy and management policy in that school. Looking through the field notes chronologically, it is clear that later interviews jumped whole sections, or needed to elicit less detail in some areas. This is the way in which "grounded theory" is supposed to work, in that certain themes start to gain prominence and, through a process of "progressive focussing" (Hammersley and Atkinson, 1983), the research begins to narrow down to the few most important underpinning arenas. However, it would be dishonest to claim that such focusing was entirely systematic or intentioned; interviewers just get bored asking the same questions and apparently getting the same replies.

Some questions also got dropped or changed because of their entirely fatuous nature. In the first rural school I visited in Zimbabwe, I asked if there were any problems with electricity. "No problems at all . . ." replied the head. I was reassured, and wrote "No probs." Then he continued ". . . as long as we teach in the stipulated hours." What he meant was that there were no problems with the electricity because the school did not have electricity. Another (urban) head did not actually want electricity in the teaching blocks because that would mean they could be used by the community in the evening. He did not want to lose control or have his rooms untidied by incomers. The phrasing of questions might mean that very important differences in interpretations of resources for schools might be lost. It is by no means clear that an input such as electricity is seen as a universal good or necessity.

The reverse side to the coin is, of course, the benefits of being able to ask stupid questions because of being a "cultural stranger," a theme which I shall discuss later. The obvious advantage of an interview over a questionnaire is being able to realize inappropriateness and clarify language before 500 puzzled replies render a question invalid. What we have learned from the process is that some sort of structure is comforting initially for both interviewer and interviewee, but that daily reflection on the way questions have to be reframed or explained not only helps the initial investigative process but provides clues to the eventual interpretative themes chosen.

ACCESS

Most research methods textbooks will talk of the issues of access—particularly in ethnography when one wants to become part of a group, to gain insider information. The notion of interviewing implies something more formalized than gaining entry to, say, a deviant gang to experience first hand their values and modes of operating. Nonetheless, the way in which an interview is "set up" is clearly of importance in interpreting the outcomes. I am able to compare three different ways of gaining access within the project. In one visit to Botswana, I approached the Ministry of Education in order to identify schools which might allow me to interview both heads and staff, and "hang around" staffrooms as well as observe lessons for a period of one week each. I wanted an urban day school as well as a boarding school, and in the latter case, to be able to stay in the school if possible. Hence the negotiations were done on my behalf by the Education Officer, who obviously chose schools where she knew the heads well and felt they would be prepared to accept a researcher. Both schools were therefore warned of my arrival, and I went on the bus unaccompanied at a pre-set time to begin the visit by meeting the principal. I then arranged a later, more extended interview.

In Zimbabwe, I requested short visits to a range of schools, simply to interview the principal. The location of the schools was again done through the Ministry of Education in Harare and in Bulawayo, but I was accompanied to the schools (in my rented car) by an education officer, in both places a schools inspector. Sometimes they sat in on the interviews, sometimes not.

In Pakistan, a Ph.D. student already on his fieldwork arranged the interviews through a contact of his, and we went together to the various institutions; it appeared essential that a "protocol" man also accompany us, using an official car and driver. We therefore swept up to the schools in a party of four, pennant flying.

The question of access, arrangement and arrival sets the tone for the entire interview, an area underplayed by texts on interviewing that focus simply on "getting permission." In Botswana, I arrived at the boarding school principal's house hot, sweaty and anxious, having been put off the bus what looked like miles from anywhere and trudging blindly across the bush in what I hoped was the right direction. The principal gave me a glass of water and serenely continued breastfeeding her sixth child. In no way did I represent a threat, and indeed I was the one who had to be reassured and calmed down. The teachers were delighted, for they had been told to expect "a doctor" and the dust-covered spectacle they encountered did not fit their apprehensions of a formidable researcher. I think I was able to gain confidence and trust reasonably quickly, as it was appreciated that I had made such efforts to come to that school.

Arrivals in Zimbabwe were interesting, but for a different reason. I realized that the enthusiasm that the education officers had for being assigned to accompany me was because they had run out of transport money for that financial year. Particularly in the rural areas, they had no way of visiting remoter schools and inspecting the teachers. Hence when I turned up in my rented car with what looked like unlimited gasoline money, they seized the chance to "take" me to as many schools as possible. In Bulawayo region, I was whisked from one school to another, with the inspector using the opportunity to observe and talk with the subject teachers while I galloped through my interview with the head. From a Western perspective with the norm of appointment systems, I was initially uneasy, if grateful, that we could simply turn up unannounced at a school and the head would drop everything to talk to me. While it is disadvantageous for a school not to have a telephone, it presents great opportunities for a visiting researcher to be able to call in "on spec." There were therefore three great benefits of having an official "minder." One was that my visit clearly had the sanction of the office, and I was always warmly welcomed; second, I was able to observe at first hand the relationship between head and inspector; and third the journeys to and between schools provided the fascinating "infilling" from the inspector on the schools themselves, the communities and on local and national education policy. The only problem was trying to remember everything as I avoided the potholes and resisted the inspector's shouts of encouragement to drive faster.

Pakistan was something else again. Here I was not only expected, but the schools often went to great lengths to prepare for the visit. At one, the principal appeared in his academic gown, and had told all the staff to wear theirs; they were all lined up on the drive as we drove up. I may have imagined the looks of disappointment as a woman appeared, but certainly my automatic reflex of extending my hand was an error I should have realized. Men do not shake women's hands in Pakistan. (I will talk more of gender and power issues later.) In all the institutions, great hospitality was provided, and I pondered the social rules about how much I was supposed to eat and drink. Yet this was a minor problem compared to the difficulties of penetrating the formalities. As my student kept reminding me, we would not have been able to gain any access to the schools without these meetings having been set up by a friend in high places. Even clutching official letters from the University of Birmingham, my student had been unable to get many interviews in other regions. Heads simply refused, or were "not available" when he arrived at the appointed time. He did not have the right place in the intricate hierarchy of connections. Yet because his friend did, and obviously carried great influence, this meant the principals were very wary of what my interviews were "really" about. No assurances of confidentiality or objective research published only in the UK would convince some that we were not spies and would not report any problems directly to the Ministry of Education or local politicians. Getting any more than factual information from the interview required all our limited questioning skills—in either English or Urdu.

On reflection, some of the best conversations were with the Zimbabwe heads, who were caught off guard and would have had no time to worry about what they should or should not say. Yet the cultural issues are the key to access. Societies vary in their degree of openness or in the importance of "face," and attempting in-depth interviews by either a local or an outside researcher is very difficult in a culture that is founded on deference and fear of nepotism. In Pakistan, we would not have gained access without the high-placed friend and the accompanying protocol man; yet the very specter of these two precluded any real disclosure. Reflective interviewing would have to be done over a very long period when trust could be established; interview questions would have to be phrased very differently.

In Taiwan, I recall similar issues of "face." Asking college principals about management problems they experienced, I simply received the reply "We have no problems." Touring the colleges, everyone was happy and smiling, offering tea, gifts, a deep interest in Birmingham. Even in the student counseling unit, everyone was smiling. It was clearly essential that a visitor was shown a perfect institution, and my attempts to elicit "training needs" met with a polite side-stepping of the question. Here, it was essential to phrase questions not in terms of dealing with "problems" or identifying "needs," but of managing change, or taking the institution into the future. Hence I found that some Pakistan principals would eventually talk of dealing with the policy of the "grant of autonomy" (similar to local management of schools in UK) if the question invited them to talk of how they were able to educate the staff to fully use this splendid initiative. Interview planning in different cultures requires deep thought and study about how people are able to "present" themselves and their institution to strangers of uncertain rank and influence.

THE SETTING

Interviews are clearly not just about the words chosen, but are conditioned by the surroundings. The setting also provides important clues to the role and style of a head, given that most interviews will take place in the domain that is nurtured by that head to match with his or her chosen front. First we can observe the signs of the material wealth or otherwise of the school, and whether the provision in the head's room matches the surrounding classrooms. It seemed indicative in one Zimbabwe school that the windows of the head's office were broken just as much as in the classrooms; this was not so much solidarity with the students as a sign of the impossibility of repairs. In another, the head's office was a largish cupboard off one of the classrooms, and shared with a clerk. The head's desk faced the door to the classroom, and as we talked, the door would swing open now and again behind me because the latch was broken. Each time, the head would pick up a pole obviously kept by his side just for this purpose, and push it closed again. Leaving aside the difficulties of interviewing when one's respondent suddenly lunges across the desk brandishing a long stick, the scene set me wondering about the relevance of time management, or visioning, or SWOT analysis, when there appears to be little incentive to fix even very basic commodities such as doors that close. "Can you get OHPs that don't use electricity?" this head asked wistfully.

Second, the offices provide obvious signals about styles of leadership. Most have the master timetable on the wall; some would also contain the only books in the school, so that both teachers and students would have to ask for them, or sign them out. I was interested, too, in the various "sacred texts" that were in use: one head pointed to the "Handbook for Primary Heads" and explained, "I am guided by the book. We have to follow that." Another had Ozigi's *A Handbook on School Administration and Management* on his desk, and confided, "I like this one—because there is an area which is very difficult—how you can deal with certain cases of misconduct . . . ." Also in constant use was the *Public Service Misconduct* set of guidelines: "I can quote it, show it to the teachers. Teachers have to read it and sign it." In such ways, the props supporting the head are apparent, plus their actual daily use of official and theoretical documentation.

The site of management is also revealed by its use by others. In Pakistan, the principals' offices were often huge, and had chairs ranged around the edges like a ballroom. Our interviews were often conducted in front of a number of other people, either brought in as deemed appropriate or who happened to be there waiting for something else. There could be constant interruptions such as when a messenger brought in a note that the head read immediately, then began to issue commands. As we left, at least three other personnel sitting in the corridor would spring to their feet, presumably also messengers or staff "on hand" to comply with duties. The image was of a feudal court, with supplicants craving an audience, and decisions made on a minute-by-minute basis. No doubt the management reality was very different, but the office was certainly symbolic of a particular interpretation of authority.

All interviews are subject to "interruptions," and it is important to record these to see what significance they might have. I would disagree with Bell on planning an interview. She says: "Try to fix a venue and a time when you will not be disturbed. Trying to interview when a telephone is constantly ringing and people are knocking at the door will destroy any chance of continuity" (1987:75). However, in interviewing headteachers, such events are not actually an interruption to the investigation, but an essential component of the process. One Harare school did have a telephone, but it was outside the head's office. Therefore, every time it rang, he had to get up to go to another room to answer it. A time management course I recall which stressed the importance of using the left hand to pick up the phone so that notes could instantly be taken with the right, again seemed out of touch with such reality.

Sometimes the interruptions give a direct lead into the data required. In Harare, one young teacher knocked at the door with some problems, and the head digressed to explain:

> The problem we face is where pupils are being difficult in class—the student teacher wants me to come in and say a few harsh words. We get them to do manual work, or in extreme cases cane them. The Ministry no longer supplies canes!

In this brief diversion, we can pick up elements about the authority of the head, about the relationship with and induction of probationary teachers, and about official and hidden discipline policies—a useful interruption from a researcher's point of view.

Interruptions therefore are a clue to culture. Holgate, after interviewing a wide range of pupils and staff in different arenas in a UK special school, concluded exhaustedly, "the only uninterrupted interview was that with an HMI, suggesting that one law of research is that the level of interruption is inversely proportional to the hierarchical status of the interviewee" (1992:53). Yet, as with the Pakistan example above, in other cultures interruptions are actually a symbol of power, as they show the extent to which an important person must be consulted about everything.

The setting may also include the ancillary rooms, if there are any. Is the head hidden away behind three layers of secretary's or deputy's rooms? Or can people enter directly from a corridor? Waiting in an outside room to see a head is also full of fascinating data. I was intrigued by a large and desperate sign on a Botswana head's door which read "No Form 2 places. No Boarding Places. No discussion on any of the above. Signed . . . Headmaster." Relationships with parents can be "read off" by the numbers waiting hopefully to see a head, whether there is a "system," whether parents can speak to a head on the telephone if there is one, or whether parents are happy or able to deal with the deputy or other senior management.

The overall context of the interview can also be instructive in terms of how many of the staff, if any, the head has informed of your visit. Does the head consult staff about the occasion, bring in relevant people, notify teachers about the presence of a researcher? Or is the authority absolute, with it not thought necessary to seek affirmation from colleagues? Again, much can be read off by the way other staff react to you when coming across you with the head.

Finally, one can find out how personal the territory of the principal is. As one explained in talking of his power-sharing with the deputy: Some deputy heads say, "I learned nothing from that head. He locks his office when he leaves. Nobody answers the phone."

TECHNIQUES

Building Trust

We should now look at specific techniques within the interview process itself to try to maximize what might well be a single occasion. The first is obviously that of building trust and credibility. There are the obvious issues of sensitivity to dress, body language or degree of eye contact which Lewin draws our attention to, particularly in Asian contexts (1990:123). Yet even within a culture in which an interviewer feels well grounded, there can be problems of offense. Measor and Woods (1991:64) tell a salutory tale of an early incident in their research on pupil adaptations to secondary school:

> Lynda spoke of the pupils to the headteacher, and used the term "kids." The head said he was deeply insulted by this language, objecting very strongly to the use of the word "kids." From that point on he closed up, and was unwilling to be interviewed or to discuss school matters.

Reynolds, too, in his research on effective schools antagonized heads on more than one occasion:

> In one school, some of the pupils went up to the headteacher and told her "we told the researchers what we thought of you, Miss X." In another school, the headteacher came into the room where the "self report" delinquency data was being collected from pupils and began to look at the considerable lists of offences pupils were writing as having committed. My reaction, which was to ask the head to leave the room, did not improve headteacher/researcher relations. (1991:197)

Here the difficulties were the balance between gaining the trust of the pupils and the trust of the head; in our research the trust to be built was in terms of what the research would be used for, and, as intimated earlier, whether senior officials might use information against the heads. This could be allayed to a certain extent by our portrayal of ourselves as simply learning at the feet of the master, a stance that Lerner a long time ago referred to as "casting the interviewee in the role of expert consultant" (quoted in Hammersley and Atkinson, 1983:110). We genuinely wanted to learn how heads coped with the daily lives of their schools, and could use our cultural ignorance to encourage them to develop generalizations and their wider "theories of action."

Cultural Stranger

This role of ignorant outsider is of great benefit in an interview process, for it enables very basic questions to be asked and explanations to be sought that would not be seen as necessary for a local teacher or researcher. Our question around how teachers are selected, for example, expected heads to want or experience far more control than they did; yet most heads accepted that staffing and promotions should be done by the office: "teachers feel they're getting a fair deal if it's done by the Staffing Officer—there's no nepotism." The effective schools literature that suggests that leadership is more effective if heads choose their own team does not recognize the reality of cultures where the weight of family ties would lead to a great deal of suspicion and resentment if heads had this freedom. It was useful to have explained to us all the intricate networks of community obligations that constrained heads and made them so reliant on the rule book to provide the excuse for non-particularistic behavior if they wanted to.

It is also instructive to examine one's own reaction to what a head sees as major and minor problems:

> Other problems are minor . . . a teacher has forgotten to go and teach a lesson, Friday afternoon, disappears, the class comes to complain that the teacher was not there. The teacher has an excuse—always, but . . .

Teachers forgetting to teach might well be seen as a major breakdown in school ethos or timetabling in a tightly knit western school worried about its place on the league tables; in schools where one feels lucky to have enough staff on roll at all, teacher absenteeism is more of an irritant than a collapse of whole school development.

Again, our inexperience of shift systems and of "hotseating" meant we could ask about the basic mechanics of this. When there are not enough classrooms, and rain means that the class with the turn under the trees is forced indoors, then the pupils go back-to-back in the same classroom. "We are forced not to teach—the children are just doing corrections, or written exercises—not group work or standing at the board." (It is interesting that "standing at the board" is seen as the normal desirable behavior.) Similarly, when there is insufficient furniture, then one child has the desk, the other the chair. "This forces them to fold the books when writing notes. We cannot emphasize neatness or cleanliness." I was interested by the repeated use of the word "forced:" the imperatives of lack of resources mean a choice of language implying strong outside control of events and actions.

Active Listening: Getting Examples

Linked to the cultural stranger stance is the technique of frequently asking for examples. A head may make a general statement that will make sense to you, but more still may be gained by requesting an instance. I was asking about what were the most difficult problems, and was given the reply, "dealing with the Ministry." I asked for an example, and the head recounted:

> One of our workers passed away, June 1989. All the rules about government transport say I can't use transport for this and that. But I discussed it with the staff, and they wanted to bring the corpse from Bulawayo. I phoned the Regional Office, could we have the school truck? They said it was OK providing it was within the limits of the budget. We were ferrying the mourners. . . . so we have to make decisions, hope to get them through.

In this brief narrative we can see how so many themes come together: the community responsibility of the head, staff consultation, negotiations with the (all-powerful?) Ministry, the inevitable constraints of funds. Again, look at the number of issues emerging from constant prompting in this dialogue:

> Q: What training needs would you say you had?
> A: Human relations—because you don't only deal with staff and children, but parents, other Ministries . . .
> Q: What sort of things?
> A: Well we have a School Board . . . to get people on the right road, you have to tell them the truth—if we are doing the wrong thing.
> Q: Could you tell me an example?
> A: When mistakes are made at the school—the teacher sends a child out—instead of the parent coming to the school to find out what has happened, go to the teacher, I call the parent to talk it over. The parents pay a building fund, $10 per home per year. I check the finances. I'm considered to be Chief Finance Minister in the community! The District Council come to check the books . . .

The real impact of training was only discovered, similarly, by pushing a head about her course:

> A: We have had in-service courses for heads. We discussed skills.
> Q: What sort?
> A: I can't remember.

Yet in contrast to asking for examples is the technique which Lewin (1990) refers to as proceeding from the specific to the general. He found in

Malaysia and Sri Lanka that more was gained by asking teachers "Could you tell me about a lesson that you taught last week?" and then trying to establish with them how typical that was, plus any underlying goals, than it was by beginning with a generalized question about their teaching approach. With the latter, teachers would come up with the rhetoric "I use a guided discovery approach" and seek examples to justify this, which might not be day-to-day reality. This was why in our interviews we did not ask "What is your management style?" because heads would all claim (as they did with Ngegba in Sierra Leone) to be "participative" or "democratic." It was better to elicit the examples and management crises first and generate the preferred styles from these.

Deciding on the direction is why it is called "active" listening. Woods (1986) in his book on ethnography in educational research provides a very useful list of thirteen different ways to "assist" the interviewee once a discussion has begun. As well as requesting examples and clarifications, there are the techniques such as: pursuing the logic of an argument ("Does it follow then, that . . .?"); posing alternatives ("Couldn't one also say. . . ?"); asking hypothetical questions ("Yes, but what if . . . ?"); checking on contradictions ("Yes, but didn't you say a moment ago . . . ?"); and expressing incredulity or astonishment ("In the fourth year?"). The skill is making these seem a natural part of conversation, and striking the balance between politeness and a little productive aggression.

Using Intimate Knowledge

All this probing relates to the role of the interviewer as a participant in the process, not a recorder. "Non-directive" questions are relatively open-ended, rather than requiring a simple yes or no (Spradley, 1979); they trigger the talk in a broad area. But this does not mean that the interviewer is then passive, allowing the stream of consciousness to flow. Certain amounts of "steering" may be necessary, to get the examples mentioned above, to clarify a point before continuing, or to bring the respondent back to the agenda. Sometimes a decision must be taken to take the opposite stance to the cultural stranger, and to confront a respondent with what one does know. Perlman illustrates this from his research in Uganda:

> I could not conduct formal interviews with most people or take notes in front of them, this was possible only with the relatively few educated people who understood my work. Others became suspicious when I started asking questions about their personal marital histories. Christians did not like to admit, for example, that they had at

one time (or even still had) two or more wives. But in those cases where I had learned the truth from friends, neighbours or relatives of the interviewee, I would confront him with the fact, although always in a joking manner, by mentioning, for example, the first name of a former wife. At that point the interviewee—realizing that I knew too much already—usually told me everything for fear that his enemies would tell me even worse about him. (1970:307)

I did not know such intimate details of heads, but I often knew about financial dealings with regional offices, and of course about other schools I had visited previously. Simply mentioning the name of another such school is often enough to set a head off explaining how his or her school is superior, more organized or better resourced and how important it was not to see all the schools as the same, or to have his or her school bracketed with another. I asked about a problem of "immoral relations" a previous head had narrated. The present head was firm: "Our kind of community does not allow that in town. In the country, the teacher is a demi-God, can do what he likes, but not here."

Ngegba (1994) in Sierra Leone was able to use this "intimate knowledge" quite successfully, as many of his headteachers he had known since boyhood, and, apparently over copious glasses of palm wine, was able to extract interesting confirmations of networks of power. His problem on the other hand was being able to "bracket" his preconceived commonsense knowledge about which of his acquaintances was a strong leader and effective head. There can be a temptation not to ask questions to which you think you know the answer.

Ball (1991:178–179) discussed this issue in his review of the methodology of *The Micropolitics of the School*. He distinguished "topic" questions from "cue" questions in order to get respondents to open up fully:

There is another peculiarity (inadequacy some might say) of the free-floating interviews. In the majority of cases the interviewees were known to me directly or were personally recommended to me. I believed that the sorts of questions I wanted to ask and the topics I wanted to address, what Hoyle calls the "organizational underworld" . . . could not be dealt with by a cold calling interview technique. I needed a degree of trust from my respondents. I needed them to take me into their confidence. I wanted to share their folk-knowledge of their institution with me. In some respects I was operating close to the level of gossip and personal criticism—the informal aspects of organization which are ritually referred to but rarely analysed in organizational theory. Not surprisingly the better I knew my interviewee the more candid the disclosures tended to be, although this was not always the case; I did find others who were willing to be indiscreet with little encouragement. The interviews were long and rambling; they contained many diversions and are full of anecdotes. My approach to questioning was based on an attempt to minimize "topic" questions and maximise "cue" questions. Thus, to pass over as much control over the substance of the interview as possible to the respondent.

He later talks, however, of similar interventionist techniques as were mentioned in the previous section—that is, after a respondent has made some general statement, asking them "Can you think of a recent occasion when that was evident?"

Ball's research had different aims from ours, in that he was concerned about revealing this underworld of a single institution, not about collecting snapshot management realities from a range of settings. However, the questions of trust and of control of the interview are relevant to both endeavors. Whether the interviewee is known or unknown, similar techniques of cueing and asking for examples can be used to attempt maximum candidness.

Shadowing

A way to combine the anthropology of strangeness with gaining intimate knowledge is the form of extended interview known as shadowing. Here the researcher accompanies the head throughout entire days or even weeks, both noting what the head does and generating the head's commentary on it. One of our researchers, Sealy (1992), did this very effectively in Barbados, spending a week each with four primary school heads and keeping a precise diary of every minute of their day. He was able to compare the amount of time the heads spent in different categories of activity—routine clerical, communication with staff, leisure, telephone, teaching, meetings and so on. The total number of different activities performed each week ranged from 113 to 194, with a daily average of 30.1 activities—almost 50% higher than Minzberg's average of twenty-two activities for the business executive. There was constant change and interruption, with few occasions for any concentrated periods of time for development planning or teacher appraisal. The lack of any school secretary, and with only one school having a typewriter, meant that a large chunk of the day was spent on paper work. Yet in similar conditions of stringency, heads managed to carve out differences in their use of time, with one head choosing to do substantial teaching, another delegating more, and a third spending ten times more time than the others counting money.

Interpretive data for Sealy came from a formal interview (with a schedule) prior to the shadowing as well as the ongoing commentary. This enabled some validation, in that claims about accountability, record-keeping, delegation, relationships with parents and so on could be checked by actual behavior and use of log books during the week. Asked about the changing role of the head in Barbados, one respondent, Mrs. Buick, stated that "It now calls for more responsibility and accountability on the principal's behalf." Sealy continues:

> It was very evident from the way Mrs Buick made her daily recordings of what happened during the day so meticulously in her diary and the log book that she viewed her task as being responsible and accountable. . . . Mr Cadalack also saw himself as being accountable to parents as he mentioned in question five. He went beyond that by adding the Ministry of Education and the community to his accountability list. Although he did not expand on this point it was clear from the close relationship which he kept with the parents who visited the school and the assistance he gave to those who requested transfer for their pupils that he was aware of his responsibility to them. Evidence of his accountability to the Ministry of Education was born out by the frequent dialogue he had with that department. (1992:29)

While asking for examples in order to "expand on a point" is useful, it obviously is no match for actually witnessing real events and behavior.

Chantavanich et al.'s fascinating study of Thai schools was also able to match headteachers' rhetoric with how they really spent their time:

> In rural schools, headmasters could remain in their position until retirement. Some, who were not interested in their academic responsibilities, could maintain their positions by concentrating on other activities, some of which had nothing to do with the schools but came with the position, whereas others were routine administrative functions such as attending interschool group test preparations, picking up teachers' salaries, attending district meetings, and procuring subsidized school materials. . . . Headmasters with a sense of responsibility usually regarded the school as their top priority and assigned

nonacademic duties to other teachers or avoided them when allowed to do so. . . . Many headmasters, however, seemed to prefer these nonacademic jobs, finding them more interesting, more rewarding and yielding more immediate results. (1990:120)

The study found many heads to be "dogmatic verging on tyrannical;" if the head was absent, the whole school ceased to function.

CRITICAL INCIDENTS

A shadower may be "fortunate" enough to witness a real crisis during the period. Yet even without being present, asking about responses to particular crises gives particularly interesting clues to both management realities and management styles. Burgess (1993:24), writing on his study of headship, called the head a "critical reality definer," and quoted him:

> "My job is not to manage today's crisis, but to manage the crisis of four months time. The settlement of today's crisis is by principles established four months before. If it isn't, something has gone wrong with forward planning."
>
> This statement was followed up with a set of principles that outlined the way in which crises or critical situations such as fires, crashes and explosions might be handled. . . . Yet this overlooked many critical situations that occur on a day-by-day basis and involve interpersonal relations between teachers and the headteacher that can assist in advancing our understanding of school organization.

Burgess quotes the anthropologist Victor Turner's argument that a suitable unit of analysis in ethnographic study may be a situation, event or crisis termed a "social drama." Again, while being present at such a drama—for example a teachers' dispute—will give the greatest insights into conflicting interpretations, a head's account will also help understanding. On what do they choose to focus? The head in Burgess' study summed up his isolation because of a division between management and unions:

> No, it [headship] is lonely . . . most heads . . . to be successful they've been gregarious, they've been social, they've organized things, and you get into headship and suddenly you find it is different and the way people approach you is different. You're on the other side of the desk . . . you leave your friends behind you and that's lonely and I would say myself that my previous deputy could move backwards and

forwards and could comfort me and strengthen me. (1993:27)

I was reminded of some of the female managers I interviewed in Botswana who had been cautious about accepting promotion because they did not want to be "over" other people (Davies and Gunawardena, 1992). As Schratz (1993) confirms, event analysis can point up not just what a head does, but the stresses, ambiguities and dilemmas of a headteacher faced with a difficult management decision.

A head in a Zimbabwe mine school interestingly referred to the following as an "unpopular decision" that he had to make:

> A teacher wants to board the 9 am bus because she has important business in town, but you say, no, you have a class.

For a UK head, there would not be a decision about whether a teacher taught her class; but in a school situated miles from town, and with teachers totally reliant on mine-workers' transport, everything appears negotiable. Heads are not all powerful, but occupy an intricate position between the vagaries of their staff, their pupils, and the Ministry. Here is another example of a crisis and a management dilemma:

> I did have one case. A teacher came in and said I have a cousin, she has a problem with fees, can you take her into Form 3. So I took her in, but she had been made pregnant by him in another school, had had her child, now he said she was sickly, that was why she was behind. The thing would never have come to light, but he was doing the same thing with the other girls . . . she set spies on him, friends of this girl informed the girl, the girl approached me, said "What are you doing with my husband?" I talked to him . . . counselling is better than spelling out the regulations. The teacher promised he would behave himself, but unfortunately I had to have him removed from the school for a drinking offence, after his pay. In the staffroom the next morning, he was sitting on a pile of exercise books, should have been teaching, totally drunk first thing in the morning. I referred him to the Staffing Officer. He tried to knock at the girls' dining room the night before. So they put him in a boys' school for his own safety. The Ministry does bend backwards a lot to help wayward teachers, it has tied our hands. . . . They have passed a Labour Regulations Act which protects workers. It is very difficult to remove someone who is inefficient.

Here the recalling of an event—or series of events—enables analysis of the degrees of freedom of headteachers, and their perception of their relative power vis-à-vis the Ministry and the legislation. A good baseline then in comparative interviewing is the uncovering of what consitutes a dilemma requiring a decision, and similarly what constitutes a crisis.

PROCESS ISSUES
Gender

Interviewing is, however, more than just a series of appropriate techniques to gather data. As intimated in the introduction, it is a conversation requiring a relationship. This relationship is clearly conditioned by a number of not necessarily controllable factors. Gender and power are the obvious ones that spring to mind. As a female researcher interviewing mostly male heads, I would be acutely aware of the swings and roundabouts in this. Females may be less threatening, and hence elicit more candidness; on the other hand, they may be not worth spending too much time with. A female colleague of mine involved in a National Union of Headteachers survey for the OECD that used an interview schedule supposedly worked on by the head in advance narrated how some male heads would merely throw it back across the table saying "Don't expect me to have had time to look at this." She felt both her (youthful) age and her sex prevented some heads from taking her and the project seriously.

On the other hand, I felt that I was able to gain the confidence of those women heads and managers that I did interview. One recounted:

> There's a tendency to look down on women heads. The community are not sure what a woman head will do. It's not a problem with the staff—I was a teacher before in this school. In the community, there's a reluctance to cooperate . . .

> Q: Is there a difference between male and female heads?
> A: Male heads tend to be bossy. I believe people should be free to express their views. I create a free atmosphere of expression. I don't want to feel I'm heading.

Yet, on reflection, male heads will also take me into their confidence if asked directly about gender. Here is a Botswana male head in response to a question about why there were so many male heads:

It starts from the top. Our bosses, all of them are old traditionalists—they can't see a wife holding a responsible position. Women don't get the recognition they deserve. Now, being a chauvinist, women have always had a submissive role. Women in this country have had a hard working role. There is a Setswana saying "You can never be led by a woman." People were horrified when Margaret Thatcher became Prime Minister. I always claim to be open-minded and understand when it comes to women's affairs, but every now and then I surprise myself how reactionary I am. I realize my weaknesses. My wife used to teach with me. We were thinking who could be Assistant Head—couldn't find one. "Trouble is, you're looking for a man" said my wife. It was true. So we started to look at women. "How come we overlooked them?" So we went down the list. We found one—very quiet, hardworking. I approached her. She said "I can't do it." I persuaded her to try. Now she's Deputy Principal. Since she started, she got confidence . . . but they are frightened to be better qualified, or earn more than their husband.

Would a male interviewer have got such admissions? More admissions? Different descriptions of women's roles? Would a male interviewer even have asked the question? Even if no firm answers are possible, the analysis of data must at least take into account the possible influence of symmetrical or asymmetrical relationships in the framing of responses.

Power

It is probable that gender is but one component in the wider question of perceptions of power. As discussed in the earlier section on access, trust will be different according to how suspicious an interviewer appears. In Pakistan, our interview team comprised middle-aged foreign female university academic and a youngish local male teacher-researcher, which I suppose covers most eventualities. Neither of us however had any "influence" whatsover in that community. At the interview, we asked permission to distribute questionnaires to the staff. All heads agreed, but it was instructive that at one school, the questionnaires were duly returned all with identical answers. They were written in different handwritings, so clearly the principal had gathered his staff together and instructed them exactly what they should write. The answers were all one hundred percent positive about the school, about the management, about the latest changes in government policy. My colleague was despondent, and said they were unusable; I saw them however as very significant data, particularly in terms of validating—or otherwise—what the principal said in the interview. It enabled us to look very closely at his claims about consultation, staff development and "the grant of autonomy" to Pakistani institutions.

Again, it is difficult to quantify the effect of real or imagined power differentials in the interview relationship; in hindsight there is a case to be made for researchers revealing as much as possible about themselves before an interview proceeds. This can allay suspicion; but it also starts the process of familiarity which makes conversation—rather than interrogation—possible.

Interviewee Agendas

One tends to think only of one's own purpose in an interview. The conventional "methodology" chapter will outline the aims of the research, the rationale for the various techniques and the objectives of the interview—from the point of view of the researcher. Rarely do we think about what the interviewee's aims and objectives are for the interview. In analyzing the data, I find it helpful to ponder on the heads' apparent agendas for the interview, what they were using it for. Under questioning, most of us will use the opportunity for a certain amount of "identity work"—presenting an image of ourselves that is consistent and manageable. Headteachers in particular have especial dilemmas and problems around power, and will want to use interviews in different ways than will classroom teachers or pupils. Even if the interviewer is non-threatening, heads are nonetheless rehearsing statements to themselves about their styles and their actions. It is not just that they want to present a good image to the researcher, they must present a viable role to themselves. The school is often seen as merely an extension of themselves—they talk of "my school," "my little community." To maximize their rewards from the interview, they need to consolidate their core identity through their talk and their presentation of self/school. As Hammersley and Atkinson point out, the interview is not just "time-out from the everyday lives of participants" (1983:125); it may be actively woven by a head into current and future management thinking.

Hence I am less worried than other writers on research about "response set" or "response effect"—the eagerness of the respondent to please the interviewer (Borg, 1981). With headteachers, it is more likely that they want to please themselves—or at least some generalized image of what a "good" head is, with which you may or may not identify. The desire to present their school in a good light creates the phenomenon of not admitting problems or training needs, as mentioned earlier; but such stances are in themselves data, and important clues to management culture. Also, heads may not know what your image is: when I asked one secondary head a "simple" factual question about how many departments there were in the school, he said, interrogatively, "Thirteen? Fourteen?" While I interpreted this as a lack of touch with his own administrative stucture, perhaps his self-image was one of the broad sweep, which should not bother with detail like how many departments there were.

Analyzing the Data

The question of sifting through the material to find the head's own agendas and power position leads on to the final question of analyzing the data from interviews. I have not talked of the differences between written notes and tape recordings, as these are covered by many textbooks, and the immediate pros and cons are I think self-evident. Vulliamy (1990:103) gives a useful account of weighing up the decision to use tapes or notes in his interviews in Papua New Guinea, based on the importance of accuracy versus validity:

> Put simply, it is better to have a limited record of a respondent's real feelings than a very accurate transcription of a series of highly guarded or dishonest responses.

None of us used tape recorders, and we relied on notes written at the time and daily field notes from memory. The quotations provided in this chapter are more or less verbatim, derived from my own personal shorthand. As with note-taking in lectures (see Davies, 1995), a personal system of abbreviations, acronyms, icons and triggers enables most of the conversation and gesture to be recorded. However, it is crucial to go over these and expand again at the end of the day before one forgets whether "Ive 0 v cty mant of t S ~" means "I've nothing against community management of the school (frowns)" or was more to do with Coventry City versus Manchester United football scores. As with Vulliamy, Lewin and Stephens's (1990) book, I also took photographs of the schools, and the heads in or outside their offices, to help recall of character and setting when doing the final analysis. But there is no substitute for trying to record as many actual words and finer choices of grammatical structures as possible: they start to reveal the subtext of the information provided.

Putting together the data from factual questions or those with specific purposes or expectations on a schedule is relatively straightforward; it is trying to extract new themes or building new models that is more risky. Language choice then is the first clue. Does the head talk of "my school," "our school," "this school?" Contrast one head I interviewed who said "It does me a lot of good to think of the school as my own little community" with the principal in Little and Sivasithambaram's (1993:102) description of an "effective" school in Sri Lanka:

> How can we really say we have been successful? Our enrollment has increased, our teachers have increased, our results are better, but look at the cramped conditions in which the children are learning . . . if we cannot increase our space, all our previous efforts will turn to failure. I'm trying to encourage the parents to help us build a temporary shelter. I'll be taking this up at our next meeting.

The continual use of the word "our" in talking of action and effort is I think not without significance.

Possessive adjectives are interesting, but so also are recurrent descriptive ones. For one urban head in Zimbabwe, the word was "hard:"

> This is a hard community here—one of the worst in Harare, a criminal element here, rubs off on the students . . . we need an inbuilt system of shock absorbers to get through the day . . . a student will claim that he has paid his fees, but he has spent it, the parents come in, very harsh . . . Or an over-zealous teacher beats a boy, the parent is furious, complains, or wants to go straight for the teacher. You have to be tough. I don't know how the lady next door manages, she is new. . . .
>
> [Style?] . . . I try to use—metaphorically—the stick. I am hard on people, dependent on the situation. I have a reputation for being tough—a hard man. I will tolerate no nonsense. . . . I am a stickler for records—this does bring me into conflict with the clerical staff, who don't see the need for filing.

Also, what metaphors or images does a head use to describe his or her role? In Burgess's (1993) study, the head used the analogy of a captain of a ship, eating separately, with his own cabin and servant, and ultimately responsible for everything that went on in his vessel. This was parallel to his view that "command is lonely." In contrast, one of the Zimbabwe heads said "I use the same skills as if I were running a factory. . . . I am not a teacher any more, I am an administrator." Not just content analysis, but textual analysis will enable isolation of significant recurrent vocabulary and metaphor which indicate a head's individual style.

A parallel endeavor is to isolate particular cultural themes that might condition all heads' behavior. For us, finance was clearly an overt concern;

what emerged as distinctive was the picture of an "effective" head as one who was able to think laterally around the use of scarce resources. Such inventiveness ranged from doing deals with community leaders to making chalk out of local clays, from creative accounting out of official budgets to letting out the school premises for funerals. The very self-serving nature of heads' agendas for interview responses meant that their strategic manipulations were a source of pride and not difficult to uncover. This creativeness then had to be put within a framework of an understanding of the local mores with regard to deference patterns, political allegiances, gendered values and traditions of what to the outsider might appear to be nepotism and corruption. Very different models of "quality" and "rationality" are implied. Ball (1991:177) said that from his data he began to form the idea of headship "as a style constructed out of interactions with subordinates;" from developing country analysis we would have to add "and superiors." Yet practical and social skills are not enough to ensure the "effective" head. We would have to concur with the findings of Chantavanich et al. (1990) in Thailand and many of the writers in Levin and Lockheed's (1993) collection that some sort of academic vision is also necessary. "You don't lose sight of your academic side—otherwise you get bogged down in whether children have enough beans and vegetables . . ."

The interview can reveal what and who the head in the end thinks the school is for:

> I try to build the spirit that it is our school, in our interests that things go properly, that type of approach, thinking of the goals of the school, better than just going by the rule book . . . the most satisfying thing is to sit back at the end of the day and say, you have achieved this, you see the results of your work, you set the tone of the school. You have goals you want to achieve . . . there is the independence given to the head of the school, to promote education in its broadest sense, physically and in a tangible way . . . lecturing you are just one of the numbers, you have your group given to you, you had no control, once you had given your lecture, that was the end of the day, but here you can change the curriculum, therefore change the quality of education, and of the children even. (Interview with Zimbabwean headteacher)

There are no shortcuts to thematic analysis. We have found ourselves going through the interview transcripts many many times, for different purposes, on different hunts. This is the philosophy of "grounded theory," where the theory emerges from the data rather than the data serving only to test preconceived hypotheses. The aim is to "saturate the categories": data are scanned to identify possible recurrent themes and then scrutinised to see whether enough instances can be established to claim that a theme is becoming "saturated." A concept can be said to be thoroughly saturated when, having gone back for more research, or having rescanned existing data for varying angles on it, no new information is coming in (Glaser and Strauss, 1967). The process also involves searching for negative instances, those examples that would challenge a hypothesis. The latter is almost more important, as it is tempting otherwise to select out only those quotations and instances that match some appealing emergent framework.

There are now computer packages to do this laborious work; I still keep to the trusty color pen system to highlight different themes. Murphy (1992), a teacher-researcher interviewing parents of children with special needs, transferred her transcripts to larger sheets of paper that she then pinned up on the wall, enabling her to scan across all the interviews. "This process was extremely time-consuming (and probably quite a clumsy method) but it gave me a much clearer picture" (1992:109). I would hold that there is in fact no quick and elegant way to get immersed in data and make the breakthrough to any exciting analysis. Our transcripts have become scored with different color pens and question marks, as we test out emergent theories; saturate our categories; look for examples of prismatic society, deviance, vision, patriarchy, covert and overt goals, multiple tasks, conflict theory, rewards, the practicality ethic, strategic dilemmas, post-independence styles, toilet provision and indeed anything which appears promising for analysis.

Indeed, from bitter on-the-ground experience, the next research project will test out the relationship between the head's vision-building and the state of the Blair toilets. . . .

REFERENCES

Ball, S. (1991) "Power, Conflict, Micropolitics and All That!" In G. Walford (ed.) *Doing Educational Research*. London: Routledge.

Bell, J. (1987) *Doing Your Research Project: A Guide for First-time Researchers in Education and Social Science*. Buckingham: Open University Press.

Borg, W. (1981) *Applying Educational Research: A Practical Guide for Teachers*. New York: Longman.

Burgess, R. (1993) "Event Analysis and the Study of Headship." In M. Schratz (ed.) *Qualitative Voices in Educational Research*. London: Falmer.

Chantavanich, A., Chantavanich, S. and Fry, G. (1990) *Evaluating Primary Education: Qualitative and Quantitative Policy Studies in Thailand*. Canada: IDRC.

Dadey, A. and Harber, C. (1991) *Training and Professional Support for Headship in Africa*. London: Commonwealth Secretariat.

Davies, L. (1992) "School Power Cultures under Economic Constraint," *Educational Review*, 43 (1):127–136.

———. (1993) "Teachers as Implementers or Resisters," *International Journal of Educational Development,* 12 (4):161–170.

———. (1994a) "The Management and Mismanagement of School Effectiveness," *Compare,* 24 (3):205–216.

———. (1994b) *Beyond Authoritarian School Management: the Challenge for Transparency.* Ticknall: Education Now.

———. (1995) *Study Skills in Teacher Training.* London: Macmillan.

Davies, L. and Harber, C. (in press) *School Management and School Effectiveness in Developing Countries.* Oxford: Elsevier.

Davies, L. and Gunawardena, C. (1992) *Women and Men in Educational Management: An International Inquiry.* Paris: IIEP.

Glaser, B. and Strauss, A. (1967) *The Discovery of Grounded Theory.* London: Weidenfeld and Nicolson.

Hammersley, M. and Atkinson, P. (1983) *Ethnography: Principles in Practice.* London: Tavistock.

Harber, C. (1992) "Effective and Ineffective Schools: An International Perspective on the Role of Research," *Educational Management and Administration,* 20 (3):161–169.

Holgate, J. (1992) "An Evaluation of a Leaver's Curriculum in a Special School." In G. Vulliamy and R. Webb (eds.) *Teacher Research and Special Educational Needs.* London: David Fulton.

Levin, H. and Lockheed, M. (eds.) (1993) *Effective Schools in Developing Countries.* London: Falmer.

Lewin, K. (1990) "Data Analysis and Collection in Malaysia and Sri Lanka." In G. Vulliamy, K. Lewin and D. Stephens, *Doing Educational Research in Developing Countries: Qualitative Strategies.* London: Falmer.

Little, A. and Sivasithambaram, R. (1993) "Improving Educational Effectiveness in a Plantation School." In H. Levin and M. Lockheed (eds.) *Effective Schools in Developing Countries.* London: Falmer.

Measor, L. and Woods, P. (1991) "Breakthroughs and Blockages in Ethnographic Research." In G. Walford (ed.) *Doing Educational Research.* London: Routledge.

Murphy, K. (1992) "Parental Perceptions of the Professionals Involved with Children with Special Educational Needs." In G. Vulliamy and R. Webb (eds.) *Teacher Research and Special Educational Needs.* London: David Fulton.

Ngegba, S. (1994) "Standards, Management and School Effectiveness in Sierra Leone." Ph.D. thesis, University of Birmingham.

Ozigi, A. (1984) *A Handbook on School Administration and Management.* Harare: The College Press/Macmillan.

Perlman, M. (1970) "Intensive Fieldwork and Scope Sampling: Methods for Studying the Same Problem at Different Levels." In M. Freilich (ed.) *Marginal Natives: Anthropologists at Work.* New York: Harper and Row.

Reynolds, D. (1991) "Doing Educational Research in Treliw." In G. Walford (ed.) *Doing Educational Research.* London: Routledge.

Schratz, M. (ed.) (1993) *Qualitative Voices in Educational Research.* London: Falmer.

Sealy, G. (1992) "The Task of the Primary School Principal in Barbados." M.Ed. dissertation, University of Birmingham.

Spradley, J. (1979) *The Ethnographic Interview.* New York: Holt Rinehart and Winston.

Vulliamy, G. (1990) "The Conduct of Case-Study Research in Schools in Papua New Guinea." In G. Vulliamy, K. Lewin and D. Stephens *Doing Educational Research in Developing Countries: Qualitative Strategies.* London: Falmer.

Vulliamy, G., Lewin, K. and Stephens, D. (1990) *Doing Educational Research in Developing Countries: Qualitative Strategies.* London: Falmer.

Woods, P. (1986) *Inside Schools: Ethnography in Educational Research.* London: Routledge.

7 IMPROVING OUR PRACTICE

COLLABORATIVE CLASSROOM ACTION RESEARCH IN LESOTHO

Janet Stuart

with Mahlape Morojele

and Pulane Lefoka

INTRODUCTION

In keeping with action research traditions, this paper has been written collaboratively. It contains three "voices," all speaking in the first person. The "I" of the first part, the first case study, and of the concluding comments and reflections, is Janet Stuart, a teacher educator who worked for a year as a consultant with a team of five Basotho teachers of development studies at post-primary level. The second voice is that of Mahlape Morojele, writing as a primary teacher-trainer and one of that original team. The third voice, Pulane Lefoka, writes as a researcher who helped set up a subsequent project supporting primary teachers to develop instructional self-reflection skills.

Qualitative research takes as important the experiences, understandings and values of participants, including the researchers. It is therefore appropriate that this account looks at action research from three different perspectives. We share, however, a common understanding of, and enthusiasm for, action research and we have tried to create a coherent picture for those who might wish to take up this approach.

EDUCATIONAL ACTION RESEARCH

Educational action research is a form of disciplined and systematic inquiry that is undertaken by the people involved—usually but not always teachers—in order to improve their own educational practice. It therefore differs from other forms of research in that the researchers, instead of coming in from the outside, are part of the situation being studied, and are themselves involved in carrying out both the action and the research. To some extent, action research, or participant research, can be seen as a research paradigm on its own, different from both the qualitative and quantitative paradigms. However, it is closer to the qualitative paradigm in that it focuses on understanding rather than measuring, and in that it takes participants' perspectives as data.

Whereas some other research traditions stress detachment and aim to be "value-free," action researchers strive to "improve" something, which implies some notion of value, and because they are themselves participants, there is always an element of subjectivity involved. Indeed, one school of action research defines it as an attempt to live out one's values more fully in one's practice (McNiff, 1988). (The question of values is an important one, to which I shall return.) Action research therefore involves the idea of "reflexivity," in which the actors, reflecting on their own ideas and actions, try to analyze what they are doing and why. At the same time, the actors seek to be open to different perspectives, by inviting other participants such as students and colleagues to comment on and critique their analysis; this is an important method of validation (see Winter, 1989, for a useful discussion).

For these reasons, among others, action research is very often carried out collaboratively. This collaboration may take several forms: a group of teachers working as a team, a single teacher reflecting on her practice with the help of a "critical friend" who watches her teach, or a consult-

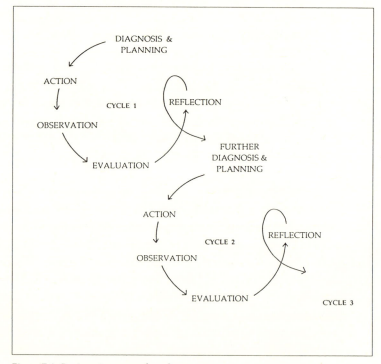

Figure 7.1. Basic action research cycles.

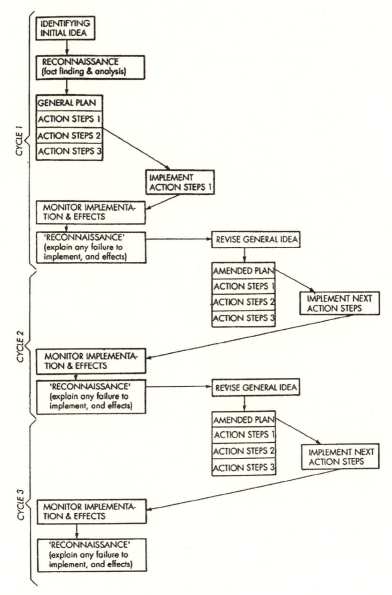

Figure 7.2. Elliott's action research cycle (Elliott, 1991: 71).

ant facilitating research by providing resources, challenge and support to the practitioners. As far as research methods are concerned, action research is eclectic. It is often appropriate to collect qualitative data—by interview, fieldnotes, tape or video recording—but more quantitative methods may also be useful, such as short questionnaires, content analysis of student scripts, or observation schedules. What is essential, however, is a reflective journal, in which the researcher records ideas, feelings, plans, actions taken, mistakes and successes, findings and preliminary analyses.

Action research usually proceeds in a cyclical or spiral fashion through successive stages of diagnosing a problem, planning how the situation can be improved, acting in the direction of the planned change, and observing in order to monitor and evaluate the results. Reflection on this process leads to further rounds of planning, acting, observing and reflecting. Many writers have suggested ways of visualizing this process. At its simplest it can be depicted as a series of cycles, as shown in Figure 7.1.

A more detailed and systematic version is offered by Elliott (1991) that adds a reconnaissance stage to verify the nature of the problem, and suggests that the action be broken down into steps (Figure 7.2).

Although one can argue about the number of stages or steps, and about how one labels them, the cyclical model is, I believe, an extremely useful and practical framework. It is above all a natural framework, in that it builds on what good practitioners do anyway. They see a problem, think of a solution, try it out and see if it works. Action research helps by slowing this process down, making it more explicit, more systematic and more rigorous.

Action research does not seek to provide conclusive answers or general laws. It is concerned with the improvement of professional judgment in situations that are infinitely varied and always changing (Schon, 1983). As such, it is concerned with individual, personal cases; it studies "singularities" rather than trying to establish generalizations (Bassey, 1983). However, case studies can highlight common principles and can suggest new ideas for adaptation elsewhere, and published accounts of action research, describing both processes and outcomes, can stimulate others to research their own practice in similar ways (Altrichter et al., 1993).

The Roots of Action Research

Action research was developed in the Western world, starting as a form of social action among deprived communities in America (Lewin, 1946) and moving thence to education (Corey, 1953). In the 1970s the Ford Teaching Project in England used it successfully to help science teachers develop clearer ideas about what discovery learning really means (Elliott, 1991). The practice was taken up more widely, along with the idea that teachers should develop the curriculum at the grassroots through taking a research stance to their teaching (Stenhouse, 1975). Networks of teachers and teacher educators grew up, sharing their experiences and understanding. The ideas were further developed in Australia (Kemmis and McTaggart, 1981) and later spread to other European countries (Altrichter et al., 1993).

Most action research focuses on practical and professional issues within the classroom and the school. Some writers, however, add a further dimension to action research, suggesting it can—and perhaps should—lead people to question and reflect on not only their own teaching but the social and political context in which that teaching is carried on. For example, Carr and Kemmis (1986:162) define action research as

> a form of self-reflective enquiry undertaken by participants in social situations in order to improve the *rationality and justice* of their own practice, their understanding of these practices and the *situations in which the practices are carried out.* (my emphasis)

In other words, such research can also take on an emancipatory role and help participants challenge unjust structures.

Potential for Action Research in Developing Countries

There are to date few detailed studies of action research in developing countries. Wright's (1988) report on work in Sierra Leone was one of the first. The flexibility of action research and its small-scale, teacher-friendly nature would seem to make it suitable. However, the nature of the education systems may not be so congenial or conducive to participant research. Action research developed in the UK at a time when the educational system was very decentralized and when there was no national curriculum; it came up from the grassroots of a strong professional culture and although it faced opposition, it was able to establish itself firmly. In most developing countries, by contrast, education systems are usually highly centralized and bureaucratic; teachers are not well trained nor is there a strong professional culture to support it. One may well ask: how appropriate is action research in such a context?

I believe that a crucial factor is the local perception of the teacher's role: are they seen as professionals or as technicians? If teachers are perceived, and see themselves, simply as deliverers of the curriculum, whose job it is to pass on knowledge in the way they are trained to do, action research is unlikely to take root. On the other hand, where professionalism is at least held up as an aim or an ideal, action research is a powerful means of enhancing and developing that professionalism, as our Lesotho experience demonstrates.

I do not think action research can be used bureaucratically, as a means of implementing top-down decisions. But in places where there are not as yet strong professional networks, a Ministry of Education can help facilitate change of this kind. An example is the Cianjur/ALPS Project in Indonesia (Moegiadi et al., 1994). The aim was to introduce more pupil-centered activity-based learning into Indonesian primary schools. The method was to involve teachers in changing their own practice through group discussions, workshops and peer observation, building on already existing Teachers' Clubs. Facilitators were trained to work at several levels. Crucial to its success was the way in which the schools were given freedom to experiment and to decide on how the changes were to be implemented.

In South Africa, by contrast, action research was taken up as an emancipatory movement at a time of great political change (Davidoff and Van den Berg, 1990). For example, Melanie Walker stresses the political as well as the personal and professional aspects of such research (Walker, 1995). She worked for three years on an action research project with primary school teachers in the Black townships around Cape Town when apartheid still ruled. One of the project's aims was to empower teachers to act against an extremely oppressive education system. She concludes that although this aim was not entirely realized, the teachers did begin to engage in a research process, becoming more reflective and flexible, more able to take some control over their own practice and change it (Walker, 1993:102–103).

It may seem from the foregoing that action research projects are always oriented towards the more "liberal/democratic" type of teaching styles (Guthrie, 1981). Insofar as students as well as teachers are encouraged to participate and reflect, thus moving the power relationships toward a more democratic and open pattern, this may well be true, while in emancipatory projects, this is made explicit. However, it would in theory be perfectly possible to carry out action research into more formal teaching methods. It is about improving the practice of teaching and learning according to one's values, not necessarily about introducing student-centered methods. It may well be that people interested in action research tend to be, at the present time, also interested in moving toward the democratic end of Guthrie's continuum, but the two are not logically linked.

Nor is it confined to certain subjects. Development studies lent itself to the approach both because of its newness and because of its epistemological base in critical inquiry, but in the literature of action research there are examples of teachers working within all school subjects. Indeed, one of the great strengths of action research is its flexibility. It has taken root among teachers in developed countries because they can use it to improve their own practice in many different ways. Similarly, in developing countries teacher-researchers do not have to take Western models as given. Our experience in Lesotho suggests ways in which indigenous models, adapted to local conditions and possibilities, can be developed. The following case studies describe what we did. In the concluding part of the chapter I will discuss what lessons we learned and draw some conclusions.

This chapter is not, however, a "recipe" for action research. There is no one "right" format. By discussing the principles and sharing some of our experiences, we hope to encourage others to try it for themselves and to develop their own appropriate path. In Africa it is said that "paths are made by walking." Action research is learned by doing.

Case Study 1: The Lesotho Action Research Group (LARG)

In 1984 I undertook an exploratory action research project with a team of development studies secondary teachers in Lesotho. The following accounts are based on what we did and how a subsequent team took the idea into primary schools.

The Lesotho Context

The Lesotho school system is in some ways a typical post-colonial one, modeled on the UK. There is, however, a longer tradition of literacy than elsewhere in Southern Africa—the first school was set up in 1833 and a vernacular newspaper appeared in 1863—and girls outnumber boys up to University level. At the time of the study, almost all children enrolled in primary school, but after seven years only about one-third took the Primary School Leaving Certificate and less than half of these went on into secondary school (Task Force, 1982). The local Junior Certificate (JC) was taken after three years, in Form C, and the Cambridge Overseas School Certificate (COSC), giving access to the University, at the end of Form E.

Unusually, education was seen as a three-way partnership between the government, who set main curricular guidelines and paid teachers; the churches, who still owned most of the schools and instilled their own ethos; and the communities, who sometimes took their own initiative to build schools. This made for an atmosphere where power was somewhat diffused, and where there was space for classroom experimentation and the exercise of professional skills and judgments. I believe this is one reason why action research was relatively easy to implement in Lesotho.

The Assumptions and Values Underlying the LARG Project

As stated above, action research involves trying to improve one's practice according to one's espoused values and it is therefore important that these be made explicit. I chose action research because I wanted my research to be useful: I hoped it might in some way help to develop teaching and learning where it mattered—in the classroom. I originally thought of it in terms of curriculum development, as the subject development studies, for which I was training teachers, was relatively new and there was no agreed pedagogy.

In the two main teacher-training institutions in Lesotho at this time (the Faculty of Education at the National University and the National Teacher Training College) there was a general consensus that interactive, student-centered teaching methods were "good" and students were introduced to these in both educational foundations and curriculum studies courses. Along with other subject specialists, I had advocated—and demonstrated—such methods in my seminars, but I was aware they were seldom practiced in schools. I therefore invited teachers who had taken my courses to collaborate with me on an action research project to investigate ways in which the teaching of development studies could itself be developed.

A team of five teachers met with me at a residential planning weekend in June. I invited them to talk first about successful methods of teaching they had used and then to identify problems they faced, together with some possible ideas to try out. Our shared experience of the University ensured there would be certain common assumptions about what "good" teaching might be, but at the same time I was aware of the dangers of imposing our own agenda. The tapes of the discussions show that I took a facilitative rather than a directive role. At the end of the two days they had generated six "guiding propositions" that were to form the research framework. These four proved to be the most fruitful:

> Students are passive in class; they do not participate actively in learning and they expect teachers to feed them with information. They can be helped through discussion, especially in small groups, and role-plays or simulations.
> Students show a lack of higher-order skills such as comprehension, application, analysis and synthesis. They can be helped through more discussion, debate, relevant literature and role-plays/simulations.
> Students believe that knowledge is "closed" or "fixed"; it is a "thing" which they "are given" rather than explorations in which they take part. This can be changed by a consistently open-ended teaching approach.
> Students find it difficult to pose questions for inquiry. They can be helped by field-trips, by interviewing guest speakers, or role-play.

In terms of Elliott's (1991) model we had identified "general ideas" and "diagnosed problems."

The aim of this workshop was that the teachers themselves should identify the themes for action research, and this was achieved. Each teacher interpreted the themes differently, and some went beyond them, but they were truly "owned" by the team, which might not have been the case had the suggestions come from me. I return below to the ways in which the teachers' ideas about "good" teaching developed.

The Program and Timetable for the Research

We agreed on an outline program whereby I would work separately with the teachers in their classrooms and the team would meet at intervals to share experiences. This was broadly adhered to, and the project took place over the academic year 1984–85 as shown in Figure 7.3.

Typically there would be a planning meeting, then I would visit the school for one or more lessons which I usually taped as well as taking notes. I transcribed the tape and sent it with the transcript to the teacher, who listened and made her own notes. We would then meet to scrutinize the evidence and share our analyses of the teaching and learning patterns. At the teacher's request, I would interview pupils about a specific aspect. The teacher would then plan the next moves in the light of all the findings. Roughly every six weeks there would be a team meeting to compare findings and discuss their significance.

It is easy, in retrospect, to describe and classify what we did in terms of three action research cycles and thus make sense of it. At the time, the process was not so clear to us. Even the start was difficult: where to begin?

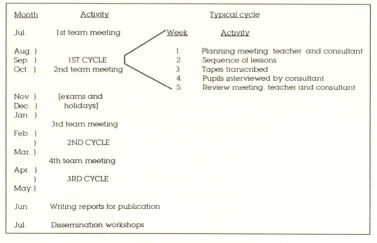

Month	Activity		Typical cycle	
Jul.	1st team meeting	Week	Activity	
Aug. } Sep. } Oct. }	1ST CYCLE 2nd team meeting	1 2 3 4 5	Planning meeting: teacher and consultant Sequence of lessons Tapes transcribed Pupils interviewed by consultant Review meeting: teacher and consultant	
Nov. } Dec. } Jan. }	[exams and holidays]			
Feb. } } Mar. }	3rd team meeting 2ND CYCLE			
Apr. } } May }	4th team meeting 3RD CYCLE			
Jun.	Writing reports for publication			
Jul.	Dissemination workshops			

Figure 7.3. Outline of project and action research cycles.

By gathering data for "reconnaissance" or by testing one of our "propositions?" In the end we simply jumped: I said I would observe a lesson for each teacher and provide feedback. This provided practice in data gathering, accustomed the students to my presence and provided some material for the teacher to analyze.

THE FIRST CYCLE

The "reconnaissance" lessons usually confirmed the problem: yes, pupils were passive, they asked few questions, cognitive levels were low. The teachers then began, in rather halting and hesitating ways, to experiment with one or more of the methods suggested: small group discussion, a guest speaker, a fieldtrip, different ways of presenting information and questioning. At this point the focus was very broad. Selected lessons were monitored and data were gathered, from their own observations, from tapes, from students' questionnaires and interview responses, and from my comments. Reflection took place in several different ways: individually, in discussion with me and others, and at the team meetings.

For example, Lomile Putsoa took her class to a factory and attempted a class discussion afterwards. Having studied the tape and transcript, she commented to me:

- It was more of a question and answer session than a discussion; there were not enough students talking. Participation was too low; I identified only eleven (out of thirty-eight in the class). Maybe I should try calling them out so they get ready to talk.

- They are looking for a consensus; they don't argue with each other. I feel these students have some potential for higher thinking skills; perhaps I am overdoing the "accepting" of their ideas to give them confidence; disagreeing might help them expand their discussion skills, but I hope it doesn't have the negative effects of driving them into their shells.

- What I want is to get them using higher order skills without my prompting them. (Meeting notes, August)

This shows the teacher learning to become more reflective and analytical. She selects data from the tape (low participation, lack of discussion, deference to teacher, evidence of thinking, together with a missed opportunity for debate); she discusses this in relation to the guiding propositions; she identifies a dilemma (it might have a negative effect) and sets up a goal (to get them to use higher order skills).

She later formalized her thinking as: "challenging students will encourage them to develop thinking skills." Now this is both a hypothesis and a plan of action. It closely approximates Donald Schon's description of good professionals "experimenting in action;" they hold "reflective conversations" with the situation, trying to "make (it) conform to their hypothesis, but remaining open to the possibility that it will not" (Schon, 1983:150). In the context of the research project, this process was being formalized, slowed down and made more rigorous. For the rest of the project, Lomile Putsoa deliberately tried out a number of ways of "challenging" her students, and monitoring the results in terms of "higher order skills." (For a fuller account, see her report in Stuart, 1985.)

Triangulation

A method often used in action research is to collect views from different perspectives: for example from an observer and the students as well as from the teacher; this is a form of triangulation. Here is an example. Tlohang Sekhamane was using the project to explore different teaching strategies with Form D (first year O Level class). First he tried sending groups to research in the library. Feedback revealed the students needed more structured guidance so he decided on a preliminary lecture on the next topic, which I observed. Afterwards, I interviewed the students, and we compared notes.

Reflecting on the lesson, the teacher wrote in his journal:

- Time — I should not attempt to squeeze so much into such a short time.
- Affective — People were attentive, but one could tell they were getting bored, either because the lesson was long or the method does not capture their interest. For the next chapters maybe the introduction should be done in three stages and not two . . . then there could be enough time for teacher to keep throwing questions to students after covering every bit . . .
- Participation — Only a few questions. Probably people would have asked more if there was enough time.

The teacher was articulating his reflections, summarizing what evidence he picked up during the lesson, hypothesizing alternative reasons for failing to reach his goals, and planning possible courses of action. Meanwhile I was interviewing a selection of the class to see what they thought.

JS	What did you think about yesterday's class? Did you feel you understood everything?
S	Yes, we understood everything, but there were some words which were new, e.g. demography.
JS	Did you enjoy it?
S	Yes, but it went on too long and we fell asleep. Forty minutes is long enough for a talk.
JS	Did you have enough time to ask questions?
S	No, by the time he paused we had forgotten what we wanted to ask.
JS	What advice would you give a new teacher from college?
S	If there is a double period, he can use the second period to ask us to ask him questions. If we don't have questions, he can ask us some, or let us go and discuss it in groups.
S	If starting a new chapter, he should tell us to go and read it first, so we know what he is talking about. If he just starts a new topic with no preparation I don't understand (general agreement).

With the students' permission, I handed these notes over to the teacher. I added from my own observations:

> First 15 minutes taken up with writing summary of the topic on the board. . . . They did not do any writing for the next hour, just listened. The language level was quite high. . . . In ten minutes you asked just two direct questions. There were a couple of "chorus" questions and answers. You went on to take each point in turn. . . . There were two pauses for questions. You took only one or two each time. During the lecture, some faces began to look rather glazed. They were very passive. (Fieldnotes, September)

It is important that the feedback is as factual as possible, rather than judgmental, which is why a tape is one of the best methods. However it is done, triangulation can enhance and deepen the teacher's own perception. Our experience throughout was that students would talk fairly openly to an observer and allow their comments to be passed on.

Observing Groups

New insights came from monitoring students involved in small group discussions. Maisang Seotsanyana's first lesson (with a low-stream Form B class) showed very low participation, so she decided to split them into groups, giving them questions to discuss. She circulated, listening, while I tape-recorded the two groups. Afterwards she discussed her observations with the class. In her report she wrote:

> From the tape I realised how this group handled a discussion and how they actually produced notes for class presentations from working in groups. I was surprised to find out that students do not engage in discussion, that they are satisfied by one answer offered from the group, after which they immediately pass to another point. . . . When the groups were asked what they do when they "discuss," answers included: "we share work and correct mistakes," "we agree" or "work together". . . . My assumption that in a discussion pupils will investigate all possible answers to a question or a situation was not shared by my groups. (Stuart, 1985: 44–45)

Here the tape was a useful adjunct but not essential. By listening and by talking over with the class their perceptions of the task, she had gained an important insight: these students had never been taught how to discuss. Subsequently she played some of their tapes back to them, explaining which parts showed discussion skills (such as listening to others, considering alternatives). Later tapes showed students putting these into practice.

At the end of this first cycle we were invited to write a joint conference paper on work in progress. This was very fortunate, as it made everyone sit down, go through their notes and produce an analytical memo (Altrichter et al., 1993) thus clarifying for themselves and each other what they had done and what they thought about it. However hard at the time, great benefit comes from putting one's thoughts on paper.

The Question of Further Cycles

When we reconvened in January after the long summer holidays I sensed some reluctance to go on. The headteacher from the mountains dropped out due to pressures of work and distance. There was a sense of "We've learnt a lot, why go on?"

Many action research projects end after one cycle. The teachers feel pleased because they feel they have gained some new insights and have done something different. Listening to the teachers' reports and discussion, I realized they had indeed come a long way. They were looking less at the students' failings and more at what they themselves, as teachers, could do to encourage better learning, e.g. demonstrate how to discuss, be more patient in explaining, challenge the students more in order to develop their thinking. A deficit model of student learning was being replaced with a framework for improving student-teacher interaction. Something had definitely changed in the teachers' minds; it was less clear how far their classroom practice had altered.

Second-Level Action Research

At this point I decided that as well as facilitating the team's action research, I would carry out action research on my own practice as well: I would monitor my own work as a consultant to try to understand what was happening with the teachers and how I could better facilitate their path to becoming teacher-researchers.

The main problem I identified was a lack of rigor: were the teachers actually doing research, or just learning to reflect on their practice? My first move was to encourage them to follow the Elliott model more closely. I pressed everyone to clarify their thinking by writing down hypotheses and "action steps" in a more precise way and to collect more specific data, particularly on student learning outcomes.

I am now unsure how far this insistence on hypotheses and on "hard data" was necessary. Some would say that it smacks too much of positivism, and that there are other ways of being rigorous (Winter, 1989). However, it did have the effect of helping them to focus on new aspects of their work and I believe that carrying out further cycles, however arduous, took their insights to a much deeper level.

Refocusing on One's Teaching

In the second cycle, for example, Lomile Putsoa decided to look at her problem in a new light. She wrote:

> I had realised in Cycle One that students' performance was below par, but I could not tell where the problem actually was. I decided to break my teaching into distinct stages, so that I could put my finger on the problematic area:
>
> a. introduce the topic by presenting a problem, giving no answer;
> b. use "brainstorming" or "buzz groups" to motivate students;
> c. involve them in some action, such as role-play, simulation, debate, guided reading, etc.;
> d. organise small group discussions in which they can use the experiences they have had;

e. give written work to see what learning has taken place. (Stuart, 1985: 22)

Lomile carried this through, monitoring and collecting data both formally (i.e. with the consultant through tapes and interview) and informally (i.e. through observing student reactions and personal reflection). Her own reflections led her to adapt the plan. She wrote:

> Initially I had not included giving students a lecture on the topic, but later I realised I was facing dilemmas I had not contemplated. Did I want students to go through long discussions every time before reaching their conclusions . . . to encourage them all to go in every direction? . . . We teach for exam purposes as well: would all students have collected enough points to answer questions?
>
> So I had to think carefully about the lecture: how to help the students without reviving their dependence on the teacher: in the end I decided to summarise the students' own ideas, with some other points, but still leave the conclusions open. (Stuart, 1985: 25)

This illustrates what Winter (1989) describes as the "dialectic critique." Lomile became much more analytical about her teaching, identifying the dilemmas and external constraints, while seeking a way out that was still consistent with the values she was seeking to implement.

Involving Students as Researchers

Lomile's third cycle was a continuation of the second, in which she focused on more specific aspects. It included trying to help the most passive students by selecting them for tape-recording in small groups.

The selection of these more passive students is an example of involving students in the research process as active participants and encouraging them to reflect on their own learning. These students had told me earlier that they were shy about speaking in class due to the fear of making mistakes in English. Giving them a tape recorder, and allowing them to erase what they wanted, encouraged them to produce much better discussions than they would normally do. This contrasts with traditional research that seeks to document students' achievement at a given moment; we wanted to document how far students could go, given the chance to practice.

There is striking evidence that all these efforts produced new patterns of teacher-student interaction in Lomile's classroom, as can be seen by comparing the two lessons in Figure 7.4.

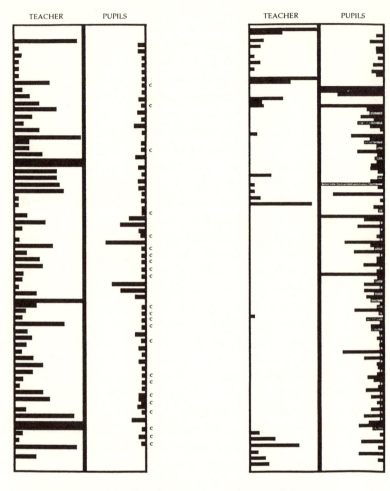

Figure 7.4. *Comparisons of pupil participation in classroom dialogue.*

Comparing Two Ways of Running a Field Trip

Maisang Seotsanyana concluded that she was presenting topics to her low-stream class in too abstract a manner and she formulated a new proposition:

> Less able students are passive when they have to learn abstract things from books, of which they have no direct knowledge; learning from first-hand experience will enable them to take a more active part in learning, and find out knowledge for themselves. (Notes of planning meeting, February)

In the second cycle, taking the topic "production," she organized a field trip to a local industrial estate of small workshops, giving the students a questionnaire to help them take notes. The class appeared eager, and asked many questions, in Sesotho, during the visit. Back in class she divided them into groups to prepare reports. While I was taping two groups she circulated among the others and seeing several had collected very little information, decided

> to arrange the report back session in such a way that the groups which had not achieved much could be helped to understand through my probing questions. (Stuart, 1985: 49)

However, the report-back lesson proved unsatisfactory. In asking the "probing questions" to try to add information to the group reports, she found she interrupted them so frequently that the class relapsed into silence. Disappointed, she sought more data.

Firstly, she asked a Sesotho-speaking consultant to give the students a short questionnaire and then to interview the class. This revealed that the students found problems in reporting in English the information they had collected in Sesotho, and that they lacked the skills of taking notes and writing reports. Secondly, she listened to the tapes of the two other groups. These shed a new light on the pupils; she was impressed by the information they had gathered and the points they raised. In a later meeting she said:

> I realised if I had listened to the tapes before holding the class discussion, I might have asked them to present differently; I would have asked the secretary of the group to stand up and read out what they had compiled, so that all this information and creativity would have been shared, instead of my leading them all the time. They were reporting within a structure which did not allow for this new information to be brought in. (Report to team meeting, March)

In the third cycle she organized a second field trip and made several changes. Instead of giving the pupils a prepared questionnaire, she spent a class period helping them to write down their own questions. After the visit, she simply told the groups to discuss what they had seen and to write a report, organizing their information themselves. The results pleased her; the pupils produced reports between 100 and 200 words long, which they read out in class and then displayed on the classroom wall (see Stuart, 1991, for a fuller account).

She had not only experimented successfully with new ways of presenting information and concepts and of organizing learning activities, she
had also learned to reflect on her own practice. As a result, she was able to

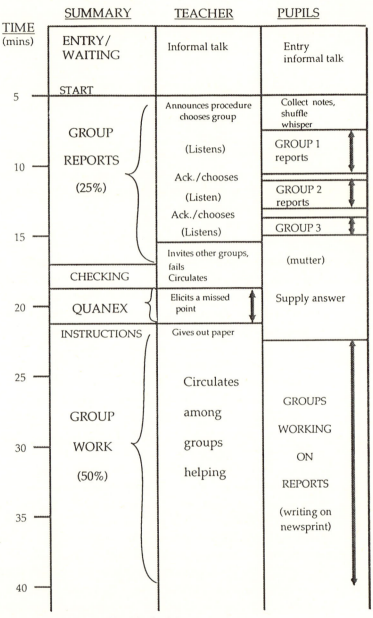

Figure 7.5. Flowchart of final feedback lesson.

trust the students more and give them more responsibility for their own learning. A significant result of the research was that rapport between the teacher and this "difficult" class improved considerably.

Figure 7.5 shows a flowchart of the final feedback lesson. This is a very different pattern from the teacher's usual style (or indeed from most Basotho teachers!) and shows how she had gained confidence in developing new methods of classroom organization.

Other Ways of Analyzing Data

Teachers regularly set and mark assignments and tests. These can become part of the data collected for the action research. Lomile Putsoa and I were anxious to get clearer evidence of how far her challenging had actually helped students to develop higher order skills. We wrote a one-page description of an anonymous "developing country" (based on South Africa) and asked students to decide whether they thought it was developed, underdeveloped, or whether they were unsure.

We scored the answers in terms of their ability to apply general criteria about development to this country and to evaluate its characteristics against such criteria. Out of thirty-six students, eleven scored at Level 4 (shows such ability), ten at Level 3 (could draw some general conclusions), seven at Level 2 (some inferences made) and eight at Level 1 (selected evidence from the text but no analysis).

As several of the team were interested in developing higher order cognitive skills and in encouraging an "open" view of knowledge, we devised ways of coding both teachers' questions and pupils' answers that would illuminate these aspects of the classroom dialogue.

1. Level of cognitive demand. We used a 12–fold category scheme, from recall of facts to evaluative judgment, which we condensed into the three levels of recall, comprehension and thinking.
2. Degrees of freedom. After the team had discussed their perceptions of open-ended teaching and independent learning, we devised a 3–point scale to evaluate the exchanges as closed, restricted or open.

- closed implies there is only one right answer;
- restricted implies the answers are limited by the teachers' expectations, or shared familiarity with the textbook;
- open implies the teacher will accept a wide range of answers, encouraging the pupils to draw on their own experience.

To illustrate, here is an extract from one of Phuthi Makhetha's lessons, in which he was aiming both to encourage his pupils to practice higher order thinking skills and to find answers for themselves. He started with factual questions about world population and the meanings of birth rate and death rate, encouraging the pupils to look up the answers. After some ten minutes comes the passage below:

com/res	T. Now is the birth-rate increasing at the moment or is it decreasing? As I said, try to
th/op	think accurately because you have to explain why you think so. Don't just say yes or no.
	B.1. It's increased *com/res*
th/op	T. Increased? Why do you say it's increased? (silence) You don't think?
	G.l. Decreased *com/res*
th/op	T. Decreased? The birth rate has decreased? Why do you think so?
	G.1. (inaudible. . . . and they don't want many children. It's not easy to . . . *th/op*
th/op	T. Her answer is that people don't want many children because when you have many children, then life becomes difficult.
	Bs (Disagreement; call out Sir, Sir)
th/op	T. That's her opinion. If you've got another opinion, then you can raise it, right?
	G.2. It's increasing. . . . Because everywhere you go you see a mother carrying a baby. *th/op*
	Pupils (laughter)
	T. That's an observation, eh? That's a good observation. Yes?
	B.2.There are not many wars . . . and the people are not killed. *th/op*
th/op	T. Is it just wars that kill people?

Key:
com = comprehension
th = thinking
res = restricted
op = open

Such coding schemes necessarily rely on a high degree of inference, and have limited value, in my view, for cross-classroom comparison and generalizations. However, they can provide useful evidence for a teacher to ponder, and can often reveal new aspects of the problem. In this case, the analysis of this lesson showed the teacher he had asked for—and got—a fair degree of cognitive skill, but that overall his questions had been relatively closed; as the following Table 7.1 shows.

TABLE 7.1

Proportions of teacher's questions in different categories in Lesson 1

Level:	Percent
Recall	47
Comprehension	18
Thinking	35
Freedom:	Percent
Closed	38
Restricted	47
Open	15

The transcript of the next lesson demonstrated that the pupils had not bothered to do the assigned reading and were relying on the teacher to provide all the "right" answers in the end. Some pupils whom I interviewed complained there was too much discussion and they preferred notes! His next cycle, therefore, involved students in setting their own questions and finding the answers. Similar analysis of later lessons showed he became much more open, but that he never again asked so many high-level questions—a problem he continued to wrestle with.

These are just a few examples of how classroom data can be gathered and analyzed in many different ways. Such methods provide relatively objective evidence of some aspects of the teaching-learning process. However, it is important not to lose sight of the less tangible but even more important aspects of classroom life, such as relationships, which cannot be measured in this way. For useful discussions of methods, see Hopkins (1985), Bassey (1986), Altrichter et al. (1993).

Going Public

The original plan had been to write a prescriptive handbook on "How to Teach Development Studies." By April, the team felt that while they had come to no conclusions about "correct methods" they had learned a great deal about improving their own teaching in their own classrooms. So they decided to write about their experiences in order to encourage others to follow a similar process of action research (Stuart, 1985). Their conclusions took the form of further propositions for other teachers to test out, such as:

> Students have the potential ability for using higher order cognitive skills; this can be developed by setting higher level questions that challenge and stretch them and by teaching them ways of tackling such questions.
>
> If students lack the necessary skills for active and independent learning, teachers need to provide training in such skills as discussion, taking notes, formulating research questions or planning and writing essays.

Comparing these with the original four guiding propositions it is clear that these now focus on the teacher rather than the student. One of the most interesting aspects of the whole study was the way that the teachers changed: from looking at how to remedy what they saw as the faults of the students, they had shifted towards analyzing their own teaching and finding ways in which they could work more effectively with students to enable them to fulfill their potential. In the process they had greatly extended their own repertoires of teaching methods, they had clarified their own conceptions of good teaching, and had begun developing "personal theories" about how to implement them. This demonstrates clearly the potential of action research for the professional development of teachers.

The next two case studies take this theme further. First Mahlape Morojele describes her own experiences as a member of the LARG team. She explains some of the work she did with her classes of student teachers, and then discusses some of the barriers she faced. She postulates how these may have their roots in the culture both of the college and of the wider society.

Then Pulane Lefoka describes her involvement with a further phase of action research, which took place in Lesotho primary schools. She focuses on ways of working with teachers who had had little or no tertiary education, and of helping them to become more reflective about their work. Her account illustrates the potentials of the approach for teacher development, but also shows clearly the amount of support needed.

Case Study 2: Reflecting on the Practice of Educating Teachers:
Mahlape Morojele

At the time of the research I had just joined the staff of the National Teacher Training College (NTTC). My task was to teach the development studies component—both content and methods—of the Primary Teachers' Certificate course. There were 250 students, the basic entry level being Junior Certificate. Some were mature men and women with some teaching experience, while others came straight from secondary school.

The invitation to take part in action research came at a time when I was under tremendous personal pressure to perform not only equally but also better than my colleagues. I was the youngest staff member and I did not have the long teaching experience that some of my colleagues had, as I had taken up the post straight from University. I was concerned about several aspects of my students' performance and I saw this as an opportunity to evaluate my own practice, lest the students' failure to comprehend was due to my teaching.

Reconnaissance

The starting point for my research was the realization that student teachers seemed unable to answer satisfactorily questions that required higher order skills. For example, they transcribed material from library books without any understanding of the text. I wondered if their inability was a reflection of my teaching! Or were there other factors?

From the propositions formulated at the first team meeting, two seemed particularly appropriate to my situation:

• students show a lack of higher order skills such as comprehension, application, analysis and synthesis.
• students believe that knowledge is closed or fixed; it is a thing which they are given, rather than an exploration in which they can take part.

First Cycle

I embarked on the first cycle of action research by exploring these assumptions. I collected data by observation, informal feedback, and analysis of student scripts, while the consultant interviewed some of the students. We audiotaped some lectures and samples of student discussion.

I started off with the topic "the concept of development." Groups of students were given the description of a village to study, and asked to identify signs of development and of non-development. An analysis of the tapes showed that the articulate students tended to dominate the discussions, and others seemed content to agree with them. Though some students were clearly capable of raising challenging issues and sustaining discussion, in general the groups tried to reach a consensus without involving themselves in debate. Here is an extract to illustrate:

A	It is said there's one big supermarket which is owned by Jandrell. Do you think it is another sign of development?	*raises a question*
B	It's a sign of development. It shows some development.	*gives firm statement*
A	Oh ya	*which is accepted*
C	There is also one butchery	
D	Do I write it down under A?	*ready agreement*
C	Yes	
A	But wait a minute, about the butchery; you're not sure how big this village is and we don't know how many it serves. It may be they need 4 or 5.	*attempts further analysis*
C	And how healthy it is.	*a new idea*
D	We have not talked about the supermarket. Even the clinic, there's one health clinic (inaudible).	*tries to extend discussion*
A	So which means we put butchery under signs of development.	*closes off discussion*

It became clear to me that putting students into groups was not enough; they needed knowledge of discussion skills.

I set up a bulletin board and asked students to bring to class newspaper cuttings and pictures that had relevance to development. I hoped to encourage them to be aware and develop an interest in what was happening around them. But the response was very poor. Only a few individuals brought pictures and there were no newspaper cuttings whatever, even though the library received newspapers on a daily basis. Why was there such a lack of initiative to look beyond the classroom? This seemed to support my assumption that students felt learning could take place only within the confines of the classroom and that they saw the teacher as the only provider of credible knowledge.

On the other hand, it had become evident from the discussions, and also from their written answers, that some student teachers showed the potential for using cognitive skills, namely separating issues, identifying cause-effect links, showing the interrelationships of variables, identifying problems, suggesting solutions, implementing and evaluating the actions. But why were they not applying these skills? Was it because their education—or perhaps cultural norms—had not encouraged them to question and analyze? I was indeed puzzled but also excited!

Reflection and Replanning

From this exploratory cycle I was able to identify areas for following up. In the second cycle the main focus was to try to create an environment conducive to independent and participatory learning that would tap the cognitive skills student teachers seemed to possess. I formulated the following hypotheses:

1.   Students will understand better if they participate fully in class, so lessons should be organized in such a way that they encourage active student participation.

2.   Students need to be both encouraged and challenged if they are to embark confidently on independent learning, so the teacher must choose methods which facilitate this.

3.   Independent learning and the development of cognitive skills can also be fostered by use of actively challenging teaching aids.

4.   An over-structured learning environment can limit the scope of understanding of the students, so the structures should be progressively reduced.

5.   Students expect tests to test recall of factual knowledge, so methods of testing should be modified to test understanding.

Second Cycle

I began experimenting with a number of teaching and learning activities designed to test these ideas. Quizzes on the bulletin board became a regular affair. No prior warning was given. The questions were mixed, some being simple recall questions while others required analytical skills. This exercise not only encouraged student teachers to read newspaper cuttings but also stimulated them to bring interesting pictures and articles.

I prepared lessons on discussion as a skill and also as a teaching method. As a follow-up, volunteers were asked to demonstrate a discussion on the topic: "What would happen if South African mines were closed down and Basotho men sent home? Discuss the good and bad effects." (There was a miners' strike at the time.)

This discussion showed that they were aware of the issues currently being raised in the media. The tape demonstrates that participants were able to put forward arguments, support them with evidence and sustain dialogue in ways that were more thoughtful and more open-ended than I had ever heard before. Asked to comment afterwards, students made pertinent and constructive points, showing they were beginning to open up and confidently critique their own actions. Some participants, however, claimed they could not express themselves fluently in English, highlighting one of the difficulties of learning in a second language.

To involve them more actively, I tried to vary my teaching methods as much as possible. For example, when teaching about "the family," I used role play and exercises based on family trees. For the topic "human needs" I presented them with pictures from other countries and asked them, in groups, to analyze the kind of life led by the people depicted, which they did well. Using another short case-study as stimulus, I asked them to explore, in pairs, the different elements of development studies—geographic, social, historical, political and economic—and their interrelationships. I was encouraged that they could produce their own analyses instead of waiting for mine.

But it was clear there was a long way to go. Although I could see their capacity for higher order skills the students themselves were still not quite confident with "why," "compare and contrast" and "critically analyze" questions, especially when asked to write their answers. Interviewed by the consultant, they claimed that such questions were "too high for their standard." Could it be because they were not articulate in English? Could it be because it was unusual for them to ask and answer such questions? They still showed a lot of dependency on the teacher; they insisted I dictate notes, and they still wanted to be given conclusions. The invitation to critique my lesson was always met with ambivalence. It was evident that a lot of work was needed in order to foster self-confidence and independent learning.

Reflections and Conclusions

Reflecting on the experience, I concluded that in demanding that students use higher order skills and in particular in encouraging them to see knowledge in a new, more open way, we were actually challenging widespread attitudes that permeate the educational and social systems; it was this that led to the seemingly oppositional behavior of the students.

Student teachers have been socialized into a system that views the teacher as the guardian of knowledge. Students fail to recognize their potential in the construction of knowledge and therefore cannot contribute toward reshaping it for themselves. Their role is to receive knowledge and thus it is not their place to critique my lesson. Their ambivalence can be seen as a form of resistance to the new culture.

The ambivalence is legitimized by the educational structure that has defined and given meaning to tutor-student teacher relationships. I too was not immune from this experience; there were times during our meetings with the consultant (who had been my tutor) when I expected her to tell me how to proceed in the next cycle. In essence I was unwittingly displaying toward her the same kind of oppositional behavior that my students were showing toward me. Yet I was unaware of my reluctance to relinquish the usual patterns of behavior and to venture into the unknown.

This phenomenon may also partly explain why my attempts to involve my colleagues in action research were futile! It became difficult to penetrate the walls of restricted professionalism that some of my colleagues had built around themselves under the pretext of being experts in their own areas of specialization. Some of them were aware of what action research entailed and how it might help educational development and yet it seemed difficult for them to transcend that level of awareness and engage in meaningful action that was geared toward transformation. To them, it appeared, action research was an additional load and thus dismissed as time-consuming.

One should not lose sight of the fact that action research has its own demands which may conflict with the day-to-day operations of the college. For example, with teaching and learning that is examination-oriented, tutors may not have sufficient time to follow up on issues identified in various cycles. Also, there were indications among my colleagues of general negativity to change, exemplified by a claim that tutors have always reflected on their work and as such action research does not offer anything new. The key issue, however, is consciously to reflect and systematize action research so that it becomes an integral part of practice.

Action research requires teachers to become researchers into their own perceptions, practices and the workplace. It requires teachers to reflect in practice and on practice (Schon, 1983, 1987). The implication that participants are capable of restructuring and transforming positively their own realities holds promise for my own professional development. Action research seeks not only to change realities but also to change the participants in the process. Furthermore, action research represents a confrontation and challenge to the hegemonic forces that prevail in the education system. To me the biggest challenge is to win over those teacher educators who seem not to have the confidence to take the plunge.

Case Study 3: Developing Instructional Self-Reflection Skills among Primary Teachers: Pulane Lefoka

Janet Stuart's project with the Lesotho Action Research Group (LARG) became Phase 1 of a series of projects conducted through the Institute of Education at the National University of Lesotho (NUL). Phase 2 was a survey of "Teaching-Learning Strategies in Lesotho Primary School Classrooms." This had no action research component, but during data collection many teachers expressed the need for feedback: they wanted the observers to tell them whether they performed according to the expected standards and, if not, to help them improve. This stimulated Phase 3. Charles Chabane, who had acted as assistant consultant on the LARG project, noted the teachers' requests, and drew up a project to introduce such teachers to simple action research techniques. Thus in 1990 the Institute of Education, with support from the Ministry of Education, mounted a project to train teachers in self-reflection skills.

The project aims included:

- to train teachers in techniques of instructional self-reflection and appraisal
- to introduce teachers to methods of self-improvement in their instructional activities

Although the project title did not bear the words "action research," this was the term used throughout the training process. It was intended to incorporate: instructional self-reflection, teacher empowerment, systematic classroom inquiry, and collaborative practice. The rationale was indeed to train teachers to improve classroom instruction using action research.

The project was able to draw on various forms of support from earlier projects. In particular, there was already a group of primary teachers known as District Resource Teachers (DRTs), whose role was to supervise teachers in multigrade schools. The Institute identified this group as potential consultants for action research; they had had an intensive training in areas such as counseling techniques and supervision of instruction. We ran an introductory workshop for them on action research and found them well able to take on this role.

Training

In sharp contrast to Janet Stuart's team of graduates, most primary school teachers in Lesotho do not have degrees and some of them do not hold even a teacher's certificate. Our training approach was heavily influenced by this fact: as well as a preliminary workshop for headteachers, we ran school-level mini-workshops, follow-up school visits, and an end-of-term workshop.

We would first explain action research, emphasizing that it is research done by teachers, in their own situation, and that it is intended to solve instructional problems and to improve students' learning. We would then introduce teachers to the action research spiral and to the steps to be followed in undertaking classroom action research. After we had explained the nature of hypotheses, the teachers carried out a practical exercise in small groups. They practiced the process by identifying a general idea, formulating a hypothesis, making a plan, and illustrating how they would execute the plan. Formulating the hypotheses proved to be the most complicated for the teachers to grasp.

As teachers engaged in this stage, we observed that they focused on students instead of on their own practice or on instructional problems. Typically, teachers would say "I have a student who . . ." or "My students cannot. . . ." It was obvious that they distanced themselves, avoiding focusing on personal and/or instructional problems. We tried to shift the emphasis onto self-reflection and self-evaluation in solving classroom problems.

We then introduced three alternatives "models" for carrying out action research. In the self-monitoring model, the teachers reflect individually on their own classroom actions, using tape-recorders. The clinical supervision model offers a carefully structured format for mutual discussion and focused observation with a colleague. Triangulation involves getting feedback from students as well as from colleagues.

Teachers clearly preferred the first to the last two; they showed lack of trust in their colleagues and fear of their weaknesses being publicly known. This confirmed that where poor relationships existed among staff members, it was difficult to use colleagues to help develop reflective practice.

In response to this problem, we developed a training module on communication skills to help teachers to collaborate and cooperate among themselves. The process of self-reflection has to be facilitated by a colleague. Through role-play teachers were shown how to develop "active listening skills," and we always observed an immediate change of attitude after this exercise.

The process of training ended with a word on documentation. Teachers were encouraged to keep diaries of their research projects. This would enable them to reflect on their experiences and above all to produce reports of their classroom research encounters. We hoped to motivate teachers to move a step forward by attempting to publish their research experiences—either in English or Sesotho—so they would be read by teachers all over the country.

Lessons Learned by the Consultants

We, as a team, also reflected on our practice as trainers. We learned from each other and from evaluation sessions. For example, we noticed that the type of example given during the "formulating a hypothesis" section strongly influenced the type of problems teachers gave. If an example was out of the education context, teachers in their small groups would come up with similar problems. Based on our reflections, we continued changing our strategies.

The workshop seating was always set out in a circular fashion. As the research team we avoided standing in front; sitting in the circle among the teachers created a relaxed atmosphere and brought teachers closer to the team. In this way we observed that the tension associated with academics from the university was eliminated.

The evaluation seminar showed teachers needed reference materials (Chabane 1991a). The handouts distributed in our presentations were not sufficient. We learned that literature was of primary importance in supporting the teachers, so in 1992 I compiled some materials written by members of the team into a handbook (Lefoka, 1992).

Reports of Teachers' Work

Although there was some reluctance to write, with persuasion over a hundred teachers did produce short reports about how they engaged in reflective practice. All of them described some problem they had identified and how they had tried out solutions, usually by experimenting with new teaching approaches or adapting their classroom management styles. These reports were edited and published in two volumes under the title *The Teacher Researcher* (Chabane, 1991b, 1992).

Examining the *Teacher Researcher* volumes closely, it becomes obvious that these reports are best understood as a form of storytelling. It would be difficult to say they illustrate systematic research, data collection and analysis. But this had not been the purpose of the project. The intention had been to train teachers in self-reflective skills and to encourage them to record their experiences in very simple language.

From their reports, we noted that teachers started to collaborate with each other. The fear of being observed was gradually disappearing. For example, Mrs. Seithleko reported with confidence that her classroom was no more a private territory that would have to be specially prepared whenever the education officer was to visit. Discussions in follow-up workshops suggested that this was the new trend. In other words, being observed and observing one another brought about confidence in teachers and freedom to discuss, share problems and document actions. In fact, over twenty teachers reported being observed by colleagues or DRTs and thirty more mentioned talking about the problems with other staff.

Furthermore, some reports showed that teachers felt freer to take risks and to experiment. Miss Montsi, for example, was concerned about the way she conducted her radio English lessons. Here is an extract from her report:

> Planning: My problem was conducting radio lessons effectively in Standard 3. I hypothesised that:

a. I did not give the learners a chance to practise first;

b. the pace of the radio lesson is too fast for the pupils, and thus they cannot cope with reading those long sentences;

c. the terminology was above the standard of the pupils.

Action: I consulted my District Resource Teacher, who then supervised me clinically, after which I made my pupils practise the sentences written on the board before the broadcast. I then prepared the material needed before the broadcast and . . . clarified words which appeared new to the pupils. During the lesson follow-up, I emphasised special problems such as pronunciation, meaning in context, etc.

Reflection: These days my pupils become actively involved in radio lessons . . . [and] enjoy them. (Chabane, 1991b: 57)

Teacher empowerment was also emphasized in the workshops. It became obvious from the teachers' reports that they were also beginning to challenge theories and practices they had had to accept in the past. Mrs. Mothae reported that although the Curriculum Centre insisted in their staff development workshops that one particular method of teaching was better than the other, she continued to merge successfully the "phonic" and "look and say" methods in teaching Sesotho.

From such reports, and from the feedback at the evaluation seminars, the team was convinced that progress was made and that the idea was being received positively. However, at the end of the first year, two particular weaknesses were noted (Chabane, 1991a). Teachers were not yet explicit enough in the action/observation part of the process. Chabane argued that the teacher researchers' reports needed to be more detailed and analytical so that the conclusion "the situation has improved" (common in the teachers' stories) should be based on what has been reliably observed during a carefully planned action. Secondly, the reports ended at the reflection stage instead of continuing into a revised plan of action.

Conventional researchers would argue that these reports are not research reports. They could show that there is little evidence of "research" in the sense of systematic and rigorous collection and analysis of data. About a quarter posed their research questions explicitly or mentioned hypotheses, but there was hardly any mention of collecting data in ways other than observation (their own or colleagues') though reports often implied that they used students' responses as a yardstick to measure improved achievement (Sebatane, 1994). Only six used a "stage" or "steps" framework in their reports and about ten analyzed the results or suggested reasons for their conclusions.

It is very important at this juncture to note that the project followed very simple steps in introducing teachers to this idea. The approach was intended for the primary school teachers with their diverse qualifications. It was a form of in-service training they had indirectly initiated. To this end we felt the project was successful, and indeed, all the evidence shows that given more time and more support they could have gone further in the direction of research.

Conclusion

The task of training the Lesotho primary school teacher in reflective skills was very challenging. Working with them required patience, understanding and being cautious. It enabled us to use appropriately simple approaches in dealing with this level of teacher. The fascinating part was the enthusiasm with which the teachers left the workshops. We concluded that action research is teacher-friendly; teachers catch it easily, almost intuitively. It is a good way of preparing for meaningful in-service, since they will be more aware of what they need (Chabane, 1991a). We feel the *Teacher Researcher* is an achievement and a starting point for engaging teachers to talk about their experiences with other teachers.

SOME CONCLUDING REFLECTIONS

The experiences related above show something of how action research can be used both to generate new understandings and to improve professional practice at different levels and in various ways. I want now to summarize some of the main benefits, look at some of the problems and discuss some of the emerging issues.

Our conclusions from both the Lesotho Action Research Group (LARG) Project and the Primary Teachers' Project were that action research is an excellent form of professional development. In particular, it helps teachers to extend their repertoires of pedagogic methods, evaluate their own teaching, clarify their values and begin to theorize about their own practice.

For example, although they had come to no absolute conclusions about the "best" methods for teaching development studies, the LARG team felt convinced that the student-centered, interactive learning methods did produce the kind of learning they were looking for and that these methods were appropriate for Lesotho classrooms. However, they had also discovered that students had first to be taught how to learn from such methods and to be assured that these would also enable them to pass exams.

An example of value clarification is the way the team thrashed out and refined the concept they called "open and independent learning" and how to apply it in class. As Lomile said long afterwards: "We knew vaguely from our training what we wanted our classrooms to be like, but we didn't know how to get there." At the end, they had a much clearer idea and had begun to develop their own personal theories about how to achieve their goals.

The Primary Teachers' Project showed how even teachers with little experience of research could use the method to try out new ways of teaching and to gain confidence in their own judgment. They also practiced new ways of cooperation, thus lessening their professional isolation and mistrust. An important result was that both groups published accounts for others to read, critique and use. To this extent, reflection had progressed into research (Stuart, 1991).

Constraints Encountered

There are, however, constraints: personal, school-level and system-wide. Although teachers involved in all these projects found action research stimulating, exciting and intrinsically rewarding, they also found it very hard work. In sum:

> A teacher who undertakes action research has to be patient, dedicated and full of perseverance . . . to keep a diary, monitor one's teaching, analyse progress or problems, admit one's mistakes, change strategy when things go wrong. . . . The most difficult part and the most basic is that many teachers still believe that they are the centre of all learning and they do not have the confidence or courage to evaluate themselves. (Lomile Putsoa, personal communication)

Some of these problems may stem from poor preparation in the training institutions. The word "research" may scare them off, as something they can't do. So a first step is to build confidence by whatever means it takes: training workshops, in-school support, positive feedback.

Within the school, there are many constraints. Particularly in developing countries, where most schooling is exam-oriented, teachers are under pressure to cover the syllabus and to prepare students for exams. They may be reluctant to set aside time for experimentation. They would rather minimize risk by staying with known methods. Students may well reinforce this by demanding to be taught in familiar ways. As Mahlape Morojele shows, this happens even at college level. It is most practical to start in small ways and within clearly defined areas or levels of the curriculum.

The attitudes of other colleagues and the headteacher may be crucial. The Primary Teachers' Project team made a point of running workshops for headteachers to ensure their support and the DRTs attempted to involve the whole staff of each school in the activities, although with only partial success. In the LARG project, although heads were supportive, no other teachers became involved in spite of the team's efforts and college tutors were similarly reluctant to join in.

Resources are also important. Although action research can be done on a small scale, audio- or videotapes are very useful in collecting data and these may be too expensive. As has been repeatedly stressed, communications, team meetings and workshops are crucial, so transport and accommodation must be paid for. If publication is envisaged, access to desktop publishing is needed.

As stated earlier, the cultural and professional milieu must also be supportive if teachers are to take on an extended professional role (Eraut, 1994). In a bureaucratic system, inspectors and education officers must be willing to allow teachers freedom to experiment and in some highly centralized systems this may be problematic. Indeed, the very idea of critical inquiry may be opposed by the wider culture. Actors may then have to choose: to move into an emancipatory mode and set out to challenge the whole structure, with political consequences, or to confine themselves to small-scale work which does not threaten accepted norms.

Personal, Social and Professional Support

As the foregoing accounts show, action research demands a great deal from its practitioners and the social context and support structures are crucial for its success. Pulane Lefoka highlights the need for training in communication skills: the importance of active listening between colleagues so that peer observation becomes constructive not judgmental. In the LARG project we found the team meetings enormously valuable in many ways: they gave mutual support and encouragement; the sharing of reflections allowed new insights to emerge; in several instances teachers picked up ideas from each other and adapted them for further use.

The role played by the consultant is an important one. The literature shows that it is rare for individual teachers to carry out action research on their own. Ideally, the consultant is not a director or tutor, still less one's line manager—experience suggests headteachers find it hard to carry out this role appropriately—but a stimulator, catalyst, or "critical friend." But at the same time action research cannot be imposed; the teachers must be partners; they must own the ideas as well as the action. Pulane Lefoka's circular seating is symbolically very important. In reflecting on my own practice, I developed the following aspects of the role: the *facilitator* (supporting, counseling), the *commentator* (analyzing, challenging), a *resource* for information and expertise, and an *organizer*, dealing with timing, money, documents, and generally keeping the show on the road.

Again, there is no one right way: each team has to develop its appropriate methods through monitoring its own practice. There is a good example from Slovenia in an article called: "Torn between action and reflection: some dilemmas of 'pedagogical support persons' in ENSI" (Pozarnik, 1993) which discusses how the consultants, as they themselves became more confident, became both less directive and more helpful to the teachers. Good action research consultants will start where the teachers are, but encourage them to become increasingly autonomous as soon as they have developed skill and confidence.

Potential Uses

Action research may well be teacher-friendly, and good teachers welcome the opportunity to reflect on practice with the help of supportive colleagues. But to keep this up systematically, to work through all stages of several cycles, to write all this down clearly, perhaps in your second language, or in a culture that traditionally emphasized oral rather than written communication, demands great dedication and/or the hope of extrinsic rewards. That is why I think that the most useful context for action research is the in-service course. In return for the hard analytical work and the written report, teachers can expect an award, promotion or pay raise. Other possibilities include funded research projects which incorporate teachers as participants, such as the Rockefeller Primary Science Project in Zimbabwe (Hodzi, 1994).

Action research does demand certain qualities. People who want neat findings and conclusive answers are unlikely to be happy doing action research. It is more likely to appeal to those who enjoy questioning, who are themselves open to reflection and to constructive critique and who are eager to revise yesterday's understanding in the light of today's new insights. By the same token, the education systems must, at the very least, be willing to allow this to take place. The potential benefits are, however, enormous—for teachers and lecturers, for their students, and eventually for the whole system.

REFERENCES

Altrichter, H., Posch, P. and Somekh, B. (1993) *Teachers Investigate their Work.* London: Routledge.

Bassey, M. (1983) "Pedagogic Research into Singularities: Case Studies, Probes and Curriculum Innovations," *Oxford Review of Education,* 9:109–21.

————. (1986) "Does Action Research Require Sophisticated Research Methods?" In D. Hustler, T. Cassidy and T. Cuff (eds.) *Action Research in Classrooms and Schools*. London: Allen and Unwin.

Carr, W. and Kemmis, S. (1986) *Becoming Critical: Knowing through Action Research*. Lewes: Falmer.

Chabane, C. (1991a) "Development of Self-Reflection Skills among Primary School Teachers in Lesotho: a narrative project report." Roma: Institute of Education, National University of Lesotho (mimeo).

Chabane, C. (1991b) (ed.) *The Teacher Researcher Vol. 1*. Roma: Institute of Education, National University of Lesotho.

————. (1992) (ed.) *The Teacher Researcher Vol. 2*. Roma: Institute of Education, National University of Lesotho.

Corey, B. M. (1953) *Action Research to Improve School Practices*. New York: Bureau of Publications, Teachers' College, Columbia University Press.

Davidoff, S. and Van den Berg, O. (1990) *Changing Your Teaching: The Challenge of the Classroom*. Pietermaritzberg: Centaur Publications.

Elliott, J. (1991) *Action Research for Educational Change*. Buckingham: Open University Press.

Eraut, M. R. (1994) *Developing Professional Knowledge and Competence*. London: Falmer.

Guthrie, G. (1981) "Teaching Styles." In P. Smith and S.G. Weeks (eds.) *Teachers and Teaching*. Port Moresby: University of Papua New Guinea.

Hodzi, R.A. (1994) "Improving Classroom Practice in Primary Science using Action Research," *Zimbabwe Journal of Educational Research*, 6 (1):55–68.

Hopkins, D. (1985) *A Teachers' Guide to Classroom Research*. Milton Keynes: Open University Press.

Kemmis, S. and McTaggart, R. (1981) *The Action Research Planner*. Victoria: Deakin University Press.

Lefoka, P. (1992) *Classroom Action Research: Materials for use by teachers in developing self-reflection and appraisal skills*. Roma: Institute of Education, National University of Lesotho.

Lewin, K. (1946) "Action Research and Minority Problems," *Journal of Social Issues*, 2 (4):34–46.

McNiff, J. (1988) *Action Research: Principles and Practice*. London: Macmillan.

Moegiadi, Tangyong, A. F. and Gardner, R. (1994) "The Active Learning through Professional Support (ALPS) Project in Indonesia." In A. Little, W. Hoppers and R. Sardner (eds.) *Beyond Jomtien: Implementing Primary Education For All*. London: Macmillan.

Pozarnik, B. M. (1993) "Torn between Action and Reflection: Some Dilemmas of 'Pedagogical Support Persons' in ENSI," *Educational Action Research*, 1 (3):469–86.

Schon, D. A. (1983) *The Reflective Practitioner*. London: Temple Smith.

————. (1987) *Educating the Reflective Practitioner*. London: Jossey Bass.

Sebatane, E. M. (1994) "Enhancement of Teacher Capacities and Capabilities in School-based Assessment: the Lesotho Experience," *Assessment in Education*, 1 (2):223–34.

Stenhouse, L. (1975) *An Introduction to Curriculum Research and Development*. London: Heinemann Education.

Stuart, J. S. (1991) "Classroom Action Research in Africa: A Case Study of Teachers in Lesotho." In K.M. Lewin with J.S. Stuart (eds.) *Educational Innovation in Developing Countries: Case-Studies of Changemakers*. London: Macmillan.

————. (ed.) (1985) *Case-studies in Development Studies Teaching in Lesotho Classrooms*. Roma: Institute of Southern African Studies, National University of Lesotho.

Task Force (1982) *The Education Sector Survey: Report of the Task Force.* Maseru: Government Printer.

Walker, M. (1993) "Developing the Theory and Practice of Action Research: A South African Case," *Educational Action Research*, 1 (1):95–109.

———. (1995) "Context, Critique and Change: Doing Action Research in South Africa" *Educational Action Research*, 3 (1):9–27.

Winter, R. (1989) *Learning from Experience: Principles and Practice in Action Research.* London: Falmer.

Wright, C. A. H. (1988) "Collaborative Action Research in Education (CARE)—Reflections on an Innovative Paradigm," *International Journal of Educational Development*, 8 (4):279–92.

8 DILEMMAS OF INSIDER RESEARCH IN A SMALL-COUNTRY SETTING

TERTIARY EDUCATION IN ST. LUCIA

Pearlette Louisy

INTRODUCTION

When I first set out to conduct a case study of the Sir Arthur Lewis Community College, I was responding to a recommendation emanating from a Pan Commonwealth meeting on post-secondary colleges in the small states of the Commonwealth that was held in St. Lucia in 1988 by the Human Resource Development Group of the Commonwealth Secretariat. I was then associated with the host institution in an administrative capacity, and was therefore a member of the group that was enjoined to prepare a practical handbook on the establishment and development of multipurpose colleges. This would be based on the findings of the meeting and include case studies drawn from the participating countries (Commonwealth Secretariat, 1988). As a national researcher, therefore, the main issue seemed to me to be one of raising questions about familiar topics. I had envisaged a study that would draw upon the views, perceptions and perspectives of those persons who were intimately involved in the planning, establishment and development of the national tertiary institution. Inquiry would be structured around themes or focus areas, along the same lines as those used by participants at the Commonwealth meeting. This would provide a common framework for future comparative analyses across the range of small states, should the call for case studies of national colleges be taken up by other researchers.

The initial decision to adopt a predominantly qualitative research approach was influenced by what I considered to be a specific concern of the study: documenting the perceptions held by educational planners in small nation-states about the "form, style and extent" of tertiary education provision in their countries; the judgments they make; the options they choose; and the contextual circumstances influencing decisions they take. I was persuaded that the insights gained from an appreciation of these perceptions could contribute to the more realistic formulation of policy options not only for the case under review but for other small states as well. These insights, together with those derived from personal experience and from a reading of the international literature on small states provided the conceptual framework for the study. The particular methodological issues that surfaced from this blend of research strategy and small-state context, and the dilemmas they presented to an inside researcher form the basis of this chapter.

INSIDER RESEARCH

Perhaps the first dilemma that needed to be resolved once I became exposed to the international literature on qualitative research methodology was my status as an inside researcher and the debate that centered around the advantages and disadvantages of researching one's own community. I had compelling philosophical reasons for becoming more involved in local research, having "collaborated" before on research projects designed and executed by outside researchers. There was strong support in the literature for my philosophical position. Crocombe (1987:133), for example, argues forcefully that since "a grossly disproportionate share of the studies of islands and island communities has been done from external perceptions" it is time for more involvement from members of the researched community itself. It has been recognized that indigenous researchers from their distinctive perspective are in a strong position to contribute to both the intellectual debate and to the process of development within their own countries without falling prey to the dangers of international transfer (Crossley, 1990). But there are equally strong concerns expressed about objectivity, impartiality and bias associated with working in a familiar setting.

The dilemma I faced is best expressed in the juxtaposition of the different approaches that the outsider and the indigenous researcher are perceived to bring to ethnographic inquiry. On the one hand, the outsider attempts to make the strange familiar, while, on the other, the local researcher is asked to treat the familiar as strange. Many writers (Delamont, 1981; Spindler and Spindler, 1982; among others) have commented on the difficulty of conducting qualitative research in familiar settings, arguing that it is easy to take for granted everyday issues and practices that require analysis from a more objective and disinterested standpoint. Outsiders as ethnographers are cautioned against "going native," so great is the concern for the impartiality which it is assumed only cultural distance can ensure. Others argue, however, that the insights that can be gained from such familiarity can far outweigh the risks. Stephenson and Greer (1981:130) in their discussion of the issues and problems confronting ethnographers working within their own culture, and of the advantages and disadvantages of knowing the community and the setting in advance, contend:

> We do not find that any of the principles underlying the problems and advantages identified are any different from those underlying problems encountered by ethnographers working in non-familiar cultures. Our problems were not different in kind, though they may have differed in intensity. Beneath their particular expressions in the familiar culture context lurk our devil-friends bias, oversimplification, prior judgement, and the human inability to separate observation from feeling. Personally, we are willing to take the risks of familiarity in order to gain understanding.

Stenhouse (1979) also sees merit in being an inside researcher, arguing that its strength lies in the critical perspective which it affords the researcher, one which is inseparably linked to the cultural location of the observer. If, as he argues, "all description derives its form from falling into place within a perspective whose structural principle is inseparable from the point of view of the observer" (1979:8), then a representation of practice seen and described through the critical objective perspective of the insider should provide a truer reconstruction of reality than one seen through the "untutored" eyes of the stranger.

The qualitative researcher's task has been described as balancing "an external, objective report with an insight into the subject's own view of the world" (Stephenson and Greer, 1981:123). When the researcher's insight and the subject's own view of the reality being researched spring from a common cultural and social experience, the findings and the conclusions derived therefrom can be stimulating and powerful. There could of course be some element of bias in the recording and reporting by an insider researcher, but no social activity is completely value-free. Our cultural bias, and the preoccupations of our time and place, King (1973) argues, are extended into our observations as so much prejudice. Thus the insider's familiarity with the meanings attached to words and acts of the researched community can prevent misunderstandings. This familiarity, Lewin (1990:211) notes, is likely to make the insider more sensitive to their perspectives. However, his counter argument that all researchers are in a sense outsiders since they have "an agenda which is over and above any participation which they have in the activities that are the subject of their research," throws the proverbial cat among the pigeons. The temporary outsider status of the insider-researcher would need to be recognized and accepted by the research subjects, if the researched activity was not to be compromised.

The debate remains inconclusive. Lewin (1990) concludes that there is no best position to be in. To him, the advantages of naive inquiry open to an outsider have to be balanced against the benefits of collegial suffering of common problems that can be expressed by an insider. In my own study (Louisy, 1993), I addressed concerns regarding objectivity and impartiality by adopting procedures for the collection of data that required minimal speculation on my part. Concentration on in-depth interviews and documentary analysis as methods of inquiry seemed to me to lessen the probability of bias associated with insider research. Other problematic areas, both of a methodological and ethical nature, would surface later in the field. While some of these are general in nature and would have universal application, many were directly related to the specific issue of conducting research in a small country setting.

THE WORLD OF THE SMALL STATE

In order to understand and appreciate the distinctive challenges of conducting qualitative, insider research in a small-state setting, one first needs to examine the particular characteristics of the small state. The world of the small state has generally been described in the international literature as being relatively constrained, remote and dependent. Benedict (1967), for example, portrays the social world of the small state as characterized by particularistic role relationships in that people in these small societies grow up within interdependent networks where the same individuals figure many times. Social relationships are therefore multiplex: there is a coincidence or overlapping of roles, in which individuals are tied to each other in many ways. Relationships in small societies, he argues, seldom concentrate on single acts or specific functions but tend to be diffuse and longlasting. Moreover the small size of the social field and an awareness of the vulnerability of small states encourage what Lowenthal (1987) describes as "managed intimacy" in which people learn to get along, whether they like it or not, with people they will know in many contexts throughout their whole lives. Such a society is therefore highly personalized (Bray, 1991)—a situation which I found to have significant implications, particularly for the issues of anonymity and confidentiality in the research exercise.

The small size of the pool from which people can be drawn to fill middle-level and top positions in administration means that such officials simply have to be multifunctional (Farrugia and Attard, 1989; Bray, 1991). Thus, with the switching of roles can come a shifting of perspective, a change in the locus of control, and perhaps even a conflict of interest. The insider-researcher who is familiar with the subjects' multiplicity of roles needs constantly to avoid "second-guessing" them, anticipating role shifts and perspectives. The outside researcher on the other hand is more inclined to accept views at face value. In the small-state setting, such multifunctional officials may find it difficult to divorce one role from the next, when their perspectives on certain issues are sought.

Another particular characteristic of small states is their transparency or visibility that exercises a significant influence over any social interaction. Making this point in respect of the education system, Brock and Parker (1985:54) observe:

> communities comprising small island states . . . have a visibility in their education due to the close proximity of officials, leaders and institutions. . . . Such visibility may be associated with notions of relevance and adaptability which are able to inform networks of communication and decision-making. In short, they are open to inspection and influence by their surrounding community to a much greater extent than in larger countries.

Bray (1991) presents the flip side of that coin. He argues that, on the one hand, systems in small states can be tremendously responsive laboratories in which decision-makers can have a strong personal influence over the whole system. On the other hand, however, education administrators and practitioners can be unduly cautious and conservative, knowing that they have a very small margin for error, and that if their actions go wrong they will have nowhere to hide. These features of small-state societies can affect the research process as much as they do everything else. To the extent that this represents both an asset and a weakness, it does present a dilemma to the researcher. To an inside researcher with both a "history and a future of colleagueship and collaboration" (Powney and Watts, 1987:184) with members of the researched community, the dilemma is even more significant.

ETHICAL ISSUES IN QUALITATIVE RESEARCH

It has been recognized that the moral fitness of a decision or a course of action in social research varies with the research context, the research problem and the research methodology (Cassell, 1980; Burgess, 1984, 1989), notwithstanding the statements of ethical principles established by professional associations to regulate the conduct of their researchers. While these ethical principles recognize the obligation of the researcher to research subjects, research colleagues, other researchers and sponsors, as well as to scholarship and to citizenship, the core ethical problem is seen as acting in the context of two conflicting values:

> the pursuit of truth through scientific procedures and the maintenance of respect for the individuals whose lives are being lived, focally or peripherally, in the context of one's research project. (Smith, 1980:192)

Accordingly, discussion has tended to center around researchers' obligations to their research subjects, and on the following ethical issues.

1.   The balance to be maintained between the public's right to know and the individual's right to privacy. In this regard, researchers are cautioned on the need to be aware of the intrusive potential of some types of research and the need to minimize as much as possible the invasion of privacy that such research can cause.

2.   The practicality of "informed consent." How much should research subjects be told about the nature of the research project? Smith (1980) recommends that people should be given the opportunity to agree in full view of aims and purposes, problems and procedures and relevant information. Burgess (1984), on the other hand, argues that such detailed information would influence the behavior of those being researched and compromise the findings of the study.

3.   The maintenance of anonymity and confidentiality. To what extent is it possible to keep confidential the identities and records of research subjects in some types of qualitative research and in certain research settings? The problem associated with anonymity and confidentiality in the highly personalized society of small states discussed earlier is a special case in point. The generally accepted principle that all research work should be open to scrutiny and assessment by colleagues raises questions as to the amount and type of information to be released to allow for such scrutiny and yet remain within the limits of confidentiality requirements.

The recognition that there is a special dynamic created between the researcher and the researched, and between the researcher, the research, the research process and the research report, argues for the existence of no standard solutions to ethical dilemmas encountered. Qualitative field research calls for consultation, negotiation and compromise. To the inside researcher, ethical issues relating to obligations toward research subjects take on greater significance. In the section that follows, I will examine some of these issues, drawing on the problems encountered and the procedures and "solutions" adopted for my own small-scale case study of the only tertiary level institution in my home country of St. Lucia.

THE RESEARCH PROCESS: INSIDER RESEARCH IN A SMALL-COUNTRY CONTEXT

The design of a research project has been described as "the logical sequence that connects the empirical data to a study's initial research question and, ultimately to its conclusion" (Yin, 1989:28). It takes into account research processes as well as research methods, focusing on issues involved in starting research, gaining access, selecting informants, and the collecting, analyzing and reporting of data. Some of these key phases and processes are here examined in the light of my own experience as a field researcher in a familiar setting.

The research project to which I committed myself involved a critical examination of recent developments in tertiary education in St. Lucia. Research into these developments from an internal perspective was to my mind both timely and necessary. Yet local initiatives in tertiary education expansion had left small-country policy-makers out in the cold, since it was widely accepted by the international community that they should be concentrating their energies and their resources on the improvements of basic education. This then was one dilemma that needed to be resolved. Should I trust the "member's knowledge" (Schwartz and Jacobs, 1979) which I possessed and go against the international current? Would I be marginalizing St. Lucia and other small states even further by pursuing that line of inquiry? Indeed many of the dilemmas that I had to resolve sprang not from problems inherent in the research activity itself, but from difficulties encountered in attempting to follow prescribed or pre-existing models, conventions and orientations. The decision paid off as the study uncovered others in small states with similar preoccupations and perspectives.

THE RESEARCH CONTEXT

Case-study research is grounded in context. In order therefore to appreciate the significance of what may be considered well-worn issues raised in this chapter, it is instructive to examine the specific context within which the study reported here was conducted.

The literature on small states has been particularly careful to avoid generalities in its categorization of the increasing number of small national units which have emerged on the international scene. Thus one reads of small states, mini-states and micro-states, depending on whether their human resource base averages five million (Demas, 1965) or less than 250,000 (Shand, 1980). With a population of 145,000, St. Lucia's position in this typology leaves little room for debate. Moreover, its 238 square-mile surface area is characterized by mountain ranges fanning out from a central ridge which runs along the entire length of the island (twenty-seven miles long and fourteen miles wide, as the blackbird flies). Settlement clusters are therefore confined for the most part to the valleys and the coastline, with 53% of the total population concentrated in the urban and suburban areas of Castries, the capital city. Not only does this settlement pattern influence the location of services but brings into sharp focus the transparency and visibility with which these services have to be managed and administered, and the close proximity in which key officials live and work.

Notwithstanding its small size, St. Lucia is the second largest and the most densely peopled of the islands of the Organisation of Eastern Caribbean States (OECS). As home for the eight-member OECS headquarters and of its Education Reform Unit, which coordinates the implementation of regional strategies and policies, the positions of key officials are open to scrutiny in a way that those of their counterparts in larger countries would not be. The fact that they hold key positions both regionally and locally point to them as logical choices in a study which attempts to investigate the internal and external imperatives shaping the current pattern of tertiary education in the country. As far as the research process is concerned, the fact of their involvement at these levels makes the issue of anonymity that much more difficult to maintain.

In the area of tertiary education, St. Lucia holds key positions in the Association of Caribbean Tertiary Institutions (ACTI), a consortium committed to resolving issues related to program accreditation and articulation, and to dealing with matters relating to institutional development and program provision. As one of the twelve contributing and participating members of the regional University of the West Indies, it has a voice and voting rights on council, the institution's highest governing body. As the central secretariat of the OECS Education Reform Strategy Unit, it directs the harmonization and articulation of the regional initiative which embraces, among others, the decision that tertiary capacity is to be interpreted in sub-regional terms: a concept that calls for collaboration, dialogue and negotiation among similar small states with differing priorities, but with the same degree of transparency in the provision and management of these.

As the hub of tertiary educational development in the OECS, St. Lucia's main institution, the Sir Arthur Lewis Community College, was a natural research site for a study which aimed at examining the factors that influenced the expansion of the tertiary education sector in a small developing state. The current international debate concerning the wisdom of encouraging the proliferation of higher education institutions and the methods of containing "fiscally unsustainable enrollment growth and a sharp decline in quality" (World Bank, 1993:iv), and the issues of quality, access and efficiency in Caribbean education (World Bank, 1992), justified the focus.

The Sir Arthur Lewis Community College is a state-owned institution established by an act of Parliament in 1985 through the amalgamation of five previously autonomous institutions. Conceived as a multipurpose, multilevel institution, it offers a mix of certificate, diploma and degree-level programs in arts, science and general studies, teacher education and educational administration, technical education and management studies, nursing education and agriculture. Its programs are geared mainly to meeting the middle-level professional, managerial and technical needs of St. Lucia, but as one of the designated Centres of Specialisation in the sub-region, it also caters, in selected areas, for students from the OECS. In developing some of the tertiary education strategies, St. Lucia has sometimes had to devise controversial planning models that have placed it at the center of international attention. The need for research of this type which involved in-depth case studies of individual systems and institutions had already been recognized (see, for example, Brock, 1988). The eventual answers to the problems of educational provision in small states, it was argued, would most probably be extracted from the findings of indigenous researchers. Indeed, much of the information available on education in small states in the international literature had been culled from quantitative surveys, conducted by external agencies, from country profiles prepared by nationals at the request of external bodies, and from perspectives gained by external "parachute" consultants on short-term visits. A detailed case study of St. Lucia would be a first step in what Crossley and Vulliamy (1984) refer to as a methodological broadening of scope, which could provide a richer understanding of the processes involved in the planning and development of tertiary education and the various perceptions held.

At the heart of the case study of the Sir Arthur Lewis Community College lie the peculiarities of the small-state context. It has been noted that the establishment of post-secondary institutions in the small states of the Commonwealth is characterized by an invariably long period of gestation (Commonwealth Secretariat, 1988). In the case of the college this lasted for nine years, followed by a further seven years of active planning. The task of planning the establishment of the institution was entrusted to a succession of individuals and committees, whose membership included some of the very persons who subsequently were selected as key respondents in the later study. The lack of spare capacity in a small system, the multifunctional nature of the positions that key officials occupy resulted in some of the same individuals serving on all the committees in one capacity or another. While their membership provided the continuity that was needed to sustain the process, it had implications for the changing views and perspectives of these individuals, as the external environment and imperatives changed, and as their own grasp of the concepts matured and found expression.

The college was selected as the research site for the study because of its familiarity, its ease of access and its status in the region as a leader in moving toward viability and credibility. It had by then been able to some appreciable extent to face the challenges associated with tertiary education in small states—a small resource base, low levels of enrollment, problems of staff recruitment, limited institutional capacity and a potentially restrictive intellectual and professional environment, all issues attributed to the constraints of scale, isolation and dependence. The study of the college was meant to provide some insight into the following five main issues:

• What were the factors that provided the impetus for the expansion of the tertiary education sector in the country?
• How has St. Lucia dealt with the constraints of scale, isolation and dependence in the development of its tertiary sector?
• What internal and external imperatives are shaping the current pattern of tertiary provision in St. Lucia?
• How may the country and its national institution enhance tertiary education provision at the national, regional and international levels?

The differences noted earlier in the perspectives held by the international community regarding the expansion of tertiary education pointed to the need for greater attention to be given to the perceptions and judgments of national decision-makers. In the case study of the Sir Arthur Lewis Community College, particular efforts were made to document the perceptions of those who were directly involved in the planning of the institution, and those who are currently involved in its development and administration. The judgments they made, the options they chose, the contextual circumstances which influenced their decisions were of particular importance.

The research was planned as a case study in the qualitative research tradition. It was designed to document the factors and processes that led to the establishment of the Sir Arthur Lewis Community College, the factors and issues that continue to shape its development and the extent to which it has considered and adopted strategies discussed in the international literature on small states. It was to be of immediate and practical use, almost in the tradition of action research, as it was expected to make a contribution to our understanding of contemporary trends in the planning and management of tertiary education in small-country settings. I needed to portray the insiders' views of these educational issues, and to juxtapose these against the perceptions of the outsider. It was to be one step forward from earlier collaborative studies by metropolitan and indigenous researchers of the type undertaken by, for example, Bray and Fergus (1986) and Attwood and Bray (1989).

The design I used was based on one suggested by Yin (1989) for a single-site case study (see Figure 8.1). It outlined the operational procedures used to collect and analyze the data as well as the sequence of and the relationship between these procedures. The development of the research questions, the selection of the respondents and the decisions taken regarding methods of data collection and analysis are discussed in a later section in the account of my own personal experiences in the field.

However, in the light of my own position as an insider, particular attention was paid to the preparation of the fieldwork. Prior to entering the field, a preliminary interview agenda was drawn up to match interview respondents with the topics and issues (the research questions) to be investigated. The match was made on the basis of the respondents' special knowledge of the topic and the nature of their involvement with the college. These respondents were drawn from the Ministry of Education, members of the planning committees and task forces, members of the Board of Governors, the senior administrative staff of the college, representatives from the private sector and labor organizations, representatives of the regional university and the OECS. The questions centered around universal issues in the international debate on higher education as well as some of particular relevance to the region, namely:

- tertiary education policy planning
- access, quality and relevance in higher education
- institutional mission and purpose
- centralization and decentralization of tertiary provision
- financing of tertiary education
- cooperation and collaboration in tertiary education
- human resource development
- future direction of tertiary education
- tertiary education and the labor market
- the impact of smallness on the provision of tertiary education

These were questions that were first framed within the wider context of small nation states. It has been argued, however, that there are many significant commonalities that center on the economic, political and cultural vulnerability of small states and on the strengths that derive from the nature of

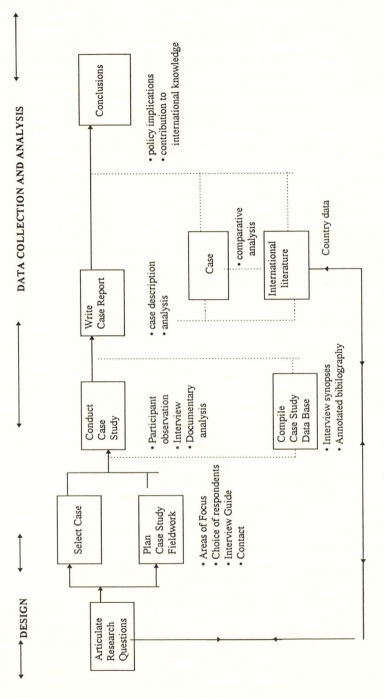

DATA COLLECTION AND ANALYSIS

DESIGN

Articulate Research Questions

Select Case

Plan Case Study Fieldwork
• Areas of Focus
• Choice of respondents
• Interview Guide
• Contact

Conduct Case Study
• Participant observation
• Interview
• Documentary analysis

Compile Case Study Data Base
• Interview synopses
• Annotated bibliography

Write Case Report
• case description
• analysis

Case
• comparative analysis

International literature

Country data

Conclusions
• policy implications
• contribution to international knowledge

Figure 8.1. The case-study research design. Adapted from Yin, R.K. (1989).

their societies (Packer, 1989). My own investigation, therefore, focused on these questions as they related to St. Lucia and to its tertiary institution.

The interviews with the respondents were tape-recorded. These were analyzed following a procedure recommended by several qualitative researchers (Bogdan and Biklen, 1992; Vulliamy and Webb, 1992; among others) that matched units of data to emerging coding categories. Although this type of "edited primary source" (Stenhouse, 1978:37) has been criticized as presenting only a filtered version of the conversations that actually take place, I found this reconstruction to be a useful record that could be conveniently accessed in case of any questions concerning the partiality of the inside researcher's analysis or interpretation. A record of the main documents consulted during the fieldwork period complemented the data generated by the interviews. Abstracts of these documents presented in the form of an annotated bibliography completed the case-study database. This record reflected to a large extent the multiple perspectives of the community of people involved in the development of the tertiary education sector in St. Lucia. The need for such a database had been strongly argued by earlier researchers for different reasons. They were concerned about the need to lay the foundations of a sound tradition of public scholarship (Stenhouse, 1978), to increase the reliability of the entire case study (Yin, 1989), or to upgrade the status of the qualitative case study from the category of "soft research." For an inside researcher, such a case study significantly enhances the transparency of the research process and can help clear the air on allegations of bias and partiality.

In the Field: A Personal Experience

I referred earlier to the small size of the pool from which one could draw people in a position to make informed comments on the issues being researched. To a large extent this dictated the type of sampling procedure used in my study. My familiarity with almost all of the possible respondents pointed to one logical choice—judgment sampling. In this procedure, informants are selected on the basis of the special contribution that the researcher believes they can make to the situation being studied. Burgess (1984), Hitchcock and Hughes (1989), Vulliamy et al., (1990) among others, emphasize the need to seek out people who possess knowledge about specialized interests and concerns in the social setting, people whom the researcher feels are integral to the scenes and situations being investigated. Such judgment sampling, however, demands that the researcher has a knowledge of the situation that is to be studied in order to evaluate the individual's position in a particular setting and their knowledge of that setting. Such insider knowledge presented me with both an advantage and a dilemma. I used this knowledge to draw up my preliminary interview guide which matched each respondent against the areas that I wanted to investigate. As I mentioned earlier, the match was made on the basis of the respondents' special knowledge of the particular issues being addressed, and the nature of their involvement with the institution or with the provision of tertiary education in the country. From this interview guide, a pool of questions was compiled for my personal use during the interview sessions. This shortened the time spent in the field by eliminating the hit-and-miss element associated with random selection from a pool that may or may not be familiar with the issue under investigation. There were times, however, when I wondered whether such a selection procedure would not shut out significant data, and thus invite criticism of subjectivity and partiality. But the personalized nature of the small society, its transparency and the multiplex role relationships of the key respondents combined to ensure that all significant interests were considered.

I entered the field therefore with an initial list of key respondents. By the end of the fieldwork, however, the number had grown appreciably. Not only did interviewees recommend others whom they knew had specialized knowledge of the issues being discussed, but most were aware of whom the others would have been. For the most part, they had all been involved at one time or other in the planning and development of the institution. This effectively ensured that the research subjects themselves, at least, were not likely to raise questions about issues of bias on my part. However, this did pose problems regarding the issue of the preservation of their confidentiality and anonymity. Commenting on this ethical issue in the context of educational research, Powney and Watts (1987:184) observe that

> the profession is relatively small and it is difficult even in large scale surveys, to disguise the identity of unique schools, colleges or even distinctive styles of educational management. Therefore it is possible that even individuals can be tracked down. Concealing the identity of informants becomes still more problematic in small-scale educational research.

Consider then the dilemma facing an inside researcher attempting to discharge the obligation of preserving anonymity and confidentiality in the context of small-scale educational research in a small-country setting, where the pool of people likely to be well informed about specialized issues is relatively small, and where such key figures are known to each other. I accepted that there was no possibility of all respondents remaining completely anonymous, though I adhered to the convention of using anonymized references to specific individuals in the report. To this end, each interview was identified by an alphanumeric code, (for example, BGV-T, 13.08.92), the first part of which identified the respondent, and the second, the date on which the interview took place. These interviews were recorded, edited, reconstructed and then prepared as the case-study database (Louisy, 1993).

The availability of a database, independent of the case-study report, may have increased the risk of betraying the confidentiality of what was said during the interviews. However, it was a risk that I was willing to take. The call had been made, justifiably so, by case-study advocates, Stenhouse (1978) and Yin (1989) among them, for a formal, independent database from which readers and other investigators could directly review the evidence collected. Such a case record, it was argued, could serve both as grounding for the researcher's own reportage and as resources for communal use by the community of educational researchers. My own reasons for committing myself to the study argued for such a record. Indeed there were times when I felt that I was perhaps more concerned about the issue of confidentiality than were some of my interviewees. Possibly because I was known to be an insider, some of them even speculated, during my interviews with them, on the positions that others would take on particular issues. In such a highly transparent society as St. Lucia, there is a very thin line between what is widely shared community knowledge and what is private business. Ethical obligations concerning anonymity and confidentiality take on very different dimensions in these contexts.

Prior involvement in the management of the institution being researched and personal knowledge of the key respondents facilitated entry into the field. However, this ease of access was counterbalanced by a narrowing of my options as far as choice of data-collecting methods was concerned. For I had decided that in order to minimize the incidence of bias that could be attributed to an inside researcher's familiarity with the setting, I would make limited use of observation so favored by qualitative researchers. My approach could therefore be best classified as "condensed fieldwork" described by Stenhouse (1982) and Vulliamy (in Vulliamy et al., 1990) as relying principally on tape-recorded interviews, the collection of documents and the limited use of observation. Such observation as took place, principally from my attendance at committee and planning meetings, was used primarily to augment, challenge or corroborate data that had been gathered in the interviews and from the documents.

Such triangulation, by taking different bearings on the issues being investigated, had the important advantage of pointing to gaps in the data which an insider could so easily have glossed over. For example, without the archival evidence in the files I could easily have missed the dissent over the name of the institution, a dissent that reflected a deep division on the part of the planners over the institution's mission and purpose. Many of the planners looked to an institution that would respond to the demand for local tertiary education created not by the expansion of the general academic streams of secondary schools, but by the silent cries of thousands of persons unable to function effectively in a modern world (Lewis et al., 1983:21). It was therefore to be an open comprehensive community college. But the Ministry of Education had reservations about the choice of the term "community college," and in a memorandum to the Cabinet of Ministers argued its point:

> The name does not take into consideration the institution's intention to offer university diploma programmes as well as part of the university degree course. Further it does not consider the possible long-term evolution of the College into a full degree-granting institution. The Ministry therefore believes that it would be desirable to select a more all-embracing name which would make alternative names unnecessary in the long term. (Ministry of Education File 11/13)

The ministry therefore proposed the name "The Sir Arthur Lewis College of Higher Education." The Cabinet of Ministers accepted the suggestion but later reconsidered and adopted the original recommendation. This issue never came up in any of the interviews, and in spite of my association with the institution, I certainly was not aware until then of this indecision.

I had anticipated that prospective respondents would have been aware of my familiarity with the case and therefore might not have felt the need, or even appreciated the reason, for going into details of facts. Yet such factual information was necessary to place their perspectives and their interpretation of events into context. The research design was therefore structured to allow for the use of documentary and archival sources for the collection of quantitative and historical data, and for the use of the interview to solicit perspectives, viewpoints and perceptions. This decision was subsequently justified in that respondents tended during interviews to gloss over certain details with the phrase "as you already know." Their assumptions were not always correct and important information may well have not been shared because it was assumed to have been familiar to me. I saw this as a reversal of the situation against which insider-researchers are usually cautioned—taking for granted, overlooking or dismissing situations that at first sight appear familiar. In this case, the research subjects were treating the strange as familiar, taking for granted my knowledge of the issues, giving "familiar value" to information I may not have possessed. I resolved this by turning to the triangulation technique referred to earlier, and used archival and documentary material to fill in the gaps. Indeed, some of the data that needed to be accessed were either so detailed or related to events that had taken place so long ago, over a period of sixteen years, that it was not reasonable to have expected them to be dealt with adequately within the course of an interview.

Familiarity with the setting brought a certain degree of informality to the interviewing process, which to my mind strengthened the case for the interview as "conversation" (Burgess, 1984). The interviews were scheduled at times and in places most convenient to the interviewees—in their offices, in their homes, on their way home from work, even on the beach, under swaying coconut trees! I felt the need to be a little more directive than is often recommended, however, as I wanted to ensure that my respondents were not making too many assumptions about what was or was not familiar knowledge to me. Yet, on the other hand, I could not feign ignorance of the broad issues involved in the case. I therefore assumed a middle position on the directive/non-directive continuum, sacrificing in the process the level of remoteness that conventional approaches suggest is necessary for objectivity in interview-based research. As noted above, I had compiled a pool of questions as an *aide-memoire* for my own use, with separate agendas covering the issues I wanted addressed in each interview. At their request, I communicated these to the interviewees prior to the sessions with them. The result was a series of lively conversations, full of substance and to the point. In this way one very practical dilemma was satisfactorily resolved.

I faced a further dilemma in the reporting of the case study findings. My reading of the literature on peer and insider interviewing had alerted me to the possibility of a change in the relationship between the researcher and those with whom there is both a history and a future of colleagueship and collaboration (Powney and Watts, 1987). It was a change I was anxious to avert. The decision to compile a case record heightened the possibility of a change for the worse if there was any insensitive reporting of the information shared. Any information given "off the record," no matter how significant to the issue, was therefore not reported. The first draft of the report was circulated to key respondents, not only for purposes of validation, but for possible reactions to the manner in which the information they provided was reported. It was safe to assume that they would have reacted to any insensitivity on my part in the way they were presented. I wanted my study to contribute to an international database on educational developments in small-nation states. It was to be of practical use both to my home institution and to others contemplating similar strategies and directions. The data therefore needed to be authentic and to be reported honestly. Yet this honesty needed to be dealt with within the context of a small-state setting and with a view to providing the research subjects with as much privacy as was possible in so transparent a community. In this small society in which people are likely to be able to identify themselves and others in the research report, there were compelling reasons for me to adopt a reporting style that was true to the data and yet not unduly intrusive of the research subjects' right to such privacy as can be enjoyed in so personalized a society. The acceptance by the respondents of the report as drafted suggested that I had managed to stay on the right side of the conflict between the public's right to know and their right to decide what the public should be told of their private thoughts and opinions. While this related only to limited circulation of the "report," I doubt whether the problem would be greater if and when it is more widely disseminated. To begin with, there had been no attempt to disguise the name of the institution—there was only one of its kind. The individuals quoted in the report would have been identifiable to themselves and to others. In some large-scale studies, the use of pseudonyms and the modifications of situations and events are common practice in reporting field studies, as it is argued that people are more open to being interviewed and observed when they learn that anonymity and confidentiality can be maintained. Perhaps people in small systems are so used to the openness in the lives they live that the researcher has less need to resort to distortion of data in relation to the reader of the complete study. In the words of one of the key respondents: "A community as small as ours has to internationalise itself and therefore make channels so that what we are creating can more easily flow out" (Louisy, 1993: 1xxvii). The logical conclusion is that the inside researcher may, in some cases, be less unduly worried about violating edicts of anonymity. The outsider, however, would need to be more circumspect, especially if there had not been enough contact with the people on the ground.

CONCLUSION

I had often wondered whether the debate about insider/outsider research was a case of much ado about nothing. I came out of this fieldwork experience with a keener appreciation of the issues involved and, more importantly, with a firmer conviction of the importance of context in qualitative research inquiry. One of these contextual issues is the cultural position of the researcher.

The insights gained from an appreciation and understanding of the local context are powerful tools in the hands of the inside researcher. I have in the previous sections demonstrated some of these—familiarity with the setting, ease of access into the field, judicious selection of respondents. It would appear to me in fact that the main feature of the qualitative research paradigm, what Filstead (1970:6) refers to as "first-hand knowledge of the social world in question" is the particular strength of the inside researcher. Schwartz and Jacobs' (1979) concept of the "sociology of the inside" and King's (1973) recommendation that educational researchers get a "view of the inside" are the types of theoretical orientations that qualitative research advocates. And this to my mind is what the insider is particularly qualified to do. It seems paradoxical, therefore, that this same claim of sensitivity to local contexts should evoke criticisms of bias, oversimplicity and subjectivity when such research is conducted by an insider. Perhaps this is the real dilemma—a concern for meaning gained from involvement in the field as against the suspicion that such meaning when interpreted from the involvement of those closest to the situation may not stand the test of rigourous inquiry. My "dilemmas" in this particular study were thus both practical and ethical in nature:

1.   Obligation to the public. Was St. Lucia's interest being served by undertaking this study at a time when international advice went to the contrary?

2.   Obligation to research subjects. Should I have told my interviewees beforehand of the topics that I wanted to discuss with them? How confidential could I have kept their views or how anonymous could they be expected to remain in any eventual publication of the report or the case database? Perhaps the nature of educational research does not hold as many "terrors" and opportunities for betrayal of trust as would some other types of social research. And what if the interviewees are identifiable in the report? Would not the research bargain into which they entered, and which they agreed with me as the researcher, prepare them for wider dissemination of their views?

3.   Obligations to research colleagues. Did the modifications that I made to the prescribed and conventional strategies bring the research community into disrepute?

A second contextual issue of relevance to my study was the small-state setting. The literature on small states has consistently argued that these countries are not scaled-down versions of larger states, but that in fact they constitute a singular consistency, with an ecology of their own. This should not be interpreted as imputing theoretical uniqueness to small systems, but as evidence that there are multiple ways of ordering society and therefore multiple ways of dealing with that diversity. The case-study fieldwork in St. Lucia raised both practical and ethical issues that suggest the need for some more flexibility in the conventional strategies traditionally prescribed for the conduct of qualitative research. As an inside researcher in a small-state setting there were some adjustments that I had to make. For example, the personalized nature of the society and the existence of particularistic role relationships noted earlier made it difficult for me to assume the type of remoteness that some approaches require to achieve objectivity or to guarantee anonymity. Allowances for such flexibility are particularly crucial as qualitative research is seen to have considerable potential to contribute to educational practice and policy in developing countries—small states among them. Such contextual differences could contribute in the long term to the refinement of the qualitative research approach, and help strengthen its claim of sensitivity to local contexts. The research experience as an insider in this small-state setting also draws attention to the need for the adoption of a reporting style that, while remaining true to the data, is not unduly intrusive of the research subjects' right to privacy. There are examples in the literature where research reporting by persons who had found their way "inside" caused quite a stir; gaining much more notoriety than these researchers had anticipated or perhaps bargained for.

This chapter does not examine to any great length the whole continuum of "inside research," focusing as it does on the specific experiences of an indigenous researcher. It is therefore not clear from my limited personal experience whether the issues that I faced as an insider in a small-country setting would be similar to those faced by an insider in a larger setting? Whatever the answers to this and the earlier questions I raised might be, it would seem to me that there is the ever present need to appreciate and recognize that it is the special dynamic created between the researcher, the research and the researched community that determines what is practical and ethical and what is not.

REFERENCES

Attwood, I. and Bray, M. (1989) "Wealthy but Small and Young: Brunei Darussalam and its Education System," *Education Research and Perspectives* 16 (1): 70–82.

Benedict, B. (ed.) (1967) *Problems of Smaller Territories.* University of London: The Athlone Press.

Bogdan, R.C. and Biklen, S.K. (1992) *Qualitative Research for Education: An Introduction to Theory and Methods.* Boston: Allyn and Bacon.

Bray, M. (1991) "Education in Small States: Growth of Interest and Emergence of a

Theory," *Prospects* XXI (4): 503–516.

Bray, M. and Fergus, H. (1986) "The Implication of Size for Educational Development in Small Countries: Montserrat, a Caribbean Case-study," *Compare* 16 (1): 91–102.

Brock, C. (1988) "Education and National Scale: the World of Small States" *Prospects* XVIII (3): 303–314.

Brock, C. and Parker, R. (1985) "School and Community in Situations of Close Proximity: The Question of Small States." In K.M. Lillis (ed.) *School and Community in Less Developed Areas*. Beckenham: Croom Helm.

Burgess, R.G. (1984) *In the Field: An Introduction to Field Research*. London: Allen and Unwin.

––––––. (ed.) (1989) *The Ethics of Educational Research*. Lewes: The Falmer Press.

Cassell, J. (1980) "Ethical Principles for Conducting Fieldwork," *American Anthropologist* 82 (1): 28–41.

Commonwealth Secretariat, (1988) *Post-Secondary Colleges in the Small States of the Commonwealth: Summary Report*. London: Commonwealth Secretariat.

Crocombe, R.G. (1987) "Studying the Pacific." In A.Hooper, S. Britton, R.J. Crocombe, J. Huntsman, and C. Macpherson (eds.) *Class and Culture in the South Pacific*. Suva: University of the South Pacific.

Crossley, M. (1990) "Collaborative Research, Ethnography and Comparative and International Education in the South Pacific," *International Journal of Educational Development* 10 (1): 37–46.

Crossley, M. and Vulliamy, G. (1984) "Case-Study Research Methods and Comparative Education," *Comparative Education* 20 (2): 193–207.

Delamont, S. (1981) "All too Familiar? A Decade of Classroom Research," *Educational Analysis* 3 (1): 69–83.

Demas, W.J. (1965) *The Economies of Development on Small Countries with Special Reference to the Caribbean*. Montreal: McGill University.

Farrugia, C.J. and Attard, P.A. (1989) *The Multi-functional Administrator: Educational Development in the Small States of the Commonwealth*. London: Commonwealth Secretariat.

Filstead, W.J. (ed.) (1970) *Qualitative Methodology: First Hand Involvement with the Social World*. Chicago: Markham.

Hitchcock, G. and Hughes, D. (1989) *Research and the Teacher: A Qualitative Introduction to School-based Research*. London: Routledge.

King, E.J. (1973) *Other Schools and Ours: Comparative Studies for Today* (4h ed.). London: Holt, Rinehart and Winston.

Lewin, K. (1990) "Beyond the Fieldwork: Reflections on Research in Malaysia and Sri Lanka." In G. Vulliamy, K. Lewin, and D. Stephens *Doing Educational Research in Developing Countries: Qualitative Strategies*. London: The Falmer Press.

Lewis, V.A. et al. (1983) *Integration of the Morne Educational Complex. Report of the Task Force Appointed by the Minister for Education and Culture*. St. Lucia.

Louisy, C.P. (1993) "Tertiary Education in St. Lucia: Implications for Small Island States." Unpublished Ph.D. thesis, University of Bristol.

Lowenthal, D. (1987) "Social Features." In C. Clarke and T. Payne (eds.) *Politics, Security and Development in Small States*. London: Allen and Unwin.

Ministry of Education and Culture (1966–1985) "Files 11/13: The Morne Educational Complex/Integration of the Morne Educational Complex, St. Lucia."

Packer, S. (1989) "Post-Secondary Education in the Small States of the Comonwealth." In *International Development Programmes in Higher Education Annex: Special Papers*. London: Commonwealth Secretariat.

Powney, J. and Watts, M. (1987) *Interviewing in Educational Research*. London: Routledge and Kegan Paul.

Schwartz, H. and Jacobs, J. (1979) *Qualitative Sociology: A Method to the Madness.* New York: The Free Press.

Shand, R.T. (ed.) (1980) *The Island States of the Pacific and Indian Oceans: Anatomy of Development.* Monograph 23, Development Studies Centre. Canberra: Australian National University.

Smith, L.M. (1980) "Some not so Random Thoughts on Doing Fieldwork: The Interplay of Values." In H. Simons (ed.) *Towards a Science of the Singular: Essays about Case-study in Educational Research and Evaluation.* CARE: University of East Anglia.

Spindler, G.D. and Spindler, L. (1982) "Roger Harker and Schonhausen: From the Familiar to the Strange and Back Again." In G.D. Spindler (ed.) *Doing the Ethnography of Schooling: Educational Anthropology in Action.* New York: Holt, Rinehart and Winston.

Stenhouse, L. (1978) "Case-study and Case Records: Towards a Contemporary History of Education," *British Educational Research Journal* 4 (2): 21–39.

———. (1979) "Case-study in Comparative Education. Particularity and Generalisation," *Comparative Education* 15 (1): 5–10.

———. (1982) "The Conduct, Analysis and Reporting of Case-study in Education Research and Evaluation," In McCormick et al. (eds.) *Calling Education to Account.* London: The Open University Press.

Stephenson, J.B. and Greer, L.S. (1981) "Ethnographers in Their Own Cultures. Two Appalachian Cases," *Human Organisation* 40 (2): 123–130.

Vulliamy, G., Lewin, K. and Stephens, D. (1990) *Doing Educational Research in Developing Countries: Qualitative Strategies.* London: The Falmer Press.

Vulliamy, G. and Webb, R. (eds.) (1992) *Teacher Research and Special Educational Needs.* London: David Fulton.

World Bank (1992) *Access, Quality and Efficiency in Caribbean Education: A Regional Study.* Population and Human Resources Division. Country Department 3: Latin America and the Caribbean Regional Office.

———. (1993) *Higher Education: The Lessons of Experience.* Washington, D.C.: The World Bank.

Yin, R.K. (1989) *Case Study Research: Design and Methods.* Beverly Hills: Sage Publications.

9 PLANNING FOR CASE-STUDY EVALUATION IN BELIZE, CENTRAL AMERICA

Michael Crossley

J. Alexander Bennett

INTRODUCTION

A central theme of this volume, and one well supported by the various contributors, is that much of the educational research that is carried out in developing countries is quantitative in nature, and dominated by assumptions characteristic of the positivist paradigm. Here it is also argued that much of this work is, itself, applied in nature and increasingly policy oriented. To a large extent this has been influenced by international development assistance agencies, and efforts to monitor the impact of prestigious, and expensive, educational development projects. As is the case elsewhere, evaluation has thus become a major concern for many policy makers, planners and researchers intent on ensuring the most cost-effective use of scarce resources in times of financial austerity (Lewin, 1991). Indeed, in the history of many developing country education systems it is not uncommon to see the evolution of ministry research and evaluation units from origins relating to specific project evaluation initiatives (see, for example, Guthrie and Martin, 1983).

Reflecting international trends and the economic priorities of lending agencies such as the World Bank (Jones, 1992), much of this work has focused upon what Scriven (1967) long ago identified as summative project evaluation. The language of both government and aid-agency documents often reveals a preoccupation with inputs and outputs, with performance indicators that can measure the extent to which project goals have been met, and with improved statistical data. This is valuable and essential work, and in many developing countries related efforts to establish effective Educational Management Information Systems are now a central component of contemporary reforms. Burchfield, Easton and Holmes (1994), for example, discuss such developments in Botswana, and recent years have seen similar developments in Belize, building rapidly upon initial Planning

Unit efforts to collate reliable data for the now annual *Education Statistical Digest* (Belize, 1994).

The now extensive evaluation literature, however, has long recognized the limitations of summative evaluation, especially when focused solely upon measurable outputs. Understanding the process of education and of innovation is also essential if we are to improve the chances of successful policy implementation—and it is recognition of this that underpins efforts to strengthen qualitative and formative dimensions of the evaluation enterprise (Tessmer, 1993). During recent decades pioneering approaches to this latter type of educational evaluation include Robert Stake's (1967) exploration of responsive, "goal-free" models in the U.S., and Malcolm Parlett and David Hamilton's (1977) influential strategy for "illuminative evaluation" developed in the UK. Researchers such as Stenhouse (1975), Elliott (1991) and colleagues have furthered such thinking by advocating increased teacher involvement in school-based evaluation, the use of detailed case studies and educational action research. Evaluation with a strong qualitative dimension is now well represented in the Western literature (see, for example, Fetterman, 1988; Webb, 1990; Broadfoot and Osborn, 1993; Tessmer, 1993; Webb and Vulliamy, 1996), but, despite its potential to contribute to improved feedback and implementation, few educational initiatives in developing countries, as yet, build substantial qualitative components into their evaluation strategies—though there is some evidence that this situation is beginning to change (Fuller, 1991; King, 1991; Weeks, 1994; Wolff, Schiefelbein and Valenzuela, 1994).

The purpose of this chapter is to reflect upon how efforts have been made in the Central American state of Belize to build a case-study evaluation component into the contemporary Belize Primary Education Development Project (BPEDP). Focus is placed upon the origins and rationale for this evaluation study—and upon the planning processes and organizational frameworks established. The discussion engages with many issues raised by other contributors to this volume, and in particular, to those relating to case-study research in a small-country setting articulated by Louisy in chapter 8. More broadly, this Belizean initiative is conceptualized as a modest attempt to strengthen qualitative aspects of educational evaluation, in a system with little prior experience of such work, through international collaboration (see Crossley, 1992) designed to contribute to local research capacity building.

EDUCATIONAL DEVELOPMENT AND RESEARCH CAPACITY BUILDING

The 1990s have seen major challenges to the nature of the relationship between development assistance agencies and national governments (see, for example, King, 1991; Garrett, 1995). Such challenges were both reflected in, and influenced by, the March 1990 World Conference on Education for All held at Jomtien in Thailand (King and Singh, 1991; Windham, 1992). The Jomtien meeting, and subsequent reports and debates, helped refocus international attention upon basic education, but have also pursued ways of improving the impact of aid-supported educational interventions. The disappointing success rate of so many project initiatives throughout the developing world inspired such thinking—and attracted renewed attention to qualitative issues and the potential of formative evaluation. Post-Jomtien initiatives also emphasize the importance of improved "partnership" between agencies involved in educational development—and of the need for research capacity building within the south to facilitate more equal relations. As King (1991:18) points out:

> In many of the poorer countries of the world, the local capacity confidently to analyse their own educational priorities, and to pursue coherent programmes of research is not stronger than it was in the early 1970s. . . . There is unfortunately little evidence for many of the poorer countries of the world that the essential skills for the evaluation and management of increasingly complex education systems are in place.

The improved sustainability of educational innovation in an international context is thus seen to be closely related to research and evaluation capacity building and improved cooperation and collaboration between north and south. Recognizing that there are limited independent financial resources to fund such collaborative research and evaluation, King (1991:25) accepts that, in the short term at least, there will need to be "continued reliance on research and evaluation that are spin-offs from agency projects." In tune with the present analysis, however, he goes on to argue that: "Hopefully, . . . such donor-aided projects will be able increasingly to encourage research and studies that are locally relevant and appropriate to particular contexts" (King, 1991:25).

It is in this spirit that the Belizean study reported here was formulated in association with the externally supported BPEDP. Before looking at the origins and nature of the study, however, it is first pertinent to provide an overview of the Belize context and of the nature of the BPEDP itself.

BELIZE: EDUCATIONAL EVALUATION IN A SMALL STATE

Belize (formerly British Honduras) is located on the Caribbean coast of Central America and has borders with Mexico to the north and Guatemala to the south and west. It is a small state in terms of both physical size and population—with a total land area of 8,866 square miles (twice the size of Jamaica) and approximately 205,000 people (Barry, 1992). A quarter of this population live in Belize City, the former capital, and in 1993, 43.9% were aged fourteen years or under (Belize, 1994:3). About 58% of the population are Roman Catholics and 34% are Protestants, with small groups of other faiths or denominations making up the total. The main ethnic groups are Creole, Mestizo and Garifuna though they are well intermixed. By 1993 over 9,000 refugees from neighboring Central American states had also settled in Belize, adding significantly to the social and educational challenges facing the new nation.

The country attained independence from the UK in 1981, though it remains a member of the Commonwealth and has a parliamentary democracy based on the Westminster system. Close ties are retained with the UK, though the U.S. is increasingly influential in all aspects of social and economic affairs. The economy is based upon agriculture (notably sugar cane, citrus and bananas), light industry and tourism. This inevitably suffers from fluctuations in world commodity prices, and the nation has not escaped the impact of the international economic recession. Administratively, the country is divided into six districts: Orange Walk and Corozal to the north; Cayo and Belize to the west and center; and Stann Creek and Toledo to the south. While English is the official language, and the language of instruction in schools, Spanish is also widely spoken, especially in northern and western areas.

The basic education system consists of two years of preschool, eight years of primary and four years of secondary schooling. Beyond this, limited tertiary education is provided by a variety of institutions including Sixth form Schools, the School of Nursing, Belize Teachers College (BTTC) and the University College of Belize. Preschool places are not widely available but primary school is compulsory and enrollments compare favorably with other Central American and Caribbean countries. In 1992–93 there was, for example, a total of 270 primary schools with 48,612 pupils enrolled, representing 86.3% of the age group overall. At the completion of primary level pupils take the Belize National Selection Examination (BNSE) which limits entry to secondary school. In 1992–93 72.4% of all graduating primary school pupils continued their education at secondary level and there was a total of thirty secondary schools with 9,457 students enrolled (Belize, 1994). Only a small percentage of school leavers progress to tertiary education and training, and of the 1,818 teachers employed in primary schools only 47% were certified as fully trained in 1992–93.

Schools are maintained and managed by a church-state partnership that dates back to 1816 when the Church of England founded the first public school. This was later formalized in the 1962 Education Ordinance and has been periodically updated since then. Three denominations (Roman Catholic, Anglican and Methodist) are most prominent in this partnership, though 63% of all primary pupils are enrolled in the 133 primary schools run by the dominant Roman Catholic agency.

Under the terms of the partnership the various church agencies are primarily responsible for the management and staffing of their own schools; while the government contributes half of the costs of school facilities and maintenance, pays teachers' salaries, establishes educational objectives, curriculum guidelines and administrative structures, trains teachers and conducts overseas formal examinations.

Relating more directly to educational research and evaluation capacity the Belizean Ministry of Education currently has no dedicated research or evaluation unit. As planning began for the present study, however, ways were being sought to improve coordination between the work of the ministry's Curriculum Development Unit (CDU) and BTTC. Both of these bodies are centrally involved in curriculum innovation, the former focusing upon materials and the latter upon staff development. CDU staff need feedback from the schools to inform their professional work and BTTC students are required to use new materials effectively and undertake minor research projects during their course of training. In addition, plans were also in train to restructure ministry functions in a way that the CDU, BTTC, Planning Unit (and new Examinations and Assessment Unit) would be incorporated in an enlarged Educational Planning and Development Division located on the combined CDU and college campus. Such developments are an integral part of the BPEDP, the main components of which are outlined below.

THE BELIZE PRIMARY EDUCATION DEVELOPMENT PROJECT

With a national education system well established and relatively high rates of primary school enrollments being achieved, by the end of the 1980s attention in Belize turned increasingly toward ways of improving the quality of the education provided. It was, for example, widely recognized that many schools had inadequate or badly maintained buildings, that they were poorly supplied with textbooks and other materials and that too many teachers were untrained or ill-prepared for administrative responsibilities. Furthermore, improved planning and management capacity within the Ministry of Education was seen to be an essential prerequisite for further progress. The 1989 Manifesto of the soon to be elected People's United

Party (PUP) thus called for curriculum reform that would strengthen Belizean national identity and improvements in "the quality of primary education . . . with more trained teachers, and access to affordable textbooks" (cited in Van der Eyken, 1994:29). It was within this changing international climate that, in 1990, Belizean authorities came together with the World Bank and the British Overseas Development Administration (ODA) in planning for the BPEDP. In the same year the bank had itself signalled its own intention to give increased attention to the primary sector acknowledging that:

> to respond forcefully to the widespread need for improved primary education, the Bank must expand its lending operations in this area and give special priority to countries considering appropriate programmes of reform and development. (World Bank, 1990:7)

The resulting BPEDP is therefore one of the first major aid-assisted, primary education initiatives to be developed and implemented in the post-Jomtien era. As such it embodies many of the emergent principles outlined above, reflects priorities expressed in the World Bank's Primary Education Policy Paper (1990), and builds upon Belize's established links with both the UK and the U.S. It is, nevertheless, well characterized as a genuine partnership between three major stakeholders. The project began at the start of 1992 as a seven-year, U.S. $12.64 million program, funded by the government of Belize (34%), a loan from the World Bank (56%) and a technical assistance grant from the British ODA (10%) (Goulden, 1994). The overall aim of the project is to improve the quality and effectiveness of primary education by enhancing teacher professionalism and activity-based learning, through activities grouped into six core components managed by a Project Implementation Unit (PIU) based in Belize City. In broad terms these components include: the building or renovation of new schools and classrooms; the upgrading and expansion of primary teacher training and field support offered by BTTC (to raise the proportion of trained teachers to 80% by the year 2000); the revision and standardization of primary school curricula; textbook provision; the development and implementation of formative and summative evaluation procedures; and the strengthening of educational planning and management systems within the Ministry of Education. This partnership for the multidimensional reform of the primary education sector thus represents, for many, a new departure in aid-assisted educational innovation—and one that will deserve more detailed research and evaluation as implementation proceeds.

The study reported here was not initially part of the BPEDP but it did have Belizean origins. Concern had long been expressed within the country that little data existed on the quality of primary education, and it was argued that research was required that could document this, along with the prevailing conditions in schools and the nature and quality of teaching and learning. One of the current writers was responsible for pursuing this brief in his capacity as head of the CDU. Initial work (see Bennett, undated) eventually became combined with more immediate responsibilities relating to the implementation of the BPEDP. This led to close working relationships with personnel from the University of Bristol School of Education—the international organization responsible for the implementation of ODA technical assistance to the BPEDP (Van der Eyken, 1994). Discussions between these two parties about ways of documenting the quality of education in Belizean schools drew attention to the potential of qualitative research, based upon substantial fieldwork, that could help generate detailed case studies of practice. To this discussion was added the need for feedback on BPEDP implementation—for data that would help decision-makers to monitor (and improve) project impact. This two-fold agenda provided the seeds of what eventually became known as the *School Case-Studies and Impact Evaluation* (Crossley, 1995). Reflecting the principles expressed by King above, plans for educational research and evaluation in Belize thus developed from an ongoing, aid-assisted program of educational reform. Moreover, local needs and Belizean personnel were primarily instrumental in initiating and determining the nature of the study. The research rationale therefore incorporated the quality brief and the call for evaluation data. Detailed studies of the process of primary education in selected schools, it was argued, could document the nature and quality of teaching and learning, articulate examples of good practice and identify problems faced in project implementation. This work would include descriptive accounts of school contexts and processes, and generate critical analysis that could contribute to formative and summative BPEDP evaluation. In conceptualizing this approach the work of Stenhouse was helpful, for he argues that research conducted from a comparative and international perspective

> will miss making an important contribution to the understanding of schooling if it doesn't participate in the current development of case-study approaches to educational processes and educational institutions [and that] . . . we develop in our field a better grounded representation of day-to-day educational reality resting on the careful study of particular cases. (1979:9–10)

In Belize no such studies existed though it was very much in the interests of the BPEDP that ways of monitoring project impact at the school level were devised. While a case-study foundation was adopted, an evaluative tone to the study inevitably emerged increasingly strongly as efforts were made to meet the requirements of decision-makers and sponsors—and to produce a research design that would focus upon the impact of core project components. To some extent this narrowed the field for, as Stufflebeam and Webster (1988:572) point out, while research and evaluation may use the same techniques:

> Evaluations often are localised, short term, concerned with solving practical problems, directed to ranking options, and rooted in value questions, and they may be of little interest outside the immediate setting. Research, on the other hand, is concerned with extending and generalising basic understandings about educational processes; concerns about immediate utility of results are secondary.

Nevertheless, in practice a degree of balance was established that, particularly with respect to the quality theme and educational processes, retained interest in broader research objectives. One further, though central, element of the overall rationale relates to the research and evaluation process itself, for the study was from the outset seen as a valuable vehicle for the training of Belizean researchers; and as a way of contributing in a practical and useful way to local capacity building. We will return to this important theme later.

AIMS AND ORGANIZATIONAL FRAMEWORK

Following the early project discussions held in 1993, progress in planning for the study was relatively rapid for a collaborative venture of this nature. This was facilitated by the already well established Belize-Bristol Link Programme that regularly brought University of Bristol staff to Belize and, of great strategic importance, located two Bristol staff permanently in country from 1992–1994 (Van der Eyken, 1994). Planning meetings could thus be convened in Belize where the attendance of senior decision-makers and key players was possible. In this way a genuine international partnership came to characterize the study from the initiation phase onwards. These initial meetings also helped clarify aims and establish a clear organizational framework.

At the most fundamental level the study came to be accepted by the PIU as a new but integral part of the BPEDP, with the following three aims being formally acknowledged (Crossley, 1995:1):

1.   to document the nature and quality of primary school education (and changes over time) in selected schools;

2.   to contribute to the evaluation of the impact of the BPEDP at the school level;

3.   to contribute to the development of Belizean research capacity, most notably within BTTC and CDU.

Start-up funding for the study was provided through two sources. The PIU secured funding for the in-country expenses of Belizean team members, and the Belize-Bristol Link supported the international travel of University of Bristol staff. This is a model that again well demonstrates the potential of north-south collaboration focused upon research and evaluation designed to meet local needs.

Returning to the staff development and capacity building dimension, the study provided an ideal vehicle for CDU and BTTC cooperation, and, as already indicated, this was a major BPEDP priority—and one that underpinned the eventual establishment of the enlarged Educational Planning and Development Division in early 1995. Collaboration was well demonstrated in the operation of the Research Steering Committee. This was a further core element in the organizational framework and one that proved to be increasingly important. This was based in the Education Planning and Development Division and chaired by the in-country Research Coordinator (then one of the present writers). It consisted of representatives drawn from CDU, BTTC, Ministry of Education, District Education Offices, Examinations and Assessment Unit and the University of Bristol. Once established, this Steering Committee was largely responsible for directing and supporting the future course of the study. Its members played an active role in the detailed research design, in the selection of schools and team members, in communication and in the coordination of various activities, including the logistical arrangements for fieldwork and research training workshops. Leadership of the Steering Committee was vested in the Chairman who was also responsible for budgeting and other financial and monitoring procedures. The Chairman was supported by a Steering Committee Secretary, who, in the first instance was one of the University of Bristol staff members located in Belize. This role was subsequently and effectively localized by a team member based at BTTC. Backing up the Steering Committee in Bristol was an additional "Research Cluster" group comprised of University staff and researchers interested in supporting this collaboration.

Two types of research training workshops were arranged by the

Steering Committee, those led by in-country personnel and those run by visiting staff from the University of Bristol. The support of locally-based Bristol staff was, however, of considerable strategic importance in the early stages of planning and start-up, helping to make it possible for six workshops to be held within the first year. Of these one was held in Bristol when a group of senior administrators from the Belizean Ministry of Education participated in a Link Programme attachment there. Details of this training follow elsewhere, but here it is more appropriate to examine the composition of the research team, before moving on to details of the research design itself. While the full research team, which included more than twenty-five members, was invited to attend all training workshops, the group was also divided into separate school case-study teams. Each of these subteams, initially consisting of two or three members, was responsible for one (or sometimes two) in-depth school studies, the details of which follow.

RESEARCH DESIGN

Four phases for the Case-Studies and Impact Evaluation were planned through the collaborative processes outlined above, with particular care being given to: (1) ensuring that the study was modest in scope and cost and (2) avoiding making unrealistic demands upon participants' time. For a small state where many key personnel have multiple roles to play (Bray, 1991), these were seen to be particularly important parameters—especially since many potential research team members were already heavily involved in the implementation of other components of the BPEDP.

The first research workshop, conceived as an open planning meeting, attracted the interest and involvement of staff from sections throughout the Ministry of Education, from the districts and from BTTC. Many of these participants subsequently volunteered to join the research team, and to this core others were strategically co-opted. The same meeting formalized the creation and membership of the Steering Committee. The latter body then became responsible for the selection of case-study schools. For this process a list of selection criteria was first established to enable a range of different types of school and content to be included. These criteria included district and location, management agency and enrollment size, extent of BPEDP involvement, examination performance, and rural/urban characteristics. The overall aim was to include schools from each of the six districts and to have a range of different types represented in the study. A degree of pragmatism also entered the equation as the eventual short list was finalized with an eye on the accessibility of each school for potential research team members. After some modifications and additions had been made, twelve case-study schools were eventually confirmed. Details of these are available elsewhere (Crossley, 1995), but the list included at least one from each district, rural and urban schools, a broad spectrum of management authorities (including the dominant Roman Catholic, Anglican and Methodist agencies), small and large schools, and those with and without major building programs under the auspices of the BPEDP.

With the basic organizational framework established, the research team identified and the case-study schools selected, preparations were made for phase 1 of the study.

Phase 1 : Context and Background

Formal letters requesting access to each case-study school were sent with the endorsement of the Chief Education Officer to each relevant principal and management agency. This also included summary details of the nature and scope of the proposed study. In some cases personal visits were possible. In all cases access was approved and fieldwork was able to begin during the third term of the 1994 school year. Very much in the spirit of qualitative research, this first phase of fieldwork was concentrated upon the collation of data relating to the context and background of each school. Guidelines for this work were drawn up collectively during an early research training workshop held in Belize City. These focused the attention of team members upon various categories of data, including location, catchment area, school history, buildings and facilities, enrollment, staffing composition, availability of teaching and learning materials, school timetable, school values and school ethos (see Figure 9.1). The structure created by these guidelines also provided a common framework for the writing up of fieldnotes on this phase—a strategy that was, perhaps, essential given the relative inexperience of team members. Indeed, the importance of agreed frameworks and common research guidelines for team coordination was increasingly acknowledged as the basic research design was refined and extended. This is an issue that is not well articulated in the qualitative research literature, where there is less of a tradition of teamwork and multisite studies. Where the existing literature was more helpful was with regard to the broad methodological orientation adopted by team members, and specific techniques for data collection. Training workshops held prior to and during phase 1 thus drew attention to the importance of team members establishing a close working relationship with their school communities, and to the potential of detailed case studies to penetrate beyond the rhetoric of innovation. It is argued elsewhere:

1. **Location**
   Name of school
   District details
   Site and situation
   Local climate
   Landscape/topography
   Infrastructure/communication/utilities
   (water, light etc.)
   Local settlements, population types and sizes
   Nature of local economy and employment
   opportunities
   Community values, politics, religions, attitudes
   to school etc.
   Local health factors
   Other relevant factors

2. **Local Educational History and Management**
   Nearby schools and inter-school relationships
   Educational history in the area
   Educational management in the area
   Relations between school and management agency

3. **School History**
   Origins and management
   Demographic details of catchment area
   Development landmarks
   Growth patterns and phases
   Involvement in previous projects

4. **Physical Resources**
   Land availability and use
   Playground space
   Commercial enterprise
   Buildings: number and condition
   New building initiatives
   BPEDP building program if any

5. **Human Resources**
   Pupil numbers by grade, gender, ethnicity,
   language etc.
   Teacher numbers, qualifications and turnover
   Teacher gender, age ranges, experience etc.
   Pupil/teacher ratios
   Ancillary staff details
   Roles and responsibilities of staff and principal
   Management support available
   Attendance records (pupils, staff)
   Non-enrollment, repetition and dropout details
   Transfer issues if any
   Examination performance in recent years
   Community support factors, PTA input etc.
   BPEDP input evidence

6. **Availability and Condition of Teaching and
   Learning Materials**
   Curriculum guides
   Annual schemes
   Textbooks (numbers, ratios per student/subject
   etc.; and loans, sales)
   Reference materials
   Library resource
   Duplicating facilities
   Basic materials (paper, pencils, etc.)
   Other materials (computers etc.)
   PTA, church etc. input
   BPEDP input evidence

7. **School Timetable and Organization**
   School management style
   Timetable details/subject allocation
   Specific details
   Multigrade teaching requirements
   Team teaching, etc.
   Extra curricular activities
   External influences
   Holidays and records of time "lost" for
   teaching
   Classroom layout and organization
   (furniture, etc.)
   School rules
   Punishment use and discipline
   School policy

8. **Shared Values and School Ethos**
   Religious influence
   Management style
   Atmosphere/relationships/commitment
   Uniform
   Civic duties, community links, etc.
   Attendance and use of training/workshops

9. **Other factors**
   Involvement in BPEDP workshops

Figure 9.1. Guidelines for the collection of background and contextual data. Source: Crossley, M. and Bennett, J.A. (1994).

Through their concern with the everyday practices of teachers and students, case-study methods are well placed to identify important constraints on innovation, which may not be apparent to policy-makers who necessarily lack a detailed understanding of the local context in which innovations are being attempted. (Crossley and Vulliamy, 1984:199)

Researchers were encouraged to visit their schools regularly, to work with teachers where possible and to collect data from a range of different sources and by a variety of methods. During phase 1 in particular, they were advised to keep an open mind to data collection and to build upon the agreed guidelines if necessary. Bogdan and Biklen (1992:58) capture the potential of a flexible and relatively open agenda well by pointing out that:

A strategy qualitative researchers employ in a study is to proceed as if they know very little about the people and places they will visit. They attempt to mentally cleanse their preconceptions. . . . Plans evolve as they learn about the setting, subjects, and other sources of data through direct examination. . . . How they proceed is based on theoretical assumptions (that meaning and process are crucial in understanding human behaviour, that descriptive data are what is important to collect, and that analysis is best done inductively) and on data-collection traditions (such as participant observation, unstructured interviewing, and document analysis). These provide the parameters, the tools, and the general guide of how to proceed. It is not that qualitative research design is nonexistent; it is rather that the design is flexible.

The phenomenological perspective alluded to here informed the broad orientation of team members, and the three basic techniques of observation (participant and non-participant), in-depth, unstructured interviewing and document analysis provided the focus for initial practical training. For each phase the "triangulation" of methods was encouraged, though it was acknowledged that this balance would vary over time with, for example, documentary sources possibly being most significant in pursuing contextual and background data during phase 1.

Phase 2 : In-School Research

Phase 2 of the study in many ways grew from the entry to the field and contextual data collation characteristic of phase 1. Demarcation of a separate phase, however, helped as a mechanism for team coordination. The focus of this phase was thus, in many ways, a natural extension of fieldwork into the study of the processes of the school itself. Officially the target was to document the impact of the BPEDP at the school level and the nature and quality of teaching and learning. These more specific objectives were consistent with the "progressive focusing" advocated in the methodological literature, though additional structure came from the parameters of the evaluation itself.

Significantly, such refinements to the overall design emerged from collective team input during a research training workshop. The analysis of BPEDP documents highlighted six main project components, each of which were intended to have an impact at the school level (see Bennett and Young, 1994). These were seen to offer the most appropriate broad categories for the structure of in-school research. Workshop members then developed a series of fieldwork questions that could provide guidance for each school team as they sought to discover the nature and extent of project impact relating to (1) school facilities; (2) planning and management; (3) teacher education; (4) curriculum development; (5) textbooks and teaching materials; (6) examinations and assessment. This process generated a set of guidelines for phase 2 (Crossley and Osborn, 1994) to complement those prepared for phase 1. Classroom observation, both systematically structured and unstructured (ethnographic), was also planned to be carried out by each school team as a way of documenting and monitoring the nature and quality of teaching and learning. Training in such techniques was therefore built into team workshops and instruments were collectively developed or adapted for team use. Principals and teachers were also identified as key informants for qualitative interviews. Again, it was stressed to all team members that any guidelines and instruments prepared in advance should not be seen as comprehensive and inflexible lists of research tasks or questions. Moreover, it was assumed that if some of the same questions were repeatedly asked on separate visits, data may begin to reveal the extent of changes over time.

Having said this, the team became increasingly aware of the fact that the very flexibility and responsiveness of qualitative research and evaluation required a significant degree of researcher initiative and creativity in the field. No guidelines could prepare for every contingency, and a tension between individual creativity and team coordination was, to some extent, inevitable. This is well illustrated with reference to the potential strength of qualitative evaluation to identify the unintended effects of educational innovation that often help observers to understand and explain the responses of practitioners involved in implementation. The identification of such unintended effects relies to a large extent upon the sensitivities, insights and abilities of the evaluators. As so often noted in the methodological literature, in qualitative studies the researchers themselves are often the key research "instruments." For largely pragmatic and financial reasons phase 2 was planned to run throughout three school terms with each subteam being required to visit their school at least four times per term and to submit a Termly Field Report for collation and review by the Chairman of the Steering Committee. In this way it was envisaged that a file of field reports (including one for phase 1) would be built up—and that summary Interim Research Reports could also be made available for the Ministry of Education by the Chair of the Steering Committee.

Phase 3 : Writing Up Case-Study Reports

While it is evident from the above account that much data analysis and writing up would begin in the field, the limitations placed on researchers' time by other substantial commitments made it realistic to demarcate phase 3 of the study as a period for formal writing up of the individual case studies. At the time of writing, detailed plans for this phase, modes of analysis to be adopted and the structure of case-study reports have yet to be finalized. The overall model for reporting and disseminating the findings of the research has, however, been outlined. This envisages the production of twelve separate school case studies, each combining data from the two phases of fieldwork: background and context; and in-school research. These it is assumed will be written by, and credited to, members of each case-study subteam. Each case study is planned to be written to a common structure and framework to provide: school descriptions, including contextual and historical details and accounts of the nature and quality of teaching and learning in practice; detailed reports of the impact of each of the BPEDP components at the school level; critical evaluations of the problems encountered in project implementation and; examples of good practice relating to teaching quality and BPEDP goals.

Reflecting Parlett and Hamilton's (1977) rationale for illuminative evaluation, it is intended that these studies will contribute to the evaluation of the BPEDP by assessing

> how it operates; how it is influenced by the various school systems in which it is applied; what those directly concerned regard as its advantages and disadvantages; and how students' intellectual tasks and academic experiences are most affected. It aims to discover and document what it is like to be participating in the scheme, whether as teacher or pupil; and in addition to discern and discuss the

innovation's most significant features, recurring concomitants and critical processes. In short, it seeks to address and to illuminate a complex array of questions. (Cited in Hamilton et al., 1977:10)

With the policy implications of evaluation firmly in mind it is argued that knowledge of problems encountered and the dissemination of accessible examples of good practice will be of direct value to the schools themselves, for the modification of project implementation strategies, and in demonstrating and communicating project objectives and experience to other schools and to other interested parties. This assumes that writers will be able to communicate their findings through disciplined and clear narrative that can be understood by a wide range of potential readers including policy makers, administrators, teachers and community members. As Yin (1984) points out, well written case studies have great potential for the effective dissemination of findings, for they can be very down to earth, attention holding and in harmony with the readers' own experience. Whether this will be possible in the present Belize context remains to be seen, but it is argued that, given continued support, the target is a realistic one and the process is valuable in itself. Indeed, from such case-study materials local school histories could also be reworked in a form suitable for use in schools—perhaps as support materials developed by CDU personnel.

Phase 4 : Synthesis Evaluation Report

The twelve separate case studies envisaged above are intended to stand alone as individual publications but it is the collective findings that hold greater potential for both evaluation and research. As the number of completed case studies builds up, the chances of identifying and confirming common trends increase. It is with this comparative analysis in mind that a synthesis evaluation report is also planned to help identify and understand reasons for BPEDP success or failure. The dilemmas of generalizing from case studies are well rehearsed in the literature but this remains a controversial and subtle debate. Guba and Lincoln (1981), for example, maintain that "fittingness" is a more appropriate concept to apply, arguing that if clear and detailed descriptions are made available for others in similar situations to read, they can assess for themselves how translatable findings are for their own context. Elsewhere, the editors of the present volume have explored how comparative case studies, as proposed here, can enhance the potential generalizability of research findings (Crossley and Vulliamy, 1984:204; see also Vulliamy, Lewin and Stephens, 1990).

It is to phase 4 and the synthesis evaluation that we can also look for more theoretically informed research findings. One line of inquiry already being pursued, for example, relates to the relevance of the Belizean studies to the international school effectiveness literature (Reynolds et al., 1994). On a more pragmatic level such reflective work will most probably be best completed by one key member of the research team who, with support, has a strong overall grasp of the study, and the time, ability and resources to link specific findings with the relevant theoretical literature.

CONCLUSIONS

In reflecting upon the origins and evolution of the Belizean Case-Studies and Impact Evaluation it is argued that much can be learned from the experience of planning for the collaborative model that has been formulated; and from the specific achievements and problems encountered. It is to these broader lessons that we now turn, in full knowledge of the fact that, while implementation has begun, whether or not the study itself will be sustained is an open question.

At the most fundamental level our work has revealed that, as in so many other developing countries, qualitative research and evaluation is not, as yet, well represented in Belize. Moreover, much of the educational research and evaluation that has been carried out has, perhaps predictably, been related to aid-assisted projects, has been conducted by visiting researchers and has not been well disseminated within country. Little significant research and evaluation capacity has yet been developed in the Ministry of Education, although school statistics are now being compiled annually and teacher education programs offered by BTTC incorporate basic research training and involve students in minor school-based projects.

On a more positive note, with the restructuring of the Educational Planning and Development Division the time is now perhaps right for more systematic research capacity building—and for efforts to complement recent advances in statistical data collation, management and dissemination with the production of case-study databases and training in qualitative approaches to research and evaluation. A recent World Bank publication on the quality of primary education in Latin America and the Caribbean (Wolff, Schiefelbein and Valenzuela, 1994:10), for example, pertinently concludes:

> Research priorities, which should be defined nationally on a consensus basis, could include: evaluating a variety of basic, applied, developmental, prototype, and small-scale innovations; creating strong formative evaluation programs; increasing "ethnographic studies" of classroom interactions; . . .

Certainly the development of local research capacity will increase the potential for more equal partnerships to characterize internationally supported innovation; and increase the chances of greater local ownership and responsibility in the spirit of the post-Jomtien debate. More specifically, as already demonstrated through the case-study planning process, research and evaluation is an ideal vehicle for promoting increased cooperation and collaboration, focused upon school contexts and processes, between personnel from the CDU, BTTC and other sections of the Educational Planning and Development Division. It is with these broad themes in mind that we conclude by reviewing first the positive lessons to be learned from the Belizean experience, and second, the limitations and dangers to be avoided, both in this context and elsewhere.

Collaboration well characterizes this Belizean study in a number of ways, pointing to some of the main strengths of the evaluation initiative as a model for others to consider (see Crossley, 1992). At the broadest level the initial Belize-Bristol Link Programme provided a sound basis for international and interpersonal collaboration related to an aid-assisted project. The importance of established links in facilitating further initiatives, such as this ongoing research, should not be underestimated. Indeed, the impact of the recent conclusion of the formal Belize-Bristol Link Programme upon the BPEDP and the present study has yet to be assessed—but, in the absence of the many support strategies that were previously in place, maintaining continuity will inevitably be more difficult to achieve.

This is also a study that, within a framework of north-south cooperation, has evolved from the outset with a high degree of local ownership, direction and support. The Research Steering Committee is a particularly notable component of the overall organizational framework that may prove useful, in principle, to others planning similar international collaborations. Further collaborative strengths include the way in which CDU and BTTC staff have worked together on a topic of common concern, and the way resources from different funding agencies have been brought together in support of research capacity building.

The latter issue points to the value of research that combines both product and process goals, for this is a study that is designed to provide research training for many individuals, while generating new knowledge and useful feedback on project implementation. Given the modest size and scope of the study this amounts to a potentially cost-effective staff development and project evaluation strategy. Beyond the immediate future there is further potential for this experience to generate the seeds of a future research and evaluation section within the Educational Planning and Development

Division of the Ministry of Education.

Pursuing the evaluation theme further the case-study plans usefully demonstrate how qualitative research methods can contribute much to the process of evaluation—especially in the context of international development projects where quantitative and summative studies remain dominant. This is not to equate case study with qualitative research, for case studies can incorporate quantitative data, and this Belizean study has also explored plans to generate related statistical surveys of, for example, changes in school examination results and the national output of trained teachers (Hyde, 1995). Where qualitative approaches are especially useful, however, is in their attention to context—and knowledge of both innovation impact at the school level and of the nature and quality of teaching and learning is urgently required in Belize, as it is in many other developing countries. Moreover, Lillis and Hogan (1983) argue persuasively that the absence of detailed case studies of schooling in developing countries is as much a constraint upon the production of valid theory as it is upon realistic policy formulation.

In this respect efforts to plan the study in such a way that varied products could result may be helpful for others. The individual case studies have, for example, been planned to emphasize locally specific findings, the synthesis report to contribute in a broader way to BPEDP evaluation, and more theoretically oriented reflection upon these findings, it is hoped, may add to research knowledge on school effectiveness and educational innovation.

If the study proceeds through all four stages, and the twelve case studies and synthesis report are well written, the narrative style of the work will help to make it accessible and useful for a wide range of readers including practicing teachers and policy makers. Beyond Belize the study may be of particular interest to other small states in Central America and the Caribbean. As the previous chapter by Louisy indicates, small states face many similar educational problems and learning from each other's experience can often be most productive. Bray (1991:101), for example, notes that "aid agencies are not always willing to examine in detail the specific circumstances of every country," and that

> Some donors and lenders find it uneconomic to prepare small projects, and therefore press small states to accept large ones. . . . The result is that large education projects are devised which severely stretch the country's absorptive capacity, or extends the administrative burdens on ministries which are already hard pressed.

The Belizean experience of innovative but large-scale sectoral reform will, in this light, command widespread interest. Looking to the problems encountered, it is already clear that the multiple demands made by the BPEDP upon key personnel in the Belize education system make it difficult for some of the same people to sustain their own involvement in research and evaluation. This is despite the fact that this potential limitation was well recognized at the outset of the study when "modest" objectives and expectations were established. Added to this, the rapid movement of personnel, including secondments and study breaks abroad, from one role to another has posed further logistical problems for the research team. This is again characteristic of small-state contexts—and a factor that deserves greater consideration by planners and administrators. In the present study, acknowledgment of such factors has led to ways being sought to minimize the demands made upon key players. These include the strengthening of case-study teams by the addition of more district-based personnel and practicing teachers. During the implementation of phase 1 (now relatively successfully completed), for example, the most effective subteams were seen to be those where a larger local team was convened under the leadership of one key player (Crossley, 1995). In Cayo and Toledo districts this included the co-opting of VSO and Peace Corps representatives—most appropriately adding a further international and collaborative dimension to the study. Where team members are practicing teachers the addition of an insider perspective (despite the dilemmas of such input) holds much potential for in-depth study. Further team strengthening is to be attempted by the coordination of BTTC trainees' school research projects with case-study fieldwork activities—a strategy strongly supported by the college principal and one that could significantly strengthen the study and the college research program simultaneously. Anticipating Smith's chapter on teamwork that follows, the Belizean experience is therefore increasingly helpful in revealing the significance of the tensions that exist between the much valued flexibility and openness of qualitative research, and the need to provide structure and guidance for team efforts—especially when members have limited training and fieldwork experience. Supporting teamwork and simultaneous staff development of this nature clearly demands sustained support and consistent and clear coordination. Recent months have thus seen efforts to increase the structure and guidance provided for team members and to plan for continuity of funding, coordination and leadership.

In concluding it is argued that, because of its very nature, there remain limits to the extent of detailed planning possible for qualitative research and evaluation. This is partly because the exact course and quality of fieldwork relies, to a significant extent, upon the abilities and initiative of the researchers themselves. To cite Bogdan and Biklen (1992:212), "One must work to achieve a balance that helps a team work together but allows each individual enough room to be creative." Careful planning can, however, help to establish a sound framework for training and fieldwork to be conducted within—and help to coordinate the activities of research teams as discussed here. It is in this respect that we hope others will find our reflections upon this early phase of Belizean experience to be both interesting and helpful for the planning and implementation of their own studies elsewhere.

ACKNOWLEDGMENTS

We wish to acknowledge all colleagues in Belize and Bristol who have contributed in many ways to the work reported here. In particular, thanks go to all research team members for their enthusiasm and input, to Dr. Santos Mahung, Permanent Secretary for Education, for supporting the initiative, to Mr. Derek Goulden, Director of the Belize-Bristol Link Programme for invaluable advice and encouragement, and to Dr. Marilyn Osborn for helpful and timely input into the research training program. The Belize-Bristol Link was funded by the British Overseas Development Administration.

REFERENCES

Barry, T. (1992) *Inside Belize*. Albuquerque: The Inter-Hemispheric Education Resource Center.

Belize, Ministry of Education (1994) *Belize: Education Statistical Digest 1993*. Belmopan: Planning Unit.

Bennett, J.A. (undated) "The Quality of Education in the Primary Schools of Belize. Indicators." Belize City: Curriculum Development Unit (mimeo.).

Bennett, J.A. and Young, R. (1994) *BPEDP Research Brochure*. Belize City: BTTC.

Bogdan, R.C. and Biklen, S.K. (1992) *Qualitative Research for Education. An Introduction to Theory and Methods*. Boston: Allyn and Bacon.

Bray, M. (1991) *Making Small Practical: The Organisation and Management of Ministries of Education in Small States*. London: Commonwealth Secretariat.

Broadfoot, P. and Osborn, M. (1993) *Perceptions of Teaching. Primary School Teachers in England and France*. London: Cassell.

Burchfield, S.A., Easton, P.A. and Holmes, D.R. (1994) "The Development of an Educational Management Information System Model for Educational Efficiency Analysis, and its Adaptation in Botswana." In S. Burchfield (ed.) *Research for Educational Policy and Planning in Botswana*. Gaborone: Macmillan.

Crossley, M. (1992) "Collaborative Research, Ethnography and Comparative and International Education in the South Pacific." In R.J. Burns and A.R. Welch (eds.) *Contemporary Perspectives in Comparative Education*. New York: Garland.

———. (1995) *School Case-Studies and Impact Evaluation (BPEDP)*. Bristol: University of Bristol Centre for International Studies in Education.

Crossley, M. and Bennett, J.A. (1994) *BPEDP Research Project. Guidelines for the Collection of Background and Contextual Data*. Belize City: Curriculum Development Unit (mimeo.).

Crossley, M. and Osborn, M. (1994) "Guidelines for In-School Research (Phase 2)." Bristol: University of Bristol Centre for International Studies in Education (mimeo.).

Crossley, M. and Vulliamy, G. (1984) "Case-Study Research Methods and Comparative Education," *Comparative Education*, 20(2): 193–207.

Elliott, J. (1991) *Action Research for Educational Change*. Buckingham: Open University Press.

Fetterman, D.M. (1988) (ed.) *Qualitative Approaches to Evaluation in Education: The Silent Scientific Revolution*. New York: Praeger.

Fuller, B. (1991) *Growing Up Modern: The Western State Builds Third World Schools*. London: Routledge.

Garrett, R.M. (1995) (ed.) *Aid and Education: Mending or Spending*. Bristol: University of Bristol Centre for International Studies in Education.

Goulden, D. (1994) "Belize-Bristol Primary Education Link Programme." Bristol: University of Bristol Centre for International Studies in Education (mimeo.).

Guba, E.G. and Lincoln, Y.S. (1981) *Effective Evaluation. Improving the Usefulness of Evaluation Results through Responsive and Naturalistic Approaches*. San Francisco: Jossey Bass.

Guthrie, G. and Martin, T.N. (1983) (eds.) *Directions for Educational Research*. Port Moresby: University of Papua New Guinea.

Hyde, M. (1995) *BPEDP Case-Study Research: Use of Assessment Data*. Belize City: AEU (mimeo.).

Jones, P.W. (1992) *World Bank Financing of Education. Lending, Learning and Development*. London: Routledge.

King, K. (1991) *Aid and Education in the Developing World*. London: Cassell.

King, K. and Singh, J. (1991) *Improving the Quality of Basic Education*. London: Commonwealth Secretariat:

Lewin, K.M. (1991) *Education in Austerity. Options for Planners*. Paris: UNESCO.

Lillis, K. and Hogan, D. (1983) "Dilemmas of Diversification: Problems Associated with Vocational Education in Developing Countries," *Comparative Education*, 19(1): 89–107.

Parlett, M. and Hamilton, D. (1977) "Evaluation as Illumination." In D. Hamilton, D. Jenkins, C. King, B. MacDonald and M. Parlett (eds.) *Beyond the Numbers Game*. London: Macmillan.

Reynolds, D., Creemers, B., Nesselvadt, P., Schaffer, E., Stringfields, S. and Teddlie, C. (1994) *Advances in School Effectiveness. Research and Practice*. Oxford: Pergamon.

Scriven, M. (1967) "The Methodology of Evaluation." In R.E. Stake (ed.) *Curriculum Evaluation. AERA Monograph Series on Curriculum Evaluation*. Chicago: Rand McNally.

Stake, R.E. (1967) "The Countenance of Educational Evaluation," *Teachers College Record*, 68: 523–540.

Stenhouse, L. (1975) *An Introduction to Curriculum Research and Development*. London: Heinemann.

——. (1979) "Case-Study in Comparative Education. Particularity and Generalisation," *Comparative Education*, 15(1): 5–10.

Stufflebeam, D. and Webster, W.J. (1988) "Evaluation as an Administrative Function." In N.J. Boyen (ed.) *Handbook of Research on Educational Administration*. New York: Longman.

Tessmer, M. (1993) *Planning and Conducting Formative Evaluation*. London: Kogan Page.

Van der Eyken, W. (1994) *Belize-Bristol Link Programme. Final Evaluation Report*. Bristol: University of Bristol Centre for International Studies in Education.

Vulliamy, G., Lewin, K. and Stephens, D. (1990) *Doing Educational Research in Developing Countries: Qualitative Strategies*. Basingstoke: Falmer.

Webb, R. (ed.) (1990) *Practitioner Research in the Primary School*. Basingstoke: Falmer.

Webb, R. and Vulliamy, G. (1996) *Roles and Responsibilities in the Primary School:*

Changing Demands, Changing Practices. Buckingham: Open University Press.

Weeks, S.G. (1994) "Educational Research, Policy and Planning: A Third World Perspective." In S. Burchfield (ed.) *Research for Educational Policy and Planning in Botswana.* Gaborone: Macmillan.

Windham, D.M. (1992) *Education for All: The Requirements.* Paris: UNESCO.

Wolff, L., Schiefelbein, E. and Valenzuela, J. (1994) *Improving the Quality of Primary Education in Latin America and the Caribbean.* Washington D.C.: The World Bank.

World Bank (1990) *Primary Education. A World Bank Policy Paper.* Washington D.C.: The World Bank.

Yin, R. (1984) *Case-Study Research: Design and Methods.* Beverly Hills: Sage.

10 IMPLEMENTING QUALITATIVE RESEARCH IN PAKISTAN

INTERNATIONAL TEAMWORK

R.L. Smith

INTRODUCTION: INTERNATIONAL AID, CAPACITY BUILDING AND RESEARCH

Like most international aid agencies, Britain's Overseas Development Administration (ODA) has developed policies that emphasize capacity building in partner countries. This is particularly true of ODA's approach to educational aid. The Education Policy Paper (ODA, 1994:2) lists six major dimensions to the agency's educational aid program—promoting human resource development, promoting economic reform and growth, promoting good government, reducing poverty, addressing gender issues and tackling environmental problems. All these objectives are couched in the language of assisting partner countries to develop local capacity to achieve progress in the selected areas. In line with this broad objective, in 1988 a Link Project was established by ODA between the curriculum bureaux of the Ministry of Education in Pakistan and the School of Education of the University of Bristol. The British Council also played a role in the project, facilitating the overseas training aspects of the link. The aim of the link was to form a partnership that would contribute to curriculum development in Pakistan in the broadest sense. Components of the project included in-country and overseas training, the provision of books and equipment—in particular, computer equipment and training for each bureau—and the development of joint research projects. Pakistani researchers were invited to spend six week periods at the University of Bristol preparing research proposals, searching the literature and seeking research partners from among the Bristol staff before returning to Pakistan to carry out small research projects. It was from such a short visit that the joint research project analyzed below was initiated. An additional component in the original project design was a plan to cluster schools to promote local curriculum development. This activity proved impossible to implement, despite agreement from both ODA and the government of Pakistan in the original project documentation. After some negotiation, the resources originally committed to this component were redirected to fund the joint research project. ODA's flexibility in responding to the request from the university and the curriculum bureaux reflects well upon the agency, and in evaluating the impact of the overall initiative the outcome of the joint research project counts as a significant achievement.

Curriculum in Pakistan is a national or federal responsibility. The provincial departments of education are responsible for the implementation of nationally agreed guidelines. The Federal Curriculum Bureau, popularly known as the "Curriculum Wing," develops the guidelines for school curricula and for the Primary Teachers' Certificate (PTC) and the Certificate in Teaching (CT). These awards are for primary school teachers and middle school teachers respectively and are offered at Elementary Colleges of Education (ECE) throughout Pakistan. Provincial curriculum bureaus contribute to the development of national guidelines through their membership of syllabus panels. There is a good deal of cooperation between the bureaus and textbooks developed in one province are frequently adopted in the others.

The Pakistan-Bristol Link Project focused largely on the issues of curriculum management and implementation. The project was conceived as one in which changing the actual content of curricula would be less the subject of joint activities than training and research in strategies for implementation. Hence, much overseas training, both short-term and for the University of Bristol's one-year Master of Education degree, emphasized management problems and issues in curriculum development. In-country seminars and workshops also focused on implementation challenges. Thus it became clear that more research would be necessary to identify important issues in the management of the curriculum. A sharper identification of the research required occurred as a result of more ODA funded initiatives, including a 1988 review of teacher education in Pakistan (Smith et al., 1988), and a further survey a year later of the training needs of ECE staff (Smith et al., 1989). ODA's own attitude to research as a key factor in educational development is reflected in its *Education Policy Paper*. The agency indicates that research projects should involve overseas partners and should define a policy direction for ODA, address a problem of interest to donors, pump-prime a wider project or form an integral part of an existing project (ODA, 1994:9). The Link Project's evaluation of the curriculum in Pakistan's Elementary Colleges of Education conformed well to these objectives. Doing qualitative educational research in developing countries is not a new activity although its history is relatively short (see Vulliamy et al., 1990). What is of particular significance in the experience discussed and analyzed below is the teamwork dimension. Not only were Pakistani researchers supported by UK-based researchers, but teamwork was built up between and within the provincial bureaux themselves.

The Context of the Research: Why Are All Those People Counting All Those Numbers?

The attempt to make a scientific study of education or, "to provide an organized body of empirical knowledge integrated by a set of tested theories" (Kitwood, 1976:76), is of fairly recent origin. Charlotte Fleming's *Research and the Basic Curriculum* (1946) was the first British example of a compendium of research which went beyond mere psychometrics, and Cohen and Manion (1989), in what has become a standard work on educational research, illustrate its popular conception by referring to it as "scientific" and noting that it would enable educators to develop the kind of reliable knowledge base boasted by other disciplines. Much educational research has thus been presented in standard textbooks as a largely unproblematic and technical process concerned with sampling, questionnaire design, interview schedules, response rates and standardized statistical techniques. An idealized model of the research process has been presented by many writers in which approaches have been carefully planned in advance, where predetermined methods and procedures have been pursued and "reliable" and "valid" results have followed as a natural consequence. Critics of this form of scientism have, however, leveled charges of reductionism and technicism. Walford (1991) also notes that much research in the natural sciences is actually characterized by compromises, shortcuts, hunches and sheer serendipity; in other words there is a romantic view of what happens in "scientific" research which may not represent the reality of what "the people in white coats" spend their time doing.

This romantic or unrealistic view has been thoroughly embraced in Pakistan. The research landscape is dominated by people counting numbers in one form or another. Not only is number-counting a way of life; the recording of these activities is both rigorous and de rigueur. Summaries, abstracts and reports of research are produced regularly by such bodies as the Academy of Educational Planning and Management (AEPAM), whose *Documentation of Educational Research in Pakistan*, 1947–90 (AEPAM, 1990) provides a compendium of educational research undertaken since independence. The listings include the output of various university institutes, government research bureaux and individual authors and researchers. Documents listed include textbooks, workshop reports, masters' and doctoral theses, formal commissioned research and evaluation reports. Some 443 documents are listed and annotated. Articles appearing in the *Pakistan Education Journal* also reflect a strong commitment to quantitative research.

It is clear from the majority of research abstracts listed in the AEPAM compendium and elsewhere that almost all contributors attempt to conform to the scientific requirements of the natural sciences such as agricultural or biological research. In another AEPAM publication, of the first fifty research studies listed, thirty-three were purely quantitative in nature and three were of a qualitative design (see Farooq, 1989). However, the rigor with which this work is pursued varies from case to case. Small samples, unclear hypotheses, little theoretical insight and confused findings characterize many reports, while the general presentation of papers follows the approved scientific model, complete with precise measurements and apparently appropriate tests for significance. There is little doubt that the researchers believe that a cumulative body of objective knowledge has been built up. In its details too, each piece of research appears to be modeling itself on a particular view of science. There is clearly great faith in mathematics as an appropriate language for summing up and interpreting social events.

Whether educational research can or should match up to this kind of scientific model or not is more than an academic argument, especially in countries like Pakistan where educational policy may be shaped by research which is little more than folklore dressed up with statistics. Research into the weight of books carried in a pupil's satchel, for example, actually led to a curriculum policy change. An integrated curriculum was developed for the early grades thus introducing a single textbook to replace several, presumably heavier, textbooks. The research itself was sadly flawed by using a small and unrepresentative sample drawn from elite schools in the capital city. However, it had the all-important appearance of scientific respectability (see AEPAM, 1990). It could be argued that the change in policy might reflect more of the micropolitics of curriculum development in Pakistan than a real faith in scientific research. But what is meant by the term scientific?

MODELS OF RESEARCH

Questions concerned with how scientific educational research is depend on how the natural sciences are viewed or characterized. Science is a means by which we are able to integrate experience through general laws and theories. No ultimate reality may be revealed but a useful basis for explanation and prediction is achieved. An alternative view might be that science is there to help us proceed through accurate observation and description to where we may make causal connections. Unfortunately, much of what passes for scientific educational research in Pakistan fits neither model. To illustrate this it can be argued that concepts from the natural sciences like mass, length and time are relatively stable, or at least scientists within the same paradigm can discuss their meanings fruitfully. The same cannot be said of terms like effectiveness, achievement, interests and so on. Yet in Pakistan they are often incorporated into heavily quantitative studies as if they were entirely unproblematic. More importantly, analysis of much of the research described in the AEPAM compendium reveals that there is not only a reliance on very elastic terminology but there is some naïvety in the selection of methods of research. To quote a direct example from recently published work—"Explaining the differences in academic achievement of students of male and female teachers in primary schools in Pakistan" (see AEPAM, 1990:20). The study quoted is preoccupied with "scientific" procedures like random sampling and relating mean pupil scores to the teacher's gender. Can it really be envisaged that a direct causal link can be found between the sex of the teacher and the achievement of the pupils? Were no other variables considered? Can such variables be successfully controlled statistically? What difference will the findings make anyway? Will there be mass transfers of male and female teachers to more appropriate classes as a result of the findings? Has this field not always proved a methodological minefield (see Simmons and Alexander, 1980)?

Further evidence for the borrowing of inappropriate models of research in Pakistan can be seen from a category of studies best labeled as "manipulative," reminiscent of the notorious work of Sherif with summer-camp boys in the United States in the late 1950s (see Cronbach, 1963). Typical of research reports conforming to the manipulative model in which groups are set against one another is one entitled "The effect of a fearful and fear-arousing message on pupil learning" (AEPAM, 1990:341), an unethical study if ever there was one, but one which fits well into a white-coat-in-a-laboratory view of research. In summary it can be stated that most of the research listed in educational reports in Pakistan has as common currency "subjects," "treatments," "factors," "variables," "correlations" and "differences." On the other hand, those at the chalk-face of education are probably more concerned with people, ideas, relationships and skills. This is more than a claim for more humanism in the humanities; educational research in Pakistan has, it is argued, created a false consciousness—the prestige of science—that has obscured the real needs of the people in education, particularly the pupils. In another context Peter Woods captures the same point and has this to say:

I am not arguing that we should not have a rigorous methodology with due attention to matters of validity, access, ethics, data collection etc., nor that we should not have tested and recognized techniques and routines. Rather that, as part of that methodology, we should give equal attention to the cultivation of mental states as conducive to the production of theory as to the collection of data. One requires liberation, creativity and imagination; the other, discipline, control and method. (cited in Walford, 1991:187)

It is these issues that lie at the heart of the problem of educational research in Pakistan.

PROBLEMS FOR EDUCATIONAL RESEARCH

Here it is argued that more educational research should be set up to address real problems, not merely to exploit a technique that happens to be available or to satisfy the research component in an aid donor's project. The massive problems of poverty, illiteracy and gender inequities, which bedevil education systems in developing countries and which are reflected in ODA's aid priorities, cry out for high quality research. An emphasis on problem-based research would be likely to stimulate the development of newer modes of inquiry that are better suited to education. In particular the quantitative survey as a vehicle for educational research has become over-dominant in Pakistan. The research component of the Pakistan-Bristol Link discussed here therefore had to contend with the quantitative, hard data paradigm characteristic of the Ministry of Education. Research reports already abound that list the number of library books available, the years of experience of teaching staff and the numbers of chalk-boards and storage cupboards per student group in the colleges of education; yet little is known of the quality of the work going on there.

If educational research is to address real problems it is also essential that the methods of inquiry are appropriate to the topics selected. The pursuit of understanding is a key issue in qualitative research. Ideas and values form a crucial element in social action and social institutions and must be understood as such. Thus Kitwood (1976:79) maintains that "in the interpretative understanding of inter-personal situations, the grasping of the significance of human actions is possibly of greater importance (than mere measurement)."

A further fundamental issue for countries like Pakistan is the fuller recognition of the potential of the teacher as a researcher. Detachment and as much objectivity as possible are prerequisites for many types of research, but there are some forms of inquiry which can best be carried out by someone who is actively and continuously involved in the practice itself. It would be hard for anyone other than a teacher to detect differences in the "feel" of a class at different times of the school day or to observe how different groups of pupils react to different teaching styles. Teachers are of course already engaged in educational research as they meet pupils, prepare lessons, solve problems—insofar as they have theories to guide their actions. They should certainly have the "tacit knowledge" of the context that Polanyi (1969) sees as essential for excellence in science.

In this last statement lies a possible answer to the question of why all those people are counting all those numbers. Social scientists and professional educational researchers, locked into a limited view of what is scientific, are simply doing what they think they ought to do, and what their peers seem to be doing all over the world. Perhaps it is the teachers' body of commonsense knowledge, systematized, tested, extended and linked to worthwhile theory that will provide a basis for more useful educational research. If research is defined as systematic, self-critical inquiry there is no reason why teachers, professional researchers or teacher educators should not be trained in a variety of approaches, and encouraged to be self-critical.

AN ALTERNATIVE RESEARCH MODEL FOR TEACHER EDUCATION: QUALITATIVE RESEARCH AND TEAM BUILDING

The curriculum for Pakistan's Elementary Colleges of Education (ECEs) has remained unchanged since 1976, despite extensive and radical change in most aspects of the school curriculum and in government policy regarding such issues as girls' enrollments. This state of affairs made the selection of the ECE curricula as a research focus a timely and logical choice. The presence in Bristol of an experienced researcher from the Sindh Bureau of Curriculum and Research on short-term research training added impetus to the proposal and a research approach was developed that would involve the staff of all the curriculum bureaux working as teams with colleagues from the ECEs. The project which developed comprised a design phase, conducted in Bristol and focusing on problem identification, literature review and project design; an initiation phase, conducted in Pakistan and including selection of local research teams (LRTs), initial training and development of research approaches; the implementation phase, involving fieldwork in Pakistan by the LRTs, continued revision of instruments and training workshops; an analysis phase, conducted in Pakistan and requiring the LRTs to develop provincial reports, later to be combined into a national report; and a finalization phase in Bristol during which the national report was edited and redrafted in English ready for publication.

This apparently neat structure hides a multitude of issues and challenges and the whole procedure took two and a half years from the first problem identification in July 1990 to the publication of the final report in December 1993. This is not to suggest that we experienced only problems and there is no doubt that the final outcome was well worthwhile. Not only was the research product well received but the process of staff development was extremely valuable. Even more important, the professionals responsible for the renewal of the college curricula carried out the analysis themselves, working in teams made up from Curriculum Bureau staff plus ECE personnel.

The Teams in Operation
The Design Phase

From its inception a chief characteristic of this research project was its team approach. Mention has been made of Iqbal Malik's visit to the UK, accompanied by Jawaid Rashid of the federal Curriculum Wing. In discussion and negotiation with Bristol staff, notably J.M. Gutiérrez-Vázquez of the Centre for International Studies in Education, it soon became apparent that a joint activity for both Research Fellows would be more productive in the limited time available for the design phase. Malik was already an experienced researcher, albeit more familiar with quantitative studies. Rashid was less experienced. Combining their time and effort made sense for a number of practical reasons, not least being the desire to start a teamwork project *through* teamwork. The Bristol Link Project staff had also developed a team or joint approach to much of the other work with Pakistan so a synergy began to develop, albeit complicated by insider/outsider, project manager/ project recipient relationships. The very issue of selecting a research strategy of a more qualitative type became a topic of some debate; Bristol staff could see the value of "thick description" (Denzin, 1989) but did not wish to push a particular line. The Pakistani Research Fellows were more comfortable with surveys and questionnaires but became fascinated by the alternatives suggested. However, the conditions were well established for a cooperative venture, not least because of the long experience with Pakistan that the Bristol staff possessed. A strong partnership developed between Gutiérrez-Vázquez and Malik as the research literature was surveyed and analyzed. It was this process, the major rationale for the six-week study visits for Pakistani researchers, which produced the design eventually adopted. Four elements or goals were identified for the research design—analysis of the two ECE curricula, research training for Pakistani curriculum staff, development of a team approach and the implementation of a national rather than provincial inquiry. These goals reflected accurately the donor agency's concern for capacity building in Pakistan. By the time Malik and Rashid left Bristol, initial reading in research methodology had been conducted and a draft research plan, including a timetable for the completion of training, piloting and revision of instruments, fieldwork, analysis of findings and writing up had been prepared. During this phase it was decided by the design group to center on the evaluation of curricular aims and objectives, selected content areas of the curricula, teaching methods in use and college assessment procedures. This investigation of the implemented curriculum, supplemented by an assessment of the perceptions of ECE principals, tutors and students, as well as by practicing teachers and supervisors, was to become the focus of the research. In addition, the internal consistency of the curriculum documents, practices and textbooks was to be examined. Finally, the congruence of the curricula with national educational policies and a set of criteria derived from the international literature on teacher education formed the external consistency dimension of the research design.

Having settled on this four-fold design—evaluation of implementation, evaluation of internal and of external consistency and assessment of the perceptions of the "users"—attention shifted to the practicalities of carrying out the research, given that there are sixty-two ECEs in Pakistan located at points as widely separated as Gilgit in the north of the country to Karachi, some 1600 kilometers to the south. It was decided that some sort of sampling would be essential and that teams of researchers working in depth with a selected group of ECEs would yield richer results than yet another mass survey by postal questionnaire. Thus the broad principles of the research exercise were agreed in Bristol—a qualitative team inquiry focusing on the four areas noted above.

Much time had been spent on discussion of the team approach and its various advantages and disadvantages. Given the desire to achieve a widespread inquiry into the issues surrounding the ECE curriculum, coordinated teams of researchers were the obvious answer. However, the five bureaux had no history of working together on common research programs. More familiar was the commissioning of research from the Sindh and Punjab bureaux—always perceived as the strongest research centers—for provincial surveys or investigations from which national strategies might be developed. The question of the leadership and coordination of five teams also arose. Curriculum is a federal responsibility and any research into its effectiveness would normally be undertaken or commissioned by the Curriculum Wing in Islamabad. Added to these organizational challenges was the logistical one of how finance would be disbursed and accounted for as the exercise got under way and expenses and honoraria were claimed.

The Initiation Phase

Initiation of the research proper began with the negotiation of procedural issues such as methods of payment to researchers for their travel and time spent on the project and approval for access to the ECEs. These and other administrative matters were agreed with both the provincial and the federal authorities. The Bristol research partners visited all the provincial centers and the Curriculum Wing in Islamabad to obtain formal approval for the research project, and in particular its qualitative approach. It was this latter issue which created the biggest initial problem, although the logistics of paying the LRTs became a bone of contention later. Enough has been said already about the prevalence of a quantitative approach to research in Pakistan's education system. The conceptual and ideological debate concerned what Bryman (1988) refers to as "warrantable knowledge," whether what the research discovered would be regarded as worthwhile. For the Bristol people, and Malik himself who had become very attracted to qualitative approaches, there was little to be gained from further mass surveys, even of opinion from staff members of the ECEs. What had emerged from the research design phase was a conviction that a combination of methods involving documentary analysis, observation and field interviews of staff within a case-study framework would yield more illuminating results.

The management of education in Pakistan is highly bureaucratic and centralized. Obtaining offical approval for the research project was no easy task in a system where the "No Objection Certificate" is a major instrument of administration. This procedure requires each official to obtain a written go-ahead from his or her immediate superior before action may be taken, a chain of decision-making which is time consuming and cumbersome. After some delay—there were nine directors of the Curriculum Wing during the fifty-four-month life of the Link Project—the broad scheme of the research was agreed with the Pakistani authorities and with ODA. Five LRTs were identified, one federal at Islamabad and one for each of the provinces—North West Frontier Province (NWFP), Baluchistan, Sindh and Punjab. Each team had two or three members from the bureau, all of whom actively participated in a series of national workshops conducted between October 1990 and June 1992. All members at the workshops collectively designed the strategy for the project, the research approach and the instruments to be used. Training was also given in interviewing and classroom observation techniques.

A little has already been said about the novelty of using teams in qualitative studies, especially teams made up of ECE staff and Curriculum Bureau personnel. One of the recurrent problems during the project was the frequent attempts by certain bureau directors to substitute new members for trained researchers who had already been inducted into the project. Team building as a major outcome of the research program was certainly more of a Bristol priority than a local one. However, the teams were set up. The LRTs then carried out training of research assistants drawn from the ECEs in their own provinces in order to plan, organize, implement and evaluate their own research. Field testing of all instruments was carried out locally. A comprehensive set of documents was produced with and for the LRTs, ranging from statements of the aims of the project to guidelines for the setting up of local research teams and guides to interviewing and observation. Some eighteen documents were developed for the research project and remain as models for future research activities. These documents included guidelines for checking the internal consistency of teacher education curriculum documents. The syllabuses for key subjects taught at the ECEs and the "Blue Book," an official Ministry of Education publication outlining the principles and objectives of the ECE curricula, were the target documents for the internal consistency exercise.

The Implementation Phase

This phase saw the beginning of fieldwork and revisions to various guideline documents. By this time some of the implications of a teamwork approach were becoming more apparent. Note has been made of the difficulties of maintaining regular membership of teams in a context where frequent transfer at short notice is a feature of government service. Bogdan and Biklen's book (1992:211) is one of the few to discuss some of the pros and cons of teamwork in qualitative research, although Patton (1990:431) also comments on this approach. The most obvious advantage quoted is relevant to the Pakistan case study under discussion—the opportunity created to carry out work simultaneously at a number of sites. Bogdan and Biklen go on to suggest that the different skills and perspectives of the team members can add a richness to the process of research, provided rivalry does not obtrude. As the implementation of the project proceeded it became clear who were the leaders, who were the individualists and who were the team players. In fact, friendly rivalry, in terms of who could report back first on successful field visits, provided an impetus when progress slowed. Certainly the project coordinator ensured that responsibilities were clearly delineated and that deadlines were observed. This last issue constituted a perennial problem. At no period during the research were team members able to devote their full time to the program. Whilst evaluating the ECE curricula they had to maintain their normal workloads. Further issues arising from the team approach are spelled out later as lessons from experience, but at this stage of the research the design team and the coordinator felt encouraged that the teams were working well and carrying out the tasks allotted to them. Even more important, they were making valuable contributions to the revision and redesign of research activities through the national workshops.

Field work focused on a purposive approach to sample design (Borg and Gall, 1983; Patton, 1990) combining extreme cases, maximum variation and critical case strategies. Characteristics of the colleges examined, such as urban/rural, female/male/both sexes, well established/recently created, high/low prestige, traditional/progressive, socioeconomic environment and geographical location were identified. The sample of colleges used represented about 12% of the existing institutions. Specific details of the fieldwork are given elsewhere (Gutiérrez-Vázquez, Smith and Malik, 1993) but, in brief, each college was visited for a two- to three-week period. During this time college documentation relating to curriculum policy and implementation was surveyed, minutes of relevant meetings were reviewed, and the quality and availability of textbooks and other teaching and learning materials were assessed. Semi-structured interviews were carried out with principals, tutors, sub-division education officers and supervisors of primary education. Group interviews were also carried out with student teachers and practicing teachers drawn from each college catchment area. Classroom observation for the whole study involved the documentation and analysis of ninety class periods in a total of eleven subject areas.

Colleges varied in their reaction to visitation as part of the research program. The LRTs usually met the principal first and then discussed the project with the whole staff. The student body was also informed about the purpose of the visits. The role of the LRT members as insiders in the research process was crucial to the success of the project, especially when the semi-structured interviews were carried out. Classroom observation was also facilitated by the easy recognition of researchers as colleagues.

The Analysis Phase of the Research

Although ongoing analysis is characteristic of this type of qualitative inquiry, the regular coming together of the LRTs provided an opportunity for joint analysis of data gathered in the field. Through this exercise the necessity to sharpen the focus of the study became evident if we were to keep the analysis within manageable limits. The integration of the research activity into the ongoing work of the curriculum bureaux was highlighted at this point by the opportune publication of a survey document, or checklist, by the Curriculum Wing. This document encouraged the researchers to review their approaches and to develop more discerning questions and issues. The process of analysis was a particularly rewarding exercise, although time-consuming. The joint development of strategies for conducting the analysis and the building up of "trees" of categories by the different LRTs which were finally consolidated into an agreed analytical tool was a notable outcome of the research and training exercise. Typically a "tree" for investigation and analysis developed from a straightforward question such as the availability of subject syllabuses at the ECEs. This question branched out to deal with the four subjects being investigated at the PTC level, the seven subjects of the CT program and their availability to the lecturers and the students—a matrix of twenty-two questions arising from the initial item. Even larger trees with more branches were developed when evaluation strategies used for the eleven selected subjects were explored. The strategy for evaluation given in the curriculum, that used in practice, those used in teaching, the issue of internal and external evaluation, the value and relevance of examination papers, suggested schemes of evaluation, follow up to the learning process and assessment of student performance were all generated by the LRTs in their training workshops. Because so much of what was being explored was new territory for the teams, real excitement was generated as the work progressed. The five provincial/ federal write-ups of this information were then combined into a national draft by the team from Sindh. The outcome was massive, detailed and reiterative—but authentic.

The Reporting Phase

This stage of the project was intensive, involving the redrafting of the report and its preparation in English. This task was carried out in Bristol by Iqbal Malik, the originator of the research program, and his main collaborator, Gutiérrez-Vázquez. Following Patton (1990) it was agreed during the report writing that the key elements of focus, balancing description and interpretation and writing with the intended audience in mind should be paramount. Many of the findings of the research were in fact negative. The executive summary indicated numerous problems with the curriculum in practice so the issue of how to present the findings as something other than a long list of faults and failings became important. Nevertheless, it was possible to draw attention to a number of valuable positive elements in the teacher education system of Pakistan. The target audience for the research was seen to be not merely the official group responsible for occasional curriculum revisions. As teams had been built up to include ECE staff then the development of critical awareness in the institutions constituted a major target and achievement. The growth of research skills among the teams within the structure of teacher education, and the identification of key staff with an enthusiasm for change and development were also positive outcomes. Perhaps most important was the willingness of the Pakistani authorities to use the research findings as part of their policy development debate, particularly in terms of an Asian Development Bank initiative to revise the whole system of primary teacher education.

In summary, it can be said that the outcomes of the joint program of research exceeded our expectations. Although the study had limitations, particularly those imposed by lack of resources and time, its findings represented the first comprehensive study of the curriculum problems of the Elementary Colleges of Education in Pakistan. In the longer term a more important outcome may well be the establishment of a national network of trained researchers, used to working as a team and enthused by more varied approaches to the research enterprise.

Lessons Learned from Teamwork and Key Factors Contributing to Success

The important leadership dimension was a major element in the success of the research project. Both Malik and Gutiérrez-Vázquez exercised a form of committed leadership which drew others along with them, rather than imposing a managerialist style. Gutiérrez-Vázquez, a Mexican of wide experience in the developing world, was able to form a rapport with the LRTs which provided the back-up and support so emphasized by Bogdan and Biklen (1992:211) as an essential part of team research efforts. The laying out of clear deadlines and tasks by the project leaders also assisted the teams in working together. Shared responsibility in drafting, polishing and finalizing reports drew people together as they prepared their analyses and worked at forming them into a national picture. The frequently interrupted schedule of meetings and workshops gave an unexpected impetus to teamwork as the LRTs began to be concerned about the success of their project; for many it was a first opportunity to exercise real responsibility and they felt sensitive to any disruption that might interfere with completion of the task. It was a cause of some regret that the project leaders and design team were unable to carry out one of Bogdan and Biklen's recommendations—researching the researchers (Bogdan and Biklen, 1992: 212). Time and resources did not enable us to analyze changes in the teams, shifts of attitude or skill development. Only impressions were left with us, to be discussed as lessons learned from teamwork.

Whether the qualitative paradigm can take root more firmly in Pakistan remains to be seen. A relatively modest input from ODA funds of a few thousand pounds for a limited project cannot be expected to evangelize a whole national research community, nor perhaps should it if we are to avoid the criticism usually leveled at those exporting their own brand of research paradigm. But the Pakistan-Bristol Link experience raises important questions concerning the compatibility of a qualitative approach with the social and cultural milieu found in Pakistan.

Qualitative research has been described as "naturalistic," "holistic" and "contextualized" (Wiersma, 1991). These characterizations form a contrast with the Pakistani view of educational research, as reflected in published documentation, with its strong emphasis on what is perceived to be scientifically objective and therefore "true" (see, for example, Farooq, 1989). There is, however, much truth in Giarelli's statement that "all knowing, scientific and otherwise, involves interpretation" (cited in Sherman and Webb, 1990:213). It is this issue of interpretation which, it is argued, lies at the heart of the apparent dispute between the qualitative and the quantitative camps and that proved a stumbling block in developing enthusiasm for a more qualitative approach in Pakistan. Sherman and Webb (1990) characterize qualitative research as focusing on context, natural settings and discoveries that lead to new insights. Experience is to be taken as a whole, or holistically—understanding experience as unified rather than made up of disparate variables. Socio-cultural patterns of experience or relationships among events are "matters of importance, not the quantification of human events" (Sherman and Webb, 1990:6). Given this characterization, experience in Pakistan with the ECE research suggests that qualitative approaches to educational research lend themselves more readily to the realities of developing countries for a number of reasons. These can be summed up under the following three headings.

The Cultural Fit of Qualitative Research

David Court traces the development of educational research in Kenya back to the "international expansion" of American social science, allied to the spread of human capital theory and the inputs of international aid agencies into such institutions as ministry planning units, bureaux of statistics and their consequent emphasis on quantitative data-gathering. Court goes so far as to characterize early educational research in Kenya as "replicating Western-based studies" (see Shaeffer and Nkinyangi 1983:167). Using Pakistan as another example is easy to see the 1960s and 1970s as a period of imported research paradigms, often linked to scholarship schemes which encouraged students from the developing world to take higher degrees in the U.S. or Europe where the quantitative paradigm reigned supreme. The examples already given of published research from Pakistan show a marked emphasis on survey-type studies buttressed with much statistical support, often of dubious technical reliability or validity. The second and even more important point is that no paradigm other than the quantitative/scientific one seems to be used. In Maslow's words, when the only tool you have is a hammer, every problem begins to look like a nail (cited in Covey, 1992:27). It can therefore be argued that the only instrument available is a blunt one. Yet a more qualitative approach has much to commend it for cultural reasons because "human behaviour is shaped in context and . . . events cannot be understood adequately if isolated from their contexts" (Sherman and Webb, 1990:5).

This is an argument for adapting research to the culture in which the inquiry is to take place. The same writers go on to argue that "qualitative researchers want those who are studied to speak for themselves" (1990:5). In cultures that value oral traditions and where kinship and relationship are of pre-eminent importance a research paradigm may be more appropriate which rests upon qualitative principles. Where the validity of educational research is concerned there has been a long history of the replication of Western models in foreign contexts. The argument here is that much of what passes for educational research in the developing world is culture-bound— but bound in the culture of North America or Europe. This argument could be extended to examine much of what goes on in schools in Africa and Asia. Cultures that have, for example, long valued cooperation and peer instruction as a means of passing on the culture to the next generation have had to come to terms with what is called "cheating" in the imported school systems they have inherited. The characteristics of socio-cultural milieu must become the starting point for those designing educational research. As Shaeffer and Nkinyangi (1983:7) put it, "knowledge of [this] environment can lead to an assessment by governments and donor agencies alike of how best to enhance local capacity to define, analyze and resolve educational problems, in short, to 'do' educational research."

The same writers go on to suggest that the essential first steps in setting up viable and realistic educational research capacity in the developing world will require efforts to generate a national research environment that will guarantee the more effective conduct and application of educational research. Too often the researcher has come in with his or her model, developed at graduate schools or research institutes elsewhere, and then has attempted to apply the technology to the context. Aware of this within the research design phase at Bristol we were anxious not to impose a view of research that would suffer the same condemnation. Again, the emphasis on a teamwork approach helped to promote the rationale for a more context sensitive paradigm. It was acknowledged during the design phase that teams would find their fullest expression as they analyzed and interpreted rich qualitative data. As Kluckhohn (1959) says, "statistics obscure the qualitative dimensions of pattern and . . . informants should be viewed not as actors whose behaviour must be measured, but as documents that reflect the culture of which they are the bearers' (cited in Sherman and Webb, 1990:80). Part of the research plan was to regard our LRT members as documents in this sense. Qualitative research strategies are above all else context-sensitive and developing a national research environment was seen to require the skills and insights of our team members as fundamental building blocks. It can thus be argued that a holistic, natural approach to human inquiry is likely to be more readily assimilated into "traditional" cultures where ways of knowing are not confined to the technical. Indeed, it was refreshing to hear the levels of debate in LRT workshops concerning what was meant by what was said to researchers in their visits to colleges. This gave a new meaning to research for people who had previously only experienced the checking of questionnaire responses or other more formal instruments.

Resource Capacities

The resource capacities of many developing countries are too limited to provide the logistical and technical back-up that heavily quantitative approaches will require. Certainly the research team experienced a good deal of difficulty of a logistical and technical nature in setting up and implementing a fairly modest piece of qualitative research. If we had taken a larger sample, used a more quantitative approach requiring computer back-up for data analysis, had attempted to train more people in research techniques, then the resources of the curriculum bureaux would have been stretched to breaking point. The heavy, if routine, workloads of the research team members would have constituted even more of a constraint than we actually experienced.

Political Issues

Political problems often present themselves in educational research. There is often resistance to the large-scale national survey and Pakistan's statistical database is, for example, notably incomplete where female enrollments are concerned. The fundamentally political nature of educational research also becomes evident in considering the cultural environment in which research takes place when there is an argument in favor of using those approaches that most appropriately fit into the culture. In this light it is interesting to note that the Mali government has a declared policy of eschewing complex research (and what is seen as individualistic research merely for personal gain or intellectual satisfaction) in favor of a search for "solutions to the numerous socio-economic problems" facing the country: "Our research will be turned toward action, toward practical realizations in order to help provide our country with simple equipment and methods . . ." (cited in Shaeffer and Nkinyangi, 1983:246). This type of political support for more home-grown research priorities may also strengthen the case for qualitative studies carried out by local personnel.

CONCLUSIONS

The practical experience gained from the teamwork approach in Pakistan has been touched upon already but may be summarized in terms of leadership, support, ownership and logistics. The Link Project was fortunate in the leaders who emerged. Their commitment and energy were essential. The growth of the LRTs into real teams over the period of the research project also created a sense of ownership. The provincial reports were produced, bound and clearly identified with the different bureaux personnel. The structured timetable of events and activities, though frequently delayed, postponed or interrupted, also created a sense of purpose and progress as activities were achieved and ticked off the checklists. However, the logistical aspects of the project were not always smooth. LRT members paid expenses and other costs from their own pockets—another mark of commitment. Permission was not always granted for team members to carry out fieldwork on time. Frequent changes of plan were necessary and flexible scheduling soon became a way of life. Despite setbacks and delays, the team research project was accomplished. The qualitative approach had generated great enthusiasm and a modest new dimension had been added to the research capacity of the bureaux.

This team experience reported from Pakistan has tried to show that research located more toward the qualitative end of the continuum may be more naturalistic, more culturally sensitive and more acceptable both to those being studied and to those responsible for generating research support and funding in many developing countries. The end of all good research must be to "converse" more effectively. It is a constant complaint of researchers that nobody reads what they produce and nobody acts on their findings. The conversation remains one-sided. Perhaps the problem lying at the root of this non-communication is compounded by the style and type of research adopted. We would like to believe that in some cases research has led to improved policy and practice. The challenging of conventional wisdom has certainly been an outcome of some research designed to find more effective ways of solving educational problems. If more effective ways are to be found through research in developing countries then there is a major role to be played by those researchers who are prepared to cultivate increased sensitivity to the context in which they are working, in order to interpret reality and to utilize fully the "documents" with whom they interact. Not only will the usefulness of research products be enhanced but team building of this nature can help to develop the research capacity that is so badly needed. In this research project all involved became mutual documents, gaining from our reading of each other and creating deep and enduring linkages.

REFERENCES

Academy of Educational Planning and Management (AEPAM) (1990) *Directory of Educational Research Projects*. Islamabad: AEPAM.

Bogdan, R., and Biklen, S. (1992) *Qualitative Research for Education; An Introduction to Theory and Methods* (2d ed.). Boston: Allyn and Bacon.

Borg, W. and Gall, M. (1983) *Educational Research: An Introduction*. London: Longman.

Bryman, A. (1988) *Quantity and Quality in Social Research*. London: Unwin and Hyman.

Cohen, L. and Manion, L. (1989) *Research Methods in Education* (3rd ed.). London: Routledge.

Covey, S. (1992) *Seven Habits of Highly Effective People*. London: Simon and Schuster.

Cronbach, L. (1963) *Educational Psychology* (2d ed.). New York: Harcourt Brace.

Denzin, N. (1989) *Interpretative Interactionism*. Newbury Park: Sage.

Dockrell, W. and Hamilton, D. (1980) *Rethinking Educational Research*. London: Hodder and Stoughton.

Eisner, E. and Peshkin, A. (1990) *Qualitative Inquiry in Education: The Continuing Debate*. New York: Teachers' College.

Farooq, R. (1989) *Research in Support of Decision Making or Policy Making in Education*. Islamabad: AEPAM.

Guba, E. (1978) *Toward a Methodology of Naturalistic Enquiry in Educational Evaluation*. Los Angeles: University of California, Graduate School of Education, Center for the Study of Evaluation.

Gutiérrez-Vázquez, J.M., Smith, R.L. and Malik, M.I. (1993) *A Qualitative Study of the Official, Perceived and Implemented Curricula for Teacher Education in Pakistan*. Bristol: University of Bristol, School of Education.

Kitwood, T. (1976) "Educational Research and its Standing as Science," *Studies in Higher Education*, 1 (1):76–83.

Overseas Development Administration. (1994) *Aid to Education in 1993 and Beyond*. London: ODA.

Patton, M. (1990) *Qualitative Evaluation and Research Methods*. Newbury Park: Sage.

Polanyi, M. (1969) *Knowing and Being*. (Edited by M. Greene). London: Routledge.

Shaeffer, S. and Nkinyangi, J. (eds.) (1983) *Educational Research Environments in the Developing World*. Ottawa: IDRC.

Sherman, R., and Webb, R. (eds.) (1990) *Qualitative Research in Education: Focus and Methods*. London: Falmer Press.

Simmons, J. and Alexander, L. (1980) "The Determinants of Cognitive Achievement in Developing Countries." In J. Simmons (ed.) (1980) *The Education Dilemma*. Oxford: Pergamon.

Smith, R.L., Thompson, G.O.B., Hough, J.R. and Underwood, M. (1988) *A Survey of Teacher Education in Pakistan*. London: ODA.

Smith, R.L., Garrett, R.M., Penny, A. and Hough, J.R. (1989) *Training of Staff of ECEs in Pakistan: A Needs Analysis*. London: ODA.

Vulliamy, G., Lewin, K. and Stephens, D. (1990) *Doing Educational Research in Developing Countries: Qualitative Strategies*. London: Falmer Press.

Walford, G. (1991) (ed.) *Doing Educational Research*. London: Routledge.

Wiersma, W. (1991) *Research Methods in Education: An Introduction*. (5th ed.) Boston: Allyn and Bacon.

11 NORTH-SOUTH COLLABORATION IN EDUCATIONAL RESEARCH

REFLECTIONS ON INDIAN EXPERIENCE

Archana Choksi

Caroline Dyer

INTRODUCTION

This chapter explores the practice of collaborative educational research between the north and south—in this case Britain and India. We discuss two studies in India, both sited in the state of Gujarat (Figure 11:1): the first on the implementation of a policy innovation in primary education; the second on a literacy project with nomads. Through these personal reflections on qualitative research from the field, we draw out a number of issues that are of methodological as well as cultural significance. We hope this analysis will be of interest to those already involved in or considering north-south collaborative work, and to those with a particular interest in India.

The most common form of north-south research collaboration is within aid projects in the south emanating from northern agencies, typically casting the north as "donor" and the south as "recipient"; contracted evaluation research is the major research output (King, 1984). While this is the dominant paradigm, it is not the only one: King (1984) points also to non-contract collaborative research and its potential; north-south academic links; and direct funding for the south from northern research councils. The type of collaboration we discuss here is non-contract disciplinary research, and the second study was specifically designed to "draw into a single complex project in the South expertise from both North and South" (King, 1984: 26). Although this paper focuses on independent academic research, it highlights aspects of practice that are of relevance to all varieties of collaborative research.

It is timely to reflect on collaborative research in the context of India, given dramatic recent changes in its national policy relating to overseas involvement in education, particularly in the primary sector. Since the early 1980s, preceding the new National Policy on Education in 1986 (NPE, 1986), and then following the 1990 Jomtien Declaration, the Indian government has for the first time encouraged states designated "education-ally backward" to seek external assistance to enhance their development, and ultimately to bring about the national goal of providing free, compulsory education to all Indian children aged between six and fourteen. In line with their own changing policies, "donors" are now concerned not only to inject funds, but also to build up technical expertise and self-reliance in the host country (King, 1992).

In these changed circumstances, opportunities for collaborative research in India will, without doubt, increase in future (cf. Davison, 1992). While this may have positive benefits in the long term, we share the concern, voiced by authors such as Crossley and Broadfoot (1992) and Fry and Thurber (1989), that it may result in a greater traffic of international consultants who are less attuned to the contextual factors which so greatly influence the acceptability and appropriateness of the policy and practice they advocate.

Successful cross-national transfer of expertise is not easy to achieve, and indeed, perceptions of expertise are themselves likely to differ. As Leach (1993:18) notes, in her analysis of northern collaboration on externally-funded development projects in Africa, "expatriates had learned a great deal about local practices, socio-cultural traditions and the bureaucratic environment in which they worked [but] what they learnt they treated as social or cultural phenomena, of little worth professionally." It seems to us that the assumption that "social intelligence" (Archer, 1980) is of limited worth is mistaken: it is a vital component of professional expertise (Fry and Thurber, 1989) and a prerequisite for successful north-south collaboration. Northern researchers working in the south need to be very sensitive to cultural nuances, in order first to locate problems in practice, as perceived by respondents, and second to work together on culturally appropriate measures to address them. Cross-cultural perceptions of problems are equally likely to be very different, and "solutions" that are culturally inappropriate may only give rise to new problems.

Since the homogenizing, top-down model of policy-formulation and implementation is dominant in India (Dyer, 1993 and 1994a), research must attempt to sensitize elite decision-makers to the heterogeneous social contexts and perceptions of other groups in such a vast and varied country. Ethnographic research can play a major part in such endeavors. In such efforts, "cultural" perceptions will typically form an integral part of the multiple social realities which ethnographers try to understand (Crossley and Broadfoot, 1992) and this is an essential policy input, since these realities will inevitably condition policy implementation.

Joint research projects sited in the south can have further benefits because of restrictions on local researchers. Our experience suggests for instance that the Indian policy establishment is generally more attuned to inputs from external or national-level sources, rather than "indigenous" research (cf. Shaeffer, 1991). For reasons of prestige and status northerners may have better access to policy makers, and may then be well placed to reflect the views of non-mainstream communities, to "speak truth to power" (Wildavksy, cited in Archer 1980), and to promote the participation of the southern colleague in such interactions. The political sensitivity of the research subject, restricted access, and the poverty of material working conditions can result in the "absence of a real research environment" (Salmi, 1984:10; discussed later in this chapter) that collaboration can to some extent address (but see King, 1984).

For all these reasons, sensitive collaborative research has tremendous potential to use a range of insider and outsider perspectives and to engage with the most influential and the most disempowered. A north-south research team will inevitably have different perceptions of the "familiar" and the "strange," the understanding of which is a major ethnographic task (Spindler, 1982). Linguistically and culturally, an insider can achieve much that would not be possible for an outsider, yet there are roles for an outsider that cannot be assumed by an insider. Collaboration can help overcome disadvantages faced by either side as a result of disparities in material conditions, political agendas and research climates; and lead to a two-way flow of cultural insight and technical expertise that can be most effectively applied to educational problems (Crossley, 1990).

QUALITATIVE EDUCATIONAL RESEARCH IN INDIA

In India, qualitative research methods in education are not yet widespread. We have conducted interviews among teachers, at various levels of government, and in university settings, and a general lack of understanding of the procedures involved in data collection by qualitative methods has been apparent. This is not to say that there is no interest in their potential, for the limitations of quantitative research in illuminating "hows" and "whys" are often self-evident. For instance, the types of insight into classroom experience and the quality of the school experience required to bring about the qualitative improvements now sought by policy-makers (NPE, 1986) cannot readily be furnished by quantitative methodologies, but are the natural domain of the interpretive paradigm underlying qualitative methods (Hawes and Stephens, 1990; Vulliamy et al., 1990).

Low awareness of qualitative methodologies can be attributed to the weak interface between field practitioners, academics and government officials; and the current rather stagnant status of research within the discipline of education (Dhingra, 1991; UNICEF, 1991). The worlds of teachers, academics, policy makers and the bureaucratic administrators of education in India exist largely independently of one another (a problem by no means confined to southern contexts (cf. Finch, 1986)). None of these expects that independent educational research should inform policy formulation and implementation. Until very recently, policy makers' data needs were largely confined to statistical evaluations of numerical progress towards set targets (Dhingra, 1991), with policy inputs from quasi-government organizations such as the New Delhi-based National Council of Educational Research and Training. This arrangement appears to bypass the need for a national educational research policy with the responsibilities and priorities of actors at various levels defined (Fagerlind and Hallak, 1991). Independent researchers have little incentive to respond to information gaps they perceive to exist in the policy-making process, since these have either not been strongly felt by policy makers, or are catered for by commissioned research; most academic studies are thus destined to remain on a dusty shelf.

There is however an awakening interest among policy makers in qualitative aspects of the school system. This was evident in a major national policy shift in 1986, which suggested that the quality of schooling could be a contributing factor in the continued difficulties of enrolling and retaining children in schools (NPE, 1986). In the wake of the 1990 Jomtien Declaration of Education for All by 2000, good ethnographic studies of primary education would be a useful policy input to determine the specific areas in which funds and expertise could most usefully be allocated.

One reason why it has been difficult for the educational establishment to follow up these policy initiatives has been the extreme shortage of qualitative studies of school processes. For, if policy makers are really to draw on sources other than statistical information bases, they need something more solid than anecdotes about practice in school (Dhingra, 1991). Equally, if research is to feed into policy-making circles, channels must be created through which the information can flow.

The weak demand for research from policy makers, and political and access restrictions that determine the choice of subject matter, have meant that universities have been slow to respond to the changing national and international scenario, in terms of both the content and type of research conducted. Educational research conducted in Indian academic institutions is almost always conducted within the quantitative paradigm. By and large, studies set out with a hypothesis that is then proved by statistical methods: it is very rare to find a study that is experimental enough to find its original hypothesis wrong. To those schooled in, and comfortable with, quantitative methods, participant observation, in-depth interviews and talking to people seem neither "scientific" nor rigorous. Qualitative research seems to suffer from a credibility gap among both researchers and policy makers; and ironically, the very accessibility of the language of qualitative research may also be a factor that weighs against it (Bogdan and Biklen, 1992).

It is difficult for either the practice or image of qualitative research in India to improve, since so little information is available in country about the procedures of conducting such research. The growing body of methodological texts that cover its procedural, ethical and other aspects is generally published in the north and these texts are too expensive for most university libraries in the south. At the moment, texts which explicitly deal with the methodology of qualitative educational research in southern contexts (cf. Vulliamy et al., 1990 and this present volume) are few and far between. Moreover, until a demand for qualitative work is generated, this circle will be difficult to break.

It is noteworthy too that in India remarkably little educational research, either in universities or government organizations, has been directed toward the primary sector. Tertiary education has, since independence, absorbed the lion's share of government funds and established itself as the most prestigious sector. To work in primary education is to choose the bottom rung of the ladder and as a result, within university settings, research on aspects of primary education is comparatively rare. The content of B.Ed., M.Ed. and higher degrees is oriented toward secondary and tertiary education, and these do not attract or encourage primary teachers. Action research conducted by teachers in schools requires a level of professional awareness that has not, as yet, been achieved, particularly among primary teachers (Dyer, 1995).

Indian researchers may also face difficulties in tackling qualitative research for reasons closely linked with their own schooling. From an early age, most education in India is imparted in order that students pass examinations that test one's grasp of received wisdom and ability to replicate it, rather than the manipulation of concepts (Kumar, 1991). Content is presented as a given, in a highly structured format: it is facts, rather than problem-solving skills, that are taught. In contrast, qualitative research is often rather diffuse, sometimes untidy, and difficult to analyze. The transition for researchers used to orderly information can be difficult to make, particularly given the shortage of information and relevant examples to draw on.

Indian social contexts tend also to be more hierarchical than in the north. For Indians, it is socially appropriate to accept the status quo and generally considered unacceptable to challenge one's elders at least until one is an adult. This contributes to a certain conservatism in the study of education, and exerts a pressure to opt for safe and conventional research topics, rather than innovative ones which may not be acceptable to the older members of the establishment, or may be challenging to the political status quo.

This combination of education and socialization often means that Indian researchers initially find it difficult to deal confidently with the loosely structured nature of qualitative research. In a collaborative context, the northerner may need to recognize these constraints and offer moral support until the southern counterpart has grown comfortable with the new methodology. Once these barriers outlined have been overcome, at least to some extent, researchers are often enthusiastic about the use of qualitative research methods in educational contexts.

NORTH-SOUTH COLLABORATION IN PRACTICE

Our collaboration began when Caroline Dyer was in India collecting data for her doctoral thesis on policy implementation in Indian primary education. It has continued on several other projects, the longest of which is currently in progress: a two-year research project "Literacy for Nomads: an ethnographic study of literacy acquisition among nomads of Gujarat" funded by Britain's Economic and Social Research Council (ESRC).

Our basic disciplines differ in many ways: one researcher graduated from Liverpool University in German and Dutch and was a teacher of English and later a journalist in Hong Kong, covering education, before beginning her Ph.D.; the other has a first degree in fine arts, several years of business experience, two M.A.s, and a Ph.D. in the ethnoarchaeology of the relationship between ceramics and society. In general, the variety in our disciplinary backgrounds is a positive feature (Crossley and Broadfoot, 1992; Kelly and Altbach, 1988). Our interests and skills complement each other and we have tried to understand and then take advantage of our differences— such as race, language, socialization—as well as our similarities—for instance gender, critical inquisitiveness—to further the research process.

Our work together in the last three years has taken us into some extraordinarily varied realms: from the corridors of power in New Delhi's Ministry of Human Resources Development to single-room schools in the most isolated tribal hamlets in Gujarat; from national-level curriculum designers to illiterate shepherds, and little children in and out of school.

The variety of these socio-economic contexts, and the socialization and value frameworks of those who live in them is startling and, for the qualitative researcher, very challenging. We have found that if we capitalize on the "critical external perspective that is so valuable in making the familiar strange" (Crossley, 1993:230; Spindler, 1982) and an intimate knowledge of the culture in which we are working, we have powerful qualitative working tools at our disposal. Our north-south collaboration as an Anglo-Indian team has many advantages, most prominently in terms of access and language, for our major research task—understanding the sociological make-up of Indian society and its implications for education.

OPERATION BLACKBOARD

Intrigued by the colonial legacy of education systems in both Hong Kong and India, and by the sheer logistics of running schools in the remote areas visited during trips to India, Caroline Dyer's research interests rapidly turned toward contemporary Indian policy-making. A preliminary literature review suggested that social policy studies in developing countries such as India tend to focus on the policy itself, while implementation is a neglected domain (Jain, 1990; Crossley and Vulliamy, 1984). With this gap in mind, and convinced of the value of qualitative work in policy studies, the doctoral thesis was designed as "a descriptive analysis of policy implementation—a documentation of process with a deliberate focus on the school level" (Dyer, 1993:3). The 1986 policy program of Operation Blackboard was selected as a case study from which implications could be drawn for the wider issues of education policy implementation in the Indian context.

Operation Blackboard was designed to improve the quality of education in primary schools. It grew out of the shocking findings provided by the Fourth and Fifth All India Educational Surveys (in 1978 and 1986) that just over one-third of Indian primary schools were single-teacher, single-room establishments, simultaneously accommodating as many as five standards. Half of the schools had neither playground nor drinking water, and 40% had not so much as a single blackboard, let alone any other teaching aids. The "Operation" therefore consisted of trying to bring all India's grades one through five schools up to a minimum standard comprising two rooms, two teachers (one of them preferably female) and a set of "minimum essential" teaching-learning aids (TLA); and funded, to a tune of more than £260 million, by the central government. Implementation was to be done by the state governments, and was clearly going to be very difficult, given the size and scope of the area Operation Blackboard covered, the ambitiousness of the policy itself, and the accumulated neglect, over the years, of primary schooling. These were some of the "foreshadowed problems" that provided initial research themes (Hammersley and Atkinson, 1983).

Once the research visa had been granted, preliminary orientation work in the field went well, assisted by relevant policy documents, a basic grasp of Gujarati grammar, and Vulliamy et al.'s (1990) *Doing Educational Research in Developing Countries*. To observe classroom practice, two weeks

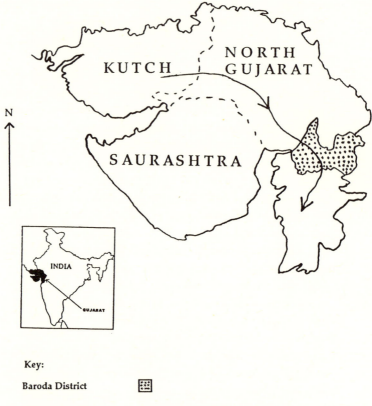

Key:

Baroda District

NORTH GUJARAT:	Area of concentration of Desai Rabaris, mostly sedentary
KUTCH:	Area of concentration of Kutchi, Dhebaria and Vagad Rabaris: Vagad and Dhebaria Rabaris migrate for the longest period per year (about 9 months)
SAURASHTRA:	Area of concentration of Bhopa Rabaris, mostly short migrations within Saurashtra
————	Migratory route of Vagad Rabaris with whom the researchers are working

Figure 11.1. Map of Gujarat, showing Baroda District, and the areas of the state where the nomadic populations are concentrated.

were spent as a participant observer in one school in a rural area of Baroda district; and two weeks in a school in a tribal area of the District; and two weeks in a municipal school in Baroda itself (Figure 11.1). It proved not to be a problem to gain orienting information from government officials, who were helpful, encouraging, and comfortable in English. But attempts to talk to teachers through the two male "interpreters" who had organized the observation periods were less successful: the first was not Gujarati, and nor was he skilled at field interviewing, visibly intimidating teachers; the second was himself Gujarati and a teacher, who was very interested in the subject and also in learning how to do qualitative research, but was not quite fluent enough in English to convey the subtler nuances of what teachers said.

Four months into the research, it was becoming urgently necessary to find someone better able to draw out insights from teachers. It proved a real problem to find people who were prepared to forfeit modern urban facilities for the insecurities of forays to villages and uncertain food and accommodation. An acquaintance's mention of someone in the arts faculty who liked going to rural areas and "talking to people" was promising, and led to a committed field researcher who was then conducting ethnographic work on pastorals' settlement patterns.

Although at the beginning it was a research relationship based on expediency—a solution to the northern researcher's problem of not speaking enough of the local language to do in-depth ethnographic interviews— this quickly changed as the insider became increasingly involved in understanding the dynamics of the educational system she herself had passed through. The collaboration also offered the southern researcher, who had suffered from the absence of available methodological information discussed earlier, an opportunity to expand her own range of data collection skills. As time went on, both researchers were increasingly drawn in to the extremely complex problematic of implementing the same centrally devised policy innovation in a myriad of different social contexts, which subsequently became a core theme of the research.

Backwards Mapping

The research strategy adopted to study Operation Blackboard was "backwards mapping" (Elmore, 1980), a bottom-up approach to policy implementation that begins "with a statement of the specific behaviour at the lowest level of the implementation process that generates the need for a policy" (Elmore, 1980:604). Unlike the top-down approach, which begins from the policy statement and works down towards the grassroots, backwards mapping switches focus to those customarily considered last—in this case, teachers. It is usually used as a pre-policy tool, but was adopted in this research as a structured approach to pinpointing outcomes and perceptions of a policy innovation at various points in the implementation process, from teachers in schools through the various levels of government to the Center, where it was conceived.

The complexity of the process, which for this innovation had two strands—the academic and the administrative—in India's federal polity is illustrated in Figure 11.2

Over 120 formal interviews were conducted in the course of one year, and these covered teachers in schools, and teacher trainers at district, state and national levels, as well as administrators in three tiers of government—local self-government, state, and national.

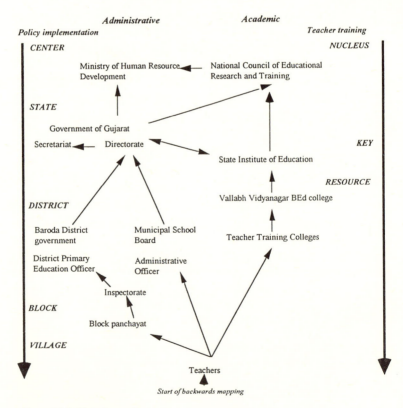

Key Bold arrows going downwards indicate the direction of policy and teacher training flow:
     arrows going upwards indicate the direction and course of backwards mapping

Figure 11.2. Mapping routes.

Backwards mapping began with the "grassroots:" teachers in schools. No access negotiations were required to visit schools, although courtesy visits were paid to the officers in charge of the district and municipal schools. The main problem at this level was one of establishing trust, as teachers were often very defensive. Their caution was related to their difficulties in implementing the program; defense of the collective identity; and their perceptions of the researchers as outsiders who had probably come to look for problems (Dhabi, 1991), since rural schools are rarely visited by anyone except the inspector, whose visits are associated with fault finding. Primary schools are, as mentioned earlier, rarely the focus of research studies. Our first difficulty was therefore that teachers did not really understand why we were there, asking all those questions, and were suspicious of us.

Second, teachers were having problems with Operation Blackboard, which as a result largely failed to have the impact on school process that it could have done. Because it did not pay attention to the needs of teachers in different circumstances, and because the training teachers received was inadequate for the shift in teaching methodology envisaged, teachers were often not really sure either how to use the teaching materials, or why they should. As a result, they were often very defensive as they tried to maintain the equilibrium of their daily teaching life which the innovation threatened to upset (see Adams and Chen, 1981; Fullan, 1991; Havelock and Huberman, 1977; Morris, 1985 for discussions of educational innovation and change). The following interview extract recorded in the research diary reflects this position:

(Background: two weeks of observation in tribal schools during which time the new boxes of various teaching-learning aids had never been opened in my presence. Other interviews have revealed the boxed tool kit is not useful for various reasons, including its very poor quality. This teacher had been observed ignoring children all afternoon and attending to administrative work—registers of his own and the children's presence—instead. He is apprehensive, and alone with 4 classes. The new boxes are stacked against the wall and covered in dust.)

CD: . . . are there any things in the kit which you don't really find very suitable?
T: No, no, it's all really good.

CD: (pause)

T: Very good.

CD: How do you use the things?

T: I use them with the children. It's very good.

CD: (points to tool kit) That tool kit. What do you think of that?

T: I use it with the children.

CD: What sort of things do you do?

T: I . . . um . . . well, I use it to show them, say, what a saw is.

CD: I see . . . for showing . . . have you ever made anything with it?

T: No . . . but it is useful.

CD: When you used it to show the children, how did you do that?

T: (Appears to see that his bluff has been drawn).

Well . . . actually . . . it's all pretty useless. (Goes on to say that he had too much administrative work, he never uses any of the things at all, that he didn't get any training and the other 'trained' teacher had never helped him).

Penetrating these defenses required a variety of tactics. An in-depth interview would usually begin with an important social prelude: trying to establish some personal connection with a teacher—perhaps by discovering a common native place, a reminiscence about school life, or an anecdote about the bus journey. It was easy to move to introducing a foreigner who was interested in Indian schools, using the "outsider" card to prompt teachers to talk about how the schools run, and initiate wider discussions. It was important to know about the nuts and bolts of school-level administration and teaching practices, for instance, to pick up on how the innovation had fitted in with, or contravened, existing procedures. It was very easy, if we wanted to elicit teachers' understandings in their own words, to use the outsider's (feigned or actual) ignorance as an excuse for seeking what often must have seemed very mundane information. Many teachers were pleased to explain aspects of their life and work which they might have assumed was self-explanatory to an Indian. On the other hand, there was always a tendency to feel that as representatives of their country, teachers should show off their best, and not mention any problems they might have. It was easier for the insider to open up more delicate areas because to confess problems to her was not seen to be betraying one's country.

We preferred to conduct interviews in schools, so as to have access to the new teaching-learning aids teachers were supposed to be using. This allowed the researchers to probe in greater depth the practical problems teachers had in manipulating the often complex aids, and to offer spontaneous assistance if appropriate. Many times after these interviews, hospitable teachers would invite us home for a cup of tea. It was during these non-official times, when teachers felt more relaxed and less guarded, that perhaps the most fruitful ethnographic insights emerged. However, teachers saw this as off-duty time so we kept the tape recorder, which we used for all interviews, off, and wrote up notes as soon as possible after leaving the site.

The formal individual teacher interviews were open-ended, guided by a set of core issues that needed to be covered in the course of an hour or so. Questions were usually descriptive, to gain general information, and structural, to understand how informants organize their knowledge (Burgess, 1984 lists question types useful in qualitative research). These interviews provided factual information but some respondents remained very cautious about expressing their feelings—an important aspect of documenting the process of change. We developed a number of useful strategies for drawing them out.

One such strategy was to appear to remove responsibility for the interviewee being the first to praise, criticize, or comment, by providing open-ended options that encouraged teachers to come up with their own reactions: "Lots of teachers we've talked to seem to feel *abc*, but we've met quite a few who feel *xyz* . . . what do you feel?" This strategy was also useful as a way of triangulating the data gained from earlier observations in schools—comparing what had been observed with what was said, and noting commonalities and discrepancies.

A second strategy was to play off the insider and outsider roles. Teachers would often make points based on common Indian experience, such as lengthy bureaucratic procedures and petty corruption. Operation Blackboard was beset by problems arising from both. In this respect it was easy to set in train a conversation that allowed teachers to come round to the impact of such problems if they wished. A teacher might confide "she won't know, but you know what it's like with bureaucrats" and the fellow Indian could then seek clarification with prompts such as "I know what you mean but *x* affects me a little differently—how does it affect you exactly?" This use of contrast questions allowed events and their meanings in respondents' worlds to be compared, in a way that is both unthreatening and socially acceptable.

Another very fruitful strategy was to be present when a group of teachers met informally, for instance at the monthly collection of pay from the group school. In India, as in other Asian cultures, it is often easier to get people to talk more openly and critically in groups than individually (White, 1992). These frank discussions, when jokes and anecdotes abounded, provided numerous underlying themes to pursue in later interviews.

Interviewing Bureaucrats

Once the grassroots interviews had been completed, the process of progressive focusing (Hamilton et al., 1977) had already begun, and themes generated at that level would continue to be refined throughout the research. Backwards mapping paid dividends immediately. It had quickly generated knowledge that could be taken to the next set of interviews; and it also allowed the identification of people who had really been involved in implementation, rather than interviewing only the most senior officer, as official top-down protocol would demand. This had a further advantage: since personal contacts are very important in Indian society, it is much easier to tackle an unfamiliar office with a named person to search out.

At district and state level, language was still an issue, since all the official files are in Gujarati. However, the then District Primary Education Officer was comfortable in English and spent many patient hours answering questions and discussing numerous issues. Although as a government official he tended to offer "correct" answers to begin with, the researcher's repeated visits to his office and obvious knowledge of the status quo in his district helped to strike up a rapport and allow him to vouchsafe information that was more personal. His words illustrated his perceptions of his role—an administrator in charge of "maintaining the establishment" with very little emphasis on academic affairs—and allowed the researcher to probe issues arising from his comments and her own experience.

It was clear, however, that he was not the man to ask about the nitty-gritty of implementing Operation Blackboard—how many new school rooms had actually been built, how many teachers appointed and so on. This was the domain of the Gujarati-speaking clerks, and required the insider's skill at creating rapport, and through that, access to the files. We paid repeated visits, and pored for hours over the figures and official correspondence, first asking general questions, and then gently pursuing the elements that did not tie up.

During these visits, we were intrigued by a cupboard that contained files we wanted to see, but was locked on every visit. Mysteriously, the key could never be located. Long after we had given up hope, the officer was transferred and, in that peculiarly Indian way, his successor was the mother of Archana's brother's friend, and the missing key was magically "found."

At the state level, we again drew on the insider/outsider combination. Possible problems of access and prestige could be overcome as English is mandatory for such senior officers, and it was thus possible for the northerner to interview the—all male, and all older—state-level officials. However, despite her explanations, the officers tended to assume they were talking to a foreigner who knew nothing about their domain. This impression, reflecting also their age- and gender-stereotyping, had to be quickly dispelled if the allotted time was not to be taken up with elementary explanations of the familiar. Initially, the power balance was very uneven, with the young, foreign, female researcher cast merely as the receiver of information, handed out rather condescendingly by the male officer. The balance could be shifted largely as the result of the insights generated through backwards mapping, and some officers made the most of this rare opportunity to receive, from an external source, information about the progress of the scheme. If a second meeting could be arranged later, senior officers were prepared to engage with the issues far more than on the first visit. This was probably largely due to mutually increased confidence now that officers were familiar to some extent with the researcher and what she was interested in, and the interviewer was clearer about fruitful lines to pursue with particular officers (see Bogdan and Biklen, 1992 for a discussion of "training" respondents to meet interviewers' needs).

Issues of status—male, senior officer and foreign female—were initially difficult to deal with (Davies, 1985), but could be manipulated to facilitate access, and the opportunity to represent teachers' views to decision-makers, something the policy had manifestly failed to consider. These state-level interviews yielded from officials at the directorate and secretariat useful information and perceptions about their roles, reactions to the policy content, and practical difficulties in implementing the scheme itself. A sense of apathy among state personnel emerged, and resentment that the center had initiated a scheme but left them with the unglamorous and difficult task of implementation.

At this level too, it was from efforts to cultivate the Gujarati-speaking clerk who had been in charge of Operation Blackboard since its inception that we could tie up the numbers, hear the gossip, and read the official correspondence. Again, the "insider" gained access by asking general work-related questions, easily done in this case by sympathizing with the sole clerk responsible for all the state-level paperwork for the scheme in Gujarat.

For the New Delhi interviews, being white and English-speaking was again an advantage. Access to officials and their files was very good, and the effort of taking the time to come to India and find out what was happening was appreciated. Unlike the state officials, all officers at this level were also interested in the outcome of the research, and aware of its value as the first study of its kind. The senior-most official interviewed was also a woman, which made for an easy rapport in the very male world of civil servants.

Interviews for the academic strand were challenging in different ways. At the three colleges where teachers interviewed in this study had taken their brief orientation programs, interviews were conducted in Gujarati, after we had discussed what should be asked with reference to what teachers in schools had reported. It was not until we mapped backwards to the State Institute of Education (SIE) that the first uncomfortable field situation emerged. There, in the first interview, in English, officials rehearsed the contents of the policy several times, but important questions pertaining to the role of the SIE in teacher training remained unanswered although this was the key institution from which all cascade training for Gujarat had emanated (see Figure 11.2). Also, despite several requests, it had not been possible to see the sample teaching-learning aids which the SIE had approved.

It was possible that language difficulties were causing these information blockages, since one or two of the people who had been involved in the program were not comfortable in English. On the next visit, both researchers talked to the people in question in Gujarati. As the interview progressed, we seemed to be going round in circles, and as we became more assertive in seeking relevant information, the officials concerned were getting more evasive. More penetrating questions enabled the researchers to discern the half-truths being offered and the officials' indifference to the enormous responsibility vested in them. We found ourselves in a serious role conflict, since we had seen the negative effect the officers' attitude had had on the lives of hundreds of teachers and children, but we tried to discipline our subjectivity: "the ethnographer must not suppress a *sense* of outrage whilst in the field, but stay and take advantage of one's rage, using it as a barometer to engage high salience" (Adelman, 1985:45). Our requests to see the kit were finally acceded to and we were taken upstairs by an informative peon; by the time we came back all the officers had had to go out on "urgent business." In effect, we had been politely rejected by the respondents on this occasion but we had—not without difficulty—retained, and allowed our respondents to retain, professional dignity (Fry and Thurber, 1989) and gained important insights into the role of this institution in general issues of teacher quality, training, curriculum development, and so on.

Interviews in Delhi were again relatively straightforward, although the "sense of outrage" was still strong, and found expression in the following incident, recorded in the research diary as follows:

> CD: (Knowing this had not been done) Did you distribute the training materials in advance so that teachers could prepare themselves?

Respondent: Yes, yes, we did.

CD: I see . . . how much in advance?

Respondent: Um, about five minutes.

CD: Do you call that in advance?

Respondent: Well, no, not really. My God, you are unusually sharp.

Some Reflections on Our First Collaboration

Since the research on Operation Blackboard was for her doctoral thesis, overall responsibility for its conduct, the notes, etc., was retained by Caroline Dyer. But it was exciting work to share, too, as it had many elements of a detective story in it. The ongoing analysis so essential to qualitative work was shaped by the discussions we used to have as we left interviews. Our individual reactions to situations and people, and the meanings we drew out, were noted in the research diary, which covered substantive and methodological notes (Hammersley and Atkinson, 1983).

An attractive characteristic of gathering qualitative data is that there are usually several "strands" of research on the go at any one time. This flexibility has many positive outcomes; one that is especially useful for northerners is that it allows them to feel that time (the perceptions of which can be a source of much cross-cultural tension) is being used "effectively" and reduces the possibility of reacting with counter-productive frustration to the inevitable lengthy "delays" in India. During data collection for this study, we would sometimes cross the then curfew-bound area of the city to try to tie up some details at the district office, only to find that the person we wanted to see was out, but there was usually something else to check on instead. This helped to maintain both the data collection schedule and cross-cultural relations.

The study would not have been so rich or informative if we had not been successful initially in encouraging reticent teachers to voice their opinions. Our experience suggests that good data at this level enabled questions at the next levels to be better directed toward practical realities. For an accurate overall picture of the policy and administrative aspects of Operation Blackboard, it was essential to gain access to both the highly visible officers, and the invisible clerks. The latter group is all the more important since, unlike officers, clerks remain in one post for years at a time, and have historical knowledge that is of great value. This dimension would have been lost without the insider's linguistic, and cultural, ability to communicate with them.

Again, it was because of the southern colleague's ethnographic interests in people and the way they relate to their environments that considerable attention was directed toward how social context might account for the outcome of the policy innovation. She suggested a second set of interviews with the thirty teachers we had already met, to find out more about the teachers themselves, focusing much more closely on factors underlying teacher attitude in general: their socialization, schooling, attitudes to the local community, levels of parental education, and so on. These data allowed very much more robust inferences to be drawn about the overall prognosis for policy innovations in prevailing conditions, rather than data confined to the particular innovation under review.

Usefully, backwards mapping reached Delhi just as revision of Operation Blackboard's guidelines, prior to its third phase of implementation, was in process. Policy makers used the researchers as a resource, and the face-to-face discussions allowed the criticism that implementation research is "long on description and short on prescription . . . desultory and strategically vague" (Elmore, 1980:601) at least to some extent to be avoided. Photographs were shown and teachers' views, along with their problems in using the new teaching-learning aids, reflected to key decision-makers. But, although interested in the research findings, the center felt that some of the problems could have been avoided at the state level, a feeling which echoed the state's perception of the center. The dilemma of state relations which underlies Indian policy-making and implementation in education thus made itself felt for the policy researchers also, since each level implied that their advice was more necessary and relevant to the other level.

Our first collaborative experience showed that each of us had a specific set of advantages that we could exploit. It was fairly easy to detect which roles were appropriate to particular contexts, and through working together, the scope of what we could find out was considerably widened. We really enjoyed the experience of "discovering" Indian primary education together, and wanted to collaborate again. In future, though, we wanted equal status and responsibility, and to design the research project together in a subject area where our substantive knowledge would be more even, building in the known strengths of both team members, and a more equitable funding status. We hoped next time to use the insights gained from the experience of researching Operation Blackboard and to work on the educational problems of a minority community, but again with a policy focus.

LITERACY FOR NOMADS

Thinking back on it, we realize that *Literacy for Nomads* was born on a bus while waiting for a flock of sheep to cross the road! As we watched the shepherd lead his sheep away, we wondered what these nomads do about education—if they wanted it at all. We were aware by now of the problems which non-mainstream communities face with primary schools, whose centrally fixed curriculum is often so ill-suited to the heterogeneous needs of the communities they serve. Do nomads send their children to school? Do they need to be able to read and write?

Some days later, we stopped at a fodder center on a main migratory route, to raise these issues with the groups we found. Nomads reported that their experience of primary schools is generally unsatisfactory, because of the schools themselves and the difficulties of leaving children at home to study while the parents migrate. The adults, from the Rabari community, were keen to become literate; they thought it would help in their day-to-day lives, and also advance their community. But not one of them thought that, because of their migratory lifestyle, it would be physically possible for them to gain access to these skills. And indeed, levels of literacy among Gujarat's nomadic Rabari and Bharwad communities—numbering some 60,000 people, most of whom do not even officially exist, according to the national census—are extremely low.

We knew that literacy and numeracy skills could be brought to nomads (cf. Ezeomah, 1982 and 1985; Gorham, 1978), and sat down to work out the options for what would be a challenging ethno-educational, action research project. This began to take shape when the Economic and Social Research Council offered financial support; we have now almost completed one year of the two-year project, which builds, both substantively and methodologically, on the experiences gained from researching Operation Blackboard.

Literacy for Nomads adopts anthropological/sociological perspectives to the study of literacy. It rejects the "autonomous model" (Street, 1984) of literacy as a national good, in favor of a close understanding of the meaning and uses of literacy in a particular social context. A major objective is to construct "an ethnography of literacy acquisition" by documenting nomads' attitudes to literacy prior to acquiring it, during the learning process, and afterwards. The teaching materials, to be developed by the researchers, will be drawn entirely from the context of the learners' lives and used to give nomads the functional skills which they themselves identify and perhaps also others that are appropriate for their lifestyle. Teaching will be done by the two researchers during a normal migration, during which time we will live with a group and teach both adults and children. The work has been divided into two one-year sections, conditioned by the nomads' migratory cycle. During this first year we have conducted trial migrations and interviews with community members, and are now beginning to prepare teaching materials. Our subsequent four-to-six months' migration with a small sample group will fill much of the second year.

The Methodological Challenges

Much of the first year has been taken up with facing the numerous methodological challenges the project has thrown up. Initially the most difficult one to overcome has been access (Delamont, 1992). Nomads are a closed social group who do not readily allow outsiders in, although once established, acceptance is absolute. To reach this position, we have had to go through many intermediaries, or gatekeepers (Burgess, 1984; Hammersley and Atkinson, 1983), whose perceptions of who we are and what we are doing have conditioned the terms on which we gain access to the target groups, thereby providing both complications and frustrations. For our first trial migration, for instance, we had to satisfy no fewer than five gatekeepers before we could even meet the man on whom all depended: the leader of the group we sought to join.

Although the range of non-government organizations' activities is rapidly expanding, most "development" in India is government-led. People who go to villages to ask questions usually do so in connection with a government activity; any stranger is thus likely to be seen—and introduced to others—as a government officer. However strenuously this is denied, there is no easy concept with which to replace the standard one since there is a widespread, and understandable, lack of any concept of research. In our case, the "local" is usually taken to be a government officer; the "outsider" is associated with an external aid agency. The problem for us as researchers has been, therefore, that people choose to respond to such "officials" in a way that will, they hope, bring government attention and relief to their problems. We become burdened with expectations that we cannot possibly even begin to fulfill. Researching the potential for working with nomads in Saurashtra, one of the three areas in Gujarat where they are concentrated (Figure 11.1), we found their attention was focused on obtaining Scheduled Tribe status, and thus access to various government benefits that, in their perception, would solve their acute water and fodder problems. While we were receptive to these problems, we would not, in the course of the literacy project, be in a position to do much about them. It was very difficult to steer respondents toward the issues in which we had the potential to interact productively; and notable that they did not perceive literacy as a useful tool in their struggle for better conditions. Interestingly, the position was very different in the area we finally chose (Kutch), where almost everyone we talked to was convinced that literacy could solve many problems.

After trial and error, we now introduce ourselves as university teachers on long leave, who would like to use the time to tackle some of the nomads' educational problems. Acceptance on these terms is a reasonably satisfactory ethical position, since it is in fact more or less true—and it earns us undeserved respect for choosing to migrate with nomads in the heat and dust, when we could be enjoying a cooler existence elsewhere. But it does highlight an ethical grey area when attempting to conduct "overt" participant observation, and one perhaps common in southern contexts: that the observation of those who do not understand what research is, and are therefore unaware of the process they are participating in, is inherently somewhat covert, whether one wishes it to be so, or not (Burgess, 1989).

Having gained access, the next step was to try to make the nomads, whose world view often does not encompass the notion of India as a country, let alone a foreign one, comfortable with us. We have had to negotiate a balance between satisfying their curiosity about us, and our desire to hear about their situations. This means answering countless queries about nationality, marital status, age, caste, salary, and so on, but these are necessary preliminaries. The researcher who shares the ethnic identity acts as a buffer zone, for it is inevitably the familiar-looking face that is addressed first. We have rehearsed many times an entry that goes something like this, with a group of men and women:

Men: You look as if you come from here?
AC: I'm from Baroda.
Men: Not from our country then (i.e. their native place). This sister?
AC: She's British. . . . Not from here.
Men: (Puzzled) . . . You understand my language, don't you?
AC: Yes, I'm Gujarati, from Baroda, so I know this language. She understands Gujarati too.
Men: Really? Good, good.
Women: Which is your caste?
AC: Bania.
Women: Jain Bania?
AC: No, Dasashrimali.
Women: What is her caste?
AC: They don't have caste in Britain.
Women: What? That can't be right.
AC: No, no, it is right . . . But she is like my caste.
Women: How old are you? . . . Are you married?
Men: Why have you come?

(Relevant explanation follows.)

One sub-text to this discussion is whether it is appropriate to offer us tea, since milk products are not given to those of lower caste, or Muslims. The arrival of bowls of sweet, milky tea signals the end of these formalities, after which we can lead into some of the issues with which we are concerned. Although this "testing" is time-consuming it is an essential cultural prerequisite, and an important investment, for it is only a smooth passage through these introductions that allows deeper relationships to form.

Being female in this context is an advantage, since a male outsider is not allowed by Rabari men to approach their women (Gala, 1993). We do not present a threat in this respect and, once accepted, are protected along with their own. In this community, women dominate family, social and economic relationships and not to be able to talk to them would be to miss critical aspects of tribal life. Conversely, we are not bound by their own gender roles (Jeffery, 1979): men have invited us, as two non-Rabari women, to sit in on all-male occasions, almost as "honorary men."

Because neither of us is from this community, and we do not share their style of dress, ornament, or speech, we have a very high profile, both within the nomadic group itself and among those with whom nomads come into contact. In this research setting, we are both, to a greater or lesser degree, "outsiders" and it is no longer only the white team member who sometimes would like to escape from the strain of being continually watched in a "fishbowl" (Bogdan and Biklen, 1992). In fact, in small Indian villages, any outsider is closely scrutinized and these attentions are tiring, perhaps the more so for the local colleague who will be expected to satisfy their endless curiosity and will answer question after question because she herself shares the cultural norms that make it impolite not to do so.

Language and Communication

Ethnographic work inevitably relies to a great extent on language, and ignorance of the language is not only "culturally offensive," as Fry and Thurber (1989) point out, but presents many difficulties in understanding another culture. Although one of our team is Gujarati, we both consider that for the nonnative speaker, listening competence and the ability to ask at least some basic research-related questions is the minimum to aim for over a long project.

While researching Operation Blackboard, the non-native speaker could, after a while, follow conversations among educated speakers and react with appropriate body language at least. Unfortunately, from the learners' point of view, Gujarati has substantial dialectic variations that provide obstacles even for a willing learner. Typically, although these nomads are Gujarati-speaking, their native dialect is very distinctive and unaffected by standardizing school language. It includes many non-standard words: *gaader* instead of *geetu* (sheep); *handio* instead of *oont* (camel). There have been amusing times when children asked to identify something in a picture have chorused an unfamiliar word, which could be either the correct answer with a dialect word, or the wrong answer altogether. Either way, the researchers have to call on an adult, for whom the ability to use standard Gujarati is a necessary skill on migration, to explain. Cross-cultural understandings take on a new dimension!

Learning these new words takes time, but it is a relatively easy chore. It is not only a matter of dialect words, however. The nomads' grammatical constructions are also different, their sentences often unfinished and complex to follow. Transcribed tapes of conversations reveal how rapidly they jump from topic to topic, taking up themes and dropping them again in the next sentence. The lack of continuous context makes it even more difficult for the novice speaker to follow discussions; the native speaker, with several years' experience of working with nomads, and with potters from the same region, has few major problems with comprehension, although she finds it tiring. It is, however, just this thought-processing strategy in non-literate people that is of great interest as a research theme, as one school of literacy thinkers argues that literacy skills enhance more "logical" thinking (Ong, 1982; Goody, 1987; but see also Street, 1984).

Interviews in this context amount to a technique of leading rather circular conversations with deliberate accents on the areas we want to explore, since this fits with nomads' own patterns of dialogue. Repetition and echoing are very much part of this patterning, and direct questions provoke responses that pick up on particular words in the question, rather than the question in its entire context and concept; answers usually refer only to the word that was picked up. Confirming, adding to and drawing out more details very indirectly is therefore the best strategy by which to gain information from these nomads, who do not share the conversational conventions held by the researchers. Inevitably, the linguistically more competent researcher bears most of the hard work of day-to-day talking and this uneven workload is frustrating: one researcher gets over-tired and the other gets mildly bored. The balance can be redressed a little in the action component of the project—the teaching sessions—where we are both actively involved in getting people to recognize and write letters and numbers; and during the writing process, the native speaker of English bears the heavier load.

This work is very satisfying: the Rabaris are extremely well-motivated students, and very patient with their own tentative efforts to master the complex Gujarati letters. We find that we are both constantly learning from them and admiring more and more their approach to life and their moral honesty.

Some Reflections on Literacy for Nomads

By its nature, *Literacy for Nomads* is a challenging project, where the roles of the researchers shift, not always harmoniously, from actively involved teacher to participant observer with varying degrees of involvement. For the nomads, we are their teachers, and this function justifies our presence, but role conflicts are inherent in the design of the project as a combination of participant observation and action research. The tension lies between the anthropological wish to observe with the minimum of intervention, and the requirements of action research—intervening and thus precipitating change. A positive aspect of our present dilemmas is that in the long term, through this research, nomads should gain the practical literacy and numeracy skills they desire and to which they would not otherwise have access, and the design of the project is such that the researchers' input can be reproduced later by community members. This is a desirable level of reciprocity that avoids the ethical unacceptability of the researcher departing with filled notebooks, leaving behind little of advantage to the respondents.

Inevitably, given the protracted access negotiations, time has also been a source of tension. The northern time-scale often seems to be threatened by one delay or another, although previous experience of research in India meant it could be set reasonably accurately. A further access-related stress for us both is the white colleague's high visibility: it is sometimes difficult to respond with a smile to inquiries from countless people on the periphery before we can meet those we really want to talk to. Inevitably too, the white researcher draws crowds when we withdraw from our group to relax, and on such occasions relaxing can be more tiring than working in the protected space of our group.

We have adapted our technology—lights, computer, recording equipment and video camera—to use solar energy for all our power requirements, and the use of a computer in the field makes this work much easier. As in our previous collaboration, writing a research diary encourages discussions of each day's events and what they might mean. This is supplemented by transcribing tapes, usually done as soon as possible so that emerging themes can be identified while there is still time to find out more, and to avoid the tedium of transcribing hours of tapes once out of the research setting. This is also a time for debriefing when there have been problems in understand-

ing in sufficient detail what has been said, and for planning future strategies. These discussions also form a control mechanism, as the discipline of
analyzing and noting down the day's events helps sustain our objectivity as
researchers. With such intensive involvement, it is an effort to keep the "familiar strange" (Spindler, 1982), and the presence of another researcher helps
create distance from the research subjects and reduce the possibility of "going native" (Hammersley and Atkinson, 1983).

GENERAL REFLECTIONS

The accounts here of two research studies have illustrated the scope and
potential of a combined north-south research team working in a developing country, and the possibilities for overcoming potential problems of access, language, and cultural appropriateness. Being female has been an advantage in terms of access and empathy, and in the practice of qualitative
research, this far outweighs the occasional discomforts for women of particularly male establishments, such as the civil service.

The notions of insider and outsider have been shown in this chapter
to be neither simple nor constant, but, by assessing the roles appropriate to
particular situations, and how each researcher is likely to be perceived by
respondents, it is possible to seek out and pursue the relative advantage of
appearing as the northerner, the southerner, or as a joint team.

As is to be expected of the process of participant observation, levels
of involvement and roles change from project to project and during the life
of a single project. Some roles are possible for only one team member: for
Operation Blackboard, the northern researcher could be in one context an
"acceptable incompetent" (Hammersley and Atkinson, 1983), and in another, an informant to decision-makers, neither of which was possible for
the southern colleague. Equally, the role of insider, used to prompt shared
Indian experience from reticent teachers and informative clerks, was available only to the Indian.

Access to the broadest possible range of respondents enriches qualitative research, both in terms of recording opinions expressed, and in the ethnographic necessity of getting an informed "feel of things" (cf. Vulliamy et
al., 1990). The range of roles available through collaborating makes very much
easier the necessary task of cultivating multiple contact points. This reliance
on individuals rather than systems is not self-explanatory for researchers socialized in the north, but it makes for easier and more enduring research relationships, even if the dependency and time-lags are uncomfortable.

The use of time is a difficult cross-cultural issue, since what may appear as time-wasting in northern eyes is indispensable social behavior in the

south. Being relaxed as far as possible about time assists in avoiding frustration and depression, and makes cross-cultural collaboration more harmonious since the southern colleague is also likely to find the standard northern pace unnecessarily fast.

In respect of both forging contacts and time, the collaborative team benefits in many ways from drawing on the southerner's cultural expertise. A southern colleague is unlikely to behave with cultural inappropriateness, possibly a danger for an inexperienced northern researcher, which promotes smooth field relationships—although, conversely, Indians are tolerant of very obvious outsiders. For *Literacy for Nomads*, the southerner's cultural expertise was the crucial resource in creating trust and the chain of contacts that allowed both researchers access to the closed nomadic community.

As a matter of courtesy and professionalism, the northerner should be prepared to learn and adapt to the norms of the south, and included in this process of adaptation is also at least some attempt to communicate in the local language, particularly if the research is ethnographic, since so much of a culture is revealed in its language. In our experience, particularly since the outsider speaks Gujarati, the regional language, far better than the national Hindi, efforts to communicate are greeted with surprise and joy, as well as amusement, and this can quickly overcome some of the initial reservations that some respondents may feel. Although it is still the native speaker who collects the important data, respondents appear more comfortable in the presence of the ethnic stranger if she can at least answer basic identity-organizing questions without an intermediary.

North-south collaboration is not always easy, for cultural assumptions are not necessarily shared and can be a source of conflict in carrying out research. A northerner working in the south needs to be highly sensitive to issues that are culture-bound, such as the use and perception of time, and personal questions, and to any role or status conflicts that may provoke tensions. Some of the most obvious of the latter can be minimized by creating as much equity as possible: in the research design, comparative levels of pay, responsibilities, opportunities to "own" and publish the research, and so on. Other collegial tensions, which inevitably arise, can more easily be confronted in such an environment, and even contribute to the research process. Some of the status differentials which provoke tensions will, inevitably, remain beyond the scope of the research team to address satisfactorily: the policy maker's belief in the wisdom of a northerner's viewpoint, for instance. However, researchers who share the view that cultural knowledge and social intelligence are a major asset, as we suggested earlier, are perhaps less likely to be discomforted by others' perhaps irrelevant perceptions of status.

As far as the professional growth of researchers themselves goes, collaboration can be highly instructive. In our case, the northern researcher, who has access both to libraries, and a supportive and critical professional constituency, has been able to provide theoretical inputs that have strengthened the qualitative field research techniques of the southern researcher, whose training was oriented toward proving points. The wealth of ethnographic data that the Indian colleague is able to collect because of her cultural, social and linguistic expertise, has in turn enormously expanded the analytical framework and understanding of the British colleague.

North-south collaboration is of particular value in its potential for covering the full scope of an educational research study using qualitative methods, in all its linguistic, cultural, and analytical aspects. The pursuit of social understanding, which lies at the core of ethnographic research, is a process of discovery. This process can be greatly enhanced by collaboration with a colleague whose perceptions of the familiar and strange are so different from one's own, for the outsider's eyes readily see the strange, and the insider's perceptions of the familiar are sharpened.

Research teams that are able to draw on a combination of what both the north and the south can offer—mixing, for instance, the advantages of advanced technology and comprehensive information networks with linguistic competence and cultural understandings—can exploit a great potential in developing the qualitative insights from which both the theory and practice of education in developing countries will benefit. Equally, a combined north-south team should be able to make a strong contribution to the development and improvement of cross-cultural theory, giving voice to the southern viewpoint that is so often excluded from northern perceptions.

REFERENCES

Adams, R. and Chen, D. (1981) *The Process of Educational Innovation: An International Perspective*. Paris, IIEP: Kogan Page.

Adelman, C.(1985) "Who are You? Some Problems of Ethnographer Culture Shock." In R. Burgess (ed.) *Field Methods in the Study of Education*. Lewes: Falmer Press.

Archer, D. (1980) *How to Expand your Social IQ*. New York: M Evans.

Bogdan, R. and Biklen, S. K. (1992) *Qualitative Research for Education: An Introduction to Theory and Methods*. Boston: Allyn and Bacon.

Burgess, R. (1984) *In the Field: An Introduction to Field Research*. London: George Allen and Unwin.

———. (ed.) (1985) *Field Methods in the Study of Education*. Lewes: Falmer Press.

———. (1989) *The Ethics of Educational Research*. Lewes: Falmer Press.

Crossley, M. (1990) "Collaborative Research, Ethnography and Comparative and International Education in the South Pacific," *International Journal of Educational Development* 10 (1): 37–46.

———. (1993) "Introduction: Comparative and International Studies and Education in the South Pacific," *Comparative Education* 29 (3):227–232.

Crossley, M. and Broadfoot, P. (1992) "Comparative and International Research in Education: Scope, Problems and Potential," *British Education Research Journal* 18 (2):99–112.

Crossley, M. and Vulliamy, G. (1984) "Case Study Research Methods and Comparative Education," *Comparative Education* 20 (2):193–207.

Davies, L. (1985) "Ethnography and Status: Focusing on Gender in Educational Research." In R. Burgess (ed.) *Field Methods in the Study of Education*. Lewes: Falmer Press.

Davison, T. (1992) "Opportunities for Qualitative Rresearch on Donor Funded Primary Education Projects: The View of a Field Manager." Paper presented to the BATROE conference at the University of Sussex April (1992).

Delamont, S. (1992) *Fieldwork in Educational Settings: Methods, Pitfalls and Perspectives*. Lewes: Falmer Press.

Dhabi, J. (1991) Personal Communication, Teacher, Harsunda School, Baroda, Gujarat.

Dhingra, K. (1991) *Improving the Information System for Planning the Quality of Primary Education: The Case of India*. Paris: IIEP.

Dyer, C. (1993) "Operation Blackboard: Policy Implementation in Indian Elementary Education." Unpublished Ph.D. thesis, University of Edinburgh.

——. (1994a) "Education and the State: Policy Implementation in India's Federal Polity," *International Journal of Educational Development* 14 (3):241–253.

——. (1995) "Primary Teachers and Policy Innovation in India: Some Neglected Issues." In *International Journal of Educational Development* (forthcoming).

Elmore, R. (1980) "Backwards Mapping: Implementation Research and Policy Decisions" *Political Science Quarterly* 94 (4):601–616.

Ezeomah, C. (ed.) (1982) *The Problems of Educating Nomads in Nigeria. Proceedings of the First Annual Conference on the Education of Nomads in Nigeria*. University of Jos, February 5–6.

——. (1985) "Land Tenure Constraints Associated with some Recent Experiments to Bring Formal Education to Nomadic Fulani in Nigeria," *Pastoral Network Paper* 20d. London: Overseas Development Institute.

Fagerlind, I. and Hallak, J. (1991) "Educational Research in Developing Countries: A Background Paper." In *Strengthening Educational Research in Developing Countries*. Paris: IIEP.

Finch, J. (1986) *Research and Policy: The Uses of Qualitative Methods in Social and Educational Research*. Lewes: Falmer.

Fry, G. and Thurber, C. (1989) *The International Education of the Development Consultant: Communicating with Peasants and Princes*. Oxford: Pergamon Press.

Fullan, M. (1991) *The New Meaning of Educational Change*. London: Cassell.

Gala, M. (1993) Personal communication, anthropologist studying Rabaris of Kutch.

Goody, J. (1987) *The Interface Between the Written and the Oral*. Cambridge: Cambridge University Press.

Gorham, A.B. (1978) "The Provision of Education in Pastoral Areas," *Pastoral Network Paper* 6b. London: Overseas Development Institute.

Hamilton, D., Jenkins, D., King, C., Macdonald, B. and Parlett, M. (1977) *Beyond the Numbers Game: A Reader in Educational Evaluation*. London: Macmillan.

Hammersley, M. and Atkinson, P. (1983) *Ethnography: Principles in Practice*. London: Routledge.

Havelock, R. and Huberman, A. M. (1977) *Solving Educational Problems*. Paris: UNESCO.

Hawes, H. and Stephens, D. (1990) *Questions of Quality: Primary Education and Development*. London: Longman.

Jain, R . (1990) "The Role of Bureacracy in Policy Development and Implementation in India," *International Social Science Journal* 123:31–47.

Jeffery, P. (1979) *Frogs in a Well: Indian Women in Purdah*. London: Zed Press.

Kelly, G. and Altbach, P. (1988) "Alternative Approaches to Community Education." In T. Postlethwaite (ed.) *The Encyclopedia of Comparative Education and National Systems of Education.* Oxford: Pergamon Press.

King, K. J. (1984) "North-South Collaborative Research in Education." In *Educational Research: Issues in Cross-National Collaboration.* IDS Bulletin 15 (4).

———. (1992) "The External Agenda of Aid in Internal Educational Reform," *International Journal of Educational Development* 12 (4):257–263.

Kumar, K. (1991) *Political Agenda of Education: A Study of Colonialist and Nationalist Ideas.* New Delhi: Sage.

Leach, F. (1993) "Expatriates as Agents of Cross-Cultural Transmission." Paper presented to the Symposium on International Perspectives on Culture and Schooling, 11–13 May, at DICE University of London.

Morris, P. (1985) "Teachers' Perceptions of the Barriers to the Implementation of a Pedagogical Innovation: a S.E. Asian Case Study," *International Review of Education* 31:3–17.

NPE (1986) *National Policy on Education, 1986.* Ministry of Human Resource Development New Delhi, Government of India.

Ong, W. (1982) *Orality and Literacy: the Technologising of the Word.* London: Methuen.

Salmi, J. (1984) "Educational Research on the Third World: A View from the South." In *Educational Research: Issues in Cross-national Collaboration.* IDS Bulletin 15 (4).

Shaeffer, S. (1991) *A Framework for Collaborating for Educational Change.* Paris: IIEP.

Spindler, G. (ed.) (1982) *Doing the Ethnography of Schooling.* New York: Holt, Rinehart and Winston.

Street, B. (1984) *Literacy in Theory and Practice.* Cambridge: Cambridge University Press.

UNICEF (1991) *Basic Education and National Development: the Indian Scene.* New Delhi: UNICEF.

Vulliamy, G., Lewin, K. and Stephens, D.(1990) *Doing Educational Research in Developing Countries: Qualitative Strategies.* Lewes: Falmer Press.

White, S. (1992) *Arguing with the Crocodile: Gender and Class in Bangladesh.* Dhaka: The University Press.

CONTRIBUTORS

J. ALEXANDER BENNETT is a former Curriculum Development Officer in the Ministry of Education in Belize, and was Head of the Curriculum Development Unit. He has had teaching experience at many levels of the educational system, including teacher training at the Belize Teachers' College and the University College of Belize. Since 1990 he has served as an adviser within the Ministry of Education particularly in connection with the World Bank supported Belize Primary Education Development project. He is a graduate of the University of the West Indies and holds an M.A. (Education) from the Institute of Education at the University of London. He recently contributed a section on the educational system of Belize for the *International Encyclopaedia of Education*, and was Chairman of the Research Steering Committee when the study discussed here began.

CHENG KAI-MING is Professor of Education at the University of Hong Kong and is currently Dean of Education. Dr. Cheng is a mathematician by training. He was a teacher and school principal, but turned to educational administration, planning, and policy analysis mid-career and did his doctorate in these areas at the University of London Institute of Education. His recent research focus has been on reforms in China's education. He has been consultant to the World Bank, the Asian Development Bank, UNESCO, UNICEF, UNDP and the International Institute for Educational Planning.

ARCHANA CHOKSI was educated in a series of rural government schools in Gujarat, India. Her first experience of a big city was Baroda, where she gained an undergraduate degree in Fine Arts from the Maharaja Sayajirao University. After several years running her own printing business, she returned to university. For her M.A. in archaeology, she worked on pastoralists' settlement patterns in Saurashtra; she gained a second M.A. in museology in 1992 and recently completed for her Ph.D. "An ethnoarchaelogical study of pottery manufacture in Kutch." Dr. Choksi has a strong interest in working with less advantaged social strata; she has also run a hobby center for children; and carried out research on behalf of India's Integrated Child Development Service. She assisted Dr. Dyer with data collection during 1991 and 1992 and is currently collaborating full time with her on a research project sponsored by Britain's Economic and Social Research Council (ESRC), entitled "Literacy for Nomads: an ethnography of literacy acquisition among Gujarati nomads."

MICHAEL CROSSLEY is a Senior Lecturer in the Centre for International Studies in Education at the University of Bristol where he is currently Coordinator for Research Students for the School of Education. Dr. Crossley was previously Associate Dean (Planning) in the Faculty of Education at the University of Papua New Guinea. He has taught in England, Australia, and Papua New Guinea; was editor of the *Papua New Guinea Journal of Education* from 1985 to 1990; and is currently a member of the editorial board for *Comparative Education*, an executive editor for the *International Journal of Educational Development*, and a corresponding editor for the *International Review of Education*. Current research interests include further methodological work on the potential of qualitative research in the field of comparative and international education, and collaborative case studies of changes in the quality of education in primary schools in Belize, Central America.

LYNN DAVIES is Professor of Education and Director of the International Unit of the School of Education, University of Birmingham. Dr. Davies also heads the Faculty Division of the Graduate School, coordinating the provision and training for research students. She has lived and worked in Mauritius and Malaysia and researched education in various parts of Africa and Asia. Particular academic interests are in school management in developing countries, gender and management, and democratic school organization. She has recently completed a book on study skills for teacher training.

CAROLINE DYER is a Lecturer in education at the University of Manchester. She initially graduated from Liverpool University in 1984 in German and Dutch; spent a year working in arts administration in London and gaining a TEFL qualification; and then traveled in India and Southeast Asia for a year. She subsequently taught English with the British Council in Hong Kong for a year, before moving to become senior reporter for education with a local English language newspaper. Intrigued by the colonial impact on educational systems, she returned to India to do some preliminary field work before applying for a Ph.D. at Edinburgh University. She completed her doctoral research on "Operation Blackboard: policy implementation in Indian elementary education' in 1993, during which time she spent a year in India. She was subsequently project manager for the first edition of the "British Resource on International Training and Education" before returning to India to work with Dr. Choksi on "Literacy for Nomads." Dr. Dyer has also collaborated with Dr. Choksi on UNICEF-commissioned consultancies and recently set up *Akshar*, a non-government organization based in India, which specializes in action research and innovation in education and literacy.

WAYNE FIFE received his Ph.D. in anthropology from McMaster University in 1992. His current research interests include education and social change in Papua New Guinea, the history of missionary education in the Pacific, and the development of bureaucratic institutions in the colonial and postcolonial Pacific. Currently, he holds a Social Sciences and Humanities Research Council of Canada Postdoctoral Fellowship at the University of Massachusetts at Amherst, where he is engaged in historical research regarding the missionary origins of Papua New Guinean education and the role this has played in the transformation of local moralities.

CLIVE HARBER is Professor of Education at the University of Natal, South Africa. He is on leave of absence from the University of Birmingham where he is a Senior Lecturer in International Education. Dr. Harber has a long-standing interest in education in Africa, particularly in regard to education and political development. He has published widely on the themes of education and political socialization and education for democracy and is currently working on a book on education, democracy, and development in Africa.

PULANE LEFOKA currently lectures at the Institute of Education of the National University of Lesotho. She works mostly with teachers in schools providing professional development training at elementary school level. This training focuses on research methods, particularly participatory action research and teaching techniques. Her main interests are qualitative research and action research and she is currently working on two studies: teachers that students regard as best teachers, and a study of school effectiveness.

PEARLETTE LOUISY is Principal of the Sir Arthur Lewis Community College in St. Lucia, a small island in the eastern Caribbean. She is a graduate of the University of the West Indies in Cave Hill, Barbados, the Université Laval in Quebec, Canada and the University of Bristol in the United Kingdom. Dr. Louisy has two main professional interests: the development of the French Antillian Creole as a vehicle for the transmission of national and cultural identity, and the development of higher education in small nation developing states. She has served as a member of the International Committee on Creole Studies, embracing the creole languages of the Caribbean, the Indian Ocean and mainland United States, and as St. Lucia's national correspondent to the Agence de Cooperation Culturelle at Technique. Her most recent work, an unpublished doctoral thesis from the University of Bristol, examines current tertiary education policies and strategies adopted by small nation states of the Caribbean and the South Pacific.

MAHLAPE MOROJELE works for the Lesotho Council of Non-Governmental Organisations as a human resource development officer. The council coordinates, promotes and supports NGOs in their development efforts. Training is one of the core programs of the council. Ms. Morojele coordinates the Management and Leadership Development Training Programme for indigenous NGOs funded by the W.K. Kellogg Foundation. The leadership training program has been designed around five themes: financial management, leadership development, management, communication, and action research. Before joining the council, she worked at the National Teacher Training College as a teacher trainer in the department of Social and Development Studies, and also taught Curriculum Studies in Development Studies to third-year students at the National University of Lesotho.

ROSEMARY PRESTON is Director of the International Centre for Education in Development in the Department of Continuing Education at the University of Warwick (UK). Dr. Preston's career has been dominated by interdisciplinary studies of the dynamics of education development in Latin America, the South Pacific and southern Africa. This has involved both statistical and ethnographic research. Themes include human resources and labor and war-related migration; policy, organizational and community studies; international consultancy as an educational process. She is co-editor of *Gender and Education*.

R.L. SMITH is a Research Fellow in the Centre for International Studies in Education, University of Bristol. His teaching career began in secondary schools, but after five years in the UK, he became a teacher educator in Zambia. University posts in Swaziland and Bophuthatswana followed, as well as periods at the Institute of Education, University of London. His teaching and research interests focus on basic education, planning and policy for developing countries and teacher education.

JANET STUART taught social studies in London secondary schools before spending six years at the National University of Lesotho training teachers of development studies. During the last year in Lesotho she carried out the research reported here, which formed the basis of her doctoral thesis. On her return to the UK, she became a Lecturer in Education at the University of Sussex, where she directed the International B.Ed. for four years in collaboration with the School of Education in the Seychelles, before becoming Chair of the Centre for International Education and directing the International M.A. programs. Dr. Stuart has traveled widely in Europe and Africa and is particularly interested in teacher education, action research, and classroom interaction.

GRAHAM VULLIAMY is a Senior Lecturer in the Department of Educational Studies at the University of York, where he teaches courses on research methods, education in developing countries, and the sociology of education. Dr. Vulliamy's interest in education in developing countries dates from 1979, when he first visited Papua New Guinea. He is a founding executive editor of the *British Journal of Sociology of Education* and of the *International Journal of Educational Development*. In recent years he has collaborated with Dr. Rosemary Webb: their first joint book, *Teacher Research and Special Educational Needs* (David Fulton), won the *Times Educational Supplement/National Association for Special Educational Needs* Annual Book Award in 1993. Their most recent book, *Roles and Responsibilities in the Primary School: Changing Demands, Changing Practices* (Open University Press), is a study of the impact of the 1988 Education Reform Act on primary schools in England and Wales. They are currently working with Finnish researchers on a comparative research project on curriculum change in primary schools in England and Finland.

AUTHOR INDEX

Subject Index

curriculum:
    implementation, 9
    innovation, 9

development theory, 44
dialectic critique, 175
disciplinary research:
and pedagogic research, 14
documentary sources:
    advantages of, 114
    autobiography as, 124–128
    committee minutes as, 128–130
    disadvantages of, 114
    dissertations as, 115–116
    and ethnography, 89–91
    literature as, 124–128
    newspapers as, 92–94, 116–119
    school textbooks as, 119–124

Ecuador, 54
epistemology, 3–7, 40, 66
ethics, 203–205, 212
Ethiopia, 13
ethnography:
    analysis in, 19
    and anthropology, 89
    and comparative education, 9–10
    and context, 87, 104, 268
    and documentary sources, 89–91
    incompatibility with teacher research, 15
    macro-, 10, 88–95
    micro-, 95–106
    origins of, 13
    and pattern, 87, 104, 107
    and validity, 108
evaluation:
    case-study, 227
    and policy makers, 221, 253
    qualitative, 222
    summative, 45, 221, 239
    and teacher research, 15–16
    traditional approaches to, 16

feminism, 46–47
fieldnotes:
    analysis of, 96–98
    coding of, 96
    fittingness, 236

Ghana, 115, 126–127
grounded theory, 136, 157

holism, 9, 87, 107, 108

illuminative evaluation, 12, 222, 235
India, 265–291
indicators, 68, 72
Indonesia, 166
informed consent, 204
insider research, 200–203, 205, 211–212, 214–215, 277–279
international education:
    and comparative education, 7–11
international transfer:
    dangers of, 7, 10, 11, 17, 18, 200, 249, 259–260
interviewing:
    and access, 137–140
    design of, 134–137, 215
    and ethnographic data, 101–102, 108, 275
    and gender, 152–153
    and language difficulties, 280, 287
    and power, 153–154
    recording of, 155, 211–212
    setting for, 140–142
    and status, 279
    styles of, 134–137, 202
    techniques of, 142–150, 277–280

Japan, 82, 83

Kenya, 116, 120, 122–123, 124, 125, 259
key respondents, 212, 215

large-scale research, 40
Lesotho, 161–197

Malaysia, 146
Mali, 262
mathematical models, 72–76
modernization theory, 10
multiple methods, 38, 48, 74

Namibia, 127–128
negative instances, 158
Nigeria, 114, 117–118, 120, 124

observation:
    of student groups, 172–173, 256

Pakistan, 137–138, 138–139, 140, 142, 153–154, 245–263
Papua New Guinea, 1, 2, 33, 42, 58–59, 87–111
paradigms, 5–6, 49
participant observation:
    experience, 54, 289
    techniques in, 95–106

REFERENCE BOOKS IN INTERNATIONAL EDUCATION

EDWARD R. BEAUCHAMP, *Series Editor*

EDUCATION IN THE PEOPLE'S
REPUBLIC OF CHINA, PAST
AND PRESENT
An Annotated Bibliography
by Franklin Parker
and Betty June Parker

EDUCATION IN SOUTH ASIA
A Select Annotated Bibliography
by Philip G. Altbach,
Denzil Saldanha,
and Jeanne Weiler

TEXTBOOKS IN THE
THIRD WORLD
Policy, Content, and Context
by Philip G. Altbach
and Gail P. Kelly

MINORITY STATUS
AND SCHOOLING
by Margaret A. Gibson
and John V. Ogbu

TEACHERS AND TEACHING
IN THE DEVELOPING WORLD
by Val D. Rust and Per Dalin

RUSSIAN AND SOVIET
EDUCATION, 1731–1989
*A Multilingual Annotated
Bibliography*
by William W. Brickman
and John T. Zepper

EDUCATION IN
SUB-SAHARAN AFRICA
A Source Book
by George E.F. Urch

EDUCATION AND
CULTURAL DIFFERENCES
New Perspectives
by Douglas Ray
and Deo H. Poonwassie

CONTEMPORARY PERSPECTIVES
IN COMPARATIVE EDUCATION
edited by Robin J. Burns
and Anthony R. Welch

EDUCATION IN THE ARAB GULF
STATES AND THE ARAB WORLD
*An Annotated
Bibliographic Guide*
by Nagat El-Sanabary

INTERNATIONAL AND HISTORICAL
ROOTS OF AMERICAN
HIGHER EDUCATION
by W.H. Cowley
and Don Williams

EDUCATION IN ENGLAND
AND WALES
An Annotated Bibliography
by Franklin Parker
and Betty June Parker

CHINESE EDUCATION
*Problems, Policies,
and Prospects*
edited, with an introduction
by Irving Epstein

UNDERSTANDING
EDUCATIONAL REFORM
IN GLOBAL CONTEXT
Economy, Ideology, and the State
edited by Mark B. Ginsburg

EDUCATION AND SOCIAL
CHANGE IN KOREA
by Don Adams
and Esther E. Gottlieb

THREE DECADES OF PEACE
EDUCATION AROUND THE WORLD
An Anthology
edited by Robin J. Burns
and Robert Aspeslagh